The Radiant Performer
The Spiral Path to Performing Power

The Radiant Performer
The Spiral Path to Performing Power

H. Wesley Balk

University of Minnesota Press
Minneapolis   Oxford

Published by the University of Minnesota Press
2037 University Avenue Southeast, Minneapolis, MN 55414
Printed in the United States of America on acid-free paper

Library of Congress Cataloging-in-Publication Data

Balk, H. Wesley.
    The radiant performer : the spiral path to performing power / H.
Wesley Balk.
        p.   cm.
    Includes bibliographical references and index.
    ISBN 0-8166-1867-4.—ISBN 0-8166-1868-2 (pbk.)
    1. Dramatic music—Performance—Psychological aspects.
    2. Singing—Psychological aspects. 3. Acting—Psychological
    aspects. 4. Self-realization. I. Title.
    MT956.B34   1991   90-34837
    792.5'028—dc20.   CIP

A CIP catalog record for this book is available from the British Library

The University of Minnesota is an
equal-opportunity educator and employer.

To all those who, in times of increasing product-fixation, helped keep the process of the traveling, singing-acting, radiant research laboratory alive—to Irene and Mary Catherine in Atlanta, David, Judith, and Bonnie in California, Shoshana in Bryn Mawr, Ann, Judith, and Debbie in New York, Francine in New Orleans, Joan and Doug in Bethlehem, Craig and Mark in Boston, Pam in Pittsburgh, Karen in Minneapolis, Bob, Phil, and the Syracuse Group, the Minnesota Opera New Music Theater Ensemble, and many others—but most particularly, with deep respect and affection, to

BEN

Contents

A Full-Spectrum Foreword ix

    Exploratory Music Theater   *Meredith Monk*....................... x

    Traditional Opera   *Andrew Foldi*................................ xii

    Musical Theater   *Joan Susswein Barber* xiii

Preface xvii

Acknowledgment... xxv

Chapter 1: Purposes and Processes, Maps and Models 3

Chapter 2: Singer-Actor Training: A Fragmented Field 36

Chapter 3. The Counterconditioned Performer 56

Chapter 4: Approaching the Whole Performer:
Developing a Science of Radiant Performing 79

Chapter 5: The Seven Lively Entanglements 99

Chapter 6: Seven Guiding Principles for Radiant Performing.......... 133

Chapter 7: Why the Singer-Actor Doesn't Practice:
Confusion about the Exercise Process 161

Chapter 8: How the Singer-Actor Can Practice:
Clarifying the Exercise Process 183

Chapter 9: The Facial-Emotional Complex I:
Exercising the Outer... 214

Chapter 10: The Facial-Emotional Complex II:
Exercising and Connecting the Inner with the Outer................ 247

Chapter 11: Exercising the Kinesthetic Mode.......................... 270

Chapter 12: Exercising the Vocal Mode............................... 304

Chapter 13: The Full-Spectrum Performer I:
  Expanding the View 340

Chapter 14: The Full-Spectrum Performer II:
  Further Up and Further In 362

Appendix A: Arbitrary Attitudes...................................... 391

Appendix B: Arbitrary Gestures 393

References... 395

Index... 397

A Full-Spectrum Foreword

The concept of full-spectrum experience is integral to *The Radiant Performer*. For example, the full-spectrum performer is one who is aware of and exercises a complete range of performance choices on as many energy spectra as possible — vocal, physical, emotional, and mental, among others.

Another important full spectrum involves music-theater style: at one end we might place exploratory, alternative music theater; at the other, popular musical theater (musical comedy); and somewhere in between, traditional grand opera. This is not to suggest that alternative music theater is never popular, that musical comedy does not explore new directions, that neither of them ever have the musical sophistication of traditional opera, or that traditional opera is never popular and does not explore new directions. As with any spectrum, any choice may interact with or be informed by any other choice on that spectrum. But these general distinctions do exist, and I use them to clarify the purpose of *The Radiant Performer* in serving them all.

This foreword will draw upon those distinctions, with three artists, each of whom specializes in a different style of music theater, addressing the issue of radiant performance. They are: from the alternative music theater, Meredith Monk, a composer, writer, singer, director, and teacher who, with the Meredith Monk Ensemble, creates and performs her work internationally; from midspectrum traditional opera, Andrew Foldi, a singer-actor with the Metropolitan Opera (among others), a teacher and stage-director, and the director of the Cleveland Institute of Music; and from the popular musical theater, Joan Susswein Barber, an actor-singer from Broadway (*Man of*

La Mancha, among others), a singer-actor with the Minnesota Opera New
Music Theater Ensemble, a director and teacher.

Exploratory Music Theater
Meredith Monk

The first time I met Wesley Balk was in the winter of 1983, when we were on
an Opera America panel discussing the state of contemporary opera/music
theater. I noticed that every time he spoke, his words seemed to mirror my
own thoughts. By the end of the session, I knew that I had met a kindred
spirit who shared many of my dreams, aspirations, and ideas of an integrated
music-theater form that could become a metaphor for a society rich in perception, emotion, and wholeness. Over the years, I had nurtured the belief
that there could be a performer who was equally at home in the arts of singing, acting, and dancing: a performer who was flexible both physically and
mentally; who could fluidly move from an aria to a dramatic scene to a dance
(or do them simultaneously), being equally at ease and expressive in each
while maintaining a sense of continuity and underlying groundedness as a
performer and as a human being. In America, in the musical comedy tradition particularly, there are some wonderful performers who are superb
singer/dancer/actors, but it is rare to find one who achieves the depth of
spirit that you see in the great performers of non-Western traditions.

In many non-Western theater forms, as well as in accounts of ancient
performance rituals, there is not the separation of music, dance, and theater
(storytelling, enactment, etc.) that we have in the West. We have become
specialists who are taught to think and to live in very compartmentalized
ways. In my own work, over the years, I had sought out performers who felt
very much the way that I did: that the voice is vitally interconnected with the
body; that the body is equally interconnected with its expressivity as a dramatic conveyor of thought and feeling. Although I was working in one of the
world's largest cities, New York, and was fortunate to find wonderful artists
(and form an ensemble) who were able and willing to explore the unknown
vocally, physically, and dramatically and to draw upon their inner and outer
resources in performance to convey what they wished to communicate, there
were many times when I felt isolated and lonely in my quest.

In 1988, I had the chance to meet Wesley Balk again. (Earlier, in the fall
of 1987, we had greeted each other in Philadelphia at a symposium on the
voice at the American New Music Theater Festival, but had little time to talk

or share our views.) The following May I was in Minneapolis working with the Minnesota Opera New Music Theater Ensemble, mounting a piece of mine, "Book of Days." I noticed from the first rehearsal the easygoing, positive attitude of the singer/actors. When I went to Wesley's classes I learned more about what was going on. The class was totally relaxed, warm, and expansive. Some of the exercises were very complex—there were signals for the face, for the body, for vocal play, for emotion. People were singing while they ran and jumped, singing while they moved two fingers and changed focus, singing upside down. Through all of this, there was a spirit of laughter and play, curiosity, thoughtfulness, and respect. I was very moved. I realized then that Wesley had spent many years developing a process and creating an environment where a holistic, healthy, creative atmosphere could be offered to artists young and old, as an alternative to the fragmented education most music theater performers receive. I felt again that I was not alone—that even though we were coming to it from different paths, Wesley and I were converging in our wish for and belief in a new way of looking at the potential magnificence of music theater as a vital and necessary part of our culture.

Beginning with the performer who is the heart, soul, and blood of the form, Wesley has inspired the participants of his classes to empower themselves to be self-generating artists who respect and care for their own processes; who support and encourage others in their growth; who continue to ask questions and enjoy learning, thereby ensuring themselves of a lifetime of renewing energy both as artists and as human beings. The nonjudgmental atmosphere of Wesley's classes created a space where everyone could take risks, could allow themselves to be vulnerable, to walk through fear to an exhilarating leap into the unknown. Participating in the classes, working joyfully with members of the ensemble who were generous, alert, sensitive, and intelligent, I knew that there was a quiet revolution going on in Minneapolis—that there was indeed a vital future ahead for music theater.

There are many people who think that live performance is dying out. As people (particularly in America) feel that sitting home and watching TV is as much as they can do after hours of unfulfilling, stressful work, the irreplaceable experience of live energy exchange that occurs in a performance would seem to be becoming a thing of the past. The sad thing is that people don't know what they are missing if they don't know what they are missing: in other words, if they haven't been exposed to it. Music theater has the possibility of being the most vital performance form. It offers the full perceptual spectrum: music, image, text, movement, light, color, object, character, environment. Pioneers like Wesley Balk are feeding new energy into this wonderful form and in turn audiences are responding by coming in numbers to something that they feel can be a healing, invigorating, stimulating experience.

The potential vitality in opera had been often diminished by contemporary performance practices (economic restrictions leading to lack of rehearsal time and inappropriate, incomplete training for the performers), by the lack of consistent nurturing for new pieces, and by continual repetition of eighteenth-and nineteenth-century pieces that, however masterful, do not reflect the complexity and multiplicity of our contemporary environment. Now—because of Wesley and a handful of other visionary teachers, producers, and artistic directors of opera companies—performers, composers, librettists, visual artists, and directors are starting to see that music theater is a viable and exciting platform for contemporary concerns, and a reflection of contemporary thought and sensibility, a medium in which to heal the yearning for integration that we all have as a birthright and that is increasingly difficult to find in the relentless speed of our world.

The Radiant Performer is Wesley Balk's offering to the music theater that we aspire to. It is as important for laypeople to read as it is for performers, teachers, and directors because what he addresses transcends the field. He is speaking of the human condition (and of human conditioning) and the way we can affirm our lives, our hearts, our minds, and our bodies, and synchronize them so that we are present and alive at every moment.

Music theater presents a situation in which everyone (the audience as well as the performers) can be openhearted, awake, and radiant. If for that one or two hours, each of us can experience feelings that we may have forgotten or see/hear things in a fresh, vivid way, then our lives will have been changed and enriched. We will go back to our daily living with a new understanding of what we are missing, what we cannot do without. We will in our own ways fight for a society that encourages healthy human interaction, a full palette of emotion, political autonomy, compassion for all living things, and the joy of play. *The Radiant Performer* is Wesley Balk's contribution to this process. The awareness and insight that it provides is an inspiration for all of us.

Traditional Opera
Andrew Foldi

In many ways, it is not too much to say that Wesley Balk is the Sigmund Freud of the singer-actor. He is the first to have probed into the unconscious (and conscious) mind of the performer to analyze, isolate, codify, and organize the multiplicity of forces that go into the creation of an individual performance in which music, singing, acting, and psychology are intertwined. In the past, these conflicting yet complementary forces have presented a Minotauran maze to the performer.

It was not so long ago that a large portion of operatic performances could justifiably be considered concerts in costume. Now, the probing and fertile mind of an innovative thinker named Wesley Balk has solved some of the mysteries surrounding the intangibles of singing-acting. Building on an extraordinarily intuitive exploration and investigation of the problem, he has developed a remarkable system (in the best sense of that word) to train the performer.

Theory is often a fascinating abstraction that is not readily related to or even concerned with pragmatic reality. For the performer, such theories seldom move beyond the status of an intellectual exercise. But Wesley has succeeded where no one else has even ventured, developing a marvelously useful way for the performer to isolate and analyze for her- or himself the many components of the craft, and then to synthesize them in actually learning how to become a better performer.

It is a unique and innovative means of helping the performer discover one's true self and then to translate that discovery into an integrated performance, a performance that might otherwise find the dichotomy of musical and theatrical elements literally destroying each other if permitted to roam out of control. How many of us, onstage in performance, have not found ourselves facing some of the following problems? By preparing for a difficult note or passage, we have dropped character for several minutes; or by totally immersing ourselves in a role, we have not been together with the conductor for many measures; or in gluing our eyes on the conductor, we have become so preoccupied with that togetherness that, through vocal carelessness, we have managed to emit some bloodcurdling sounds!

Through Wesley's insights, the performer has a tool to address these problems for the first time. In recent years, of course, others have tackled this issue; but no one, I think, has succeeded as remarkably as Wesley Balk, the radiant originator.

Musical Theater
Joan Susswein Barber

Like many readers of this book, my first exposure to Wesley Balk and his ideas was through his writing. I was a professional actress and singer in musical theater, who had temporarily abandoned my pursuit of a performing career because I felt powerless—like a child, who was always at the whim of whatever director, teacher, casting director, or producer happened to be in charge at the moment. I decided to take more control of my career and started directing and teaching myself. But then I found that I was on the other end of the power struggle and realized that it was equally frustrating: I, too, found myself playing God with powerless though talented performers. I could manipulate them into emotional states so their acting and singing communicated to an audience, but what did they come away with except a greater reliance on me?

Then I came upon a copy of *The Complete Singer-Actor* in the Drama Book Shop in New York and began reading it. It was inspiring, but how could I put the exercises into practice all by myself? By chance I learned that Wesley Balk was giving a workshop in Philadelphia. I was overjoyed: now I could meet the author himself and find out how to do "it."

But I was surprised and disappointed to learn that he had written a new book on the singing-acting process called *Performing Power*: perhaps the new material replaced the old and was no longer applicable to my needs. When I got to the workshop, I found I was the only "actor"—the rest were "singers." My assumption that the new techniques were probably not for me was reinforced. How wrong I was! Gently, and with compelling examples, he began to address all the performing, directing, and teaching issues that concerned me. The guilt for "not thinking the right thoughts or feeling the right feelings" onstage; the problem of being a method-trained actress in the stylized medium of musical theater; the vocal strain and fatigue that resulted from eight performances a week, playing intense dramatic roles in a musical; and the feeling of a lack of power that led me to leave performing in the first place: all these and more were exposed to the sunlight of performing power. Through the process of simple, playful exercises and some pretty hefty personal attitude changes, they have ceased to be problems.

Since that first meeting, I have read *Performing Power*, become a member of the Minnesota Opera New Music Theater Ensemble, attended the Wesley Balk Summer Opera Music Theater Institute, and have become acquainted with the new concepts and processes of *The Radiant Performer*. My performing, whether in cabaret, musical comedy, new music theater, operetta, or recital, has grown and continues to grow enormously and to radiate increasing power. People who have seen me perform year after year in musicals and theater frequently approach me and say, "You're better than you were last year. How can that be?"

But even more important to me, I have learned to incorporate into my teaching and directing almost all of the ideas, exercises, and principles I have learned in working with Wesley. My students range in age from ten years to middle age and every single one of them has grown as a performer and as a human being in ways beyond expectation and prediction. They perform in high school and college musicals, professional operettas, films and cabarets, in classical theater and television, and for their own delight and pleasure.

The attitudes of nonjudgmentalism, playfulness, and respect for the individual that I have learned from Wesley Balk's writing and teaching have enabled me to gain a new love for the art of singing-acting and for all those who pursue it. It works. It's not easy to do. It's an ongoing lifetime process. It's tremendous fun. It's scary. It's life affirming and life changing. And it's probably in the process of change right now, as is Wesley himself. I recommend *The Radiant Performer* to anyone interested in power, love, freedom, play, musical theater, self-awareness, and growth.

Preface

The Radiant Performer (*RP*) is the third volume in a trilogy that includes *The Complete Singer-Actor* (*CSA*) and *Performing Power* (*PP*). I would like to clarify the evolving process from which the three books emerged, specifically differentiating between their intentions. The cycle during which they were written began in the late 1960s when the "movable laboratory" with which I do research into the singing-acting process sprang into being in Minneapolis. In addition to the insights that arose from that process, I also had a number of interactions with the music-theater field as a whole—as the artistic director of the Minnesota Opera Company—which also contributed to the intentions of the trilogy. I will examine that relationship with the field below, but first the intentions of the books.

This preface reflects those intentions and is part of a continuing conversation with myself about what, exactly, I am doing in exploring the interaction of the singing-acting process with the human energy system. When *PP* was published (and *CSA* was reissued in a second edition) I wrote a preface for each of them, talking to myself all the while, speculating about the nature of this third book that I considered calling *The Synergistic Performance*, a title that, however accurate to my intentions, is too ponderously academic by half.

In the preface to *CSA* I said that the exercises in it are its experiential core. Without a direct experience of those exercises, the book would remain in the realm of philosophy: it might be inspiring, accurate, and significant, but it would not possess the only thing that lifts performance philosophy beyond itself—living energy. That is still true of any book on performance, including this one. The question concerns the nature of the exercises and to whom one is speaking.

While that call to actual exercise (rather than just reading about it) concerns the performer, *CSA* as a whole was addressed primarily to the teacher of the performer: It says in effect, "Here is what to do in the studio when working with the singer-actor; here is a coherent way of viewing music theater and the singer-actor; and here are exercises that can allow that point of view to be realized in actual performance." The exercises were mainly devoted to freeing the singer-actor of inhibitions that blocked the singing-acting process. They continue to be useful (I expand upon some of them in this volume), but they do not develop the singer-actor's instrument as a whole. They could not have done so at that stage in my understanding of the human energy system and how it is challenged in fulfilling the needs of singing-acting. That understanding has continued to evolve and expand through research in my movable laboratory.

As that process unfolded, I began to shift emphasis from the authority figure of the teacher to the performer. *PP* approached the performer's personal exercise process more directly, addressing the performer as fully as the teacher: "Here is a new view of the functioning of the human energy system; here is how that system works as it communicates in life and performance; and here are some implications for the exercise of the performance process that arise from these new awarenesses."

In *RP* I go for the exercise jugular, addressing the performer directly—with the teacher as an understood listener: "Here, for the first time, is an integrated view of the concepts explored in *CSA* and *PP*, a view that puts performers directly in charge of their own development and gives them the means to continue to expand their performing process for as long as they wish. This is accomplished by understanding and acting upon the following concepts: (1) the radiant performance the performer wants to create; (2) the demands music theater and singing-acting make of the performer; (3) the conditions of the music-theater field in which the performer is trained to carry out those demands; (4) the conditioning of the human energy system by that music-theater environment and by society as a whole; (5) the ways that conditioning interferes with singing-acting and radiant performance; and, finally, (6) what the performer can do about all that: an exercise process for total performance that gives performers a new measure of control over their own growth and development, and allows them to serve the arts of music-theater and singing-acting with increasingly radiant performance as long as they wish."

The major part of *RP* has to do with the personal exercise process itself—the vehicle with which the move toward radiant performance is made: developing the performer's awareness of the conditioning against such an exercise process and of why there has never been a means of doing so; creating a free and healthy space within the performer so such an exercise process can function beneficially; clarifying for the performer what needs to be exercised in the human energy system and how to do it; and finally, putting it all together, making a total performance exercise process available for every performer's personal use in moving toward radiant performance.

That shifting focus—moving from the teacher in *CSA* to the perfomer in *RP*—was a natural response to my own experiences in the music-theater field. Shortly after the publication of *PP* I chose to direct opera less and less in order to have the time and energy to contribute in a different way to the field as a whole. It wasn't a difficult choice to make. In Peter Brook's *The Shifting Point*, there is a section devoted to his work in opera (aptly entitled "The Forty Years' War"). Brook says that the reason for Rudolf Bing's success as a general director in opera, and specifically at the Metropolitan Opera, "was that he was so easily bored by bad opera that he took on this nightmarish job so as to get himself a few tolerable evenings. Most opera intendants sit smugly in their boxes enjoying bad performances. What made Bing so remarkable was that he was more impatient and more critical than anyone. Before you could complain about anything he was already outraged. I know of no one else from whom I gladly accepted such terrible working conditions" (p.175).

I also have that capacity for easy boredom with bad opera production, but it seems to me that much of the badness flows directly from the working conditions themselves. From the beginning of my work as a director of opera I often suggested publicly that I disliked opera, with the immediate proviso "the way it is usually produced." People who objected to my exploratory and experimental work as a director took the first part of that statement out of context to prove that the reason I did all those strange things was clear: since I had said I hated opera, I wanted to destroy it. (Why, possessing such an attitude, I would have chosen to enter the field in the first place was never made clear.)

And I did dislike it and wanted to see it done away with—as it was usually produced. I wanted to experience more often the power of the music-theater form in its full potential—in Sir Tyrone Guthrie's assessment, as "the most extraordinary experience the theater can offer an audience." *CSA* was a part of that movement toward change in the opera-producing environment. I was saying, in effect, "Imagine what this astonishing form could be, what incredible potential it has, and how we have been abusing it! Why don't we all get together—teachers, directors, coaches, and conductors— and do it right! Let's give opera the attention, care, and support it deserves. If we do, it will reward us and its audiences in ways we can't even imagine!"

But the opera-producing environment has a power of petrification in direct proportion to its potential to dazzle. The size and multiplicity of resources required to realize the potential of opera ensure that such realizations will be rare indeed. It can be a powerful and compelling form, but it generally remains what the compounding of commercial inertia and artistic confusion would lead one to expect: a large and stagnant pool of aesthetic sludge.

Although I knew that, I threw myself nevertheless into trying to change a part of the production environment with full awareness of its intractability. For a few brief years in Minneapolis-St. Paul, the Center Opera Company (which became the Minnesota Opera Company) was moving in directions that seemed important to me (and that were also regarded as significant on a national level, even while the company remained "the best-kept secret in the Twin Cities").

The efforts of the company included the establishment of a resident ensemble of artists who took classes and worked together over extended periods of time to expand their individual processes and develop their ensemble interaction. The company also sponsored the first professional nine-month training program for apprentice artists. (Both efforts were widely imitated by other opera companies in subsequent years.) These training endeavors were part of my "moving laboratory," which also included my teaching at the University of Minnesota; my private coaching, directing, and teaching of singers and actors in all stages of development; and my other work in professional and educational theater and music theater.

But the chemistry of innovation and evolution in an expensive public art form like opera needs but subtle alteration in its ingredients to begin inexorably reverting to stasis and conformity. A company based on the idea of a resident ensemble of artists, working mostly on new pieces in a small and inadequate theater that necessitates—nay, insists upon—modest production requirements and minimal orchestral resources may seem, when it is highly successful in such circumstances, to be deserving of more, of larger and therefore better resources. "If it is that good when it is small, how much better it will be when it grows up!" Or so went the logical and, though none of us knew it at the time, totally fallacious reasoning.

The logical course was eventually followed: a larger, more attractive theater was found as a fitting reward for the excellent work the company had been doing in such unprepossessing facilities. During the next few years the hidden fallacy slowly became clear (although there are many who have yet to understand what happened): those new, "more adequate," and seemingly more appropriate, comfortable, and suitable facilities forced a change of climate on the company that parched and withered the roots of its vitality.

Bigger, as we have been relearning repeatedly in this century, is not necessarily better. A bigger house means bigger everything: orchestral resources, scenic requirements, choruses, costume expenditures, and voices (which may have to be imported, thus bringing into question the whole concept of a resident ensemble). And those increased resources are not only bigger, they are also more expensive. This necessitates saving money on one hand — by reducing rehearsal time — and making more of it on the other — by producing more pieces from the standard repertory, which presumably guarantees greater ticket income (while it simultaneously reduces the number of production slots available for new pieces).

Thus, in one stroke, all the following were put at risk: the production of new, untried, and unknown pieces (especially small-scale pieces that are not appropriate in a large house); the resident ensemble concept (not every ensemble member is appropriate for standard works, nor will they necessarily have the size voice for the new, larger house, however splendidly they may have functioned in the more intimate setting); the apprentice training program (it costs money, it earns nothing, and besides, "apprentice artists only sing chorus"); and sufficient rehearsal time to achieve the kind of excitement in production that would put to the lie all thoughts of opera as a moribund theatrical form.

Speaking of the art form itself, it is important every so often to remind ouselves of the real *purpose* of the music-theater form (as distinct from the various by-products that result from the movement toward its purpose). The fundamental purpose of the art of music theater is to provide its audiences with access to a consciousness-expanding interaction with higher energies. This is the most important kind of entertainment one can experience, and its stylistic scope includes everything from broad farce to high tragedy, from traditional opera to experimental music theater.

To allow the art of music theater the time, space, and energy it needs to fulfill this purpose requires financial support beyond the capacity of the form to earn it. This is a given for all endeavors that focus on experiences with energy beyond the materialistic level of economics. But when money and size become the issue rather than the needs of the art and its audience, the art is reduced to the materialistic levels imposed upon it. At those levels music theater no longer fulfills its higher purpose, and one may as well ask it to pay its way, since its only justification at that level of reduction is its capacity to do precisely that.

This is not to say that music theater or any other form of art should not interact with the marketplace; it is simply to be clear about the issues involved: What is the purpose of the art? What are the purposes of money-making? And what happens to the art when there is not a balanced choice honoring both ends of the spectrum created between the art and the marketplace?

The art dies from an imbalance in either direction: it dies from outer causes if it makes no money by refusing to honor the needs of the marketplace; it dies from within if it tries so hard to serve the marketplace it loses touch with itself and its purpose. The important thing is that we be clear about the situation and don't counterfeit having our soul when we have sold or lost it.

I mention all this as a part of the pressures that led to *PP*. That volume can be seen as a part of the movable laboratory's efforts to deal with the increasing economic restrictions on the rehearsal process by greater clarity and efficiency of rehearsal-teaching. (The stage directors of opera have always been teachers as well. Whether they like it or not, they are teaching as they direct—either by omission or commission. Singing-acting is far too complex for the unguided efforts of most performers to simply "be edited" by directors and conductors—unless one is content with the unintentional theatrical stereotyping of which the form is generally and not unjustly accused.)

To some extent the training concepts in *PP* allowed a fuller rehearsal process: with the new tools I had developed, I was able to conduct impromptu classes in the course of rehearsals. On occasion, some remarkable performance growth was experienced, and performance standards achieved that were equally remarkable under the less-than-perfect developmental conditions of rehearsal.

On the whole, however, the intransigency of the form in its new (to the Minnesota Opera) elephantine proportions became more and more frustrating. The field as a whole had asserted its inertia. (Fortunately, the current Minnesota Opera leadership became aware of what had been lost and is exploring ways of creating new support for those aspects of the art. The recent development of the Minnesota Opera New Music Theater Ensemble—dedicated to the creation of new works, the presentation of a broader range of repertory choices, and the encouragement of an innovative touring and education program [including the potential reestablishment of a young artists' training program], have turned what might have become a typical regional opera company in the direction of becoming a full-spectrum music-theater organization.)

However, my response to the initial change of direction was to let go of attempts to reform the environment. Instead I focused on the essence of the music-theater form: the performer.

In peeling the onion of operatic performance, the final layers—in the time-honored description—are planks and a passion. The planks—the place of performance and its audience—can be as simple as that, but they are not the essence of the form. They are simply a means of allowing the passion—the emotions and feelings of the characters as communicated by the performers—to be experienced by the audience. Those passions, in turn, depend for their communication upon the performer's voice, body, and face: the next layer in the performance onion.

As we peel away that layer, we find that within the voice, the body, the face, and the emotions are other energies of increasing refinement and power. Continuing within, peeling as we go, we find at the core of the human energy system *its* essence: radiance—the fundamental, universal energy of wholeness that informs and supports everything we do. Just as the human energy system is the essence of the music-theater system, radiance is the essence of the human energy system. Thus our radiant wholeness is the supporting energy and essence, not only of the performer's process, but of the music-theater form itself—the essence within the essence.

Having tapped that synergizing wholeness, the performer can allow the qualities of radiant performance to flow into the music-theater environment and begin transforming its qualities. Rather than changing the environment so that the performer might grow and develop more fully, we can allow the development of the performer to create an energy field of greater wholeness that can interact with and *become* that environment. This, in turn, can allow other parts of that environment to expand toward greater wholeness as well. It is a fundamental energy principle: If you change the essence within the environment, you change the environment itself.

This does not mean giving up our continuing efforts to transform the external environment—from the outer to the inner—for that supports synergistically the move from inner to outer. Thus we do not discard teachers, coaches, directors, conductors, and guides in general—for they are all parts of the whole and can contribute greatly to the move toward greater wholeness. But we can support that move more fully by freeing ourselves from the addictive authority dependence that has long plagued the field as a whole. If the essence of the music-theater form the performers—are to allow that form to be fully expressed from the essence of themselves, then the essence of each performer must be opened by free human energy systems—systems capable of allowing that radiant essence to be expressed in performance by their voices, emotions, faces, and bodies; systems free to allow the unfolding of radiant performing.

When that happens we will have not only radiant performing, but a newly empowered form whose potential we have only occasionally glimpsed. Those glimpses can and will expand into a sustaining vision if we simply use the tools and techniques that are now available.

Acknowledgment

There is no way of fully acknowledging the contributions of Dr. Barbara Ray to my life, my work, and to this book. This is not to say that she bears any responsibility for how I have interacted with and interpreted her teachings, or for any of the contents of *The Radiant Performer*. The responsibility is totally mine, as is the gratitude for her inspiration.

There are two specific areas in which Dr. Ray teaches and works with the whole process of the human being: she is the world's foremost authority on The Radiance Technique®, a technique for accessing and directing universal energy to release stress and balance energies (described in greater detail in this book); and she teaches and writes about The Awakening Journey®, a wholistic approach to personal process and growth.

I have been privileged to interact extensively with Dr. Ray's work in both areas. I have studied to the Fifth Degree of The Radiance Technique, and have participated in many of her classes and seminars in The Awakening Journey. Both experiences have had a profound influence on me and on this book.

The Radiant Performer is my attempt to translate some of Dr. Ray's work with the whole human being to a specific and more limited area of human endeavor: acting and singing-acting. In so doing, I have drawn upon many other sources as well, including authors first encountered in Dr. Ray's classes, and on my own three decades of work with the singing-acting process. Dr. Ray's teachings on a higher level provide whatever coherence the book may have as it weaves these various strands together in describing a process that allows an opening to radiant performing. Any shortcomings in the translation of her teachings are mine.

In addition to drawing upon that continual underlying support for the process of this book, chapter 14 includes extensive quotations from Dr. Ray's book, *The Expanded Reference Manual of The Radiance Technique*®. That chapter—pivotal in this volume—provides ongoing guidance for me and my work with the radiant performer in each of us.

The Radiant Performer
The Spiral Path to Performing Power

Chapter 1

Purposes and Processes,
Maps and Models

There is one word which describes what you should bring on to the stage with you in this part. Radiance. *And don't be frightened of it, pet, and don't let self-mockery guy you out of it.*

Laurence Olivier, from a letter to Joan Plowright
on her opening in the title role of Shaw's *Major Barbara*.

Vision, Actuality, and Process:
The Path to Radiant Performing

We might well apply the late Lord Olivier's injunction to all roles, spoken or sung, regardless of the outer qualities of the character. For example, in later chapters we will examine a specific radiant performance that occurred in Olivier's portrayal of Othello—a character far from conventionally "radiant." But our use of the word *radiance* will expand upon Olivier's; we will use the term to speak of the fundamental, universal energy of the whole that encompasses and supports all other partial energies. From this perspective, all performance and all of life manifest radiance to some degree. As we fulfill our performing potential through the process clarified in this book, we can also learn to open more fully to that radiant energy.

We can do that with a very specific, practical, and pragmatic developmental process. But for that process to be significantly energized, we need a vision, a purpose, a destination toward which the process will carry us. We also need a clear sense of where we are now, of the present state of our personal performing systems and the environment in which they are developed. With a clear destination, a knowledge of where we are now, and a path to

3

follow, we have the ingredients to begin the journey. Let us begin with our destination or purpose.

We will view that purpose on three levels: the fundamental purpose, the primary purpose, and the secondary purpose. The *fundamental purpose* of our journey is to allow the performer to open to and sustain radiant performing with increasing consistency. The *primary purpose* is to allow the performer to fulfill his/her performing potential at each point on that journey. The *secondary purpose* is to create an exercise process to serve as the vehicle for the journey.

A word here about the words *radiant performer* and *radiant performing*. In *Wholeness and the Implicate Order*, the physicist David Bohm discusses how the structure of language contributes to the general fragmentation of thought and experience in society (a subject I will expand upon below). As he describes it, our use of language, by separating verbs and nouns—the performer from the performing—creates an inappropriate, inaccurate, and fragmented model of experience: the performer *is* the performing, and the performing is the performer. The performer/performing is a continually un-folding process. Yet, "in the ordinary mode of language, truth is taken as a noun, which thus stands for something that can be grasped once and for all or which can at least be approached step by step" (p. 41). Without pursuing Bohm's creation of a new mode of language in which "movement is to be taken as primary in our thinking and in which this notion will be incorpo-rated into the language structure by allowing the verb rather than the noun to play a primary role" (p. 30), we will let that view inform our description of our fundamental and primary purposes. Instead of radiant perfor-mance—a finished product—or radiant performer—which can seem to im-ply a finished product—we will use radiant performing—a continuing pro-cess. (A description of a radiant performer, as another way of viewing our destination, is given at the end of the book.)

Each of the three purposes interacts with and supports the other two. Radiant performing only occurs when there is fulfilled performing potential (FPP); the exercise process (EP) depends upon knowing how it serves both radiant performing and fulfilled performing potential; and fulfilled perform-ing potential can best be realized by pointing beyond it to radiant perform-ing. Since radiant performing can occur during moments of fulfilled per-forming potential—by definition, one's best performance at any given point on the journey —any performance can be radiant, however briefly. In the accompanying illustration, PRP stands for potential radiant performing.

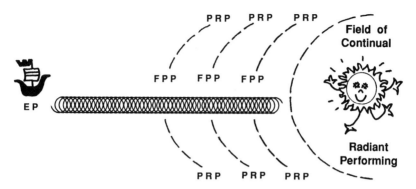

With that overall view of the journey, let us clarify the nature of each of its parts, beginning with the question that, no doubt, has already entered your mind: What is radiant performing?

There is a phenomenon in life and performance that produces a radical shift in the quality of the experience and the performance. It has been called the peak experience or the experience of flow. When it occurs during the acting or singing-acting process, it is what we will call radiant performance. In such a performance there is a transcendence of ordinary performing limitations that is more than subjective: it is manifested in the quality of performance as perceived by others. For example, in Olivier's radiant performance, the cast knew it was happening and was watching from the wings.

Beyond that, there is no way to answer the question experientially, any more than one person can tell another what chocolate tastes like. But when it happens—when we are in the presence of radiant performing, or eating chocolate—we know it. However, short of actual experience, we can sense the qualities of radiant performing by describing the conditions that make it possible.

Radiant performing is made possible in moments of fulfilled performing potential, when all the parts of the performing process—mind, emotions, voice, body, and face—are synchronized, integrated, and aligned. In terms of laser technology—which deals with light and radiance—radiant performing becomes possible when all the parts are coherent and synergistic. When the mind is one with the mind of the character being portrayed, is "in love" with the character, and is free of its potential controlling interference with the other parts of the performing process; when the emotions are also at one and in love with the character; when the voice, body, and face are each free to respond to and express the character's thoughts and emotions with their full potential power and flexibility, and are also free of any interference with each other's process and can work together as a coordinated and integrated team; when all this is so, we have fulfilled performing potential and the conditions for radiant performing. Preparing those conditions is our primary purpose, which is complete in itself; *and* the primary purpose may be transcended and expanded upon by radiant performing—our fundamental purpose.

When those conditions are present, an entirely new energy event may occur: the performer may open to a wholeness, a power, and a radiance that transcends the sum of the individual parts. Such a performance cannot be achieved, predicted, or preevaluated by the mind, for it comes from the whole, and is unknowable from a partial perspective. One cannot practice such a performance, nor even exercise for it as such: one can only prepare the conditions under which radiant performing can occur.

That preparation is accomplished with an exercise process that allows moments of fulfilled performing potential—the best performing possible at any given point on the journey. As we will see in the following section of this chapter, there has been no exercise process vehicle to serve that primary purpose. The journey has been made, of course, by performers of enormous talent and courage; but it has been unnecessarily difficult because of the lack of a supportive exercise process. Creating that vehicle—our secondary purpose—is vital in fulfilling the primary and fundamental purposes.

It is a synergistic trio of purposes: the secondary purpose (exercise process) fulfills the primary purpose (fulfilled performance potential), which may in turn be transcended by the fundamental purpose (radiant performing): the exercise process creates fulfilled performance potential, which then allows radiant performing; and the destination of radiant performing energizes the vehicle of exercise process and encourages performances of fulfilled performance potential.

Returning to our journey metaphor, we now have a sense of where we want to go (our fundamental and primary purposes). We also know that we will need to create a means of getting there—an exercise process (our secondary purpose). But there is one vital ingredient in planning any trip that is so obvious we might miss it as we begin this metaphorical voyage: we have to know where we are and the traveling conditions in order to know what direction to go and what kind of vehicle to use for the journey.

For example, if we want to go to New York City to see the Statue of Liberty, the direction we take and mode of transportation we use will depend on where we actually are. Someone from Miami might say, "Go northeast by car about 1,300 miles or so"; a Chicagoan, "Take a plane east"; a

Bostonian, "Take the train south"; a German, "Take a ship or plane west"; and the captain of a ship at sea—which, as a metaphor, is closer to our situation—would have to assess the reality of his situation and determine where he was on a daily basis: depending upon the winds and waves, he might have to head northwest for a time, then southwest, sometimes seeming to contradict previous directions in order to keep aligned to his destination.

The traveling conditions are also essential information. If the weather is stormy, the roads are icy, the sea is rough, the route is mountainous—all this will affect the kind of vehicle we choose and how we equip it. And our response to these conditions—whether we know how to drive, whether we get car-, air-, or sea-sick, how often we need to stop and rest or eat or snack, how much we like to travel, or how resistant we are to it—all these conditionings are also important factors in our journey.

Assessing reality—knowing where we are at all times, which includes location, traveling conditions and our own conditioning—is the third vital ingredient on our voyage. We must be honest, and address what actually is in all three areas. It is no good for the captain of a ship to say, "I think we are 700 miles due east of New York, the seas are calm, my ship can cover 500 miles a day, and we have fuel for three days, so we will see the Statue of Liberty by tomorrow morning," if he is in fact 2,000 miles away, far to the north, the seas are stormy, his ship can only cover 200 miles a day, and his fuel supplies need immediate replenishing. His inaccurate assessment of reality may lead to serious problems: instead of a sunny view of the Statue of Liberty by the next morning, the ship may founder on a northern Canadian shore or even strike an iceberg. Under the circumstances, the captain's best recourse—once aware of the actual situation—would be to radio for help from the Coast Guard, which could supply him with fuel and guide him out of the difficult situation.

With that vital third ingredient, we have what we need to plan and begin our journey: knowing where we want to go, knowing where we are, and creating a means of transportation. We will refer to these three ingredients as:

Aligning to Purpose (Radiant performing with an itinerary of fulfilled potential peformances on the way.)

Assessing our Reality (Our current performance capabilities and limitations—our conditionings—as well as the conditions of the field through which we will travel and perform.)

Activating the Process (Creating an exercise process to get us from where we are to where we want to go.)

There will also be:

Assisting Tools   (Maps, models, concepts, and techniques to
                                   help us in dealing with each step of the
                                   journey.)

This book, chapter by chapter, relates to these ingredients as follows:

Aligning to Purpose: Chapters 1 (clarifying the concept), 2 (mapping the
opening), 13 (preparing for the opening), and 14 (nurturing the opening).

Assessing our Reality: Chapters 1 (the missing exercise process), 2 (the
conditions of the music-theater training field), 3 (the conditionings of
the performer), 5 (the manifestations of those conditionings), and 7 (the
blocked exercise process).

Activating the Process: Chapters 8 (the exercise concept), 9, and 10 (exercising the face and the emotions), 11 (exercising the body and gestures), 12 (exercising the voice), and 13 and 14 (exercises for opening).

Assisting Tools: Chapters 1 (maps, models, guidelines, definitions, and
concepts), 4 (tools for aligning), and 6 (tools for assessing and aligning).

New Descriptions

In addition to the foregoing map and description of our journey, there are
several models and some terminology I would like to have available for reference during the trip itself. In trying to create new ways of seeing and talking about old challenges, it is useful to devise new models and concepts and
to coin new words. Sometimes those words are jargon—they do less well
what existing words can already do—and they fall by the wayside; others
serve to better clarify a piece of reality that had been obscure, and they become common parlance. I play with these new words and descriptive models
in attempting to light up, for myself and others, the parts of the performing
terrain we are exploring. I don't take any of it too seriously (feeling, as I do,
that what I'm doing is too important for that), and I sometimes refer to myself in seminars and classes as a man followed, wherever he goes, by a cloud
of potential jargon.

Beginning first with the models, there is a trio of pentagons that will
serve as reference points throughout the book. The first is a model of the
relationships between the arts of music theater and singing-acting, the envi-

ronment in which these arts are practiced, and the effect of those two factors on the performer. The other two pentagons are models of the human energy system and of the process of preparing for performance, and will be dealt with in later chapters. There will be other models as well, but without further discussion, let us begin with the first pentagon.

The Pentagon of Potentiality

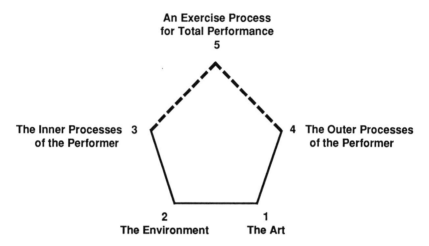

An Exercise Process
for Total Performance
5

The Inner Processes 3
of the Performer

4 The Outer Processes
of the Performer

2
The Environment

1
The Art

Each of the five points of the pentagon of potentiality represents some aspect of the arts of music theater and singing-acting. If those five aspects were to interact fully and synergistically, both arts would be realized with a power we have yet to experience from the music-theater form. There is immense potential in music theater and singing-acting, potential not yet totally fulfilled except on rare occasions. Those occasions could become the norm rather than the exception; hence, the pentagon of potentiality.

Point 1 represents the specific demands, requirements, and conventions of music theater and singing-acting. What does the opera/music-theater form ask of the human being? What are the potentials of the form? What, exactly, is singing-acting? What specific challenges and opportunities does it present the performer? What can the performer become in fulfilling the potentials of music theater?

Point 2 represents the environment of the world around the form and the performer: the conditioning of society and education that is visited upon us all, the specific educational and training processes with which the singer-actor must deal, as well as auditioning, rehearsal, and production procedures, as they interact with the training.

Those two points make up the bottom line literally and figuratively: the art itself, and the environment around the art. The rest of the pentagon concerns the performers, their internal and external energy systems, and how those systems are developed within the environment of point 2 to fulfill the challenges and potentiality of the arts of point 1.

Point 3 covers all the internal factors that affect the performers: their thoughts, emotions, attitudes, and conditionings, as well as other less commonly familiar energies. How have performers been conditioned by the societal, educational, and artistic environment of point 2? How do these conditionings assist or interfere with performers as they try to fulfill their art? What do performers "think" they need to do (as differentiated from what they *actually* need to do) to realize the potential of themselves and their art? How many of the authority figures and judges of point 2 have been consciously or unconsciously internalized — made a part of point 3 — by the performers?

Point 4 represents the external energy system of the performer. The inner processes of the performer in point 3 remain invisible and inaudible until they are translated into tangible communication by the resources of point 4. Together, points 3 and 4 represent the full spectrum of energies of the performer, from the most subtle, powerful, and radiant inner energy resources to the most palpable, direct, and compelling outer communications. While we will focus upon different parts of that total system at different times, our underlying concern is always with the whole performer, and how *all* the parts of the whole can be more fully developed and integrated to serve the whole.

As we move about on the full spectrum of performer energies created by points 3 and 4 — from inner to outer, outer to inner — there are further questions. How do the conditionings of point 3 affect the external energies of point 4? How has that external communicating system been conditioned by the training processes of point 2? How well equipped are the communicating energies of point 4 to serve the artistic requirements of point 1?

Point 5 is a crucial one. It represents the exercise process for the full spectrum of performing energies encompassed by points 3 and 4. The function of point 5 is to develop and expand the capacity of those energies to fulfill the artistic and performance needs of points 1 and 2. The dotted lines symbolize the fact that there is no exercise process for the total singing-acting performance. Creating such a process, bridging that gap, is a fundamental need of the music-theater field, and the secondary purpose of this book.

The purpose of the pentagon model, in turn, is to sustain our awareness of the interconnectedness of its various points in performance: between points 3 and 4 (the inner and outer processes of the singer-actor); between points 3 and 2 (the inner processes of the performer and the conditioning of that process by the music-theater and societal environment); between points 4 and 1 (the communicating process of the performer and the needs of the art); between points 1 and 2 (the needs of the art and the environment that surrounds it and does or does not fulfill its needs); and, returning to the whole performer, between points 3, 4, and 5 (the exercise process and the development of the performer's inner and outer processes through practice) so that the needs of singing-acting and music theater [point 1] may be fulfilled within the context of their environment [point 2].

In addition to the triangle relationship between 3, 4, and 5 (the whole singer-actor and the exercise process) mentioned above, there will be others that will offer insight, such as the 1-4-5 triangle in which we exercise — point 5 — the projective modes — point 4 — to fulfill the demands of singing-acting and opera/music theater — point 1. Or the 2-3-4 triangle, which might be called the conditioning triangle: the societal and educational conditioning of 2 is internalized in 3 (the inner process of the performer) and manifested in 4 (the external communicating system of the performer). These are some of the many ways of viewing the interrelationships of the parts of the pentagon, each of which contributes to its primary purpose as a referent for awareness.

Moving from the Known to the Unknown:
The Spiral of Expansion

Another model useful in clarifying the learning and growth process represents that process as a movement from the known to the unknown. Of the learning process, Barbara Ray has said:

> In essence, learning is moving from the known to the unknown —
> you have truly learned when you are different and are acting and
> relating differently from before learning. Learning involves the
> discovery process and the willingness to move into the unknown
> with the entire body-mind-spirit dynamic and the ability and

capacity for such movement. (*The Expanded Reference Manual of The Radiance Technique®* [*ERM*], p. 65)

This model has two aspects: movement to the outer unknown (new ways of using and combining the voice, the body, and the face), and movement to the inner unknown (new ways of thinking, imagining, feeling, observing, and opening to the energies of intuition, higher consciousness and wholeness). The movement to the outer unknown can be seen in the accompanying illustration.

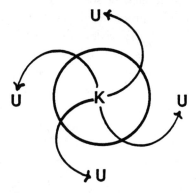

Within the circle is the known; outside it is the unknown. The circle defines the boundaries of the known—what the performer is already capable of doing with the voice, body, and face; it also defines the barrier to movement outside that known. Thus the boundary-barrier of learning and growth is defined both by the existing capacities of the performer and by the conditionings limiting that capacity.

The movement to the inner unknown, which also deals with those conditionings, is illustrated as

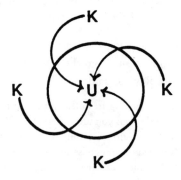

Putting the two movements together in one image gives us

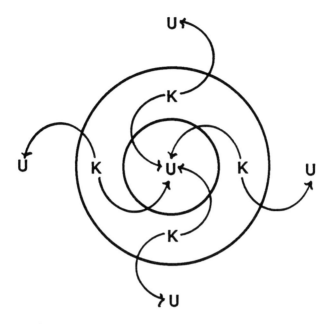

Moving from the known to the unknown is always challenging, even frightening; it takes support and courage to do so consistently. The curved lines moving past the boundary represent movement into the unknown. Their curvature suggests ways of approaching the boundary-barrier that come at it from unexpected angles, transcending it perhaps, rather than by direct, linear assault.

Making that move of transcendence, whether to the inner or to the outer, can happen in several ways; but all of them must involve coming to *know* the unknown through direct experience. We sometimes create the illusion of learning and moving into the unknown by having

> taken the unknown and tried to fit it into, define it, analyze it and/or categorize it according to what [we] already know. This limiting process is characteristic of current western mentality and defeats the possibility of actually learning something new, something more—and prevents any movement into the unknown. The unknown is not an extension or a continuation of what is already known—the unknown is something else. (Ray, *ERM*, p. 113)

Thus it is not enough to simply have *knowledge* of the unknown—nor is it even possible. We must come to *know* the unknown through direct experience—and the preevaluation of the unknown that can occur when we think we have knowledge of it will interfere with the process of actually coming to know it.

Of the many distinctions and clarifications we will explore in this book, that between knowledge and knowing is one of the most significant. It is an obvious, common-sense distinction—made clear in adages such as "experience is the best teacher"—but one whose meaning is often ignored even as we deal with its very subject: how we learn and grow.

Knowledge and Knowing

As an example, we can have knowledge about some aspect of the field of music theater—say information about the character of Carmen. We can have knowledge about her mental, emotional, vocal, and physical qualities without knowing them through actual experience. We can, of course, experience those qualities in our imagination—a kind of indirect experience—and come to know it on that level. That is the audience level. Imagining is also a vital step for the performer; indeed, a necessity, for the leap into unknown experience is encouraged by some sort of imagining—or image making. But for the performer that image must be tangibly realized; until it is it remains a part of the whole process of coming to know Carmen. The image must be realized by the performer's direct experience of the character through her own body, voice, and emotional processes. And that involves moving from the known of one's own experience to the unknown experience of another person or character—in this case, Carmen. And whatever the nature of what one has imagined about Carmen, the direct experience of it with the body, face and voice can and probably will differ. Otherwise one may be forcing the unknown to conform to one's imagined prediction of it—thereby blocking a true perception of the direct experience.

Note that there are three distinct stages in the knowing process, any one of which can be complete in itself. To have knowledge is not a bad thing, but it is not knowing. Knowledge imaginatively experienced is another stage, also complete in itself—and, as we will see, in some fields of endeavor that level of knowledge is equivalent to knowing. But there are fields in which the final stage of knowing through direct experience is unique unto itself. Performance is one of these, and for the performer, stopping at the first stages of knowledge without direct experience is, again, like trying to know a piece of chocolate without tasting it.

These distinctions are crucial in any learning situation that involves the communication of knowledge—this book, for example, or any classroom or academic situation. In some cases knowledge is all that is called for. In academia this may mean that knowledge is the only thing we can easily test. For example, knowledge of history or mathematics can be tested and measured with little difficulty. I do not suggest that merely having testable knowledge in such fields represents the wholeness of the field itself; there is a level in history and mathematics involving knowledge imaginatively experienced that is on a higher level than knowledge alone. It is experienced by the artists in those fields, and it takes them beyond knowledge to a different kind of knowing. But testable knowledge as information is a necessary foundation for making that move to the knowing of knowledge imaginatively experienced. And this is where things get sticky in teaching the arts.

In singing, acting, painting, sculpting, dancing, playing an instrument, or singing-acting, the relationship between knowledge, knowledge imaginatively experienced, and knowing is more complicated. One can have immense knowledge (and even a deep imaginative experience of that knowledge) about any of those arts without being able to experience them directly. And in those fields, to know them *is* to have experienced them directly.

Conversely, one can experience those performing arts directly—know them—while having relatively little knowledge about them. To portray Carmen, for example, a singer-actor might have memorized the words and the music, and have no further knowledge of Carmen's character—beyond what the words and music suggest—nor of acting theory, of music theory, of the opera as a whole, of the style of Bizet, nor of any other musical, dramatic, or historical background information. Yet lacking all that, the performer might still be able to give a "knowing" and powerful performance of the character of Carmen.

It is true, of course, that those missing pieces of knowledge could allow the performer to give an even more powerful performance. This is in fact the article of faith behind all teaching in the performing arts. Yet it is equally and demonstrably true that those same pieces of knowledge can actually diminish the power of that performance unless they are transformed into knowledge imaginatively experienced, and from there into the knowing step of direct experience. (And, of course, the only way all that knowledge can be so transformed is by actually rehearsing with it—by moving into the unknown with it, and learning how to exercise it so that all its parts *can* be transformed from academic knowledge to flesh-and-blood knowingness.)

There is widespread confusion about this relationship of knowledge and knowing in performance. For example, Performer X gives a stunning performance. When asked how she managed to do it, she says that she did intense research into the psychological makeup of the character, interviewing psychiatrists and reading extensively. The implication, of course, is that the power of the performance is a result of having done that research, which would mean that anyone doing the same kind of character research would also give a stunning performance, which is obviously nonsense. In fact, another performer might be bogged down and inhibited by doing the same kind of research (and many performers are). Let me emphasize that this does not mean one should *not* do the homework. I mean only to be clear about the difference between the knowledge state of the homework, the performer's imaginative experience of it, and its actual realization as experienced knowing in performance.

Knowledge as we are using the term is verbal; knowing is pre- and transverbal. The performing energies of body, face, and voice are mostly preverbal; the higher energies of intuition, higher consciousness, and radiance are transverbal; and between them stands the mind, creating knowledge through imagination, through reading and analysis of verbal sources, and then allowing the performing energies to transform it all into knowing.

Knowledge is also pre- and postexperiential; knowing is experiential. For the performer, knowledge is valuable in proportion to one's capacity to translate it into the experience of knowing performance, or for energizing the move toward knowing. Radiant performing is an ultimate act of experiential knowing that cannot be translated into words, and is therefore inaccessible to verbal definition by the mind.

When Olivier was told that his (radiant) performance in *Othello* was extraordinary, he replied dejectedly, "Yes, I know, but I don't know how to do it again." It was the frustrated voice of the mind unable to define the knowing of radiant performing in verbal knowledge terms, and thus unable to dictate its recurrence at will. As with the taste of chocolate, words are left behind at the gateway to knowing; some of our most important experiences— including falling in love and radiant performing—transcend reduction to verbal knowledge.

The important thing is to be clear about the difference between knowledge and knowing; to recognize the value and uses of each; to honor each for what it is; and to allow them to be no other than what they are. The taste of chocolate is not better than a recipe for making fudge, it is different. Without a recipe there would be no fudge; the purpose of the recipe is to create that experience. Without the creation of actual fudge, there would be no taste of chocolate, and the recipe would serve no purpose. The relationship between knowledge and knowing can be equally interdependent and mutually supportive.

In performance, for example, that relationship depends upon what we might call the "transparency" of the performer—the ability to allow knowledge of character to be perceived through the face, body, and voice without interference or unintentional modification. Lacking such transparency (which, as we will see, can be developed through exercise), the movement from knowledge to knowing will be dimmed, fuzzed, or otherwise obscured. The major challenge of this book is to deal directly with the movement from knowledge to knowing for the singer-actor: How to allow the transformation of mental information into powerful communication and, ultimately, into radiant performing.

The reversal of this movement from knowledge to knowing—that is, the demonstration of knowing by the teacher for someone else (the student) who then has knowledge of the outer effect of that knowing—is very often a part of the teaching process. That reversal does not actually teach the student observer to know the process, although it can be useful information, and does provide a model. But the teacher's capacity to demonstrate knowing does not guarantee the ability to teach that knowing. The old saw, "Those who can't *do* it, *teach* it," has an equally significant, less-often-cited corollary: "Those who *can* do it, are often *unable* to teach it." I made up the corollary from direct experience with the students of gifted "knowers" who were also teachers. One of the finest music-theater performers I know teaches as well, and the performances of his students in no way reflect his own extraordinary performing—sometimes almost the contrary.

To nurture the knowing process in someone else is an art that may have nothing to do with one's own capacity to demonstrate that knowing (which is what performing is). One may "do it," and assume that that demonstration of knowing has transmitted the knowing and made it a direct experience for someone else; and if that were so, every audience member that witnessed a great performance would become a great performer as well, which is another piece of evident nonsense. Again, while those experiences are useful and vital, it is important to be clear about the essential differences between the various stages of knowledge and knowing.

For the student with little or no experience, that approach can also create the illusion that he or she, having observed a demonstration of knowing performance, will also have access to a similar kind of performance knowingness, either by following the instructions of the teacher-performer, or by imitating parts of the outer process of the performance itself. But if the student does not have a coherent, integrative view of the total performance process—inner and outer—that kind of teaching will produce more authority-dependent mannequins than powerful performers, and will continue to spread confusion concerning the movement from knowledge to knowing.

The spiral of expansion, then, deals with the knowing-knowledge complex on several levels. One approach is to move into the unknown by first acquiring some knowledge about that unknown (reading about Carmen's character); then to experience that knowledge imaginatively; and finally to have a series of direct experiences in realizing that knowledge (of the character of Carmen) through the use of the body, the voice, and the emotions, thus coming to know it.

In another approach, one can simply move into the unknown with the body, the voice, and the emotions (without having read about the character of Carmen or defined in terms of knowledge what one is trying to communicate) and have an energy experience that will then interact with whatever knowledge one already possesses (for example, the words and music of an aria from *Carmen*).

Or one can use a combination of both approaches—and one is always doing that to some extent, for there is always some knowledge available to the person or one could not perform at all; and each exercise or performance can always be experienced as an unknown, as if one were doing it for the first time. In addition there is the inner unknown (how Carmen might feel) and the outer unknown (how she might act), which are in constant interaction.

But in all cases, the way in which we approach that movement from the known to the unknown is crucial, as is our clarity in recognizing where we are on the path from knowledge to knowing, as well as in recognizing the distinctions between them.

Like the pentagon of potentiality, the spiral of expansion is a means of heightening our awareness. In this case the awareness is about two crucial but often unrecognized challenges in the development of the singer-actor: the movement from the known to the unknown, and the movement from knowledge to knowing.

In moving into the unknown, then, there are two basic approaches: planning oriented and serendipity oriented. In the first case the following sequence applies:

1. Acquire knowledge of the unknown territory you wish to move into by reading about it or being told about it ("Carmen moved sinuously, with undulating hips, singing with a dark, velvety tone with half-closed eyes,") or by having it partially demonstrated or watching a performance, film, or rehearsal of it, or imagining how you might do it.

2. Do what you have read about, heard described, seen, or imagined.

3. Practice doing it until it becomes a known. (It may be usable before it actually becomes a known.)

In the serendipity-oriented approach, the following sequence applies:

1. Play into the unknown of Carmen's behavior with the voice, the face, and the body. Don't plan—simply *do* things you have never done. Do this several times.

2. From the experience of doing it, select those that seem to be the most potentially useful and do them again.

3. Practice them until they become a known. (Again, they may be usable before they become known.)

One can also apply this three-step process to the expansion of personal performing capacities.

1. Map yourself: make a description of your known in each mode— what you can already do. This will also define your unknown in each mode.

2. Describe an unknown behavior of the voice, the face, and the body, and do it.

3. Practice that behavior until it becomes a known.

or

1. Play into your own unknown in any mode several times.

2. Select one of the unknown behaviors (the most threatening, the most uncomfortable, the most unfamiliar, or simply the one you like best) and do it again.

3. Practice that unknown behavior until it becomes a known.

This emphasis on actual exercise affirms the fact that this book is knowledge (useful knowledge, I think, but knowledge nonetheless). To make it into knowing, one must follow its instructions and begin exercising one's total performing process. Such exercise is a major part of moving from the known to the unknown, and transforming knowledge into knowing.

Playing with Language: Naming MIM, PIM, and HOBS

The distinction between knowledge and knowing can also remind us of the function of language, which is a primary means of acquiring knowledge. We move from knowledge to knowing, and we can also move from knowing to knowledge. We can come to know something through direct experience, and can then attempt to translate that experience into words. We turn experiential knowing into verbal knowledge in attempting to communicate it to others; and however brilliantly we do it, that verbal version of our knowing is inevitably a reduction of the original experience.

This is not to attack the uses of language—useful, vital, and wonderful tool that it can be—but to recognize the fact that all language is a reduction of experience. For the gifted writer, it may sometimes seem that language expands an experience, but that is an illusion: language may distill an experience, empower it in a different way, make us feel it differently, even more strongly, but it remains a reduction—glorious, but a reduction. (And since all thought tends to be verbal, thought, too, is necessarily a reduction of experience.)

New words are attempts to open up the reducing valve of language just a bit—to allow a little more experiential reality to be caught in the sieve of words—and to allow the partiality of the verbal to open more fully to the wholeness of experience. For example, I needed a word to describe more fully the quality of performance I wanted to experience from singer-actors. There were a number of individual words that described parts or aspects of that whole experience. I wanted the performer to seem to be believable, to seem to be real or convincing, and to seem to be genuine, natural, or authentic—that is, to give a performance that seemed to come from his or her particular sense of personal power. But there wasn't a single word that encompassed all those meanings, so I made one up—a portmanteau word in the style of Lewis Carroll. The kind of performance I wanted to help singer-actors move toward is one that is *a*uthentic, *re*al, and *b*elievable: *Areba* (uh-ree'-ba). The word caught on in my classes, and became a verb as well—*to arebacize*. I will use the coinage throughout the book to refer to the qualities it enfolds.

Another coinage that had a life of its own was a name I gave the mental-intellectual part of us. That is the part that uses words and, according to recent research, spends 75 percent of its time talking to us and about us in negative, judgmental ways. Since we can call it the mental-intellectual mind (or mode), the acronym is MIM. I referred to it in a morning class in one of my institutes, and by that afternoon, participants were using it as common parlance. It seems to be clarifying and comforting to have a way of identifying, referring to, and personalizing that invisible and inaudible (except in our own heads) part of ourselves.

Since then, MIM has become an increasingly useful way of referring to that word-oriented part of our minds that observes, analyzes, remembers, imagines, and chooses. These are all useful and vital functions, and each of them can be used negatively as well as positively. MIM is always picking up information and knowledge through observations, and those observations can be made with judgment—instantly labeling the information as good or bad—or detachment—simply being aware of the information with minimal evaluation. In order to make choices, MIM can then analyze that information. The analysis can focus on reductionism or synthesis: mistaking the part for the whole on one hand, or seeing each part from the perspective of the whole on the other. Since MIM is always relating to the past or the future (when one is truly in the present, MIM is transcended—as in radiant performing), it can operate positively or negatively in remembering the past and imagining the future. In remembering, it can also be judgmental or discerning about the choices it has made. In imagining, it can worry, pre-evaluate, and be afraid of what is going to happen, or it can prepare for it playfully, creatively, and expectantly, knowing that it will be able to handle whatever occurs. At this point we will deal with the negative aspects of MIM's power, and the importance of releasing those conditioned habits of judgmentalism that cripple our positive use of the past and the future. Later we will examine the positive uses of imagining as a fundamental singing-acting tool.

MIM is a part of our performing energies that we sometimes mistakenly identify with as the whole of our mental processes. Referring to it as a part has allowed the performers with whom I work to identify MIM as only a part of themselves, and not mistake it for the whole. Equally important, they have been able to dis-identify with MIM when it is not functioning in a useful way (which, for performers, seems to be a remarkably high percentage of the time.) Because so much of MIM's conditioning is negative, I stress in my classes that MIM is not a villain, but simply an energy that can be used positively or negatively, as described above. Further, we can increase through exercise the proportion of time MIM spends in useful, supportive activity. MIM is a powerful part of us, a talking part of us, a two-edged sword part of us, and a part of us to recognize as such and not as the whole. By giving an identity to our parts we can allow ourselves to experience them *as* parts and not as the whole. Since MIM understands language so well, we can also speak to it in developing, expanding, and transforming our total performing process.

It is ironic that MIM plays such an important part in this book, with its strongly verbal-analytical approach. Much of what I am trying to do is to release the total performing process from judgmental dominance by MIM, which initiates the major interferences with that process. Why, then, I have asked myself, does MIM seem to be so necessary in freeing that process? For example, in the ten-hour seminars that simply introduce the performing power ideas, most of the time is spent in clarifying concepts with only a brief time for exercises. I have often eliminated some of the explanation, but inevitably I have to present the excised material anyway, in response to questions. In longer seminars I am able to do both, but the amount of MIM-based clarification remains fairly constant. It is encouraging that, despite all this talk, seminar participants always feel inspired and excited. The new level of understanding gives them a vision of what can unfold for them and for their performing process. Nonetheless, for a long time I was concerned about MIM's important role in the process.

My concern was that in drawing on MIM so extensively, I might be reinforcing the very thing I am trying to release. Another image gives a more accurate view of the situation: When you are in a cage, you may have to use the same technology to get out of the cage as was used to create the cage in the first place. MIM created the cage of our conditioning, and it seems that MIM is helpful in dismantling it. Dismantling the cage doesn't mean you will necessarily move out of it, of course — it only gives you permission to do so. To actually move out of the cage depends upon the use of other energy resources that are not verbally and intellectually based. But to use those resources, you must dismantle the cage. Part of this book is about dismantling the cage; the rest is about moving out of it once the bars are down.

That suggests viewing the process as a spectrum — a concept integral to our work. In this case, the spectrum has analysis at one end and synthesis at the other, and encompasses all the choices in between — each a blend of those two seeming contraries. Analysis is taking things apart to understand them better (a task that MIM especially enjoys); synthesis is putting them back together again. One is concerned with the parts, the other with the whole. Our civilization has been on an analytic-reductionist binge for several centuries now—examining things in smaller and smaller parts in order to understand how life and the universe work. Any complex system needs to be analyzed and understood part by part in the process of coming to know it. But life doesn't work in parts—it works in wholes. Whatever system we are analyzing must also be synthesized and experienced as a functioning whole before we can know it fully.

Singing-acting is just such a complex system. Lack of clear analysis has led to confusion about it. Analysis can also lead to potential fragmentation, but the analysis must be pursued until the real relationship of the parts to each other and to the whole is perceived. Simultaneously, one must pursue the process of synthesis—of understanding singing-acting from a direct experience of the whole—by actually doing it. For the greatest vitality, analysis and synthesis must always interact with each other: we must take the process in question apart *and* put it back together; and the more fully those two functions mutually support each other, the more powerful and whole the total process.

In addition to MIM, there is that part of us that experiences emotions. My feeling that the verbal mind and the emotions were two separate parts of our inner system was given validation by research by Dr. Joseph Ledoux at the Center for Neural Science at NYU. His findings suggest "that certain emotional reactions occur before the brain has even had time to register fully what it is that is causing the reaction; the emotion occurs before thought. That view is a direct challenge to the prevailing wisdom in psychology, that emotional reactions follow from thoughts about a situation." As Dr. Ledoux said, " 'Emotional reactions and emotional memories can be formed without any conscious, cognitive participation at all because anatomically the emotional system can act independently' " (*NY Times*, August 15, 1989).

We will explore the implications of those findings more fully in chapters 9 and 10. At this point we will simply name the inner emotional part of us, IMP, which, while not acronymically perfect, is perfectly appropriate for such a changeable, unpredictable, and hard-to-control part of our energy system.

If IMP produces a flow of anger, MIM can observe that anger, judge it, and try to control it. Observing both of those processes—IMP's anger and MIM's reaction to it—is another energy character I will call HOBS (our *higher observer*). HOBS assists MIM in seeing things from a full-spectrum perspective, in blending analysis and synthesis, and in describing rather than judging. As IMP feels anger, and MIM feels guilt for the anger, HOBS can help MIM see the anger simply as energy with many choices for release, and aid MIM in dropping the guilt and concentrating on choices in transforming and directing the energy of IMP rather than trying to repress it.

As with MIM, HOBS is different from what it observes, and that power to observe and become more aware increases with practice. We will suggest specific ways to expand the capacity of HOBS for observation and awareness, for they are primary resources in nurturing our growth process. Awareness, all by itself, creates change. If we couple that awareness with specific exercises which grow from it and act upon it, we have the basis for a powerful developmental process.

Initially MIM creates a field of awareness that focuses and motivates the exercises for the other parts of the human energy system. Then, as our awareness expands, HOBS comes into play as a perception of MIM. At that point it becomes possible to exercise MIM as well as the body, the voice, and the face. And even without actually exercising those parts, the awarenesses generated by MIM and HOBS will begin to create change; *with* specific exercises, those awarenesses are multiplied in their potential for growth— exercise and awareness interact with each other in a classic instance of synergy.

Another invisible, inaudible part of our energy system is the intuitional plane. Barbara Ray describes this as:

> a part of your Being of a different and higher vibration than the mental plane, [and] which gives insights and a kind of knowing without conscious reasoning or thinking processes. In higher consciousness, this plane is more expansive, of less form, and less limiting than the physical, emotional or mental planes and functions in a different way according to its inherent nature.
> (*ERM*, p. 57)

In addition to using HOBS to blend analysis and synthesis, and to move out of the dismantled cage of confusion, we can also open to our intuitive energies. Since there is no agreed-upon name for those energies, I devised another acronym that unfolded as follows.

From the intuitional plane flows creativity and imagination. "Enhanced capacities of imagination and creativity are often described as unlimited and playful" (*ERM*, p. 55). Since the capacity for true play is such a significant part of the developmental process, and since play is strongly linked to the freedom of intuitive impulse, I wanted to keep play in the name. I call those energies the *playful intuitive mode*, or *PIM*. The P could also stand for any of the other seven guiding principles for radiant performance (see chapter 6). Thus, the purposeful, processing, practicing, playful, persistent, patient, potential intuitive mode. *PIM* it remains in all those cases, and thus we have a name for that creative, imaginative, nonverbal, bright-idea, "hunch" capacity. Although we may not be able to exercise and develop PIM's power directly, we can learn to open ourselves more freely and fully to the flow of PIM's energy in serving the performing process.

I will refer to MIM, IMP, HOBS, and PIM freely, as well as *areba* and any other coinages, where they are useful for clarification. If those creations are unuseful jargon, they will languish on these pages, mourned not by me (and certainly by no one else). But if they contribute something playful or even illuminating to our exploration, it is worth the bit of language-stretching involved.

Energies We Know: Parts of the Whole

Language is also challenged in attempting to describe levels of energy that lie outside the realms of the intellectual-verbal. Expanding and clarifying concepts about our vast nonverbal energy resources is one of the functions (along with awareness) of our third model. Readers of *Performing Power* will be familiar with the cast of energy characters that were used to visualize the projective-modes concept: the kinesthetic mode, the hearing-vocal mode (which I will now call the vocal mode), and the facial-emotional mode (to be called the facial mode). They comprise point 4 on the pentagon (p. 9) — the visible and audible part of the human energy system.

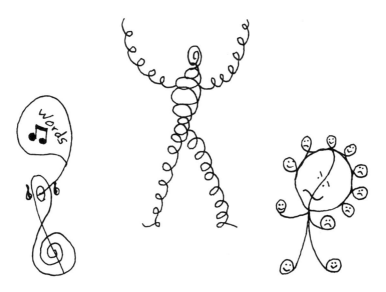

Within point 3 we found their coach, the newly dubbed MIM, the mental-intellectual mode.

We also have IMP—the inner emotional process—another member of the invisible, inaudible cast of point 3.

(Note that there is one slight alteration in the visualization of MIM: in *Performing Power* it was shown to be speaking words; the fact is, MIM depends upon the vocal mode to utter the verbal thoughts as spoken or sung words. IMP contributes the emotional feeling that is communicated by the *music* of the vocal mode—which also contributes nonemotional modifications of the literal meaning of the words. Both MIM and IMP depend upon the facial mode for further clarification of both thought and feeling, IMP interacting with the face in what we will call the facial-emotional process. Those three parts of the total facial-emotional system will be discussed in detail in chapters 9 and 10.)

We also had the intuitive mode, now called PIM, the playful intuitive mode:

In addition we now have HOBS, which does not use language, but simply observes all the other energy processes with benign, detached interest.

As a further distinction, we will refer to MIM, HOBS, PIM, and IMP as *guidance modes*, and the others as *projective modes*. Being invisible and inaudible, the guidance modes depend upon the projective modes to do the actual communicating.

Each of these energies represents a different part of the human system. Most people have experienced them as such — especially the body, the voice, and the face. But even the differences within the invisible/inaudible interior energies are commonly experienced. As in our previous example, we may be angry (IMP) and also aware that we are and think we shouldn't be (MIM). Simultaneously, we are also aware (HOBS) that MIM is judging IMP; and in the midst of all this, we suddenly know the answer to an old problem (PIM) that we have not been consciously thinking about.

All these energies, however, are part of and come from a whole energy greater than their sum. That energy of the whole is more elusive to MIM, since agreed-upon words to name our inner energies are less readily available as we move within. There are, nonetheless, more than 2,000 different ways of designating that energy of the whole, including universal energy, light, mana, bioplasmic energy, life-force energy, and so on. We will refer to that universal, whole energy as the *Radiant Whole*.

While the energies of the Radiant Whole are always within us, supporting us unconditionally, waiting to be opened to more completely by the partial energies, they are truly beyond the senses: they are transcendental, simultaneously everywhere and nowhere (thus the words *whole-hole* can imply everything and nothing). In short, there is no way to visualize or talk about such energies in a concrete, three-dimensional way. With that understanding, I propose to visualize them anyway. Introducing the final and all-encompassing member of our cast of energy characters, the Radiant Whole!

And while the Radiant Whole is ordinarily beyond our conditioned capacity to sense it, it is nonetheless integral to all of us — we wouldn't be alive without it. Although we are less familiar with it than with the energies of, say, the body or the emotions, it is always there, supporting, guiding, and informing us — we simply aren't as conscious of it.

Among the many descriptions of the Radiant Whole is that of Richard D. Carson in his book, *Taming Your Gremlin*. In discussing who you really are, Carson begins with what you are not. Among other things, you are not your body, your feelings, your thoughts, your personality, or even some complex combination of these variables (including, I would add, your voice, or your creativity). Nor are you the roles you play in life — singer, performer, actor, singer-actor, husband, mother, nice person, dedicated student, or lazy bum. You are neither your projective modes, nor your guidance modes, nor any of the many roles you play in life and on stage. The real you is your Radiant Whole, which, as Carson puts it, is:

> a pure life force (which) is not limited by your concepts and ideas
> about who you are. It is the real you that is able to experience
> and enjoy the body in which you dwell, the external physical
> world in which you live, and the thoughts, memories and fantasies
> your brain creates and stores. I do not know all that there is to
> know about the real you (or the real me, for that matter), but I
> have experienced enough to know that the real you is beautiful
> beyond your most creative fantasy, and allowed to do so it will
> guide the evolvement of your life in a manner that will feel
> terrific. (p. 3)

Experiencing Wholeness: Radiant Performing

Conscious experience of the real you — of the Radiant Whole, of your inherent wholeness — is unusual, but it is more common than one might suspect. In Abraham Maslow's studies of what he calls the "peak experience," there is an insight into the quality of that experience of wholeness and the Radiant Whole.

Maslow questioned many people about "the most wonderful, most ecstatic experiences of their lives." He used the generalized term *peak experience* for all of them, which included everything from the experience of love, creativity, and insight to aesthetic, orgasmic, and mystic experiences. To his surprise, no matter what the origin of the experiences, they were described in about the same way — all had vital qualities that were virtually identical.

> An essential aspect of the peak experience is integration within
> the person and therefore between the person and the world. In
> these states of being, the person becomes unified; for the time
> being, the splits, polarities, and dissociations within him tend to
> be resolved; the civil war within is neither won nor lost but
> transcended. In such a state, the person becomes far more open
> to experience and far more spontaneous and fully functioning. . . .
> (*Motivation and Personality*, p. 163)

"It is," says Maslow, "as if in the peak experience we accepted and embraced our deeper selves instead of controlling and fearing them" (p. 164).
Since our deeper selves include HOBS and the Radiant Whole, one might
wonder why we would fear them. But, as we will see, the unintegrated parts
of us—which include, most especially, MIM—*do* fear the wholeness they
cannot understand and control.

In the peak experience, the person "becomes more a unity, more integrated, and self-consistent . . . more completely himself, idiosyncratic,
unique" (p. 164).

> And since he is so, he can be more easily expressive and
> spontaneous without effort. All his powers then come together in
> their most efficient integration and coordination, organized and
> coordinated much more perfectly than usual. Everything then can
> be done with unusual ease and lack of effort. Inhibition, doubt,
> control, self-criticism, diminish toward a zero point and he
> becomes the spontaneous, coordinated efficient organism,
> functioning like an animal without conflict or split, without
> hesitation or doubt, in a great flow of power that is so peculiarly
> effortless, that may become like play, masterful, virtuoso-like.
>   To put it simply, he becomes more whole and unified, more
> unique and idiosyncratic, more alive and spontaneous, more
> perfectly expressive and uninhibited, more effortless and
> powerful, more daring and courageous (leaving fears and doubts
> behind), more ego-transcending and self-forgetful. (p. 164)

Such a state of being describes what we will experience in radiant performing—when all our energies come together in a coordinated, synergistic
interplay that transcends their separate capacities and allows them to become "more whole and unified." In this view, the peak experience of radiant
performing is a direct apprehension of the Radiant Whole: it opens to our
inherent wholeness and transcends the power of MIM or any other partial
energy to control it. Like all peak experiences, radiant performing cannot be
made to happen. As we pointed out at the beginning of this chapter, one can
only create the conditions that prepare for it, open to it, and allow it to un-

fold. Such performing transcends the ordinary performing experience for the audience as well as the performer; it also surpasses the capacity of MIM and its words to adequately describe it.

If the peak experience of radiant performing is to happen within the context of an art like singing-acting, it requires a degree of technical skill high enough that the demands of the role in question need a minimum of MIM's conscious attention. I will refer to the radiant performance given by Laurence Olivier in *Othello* in 1964 at various points as we proceed because it relates so profoundly and specifically to our subject.

This radiant performance involved an actor at the peak of his capacity; an actor, moreover, who may have had the greatest degree of technical skill—including a masterful command and coordination of his voice, body, and emotions—of anyone in this century (some might say of all time). This expertise was acquired through decades of practice in a career unique in its alternation between roles and media that compelled Olivier to develop his whole instrument: classical theater (voice, body, and emotions), and realistic films and television (facial and emotional processes). The performance was in a role that many great actors have called unplayable because of its enormous demands. The vocal requirements alone make it a true singing-acting role.

It was a controversial portrayal, but "the majority of critics judged [Olivier's] Othello to be a stupendous achievement and most especially they saw it as a dazzling display of virtuosity" (Cottrell, p. 339). Even those who criticized it accepted it as an enormously significant production—"There was a sense of theatrical history, of legend-making in the air" (Holden, p. 379)—and no one could deny that it was a performance of tremendous power. Franco Zeffirelli, the noted opera and theater director, said it was "an anthology of everything that has been discovered about acting in the last three centuries. It's grand and majestic, but it's also modern and realistic. I would call it a lesson for us all" (Cottrell, p. 340).

One particular performance in the run of that production has become legendary. It was so transcendent that the cast gathered to watch from the wings when they were not onstage. No one spoke to Olivier during the performance for fear of breaking the spell, but afterward they went back to his dressing room. By various accounts, he was dejected, angry, and terrified: he did not know how he had come to give such a performance, and therefore he had no way of being able to do it again.

By the very nature of his intense and highly polished technical training, Olivier was accustomed to being in control—it was a need he insisted upon as part of the craft of acting. But when, as I view it, all the lower, controllable energies—the mind, the body, the face, the voice, and the emotions—fell into total synchronization, his whole system became one, he opened to the flow of the whole and had a peak-experience performance that was radiant from beginning to end. But it was a performance his mind (MIM) could not control—and after it was over, MIM, uncomprehending, was alternately terrified, angry, and dejected.

Olivier had no model for such an event, nor has there been one generally available. Had he had such a model, it could have included the understanding that if and when such a performance were to occur, the performer might experience it as simultaneously transcendent and terrifying. The terror comes from the mind thinking it has lost control, and in truth, it has. It has done everything it can to create the best performing it can envision, and yet, seemingly independent of its efforts, there is performing of a power it does not understand and cannot control. Yet all the efforts of the mind and the rest of the performing process are vital contributions in preparing for that new and unknown energy event.

If the mind clings to the illusion that it can and should be controlling the whole process, it will naturally be frightened when, as the synergistic wisdom of the whole takes over, the mind seems to lose that illusionary control. Guided from a level of knowing the mind cannot grasp, the radiant performance that ensues is the most powerful and secure performance possible. Since the experience is unknown, the mind may fear and resist it, as well as feel out of control. But if the mind knows all this in advance, it may be able to relax and enjoy the radiant opening if it happens, and even come to love it and open to it willingly in the future.

With this understanding, Olivier might have been able not only to accept, but to rejoice in such opportunities to release control to a guiding intelligence far greater than his own. It would have meant letting go of a great deal that Olivier's MIM, with its control of all that rigorously trained technique, might insist was necessary. But, and this is the point, the letting go or, better, the opening to that source of infinite intelligence—the Radiant Whole—could and *did* create a performance that transcended all the control efforts in the world.

Simultaneously, and this is a second major point, that radiant performance was interdependent upon a finely tuned, carefully trained, technically virtuosic instrument with the voice, body, face, emotions, and mind all in a synergistic coordinated relationship and capable of fulfilling the extreme demands of a difficult role. On one hand, it is "Go with the flow," but on the other, the flow can't happen without an instrument to receive, translate, and transmit it through an appropriate role.

To recapitulate: the primary purpose of this book is to create the conditions—fulfilled performing potential—under which radiant performing—the fundamental purpose—can occur. Exercising for that primary purpose—the secondary purpose—will involve not only preparing the performer's total instrument to open to, allow, receive, and communicate radiant performing, but also learning to let go of the counterfeit control needs that block it. It is also supportive to the primary purpose to know that when radiant performing occurs, it will be a different experience from anything MIM could have predicted.

The performing power technique is a science of the human energy system that serves the three purposes on the journey to radiant performing. That journey can be supported even more fully by another science of whole energy—The Radiance Technique®—which allows us to draw directly on the energies of the Radiant Whole.

Direct Access to the Radiant Whole: The Radiance Technique

In the final chapter of *Performing Power* I discussed briefly The Radiance Technique (referred to at that time as *Reiki*). As I explained it then, The Radiance Technique allows the individual to access, amplify, and direct the universal energy (the Radiant Whole) within the human system, increasing its availability for use by the physical, emotional, mental, creative, and higher consciousness systems, thus assisting in integrating and balancing the energies of those systems. The Radiance Technique allows us to draw more fully upon our Radiant Whole—the inherent source of our entire system of human energies—and to do so consistently and reliably. As Dr. Barbara Ray, the world's foremost authority on The Radiance Technique, has put it:

> The inherent *purpose* of The Radiance Technique is to give direct access to transcendental, universal, radiant, Light-energy. This transcendental energy science accesses a total, non-partial, non-fragmented, universal cosmic order of energy which *is not at all* the same as the non-universal, partial, lower vibrational energies which are commonly familiar to us. (*Official Handbook of The Radiance Technique®*, p. 4)

We will discuss the relationship of The Radiance Technique to the performing process more fully in later chapters (especially 4 and 14). While it is not necessary to have studied The Radiance Technique to use the processes and exercises described in this book, doing so will support them in a significant way.

Using The Radiance Technique will not automatically result in a peak experience, nor will drawing upon it while performing guarantee a radiant performance. The peak experience of radiant performance is interdependent upon the capacity of the whole system to create a fulfilled performance potential. In simple terms, if you cannot sing a high C, the use of The Radiance Technique while attempting to do so will not result in a radiant performance. And since radiant performance involves the whole, the high C is not the only factor in question: the body, the face, IMP, MIM, PIM, and HOBS, and their individual and coordinated abilities are also crucial.

It is also true that as we develop all the parts of the whole performing process and create the conditions for radiant performing, we can be supported and guided by the use of The Radiance Technique. While we are *always* in contact with the Radiant Whole, our awareness of it is obscured by our conditioning. (As great teachers have told us through the ages, we are already enlightened, whole beings—we simply don't know it.) When our access to that wholeness increases, we may or may not be aware of it. This does not mean that the increased access is not there; it is simply that our perceptual capacity has not yet opened to it. Thus, regardless of our level of awareness, using The Radiance Technique *does* guarantee increased support from the Radiant Whole at any time under any circumstances.

As we develop our capacity to create the conditions that allow radiant performing, our openness to the energies of radiance will be enhanced by the degree of trust we have in their ongoing support. We can create a synergistic relationship with the Radiant Whole proportionate to our capacity to open to it on all levels of energy—including that of trust.

In its flowing, luminous freedom, the Radiant Whole is also a model for a creative, energized, joyful, flexible, open, unlimited, enthusiastic, and expansive approach to life and performance. The radiant performer is one who is on the journey toward ever more radiant performing, and who uses the performing power technique to create conditions which allow that kind of performing.

While no two experiences of performing will be identical, they will all expand the vision of what it means to be human for performers and audience alike. In *Acting Power*, Robert Cohen asks the actor who reads his book to "set his sights at the highest, at greatness itself. Nothing less will really do" (p. xi). In affirming that journey toward greatness, we may envision something beyond it: a potential of wholeness to which we may open at any moment as we perform, a wholeness that adds impetus to the movement toward greatness, that expands audiences as well as performers when it is experienced, and that, in the transcendence of radiant performing, supports and encompasses all other goals.

Chapter 2

Singer-Actor Training:
A Fragmented Field

The Whole and the Parts

The pentagon of potentiality is the overall system of parts—the arts of music theater and singing-acting, the environment within which those arts are practiced, and the processes of the singer-actor—within which the singer-actor functions. As we have seen, the pentagon is incomplete, not whole: there is no exercise process, nor aesthetic view to connect it all. However, since all the parts are interconnected, incompleteness in any part or a disconnection of any part from the whole will be reflected in the other parts. If there is any partiality or fragmentation in the larger system of music theater, singer-actors may find themselves losing personal power and losing connection with their own wholeness as a result.

The pentagon of potentiality, then, is a whole system. And each point on the pentagon, each part of that total system, is also a system within itself. Each of those subsystems must also function in wholeness for the health of the larger system. The singer-actor, of course, is one of the subsystems—perhaps the most significant of them all.

In *The Complete Singer-Actor*, I addressed the concept of the whole performer, the performer who has integrated all the parts of his or her system into a synergistic whole. At that time, however, I had no clear description of the total singing-acting process, no comprehensive way of exercising that process, nor a clear sense of the other parts of this pentagon of potentiality. The description of singing-acting is now clearer, the exercise process is constantly expanding, and I return once more to the concept of the singer-actor in the context of the other parts of the larger system.

But I will no longer refer to the *complete* singer-actor—there is no such thing. A final, finished-product state of being for any living person, performer, or process is neither attainable nor desirable. Perfection is not possible and perfectionism, as we will see, is a blighting, addictive characteristic that effectively prevents what it purports to achieve. To be complete, finished, a product, is not the issue. The issue is the process of the singer-actor, who is always moving toward greater wholeness as a performer and toward performances of increasing fullness, fulfillment and radiance; the singer-actor as an unfolding subsystem-part in interaction with the other parts of the whole system.

In *Performing Power*, the concept of synergy played an important role in helping define the singer-actor as a system of interacting parts. Synergy is the property of any system—a human being, an organization of people or things—in which the parts of the system working together create a whole greater than their sum. A performer whose parts are synergistically interacting to the full extent of their capacity to do so is, by definition, giving the most powerful performance possible. *Performing Power* defined what those parts were, described the singer-actor in a new way, and approached the process of exercising those parts and their interrelationships. In developing the exercise process of the radiant performer we are also developing the missing subsystem on the pentagon of potentiality and thus increasing the potential synergy of the larger system of music theater.

In this volume we will expand our view of that synergistic interaction between the whole and the parts. The radiant performer is one who manifests the radiant wholeness of the human system when performing, a radiance that is inherent in that system (though seldom experienced directly), and that enhances and empowers whatever communicating choices the performer may make (as well as supporting any other parts of the whole music-theater process—the other performers, the audience, the work itself—with which it interacts).

This implies that radiance in performing is a natural thing, even the birthright of the performer. It is. And yet it is seldom experienced in its fullness; radiant performing remains a rare event. What blocks it? What prevents the power of that inherent, natural, universal energy from flowing freely into radiant performing? We will examine in detail the ways we block the flow of the Radiant Whole in performance, and how we can exercise and develop our capacity to release those blocks and allow our radiant power to expand freely and fully as we perform.

But first let us look at the larger system of the pentagon of potentiality to clarify some of the ways we can (and do) block our potential for radiant performance.

Partiality and Fragmentation: Mistaking the Part for the Whole

One of the many ways we interfere with our radiant potential is by viewing the performance process from a fragmentary perspective—by mistaking a part of it for the whole, thus losing the capacity to interact fully with the other parts of the whole and with the whole itself.

David Bohm, the physicist, has discussed the issue of fragmentation and wholeness with remarkable clarity. He finds implications in the concept that go far beyond the field of theoretical physics. "Our fragmentary way of thinking, looking, and acting . . . has implications in every aspect of human life. . . . fragmentation seems to be the one thing in our way of life which is universal, which works through the whole without boundary or limit" (*Wholeness and the Implicate Order*, p. 16). We try to separate the world into fragmented parts "beyond the domain in which to do this is appropriate" and to "divide what is really indivisible" (p. 15).

For example, those of us teaching or coaching the singer-actor may attempt to isolate one part of the total singing-acting process, possibly the voice, and let it stand for the whole. ("Don't worry about acting—the voice is all that counts.") Or we may try to find the total answer in some other part of the whole process—in the body, the emotions, or the mind. Each one of us may bring a partial and potentially fragmented perspective to the teaching process, which performers must then try to put together with the other parts on their own. If several of us are doing this with the same performer (and that experience appears to be universal) he or she—lacking an integrating view of the whole—is likely to end up deeply confused about the nature of the whole system of singing-acting and music theater, the nature of the parts of that whole, and the relationship between them. As Bohm puts it:

> Fragmentation is in essence a confusion around the question of difference (partiality) and sameness (wholeness), but the clear perception of these categories is necessary in every phase of life. *To be confused about what is different and what is not, is to be confused about everything.* Thus it is not an accident that our fragmentary form of thought is leading to such a widespread range of crises, social, political, economic, ecological,

psychological, etc., in the individual and in society as a whole.
(p. 16)

(And, we might add, on all levels of education, including that of the singer-actor.)

Let us look at another model of the systems concept and the relationship of the whole and the parts. In working with the concept of disease and health, there has been an increasing awareness in the past two decades that in treating illness overemphasis on any given part, or lack of attention to the whole relationship of the parts, can prevent us from getting well. We may "cure" the sick part; simultaneously, it is very useful to give attention to the other parts that interact with the sick part. Any lack of health in the human system will include, besides the physical manifestation of it, the emotions, the mental processes, the habits and conditionings of the person, the air one breathes, the food one eats, the environment, and how all these parts, and many more, interact. Leave anything out in considering the total system and you may not understand why things are in a state of ill health (or wellness). You may have strengthened an obviously weak part of the system, you may have removed an interference between parts of the system, you may have stamped out the germ that caused the ill health, you may have done all these things and more, yet you may not have alleviated the illness itself. It will be impossible to develop a higher degree of wellness in the system because you have not altered the interactive weakness that allowed the illness to develop in the first place.

If we insist that one part is really the whole (e.g., "There's nothing wrong physically, it's all in the mind," "Just replace the heart," "Take medication to block the pain,") we consign a substantial portion of the population to an ongoing state of disease, when they could be helped by attention to the whole and to the interconnectedness of all the parts making up that whole. Enormous progress has been made in medicine and science during this century in opening to the larger, systemic view of life that acknowledges the essential interconnectedness of all things: the wholeness of humans and their many parts, including hitherto unknown processes and energies that are being acknowledged and studied for the first time in modern Western history. The human being is being viewed as an integral and participating whole-part within the greater wholeness of nature and the universe. The systems view of life has given us a remarkable concept for examining and re-examining all organic processes, including, of course, the process of singing-acting.

Singer-Actor Training: A System of Fragments

The singing-acting process is a particularly clear case of the parts and the whole. The parts of that process—the voice, the body, the emotions, the thoughts, the imagination, and other levels of energy—are variously exercised by different experts—voice teachers, musical coaches, conductors, stage directors, movement or dance instructors, acting teachers, etc. But there is no one person who can tell the performer how to exercise all these parts together, let alone how to integrate them. This creates fragmentation, which makes the part-whole relationship a harmful one. Fragmentation can arise when the part is disconnected from the whole and from the other parts, or when the part is mistaken for the whole. Let us examine this process of fragmentation as it affects a young singer-actor on her daily journey through the necessarily partial and potentially fragmented field of music-theater training. We will begin with the voice lesson.

From her voice teacher our young singer-actor receives (let us grant) much useful information and experiences genuine vocal progress. But she is also told to hold her mouth in a certain way "for the best resonance" and hold her arms slightly akimbo—"like electric elbows"—because it "looks more energized." (All quotes come from actual situations.)

On to the musical coach, who works for a certain "excitement in the sound, a bit of a buzz" (which doesn't feel especially good and seems to contradict the voice teacher's instructions).

Next comes movement class, where work is done with postural alignment ("Tuck in those buns and hold them,") and use of gestures that "must come from the base of the spine." (The posture asked for is also different from that asked for by the voice teacher.)

From there to acting class, where the focus is on developing the character from within, drawing upon intense personal experiences from the performer's past. Although she thinks it would be difficult to sing with all that tension, she is told "the feeling has to be there or you'll end up phony."

Language and diction class comes next. Here the emphasis is on the German umlaut sound and the necessary shape of the mouth to produce it correctly (which is also different from the instructions of the voice teacher).

Finally, rehearsal for an approaching performance. The director keeps asking for "more involvement, more commitment, more emotion," while the conductor says, "Watch me for the cue," and demands a gradual diminuendo while the performer is running around a chair—per instructions from the director. When the performer tells the directors she is getting hoarse from emoting as requested, the director replies, "I don't care about that—you've got to learn to act—then you can worry about singing!"

None of these instructions are necessarily right or wrong—they are simply partial statements that, if disconnected from the whole (as some of them obviously are), become fragmented. But without an integrating, wholistic point of view for the singing-acting process, all such partial instructions will tend to become fragmented unless they are intuitively connected to the whole by the teacher or singer-actor.

The nature of the music-theater field is such that we are all part-teachers in working with the singer-actor, and our responses to that fact form another full spectrum. At one end is the isolationist approach, in which part-teachers focus exclusively on their specialty (and can mistake it for the whole), with minimal interaction with the other energies of the whole system. At the other end of the spectrum are the integrationists: part-teachers who attempt to teach the whole, or other parts of the whole, whether they have the expertise or not.

As in all cases of polarized choice on a full spectrum, both of these fixed choices can create problems. The total isolationist is attempting the impossible: like it or not, all parts of the human energy system are interconnected and the isolationist approach diminishes the support each of them can provide to the others. The voice especially needs a supportive, whole relationship to the rest of the system. The integrationists are moving in a useful direction, but can also encounter difficulties if they do not have a clear understanding of the nature of the parts they are attempting to integrate with their specialty. There are voice teachers, for example, who work with the emotional process as an essential underpinning of the vocal process without understanding the conditioned, entangled relationship of the emotions, the body, and the voice.

The relationship of the parts and the whole in music theater is a complex one. It requires ongoing clarification to keep from being pulled into either-or, all-or-nothing polarizations. It is not the parts versus the whole, for the parts make up the whole. And, in a healthy system, the whole is greater than the sum of its parts—particularly the sum of those parts we are aware of, for there are other parts we may not yet know. It is the parts *and* the whole, and we must honor both simultaneously in spite of the tendency to control complexity by focusing only on parts. That does simplify things but, as we have seen, it can lead to mistaking those parts for the whole, or keep us from relating to the other parts that make up the whole. In both cases, fragmentation is the result.

The Missing Model for Integration

The question for the part-teacher in the field of music theater is: Can we sustain both concepts—the part *and* the whole—in our awareness without pitting one against the other? Doing just that is vital to the development of the singer-actors with whom we work, as well as to the health of the field as a whole. While there are some who are able to do that—and even that is a rarity—there is no one who can teach all the parts. Nor should any one person be expected to possess the breadth of perceptions and training necessary to integrate a total, wholistic view of the singing-acting process into their own work. I make no claim to possess such a breadth of knowledge: like everyone else in the field I am a part-teacher.

It would have been helpful for all of us part-teachers if there had been an integrating aesthetic—a model—that allowed us all to interact with each other more fully even as we taught our own specialty. Unfortunately, however, there has been no such model available. And while there are those special, rare teachers who have managed to transcend the lack of such an integrating model through the use of their own intuitive resources, what about the rest of us? What can we do?

Fortunately, it is not necessary to know how to teach all the parts, nor have the intuitive skills to integrate them without a model, in order to create such a model; if it were, I would not even address the issue. To do so, we need only go to the concept of the whole itself. There we will find the basic energy principles to guide us in creating a model for the singing-acting training process, a model that will also allow teachers of that process to interact more fully with each other.

As we begin to evolve such a model, and to find an integrating view for the singing-acting process, we will examine each part of the whole system of music-theater interaction as suggested by the pentagon of potential. We will begin by asking where the demand for singing-acting came from in the first place: Have singers always been asked to be actors as well? Knowing the origins of that demand may clarify some of the confusion around it. Then we will consider point 1 of the pentagon—the requirements of the form itself: what music theater asks of its performers. From there we will move to point 4—the external energy system of the singer-actor, which must be trained to fulfill the requirements of the form. Next, we will move to points 2 and 3 and consider the effect of the societal and music-theater environments on the singer-actor as he or she practices the art and exercises his or her system to fulfill its needs more fully. But first, the historical origin of the demand for singing *plus* acting.

Stanislavski Comes to Town: A New Demand for Singing-Acting

A key event in the evolution of that demand may have been the visit to New York City in 1923 by Konstantin Stanislavski and the Moscow Art Theater. While not everyone was swept away by the troupe's acting (critic Stark Young was among those whose appreciation was restrained), many were dazzled by what they perceived as a new kind of realism and a fresh sense of theatrical believability. And while there was, without question, genuine power in those performances, a part-whole confusion may also have been involved in the evaluation. Consider the following.

The audience was able to understand two of the projective modes accurately—the kinesthetic and the facial. But even that understanding was obscured by the relationship of those two to the vocal mode. Within the vocal mode itself, only the *music* of the language was understood, and even that was interdependent upon knowing the *meaning* of the words as well. The situation may have been similar to a phenomenon sometimes experienced in acting classes.

Actors who speak more than one language will often do a scene in the original language of Molière, Goethe, or Lorca. These actors, whose level of talent is well known to the other members of the class, will seem to give their finest performances ever. They will display a freedom and power that surpasses their usual efforts. The reason is clear: one of the basic ways we judge the believability of acting is by how convincingly the actors speak. And we are convinced by the musicality of the language—by how it sounds—not by the words themselves.

With a language we don't understand, there is no way of telling whether it has the nuance and subtlety of musicality that, in interaction with the meaning of the words, makes our own language ring true or false. In watching the scene, we simply relax and enjoy the musical novelty of the foreign language (since it's only a scene, there is no long-term investment) without worrying about its moment-to-moment credibility. The actors in turn are not constrained by nuances or inflections—or if they are, they know that we, the listeners, are free of that judgmental burden. The word-oriented judgmentalism that plagues performance is momentarily set aside. Without that burden, the performing process acquires a new energy and becomes a different and enjoyable experience for both performers and audience. These kinds of circumstances may have contributed to the American enthusiasm for Russian performances. In addition there was the stylistic contrast to the American acting style of the time, which is said to have been less realistic and more highly stylized.

In any case, a number of Americans journeyed to Russia in the following decade to learn more about the acting style they had seen. It was there that they encountered and were strongly influenced by the work of Stanislavski. Since they were not in Russia long enough to grasp the *total* view of Stanislavski's work (and his explorations were in continual process then and for the rest of his life), they brought back to this country a *part* of his total exploration. (Once again, we encounter the part mistaking itself for the whole.) The brilliance of Stanislavski's total investigation of the acting process is not in question; what is at issue is that only a narrow slice of his total system was brought back to this country. Whether intentionally or not, that part came to stand for the whole. We created an American acting tradition that grew from one aspect of Stanislavski's total work. One of his books, *An Actor Prepares*, became the basis for the dominant view of acting in this country for several decades. And when a fragmented way of thinking about a system leads us to mistake the part for the whole, ill health in that system is not only possibile, it is highly probable.

In the case of the Stanislavski system, the part, or parts, that were mistaken for the whole were the inner processes of the actor — MIM and IMP. The outer processes — what the voice, body, and face actually did to communicate those inner processes — were relegated to the province of technique, and concern for them was labeled variously as external or artificial or imposed. (The rest of Stanislavski's trilogy — *Building a Character* and *Creating a Role* — were translated later, and although they dealt extensively with external technique, it was too late: the internal imbalance had been established.) Even today, the words *technique* and *external* have negative connotations for most actors and singer-actors who have taken acting classes.

Rebalancing the System: Releasing Shame and Guilt

The pentagon of potentiality purposely places the inner and outer processes at opposite points, not because they are a duality (they form a full spectrum of interconnected choices) but because we have created a situation in which that potential duality is emphasized. We need to be aware of, acknowledge, and accept that erroneous view in order to transform it. The part that has been mistaken for the whole must be reconnected with the rest of the inner-outer spectrum in our understanding. We can clarify the confusion between the part and the whole with a visual representation that tells us something further: without an exercise process to hold the two together, the two points could sag further and further apart as guilt and judgment weigh down the inner resources of point 3, while from lack of clear and specific attention, the external resources of point 4 atrophy and rigidify.

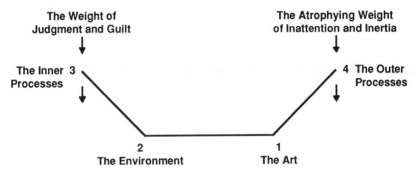

The Weight of
Judgment and Guilt

The Atrophying Weight
of Inattention and Inertia

The Inner 3
Processes

4 The Outer
Processes

2
The Environment

1
The Art

The duality we have created between the inner and outer processes through this part-for-the-whole mistake has weighed down a generation of actors and singer-actors with an astonishing amount of guilt. Several years ago I began asking each of my classes, "How many of you have ever felt guilty for not having the 'right' thoughts or feelings in performance?" Out of more than 1,000 performers, all but one raised their hands with no hesitation, usually with rueful smiles and often with some bitterness. (The single exception was a performer who worked exclusively with life-size puppets, manipulating them physically and singing for them—but for whom she had no personal mental or emotional responsibility.)

In *Performing Power* I discussed the mind-reading school of directing that insists upon the primacy of the inner-to-outer process. Once we make the mind-reading assumption that if the performer is thinking the "right" thoughts and feeling the "right" feelings, those thoughts and feelings will be projected automatically by the outer processes, we have a potential guilt gap. If the outer processes do *not* reflect what the director (or the text) asks for, then the performer is clearly not thinking or feeling the right things. Now the performer may *think* he is doing so (and may be correct, but that does not guarantee that what he is thinking and feeling will actually be projected). If he does think so, he may be defensive if he is asked to do what he already thinks he is doing. But even if he doesn't think he is thinking and feeling the right things, it is unlikely that *trying* to have those right thoughts or feelings will produce the corresponding external results—since that is what he was already trying to do. The very attempt will create a downward spiral of self-consciousness that will short-circuit the process.

Playwright and director David Mamet has said, "Most acting training is based on shame and guilt" (Bruder and others, p. ix), and that, too, is a comment greeted by actors with a sense of belated recognition. Unfortunately, we have managed to transfer that classroom guilt factor—the result of our mind-reading maladaptation of Stanislavski's work—to performance itself. The anecdotes that pour forth once that particular nerve is touched would themselves fill a book. One example will suffice for the moment.

A performer who had been acting professionally for twenty years said, after becoming aware of and applying the performing power techniques to actual performance, "It was the first time I had fun while performing in twenty years, and the first time I didn't come offstage beating up on myself for what had or had not been going on in my head while I was acting. Not only that, colleagues and audience members who knew my performance level told me it was the best work they had ever seen me do."

There are any number of possible reasons for the gap between what is happening on the inner level and what actually gets communicated by the outer. The years of control conditioning the performer has undergone may not allow the clear communication of those particular thoughts or feelings; or, self-consciousness may interfere as the mind tries to get itself to do something even as it is watching itself trying to do it. Mind-reading games are mind numbing: they are rarely accurate and seldom useful (even when they are accurate). Trying to assess the relationship between what is happening on the inside and what is being communicated on the outside is like trying to know the people in a house by the color of its paint or the style of its architecture: both paint and architecture may have been created by someone else (as our conditionings are); and even if the owners of the house built and painted it, there is a vast range of interpretation possible (a smile or a scowl can conceal, believably, a host of other, contradictory inner qualities.)

We will explore the ramifications of this inner-over-outer, part-equals-the-whole error in later chapters, and offer expanding developmental exercises to reintegrate it. For the moment we can simply note its ubiquitous presence among singer-actors (as well as actors) as they attempt the singing-acting juggling process.

Sing and Act: The Undefined Demand

Stanislavski's wholistic view of the acting process, from which we excerpted this particular bit of fragmentation, sprang in turn from the new realism of the late nineteenth century. In this view, realism came to stand for the real, the believable, the true and, finally, the Good. It infected the American theater in the thirties and forties through the efforts of the Group Theater and the Actor's Studio, spreading to American music theater and opera during the fifties. For the first time, opera came to Broadway (via Menotti), and opera producers began to yearn for a larger slice of the theater audience. By emulating what seemed to be the drawing power of movies and nonsinging theater, a more realistic approach to music theater was seen as a means of increasing the audience size.

That growing lust for realism — which had long since taken over the acting tradition — finally reached the singer-actor. Since it was, and perhaps still is, difficult to dispute the proposition that all the theatrical arts should seem to be real and believable, and that the ultimate burden for that believability falls upon the actor, the same burden in music theater had to be assumed by the singer. If the new realism was to revitalize music theater, it had to do so through the performer. Thus, for the first time in history, the singer was told, in effect, "It is no longer enough to simply sing well; from now on you must sing and act simultaneously!"

I have recounted the effect of that implicit command on the succeeding generation of singers in *Performing Power*. Here we may simply reiterate the basic error of omission: we asked singers to do something that we had not defined. They had been singing in their auditions (and rehearsals and performances), but suddenly we asked them to do something different: to sing *and* act with conscious intention: to become complete singer-actors. However, we neglected to do one important thing: we didn't tell them how to do it. We did not describe the process of singing-acting.

Everyone assumed, I suppose, that if you knew (or thought you knew) what acting was and what singing was, you simply combined the two. But the matter is not simple, and the idea of simply combining them is not useful or accurate. As I have pointed out on numerous occasions, singing is one art, acting is another, and singing-acting is a third; while the third draws upon the first two in important ways, it also differs from them significantly and is not a simple sum of the two. The relationship is a synergistic one: singing and acting come together in singing-acting to create a whole greater than their sum.

This is a more subtle instance of the part mistaking itself for the whole: here it is the *sum* of two parts being mistaken for the whole. Singing and acting, which are wholes in themselves, become parts of a greater whole when they come together in singing-acting; that whole is greater than a simple combination of the two, and if attempts to simply combine the parts are mistaken for the whole (as they often are), ill health on some level is the potential result for the singer-actor.

Since we had not defined the task of singing-acting clearly then, let us do so now by turning to point 1 on the pentagon of potentiality—the demands music theater places on the singer-actor. Then, by examining the gap between the nature of singing-acting and the capacity of the human energy system, we can begin creating exercises that will reduce that gap.

The Demands of Music Theater and Singing-Acting

What does it mean when we ask singers to act as well as sing? To answer that, let us examine some of the characteristics of the singing-acting process.

First: It is a public act that is performed for other people.

Second: It is an act in which the performer pretends to be someone other than who he/she is.

Third: Singing-acting involves the voice, the body, the face, the mind, and the emotions of the performer.

Fourth: It is an unnatural act; that is, it involves the voice, the body, the face, and the emotions at energy levels and in combinations that are not practiced in life. Further, there are no models in life for the singer-actor. The unusual level and combination of energies that make up singing-acting are seen nowhere but in the act itself. (And there are very few performers who can be usefully emulated, because we have no wholistic way of viewing performance that separates the useful from the unuseful.) There is so much confusion around this point, it is worth examining more deeply.

Unnatural in this context is not intended pejoratively: it is the very unnaturalness of singing-acting that is its greatest glory. A person doing something as technically demanding as singing-acting, doing it well, and *seeming* to do it naturally is a miracle of the human energy system. But it is easy to mistake the nature of the act itself for the effect we want to create in performing it.

In *The Shifting Point*, Peter Brook says:

> The greatest challenge now, at this point in the twentieth century,
> is to replace—in the minds of performers as well as audiences—
> the idea that opera is artificial with the idea that opera is natural.
> That's really the most important thing, and I think it's possible.
> (p. 169)

And so do I, but we must be clear about the difference between the act itself
and the effect it creates. Brook is as aware as anyone of the distinction I am
making, but without clarification that statement can be confusing. I agree
with it totally so long as we understand that it is the *effect* of the act that must
seem natural, even though the necessary techniques that create it are not.
Those vocal, physical, and emotional techniques *and* their coordinated interaction must be accepted and embraced for all that they are and what they
require. Achieving the effect of naturalness under such technical demands is
an immense challenge for the exercise process. It is the subject of this book.

Fifth: Part of the unnaturalness of the act is that we are doing it for
others—for audiences, for our teachers, directors, coaches, and conductors—as well as for ourselves. How we feel about what we are doing or what
we think we are doing may be less important than what we are actually doing
and how clearly that communicates what we intend to be doing. This will
raise the whole issue of authority dependency and judgmentalism, both to be
considered in greater detail when we examine points 2 and 3 on the pentagon of potentiality.

Sixth: Each of the three projective energies involved—vocal, physical,
and emotional—functions differently from its normal process in life. Of
these three, the voice is the most highly stylized and unusual in its deviation
from naturalistic use. The emotional demands of singing-acting, while not as
extreme as the vocal demands, are nonetheless far more intense than in everyday life. And the body, rather than acting upon the intensity of the vocal
and emotional energies, is usually required to remain relatively inactive, even
while maintaining a highly energized state of readiness and support for the
singing process.

Seventh: Time is altered in the singing-acting process. A ten-second
event in real time can become a ten-minute event in music-theater time.
Most acting problems in music theater can be traced back to this fundamental convention of the form.

Eighth: The singing-acting process is seldom if ever exercised in its totality. In virtually all situations where the total act is called upon—which
means every time a singer opens her or his mouth to sing and is seen by
someone—there is pressure to produce the best total product; this is partic-

ularly true in rehearsals and classes, yet the exercise and development of the singing-acting process cannot fully unfold in those kinds of product-oriented situations.

Ninth: It is an act that no single expert can teach in its entirety. A voice teacher can help develop vocal power, an acting teacher the capacity to act, a movement specialist the ability to use the body, a coach the development of musical or dramatic interpretive skills; but until now there has been no integrative view allowing individual experts to integrate their separate parts of the process with the whole, even as they develop the individual part for which they are primarily responsible.

There is a paradoxical corollary to this one-part, one-teacher situation. Although no single person can teach the total process, every coach, director, or teacher who works with a singer-actor while he or she is singing *is* working with the total process—and therefore is teaching it as well, whether they like it or not. Since the face and body are present and functioning whenever the singer-actor is singing or speaking, the coordination of the three energies is being practiced, developed, and taught, whether consciously or unconsciously. The only question concerns the quality of that teaching.

Let us reiterate our responsibility: as part-teachers, we are not responsible for teaching all the parts, but simply for awareness that those parts are always interacting; as our awareness develops, we become increasingly capable of helping singer-actors improve the way they interact.

Otherwise, it is as though we tried to teach people how to juggle three separate objects—a ball, a block, and a knife—by teaching them to toss and catch only one object at a time, never asking them to do it with all three at once. Learning to toss up one object and catch it with skill and ease is an important part of the total process of juggling, but it is only a part. Yet having taught our performers singing-acting/juggling in this partial way, we push them out on the stage and say, "Go ahead! Toss all three objects up at once and don't drop them—keep them in the air! Use the voice, the body, and the emotions in all the different ways we have taught you, only now put them all together simultaneously, on your own!" It would be surprising if a juggler taught in this way were able to juggle at all. It should surprise us no less that the energy processes of singing-acting are so often dropped (or not even put into play for fear of being dropped). A few jugglers, under the pressure of performance, might figure out how to do it on their own; others might have seen someone else juggle and have a sense of how to do it; but the vast majority would find it difficult and frustrating, and would probably feel guilty for not being able to do it.

The analogy is only too accurate: we have been giving the singer-actors voice lessons, acting lessons, musical coachings, movement classes, and a limited number of actual performance opportunities; but we have provided no approach enabling performers to practice combining all those parts on their own. And to this overwhelming challenge, we have inadvertently added a burden of guilt: singer-actors feel judged for not being able to do what we have failed to teach them. The combination of an undefined task and implicit judgment for not fulfilling that task has created a widespread sense of frustration and a lack of fulfillment among the hundreds of young singers (and actors) I have worked with in the past few years. They are generally unable to articulate it, but the feeling is clear: somehow things are not what they could be, something is missing and there is an underlying feeling of dissatisfaction with what is happening to them.

The Loss of Personal Performing Power: Fragmentation in Action

This feeling of loss was substantiated by a survey sponsored by the Ford Foundation. In the summer and fall of 1984, two experts, in music and theater, visited and examined the best professional singer-actor training programs in this country. They interviewed staff and performers in each program, attended classes, coachings, and rehearsals, and compiled the resultant information for evaluation by a select committee of music and theater professionals. The preliminary report had one conclusion unanimously agreed upon by all the staff and performers interviewed: all those training programs *were robbing the singer-actors of their personal power*!! This was a shock to the committee responsible for the evaluation (and continues to be so for everyone who hears about it). I was less surprised, having been aware for some time of the effect of the music-theater training process on the singer-actor. I am more surprised that, to date — January 1990 — nothing has been done about it, even though that was the purpose of the survey: to find out what was amiss so it could be corrected. At the same time I understand the enormity of the challenge and the lack of an accepted point of view that would allow action to be taken.

It should be noted and emphasized that there is no one to blame for this state of affairs: no individuals and no groups. Part-teachers of all the disciplines may be doing excellent work in their individual areas. The difficulties arise where the parts interact with each other. Singer-actors receiving different kinds of instruction and information can be confused by seeming con-

tradictions between them, even though none may actually exist. But it is ev-
idently up to the singer-actors to integrate the parts and reconcile those
seeming contradictions, even though they have never been taught to do so;
and without a unifying, integrating concept, how is that possible? If the instructors do not help them do it, can we expect performers to do it on their
own—to juggle without instruction?

This is a concrete example of the effects of fragmentary thinking on in-
stitutional and personal levels. As Bohm puts it:

> It is not an accident that our fragmentary form of thought is
> leading to such a widespread range of crises . . . in the individual
> and in society as a whole. Such a mode of thought implies
> unending development of chaotic and meaningless conflict, in
> which the energies of all tend to be lost by movements that are
> antagonistic or else at cross-purposes. (p. 16)

While the Ford Foundation committee was understandably dismayed
by evidence of the damage done by institutionalized fragmentation of
thought, that in itself is reflective of an additional problem: we are not only
fragmented in our thinking, we are largely unaware of it.

> One might go so far as to say that in the present [fragmented]
> state of society, and the general mode of teaching science [or any
> subject, including singing-acting], which is a manifestation of this
> state of society, *a kind of prejudice in favour of a fragmentary self-
> world view is fostered and transmitted (to some extent explicitly
> and consciously but mainly in an implicit and unconscious manner).*
> (Bohm, p. 15; my italics)

I first became aware of the damage created by this systemic fragmentation in observing the premature deterioration of many young singers, a phenomenon I analyzed in some detail in *Performing Power* in "The Case of the
Disappearing Divas." To better understand this distressing state of affairs,
and to become aware of choices we can make to change it, let us return to
the pentagon of potentiality, and examine the interaction of the external energy system of the human being with the needs of music theater and singing-
acting.

The External Energy System of the Human Being

With our description of singing-acting, we have some sense of the total projective energy demands a human being is confronted with when asked to
sing and act simultaneously. The next step is to explore the energy-project-

ing capacity of the human being: how does the human condition affect the efforts of the singer-actor? How does it limit those efforts? How can we exercise and transcend those limitations? The performing power technique approaches those questions through the concept of the perceptual and projective modes. *Performing Power* presented a detailed description of that concept, which will be expanded upon in chapter 5. What follows here is a brief summary of the idea.

Of the five senses (hearing, seeing, touching, tasting, and smelling) the first three are the primary means of communicating with other people. Perceptually we hear, see, and feel (physically touch or empathize with) other people. Thus we have the hearing mode, the seeing mode, and the kinesthetic mode. Corresponding to these perceptual modes we have three projective modes, which communicate with their perceptual parallels. Projectively we speak/sing to the hearing mode, we communicate mental and emotional messages to the seeing mode, and we move/gesture/touch in sending messages to the kinesthetic mode. In *Performing Power* I called these projective modes the hearing-vocal mode (now to be called the *vocal mode*), the facial-emotional mode (the *facial mode*), and the *kinesthetic mode*. All communication (apart from extrasensory perception) is based on some interrelationship of these three perceptual and projective modes.

We can view the projective modes as three channels for the flow of energy from the performer to the audience: the voice, the face, and the body. For maximum performing power those three channels need to be open to the highest possible energy flow, either independently or in various combinations. Very few performers are perfectly balanced in projective mode strength—some modes are stronger than others, and the degree of coordination between them varies enormously. Every performer can benefit from a more balanced projective mode relationship and from improved coordination between them.

Of equal importance is the fact that the projective modes can interfere with each other's energy flow as well as with their own. These interfering patterns can be thought of as disagreements as to which of the three should do the communicating in any given situation. We will refer to these interferences/disagreements as *entanglements*. Releasing and transforming entanglements between the three communicating processes is one of the most significant single factors in developing the performing power of the singer-actor.

An entanglement between the projective modes can be defined as follows: If a change in the quantity or quality of energy through one communicating process demands a change in the quantity or quality of energy through one or both of the other two, that is an entanglement. For example, when the typical young singer begins to sing (therefore changing the quantity and quality of energy in the vocal process), there is often a change in the facial process as well: the eyebrows lift or knot, the face looks anxious (or uninvolved), the eyes squint, and there may be other changes in the facial musculature. If those changes are involuntary and can't be controlled (or if it takes special effort to control them), there is an entanglement between the vocal process and the facial process.

If the performer wishes to express a strong emotion with the facial process and the shoulders rise, and/or the breathing changes, and/or the body reflects a state of tension, and the performer has no choice in the matter, there is an entanglement between the facial and kinesthetic processes.

The question is always one of choice: if the performer has no choice in how a change of energy in one process affects the others, that is an entanglement. Thus an entanglement limits the performer's range of possible choices (as well as diminishing her or his personal performing power in more tangible ways). Once an entanglement is not a necessity, the performer can choose to use that entanglement statement in defining a character. For example, tensing and lifting the shoulders in fear is a power-robbing entanglement as such. It invariably interferes with the breathing and creates other muscular tensions in the head-neck and upper torso that can interfere with the voice itself. But once the performer is free to express fear *without* raising the shoulders, she or he can choose to raise them freely without held tension, for the purpose of a particular characterization. This will not interfere with the breath or the voice—a sort of displaying one's tension cake and eating it too.

Entanglement, then, can be seen in two ways: it is both a way of controlling the flow of communicating energy through the human system and confusion about which communicating channel is the appropriate one at any given point. In either case the condition of entanglement interferes with the free flow of communicating energy through the human system. This interference becomes increasingly evident whenever either the quantity or quality of that energy is out of the ordinary. That, of course, is one of the prime characteristics of the singing-acting process: it is an unnatural, out-of-the-ordinary change in the quantity and quality of energy flowing through all three projective modes.

If we put the human condition of entanglement together with the demands of singing-acting, the challenge becomes clear: on one hand we have a form that requires for its fulfillment extraordinary energy expenditures from the human energy system; on the other hand, we have a human energy system that has been precisely and universally conditioned against making such expenditures. Many of the ills that afflict the singing-acting process — the guilt, the frustration, the lack of fulfillment, the loss of personal power that the singer-actor experiences in undergoing the very training that should expand that power, and the actual vocal damage leading to the disappearing divas syndrome — flow directly from this incompatibility between the human system and the demands placed upon it. And without an exercise process to reconcile that incompatibility, the ill effects will continue.

To begin moving toward such an exercise process, we must move beyond points 1 and 4 on the pentagon of potentiality (the needs of the art and the nature of the human communicating system) to points 2 and 3: the societal and music-theater environment surrounding the singer-actor, and his/her inner processes. It is the interaction between points 2 and 3 — especially the singer-actor's absorption of the conditioning of the music-theater environment — that leads to the entanglements.

Chapter 3

The Counterconditioned Performer

The Environment of Music Theater

In responding to the needs of the arts of music theater (including those of the singer-actor), those in charge of the environment (including me) have inadvertently fragmented the training and exercise process. We, the teachers, directors, conductors, and coaches of the singer-actor, find ourselves in a noninteracting context (whether we like it or not), which has created an environment of partiality and fragmentation. This environment in turn has powerfully affected the conditioning of singer-actors as they internalize that fragmented process.

The performer has been further affected by the fact that no total exercise process has emerged from the fragmented environment—nor could we reasonably expect one to have done so. The fifth point on the pentagon—the exercise process—remains unfulfilled. The lack of a wholistic perspective in the environment has blocked the evolution of a way to exercise that could not only function effectively for the performers, but also allow the authority figures on whom they have come to depend to interact synergistically in guiding them.

If such a wholistic frame of reference were available, and an exercise process were to evolve from it, singer-actors would be able to use it *on their own* in developing their performing process. As evidence that such a frame of reference does not exist, I have asked hundreds of singer-actors (and actors) whether they have a means of exercising their total process on their own, with no one else present. I have never received an affirmative reply. This means that the only time performers can exercise and develop their performance process is in rehearsals, coachings, classes, or lessons, all of them—with rare exceptions—product-oriented situations in which performers, concerned about an authority figure's evaluation, are trying their best to give their most acceptable performance.

Such authority dependence is a shocking limitation to anyone's growth. None of those product-oriented experiences is conducive and/or appropriate to genuine exercise. Performers in those situations will tend to do what they can already do: they will remain in the known, within the boundaries of the familiar and safe. But since, as we have seen, all learning and growth involves a movement from the known to the unknown, product orientation places a powerful restriction on the developmental process. In the current situation, virtually all the performer's potential practice time is confined to situations that inhibit movement into the unknown (except on the insistent guidance of a good teacher, director, or coach). This means being dependent upon someone else for the development and expansion of one's personal performing power and, in turn, giving up self-responsibility for one's own growth, which can only truly come *from* self-responsibility.

Authority dependency is a prime conditioning in almost every young performer educated in our system: they can only learn and grow under someone else's direct guidance. Having been provided with no way of genuinely exercising their own process—and by genuine exercise, I mean doing something you can't already do, which means *not* turning out your best product—young singer-actors have become totally dependent upon outside authorities for the development of their performing capacity. And not only is that psychologically limiting, it is also time-scarce: the time they can spend with teachers is minuscule compared to what they could spend exercising by themselves. That is not a healthy situation to promote normal performing health, let alone one that leads to radiant performing.

An Addictive Training Process in an Addictive Society

The training, rehearsal, and performing environment of music theater that surrounds and conditions the singer-actor is, in turn, encompassed and conditioned by society as a whole. In Anne Wilson Schaef's important book, *When Society Becomes an Addict*, she presents a dismaying and—it seems to me—inescapable case that the societal system in which we all live is in fact an addictive system: society as a whole has all the characteristics and exhibits all the processes of the addictive individual, and it functions in precisely the same way. In drawing this parallel, Schaef expands upon the usual concept of addiction, pointing out that while we ordinarily think of an addiction in relation to a substance—a chemical or a food—there is also such a thing as process addiction.

A person hooked on a process is addicted to a specific series of actions or interactions, such as accumulating money, working, gambling, sex, worrying, religion, and the like. The process causes us to say or think things that are inconsistent with our personal values, and these actions will become progressively more compulsive and obsessive. Moreover, an addiction seems to relieve us of responsibility for our lives. Under its illusory hold, we assume that we will be taken care of by someone or something outside ourselves—that some external force will magically appear and make things all right.

The concept of addiction has a special relevance to the arts of music theater and singing-acting training. The system of training, audition, rehearsal, production, and criticism that we have created to serve music-theater and singing-acting is a miniaturized and intensified version of the addictive system of the society surrounding it. Music theater makes demands on human energies that uniquely illumine the human condition. As the human system strives to fulfill the art of singing-acting, its negative and positive conditionings are revealed and magnified beyond the dynamics of ordinary life. The energy challenge to the singer-actor is so complex and intense that any grit from society as a whole becomes boulder-sized in the music-theater context. Thus it is useful to include some understanding of the societal conditioning that affects both the singer-actor and the music-theater environment.

Schaef uses the concept of the hologram to clarify how the individual characteristically functions within the addictive system. Each part or piece of a hologram contains the entire structure of the whole. The part is not only a part, for it has the total pattern, process, and functioning of the whole imprinted within it. In the context of a social system, the system—the whole—is like the individual and the individual—the part—is like the system. An addictive system, then, is like the individual addict within it and has all the individual's characteristics. And any individual living within that addictive system, unless aware and recovering, will demonstrate many of the same characteristics.

In this view we all carry a pre-existing burden of conditioning from that larger addictive system into whatever else we may be doing—including the process of singing-acting.

As we have seen, the first challenge to the fulfillment of the singing-acting process is the human condition of energy entanglement. That entangled condition is, in turn, a reflection of our societal conditioning as a whole; and it interferes with our communicating energies in a way contradictory to the needs of singing-acting. To fulfill the singing-acting challenge and move toward radiant performing, we must exercise our entangled condition, releasing and replacing its interfering processes and developing its capacity for a free flow of communicating energy. We will be assisted and motivated in that exercise process by a clear understanding of how our entanglements were created, how they relate to the addictive characteristics of society, and how they are further intensified by the music-theater environment in which performers are trained, employed, and presented.

Schaef's extensive list of the characteristics and processes of the addictive system illuminates the challenges of the music-theater environment and the singing-acting process. The following selection from that list is purely descriptive; it is not an accusatory, finger-pointing invitation to a guilt trip. It is meant simply to allow us to become aware of, acknowledge, and accept things as they actually are. With that increased awareness we will be better able to understand and deal with the addictive processes, and to exercise, release, and transform the entanglements they spawn.

That both our society and the music-theater environment are in the state of conditioning suggested by these addictive characteristics and processes is the experience of everyone with whom I have interacted in the field of music theater. Anyone in that field who is not affected by those characteristics in some way, either in themselves or through interaction with others, is indeed fortunate (and probably unique). This section of the book is addressed to those who *are* so affected and who wish to expand their awareness, acknowledgment, and acceptance—and thus their capacity to move beyond that state of being. They can choose to begin releasing, replacing, and transforming their conditionings and entanglements, thereby beginning the move in the direction of radiant performing. Without that process of awareness, acknowledgment, and acceptance of what is, we are either unconscious of it (and therefore its victims), or we deny and repress it (which also makes us its victims). But if we take those three steps, exercise and transformation are possible. We begin with awareness.

The Conditioning of the Singer-Actor as Reflected in the Addictive Characteristics of Society

The Process of Dualism

This is the final addictive process in Schaef's list, but it is so central to our topic that I put it first. As Schaef says, "If there is any process that is basic to all characteristics and processes of the Addictive System, I suspect this may be it" (p.112).

Consider the arts we are exploring: music theater and singing-acting. The words themselves suggest the oppositional qualities of duality, and practice in the field tends to enforce them. When I discussed the great law of opposites in *The Complete Singer-Actor*, it was a response to the dualism inherent in the form. That law might be put in this way: the greatest vitality to be experienced at any point along a spectrum of energy is through the interaction of the opposites that form that spectrum. Thus, on the spectrum formed by discipline and freedom, the greatest vitality is experienced at any point by the interplay of both discipline and freedom. Similarly with the music-theater or singing-acting spectrums: the greatest power in both arts is when the singing is informed by acting, the acting by singing, and the two become a unified whole.

Conversely, the more one polarizes along any spectrum, the more one saps the power inherent in the synergy of opposites. Relating to a full spectrum of possibility as we exercise our energies allows duality to be a tool for expansion rather than a struggle that diminishes our potential. The polarities of any spectrum of energy use can become mutually supportive and create a whole greater than the sum of their seemingly oppositional parts.

But this is not the conditioning of music theater or of society as a whole. Instead, polarization is intensified. We are trained from birth in dualistic thinking. Our parents, our schooling, and society as a whole thrust duality upon us: either/or choices dominate our lives — good or bad, pass or fail, this or that, right or wrong, in or out, off or on, alive or dead, and so on *ad infinitum*. This kind of thinking allows the addictive system to oversimplify our dealings with an increasingly complex world. It gives the illusion of control over what is in fact a universe in process. Dualistic thinking does not reflect the reality of a living process, and when we think we can divide that live complexity into two simple aspects, it feeds our illusion of control.

The error of dualism is another version of the part mistaking itself for the whole: one is forced to choose one end of a whole spectrum, and let that polarity-part be defended as the whole. The conductor and the director may feel they have to choose either music *or* theater, the performer either singing *or* acting and, in our training programs, each authority will encourage the performer—consciously or unconsciously—to honor his or her specialty over the others.

When we think dualistically, then whatever we say is right makes the opposite wrong. We divide the world into pairs of opposites, which must exclude each other. There is no recognition that there are other alternatives: both opposites may be possible choices in certain circumstances, or there may be a whole range of alternatives between them. But the process of dualism denies the possibility of even considering the inclusion of other choices.

In this book we will transform the concept of duality from a negative, polarizing process into a powerful exercise tool through the full spectrum concept. It is vital to do so, for dualism is inherent in three-dimensional life and music-theater, and unless we transform the tension-energy of dualism into a developmental tool, it can thrust us into the process of judgmentalism, another primary characteristic of the addictive system.

Judgmentalism

Judgmentalism interacts with most of the other characteristics of the addictive system. Since it is particularly and intensely evident in the music-theater environment, judgmentalism was also an important subject in *Performing Power*. The compulsive need to make negative judgments creates virtually all the other entanglements and is a delimiting and debilitating factor for performer development generally.

Descartes had it wrong: It is not "I think, therefore I am"; rather, it is "I think, therefore I judge," or so it seems in the twentieth century. Perhaps life was less judgmental in the seventeenth century. The virus of judgment has become a veritable plague in our own time.

It is clear, I hope, that I do not mean judgment in the sense of discernment and awareness, but in the sense described by Barbara Ray: judgement as "prejudices or emotional or mental assessments of partiality—of the part as though it were the whole—not seeing the whole and the correct relationship of the part to the whole" (*ERM*, p. 62).

Robert Fritz, in his book *The Path of Least Resistance*, takes aim at what he calls the outlawing of judgment by "New Age Newspeak" (p. 251). He rightly insists that judgment, in the sense of "the ability to make significant distinctions[,] is one of the prerequisites of the creative process" (p. 249). One can only agree: making distinctions, discerning differences, and making clear descriptions so that artistic, creative choices can be made are all vital capacities on the path to radiant performance.

But it is when judgment becomes generalized and predictive that problems occur. And in the case of performers, self-judgment is almost invariably not only generalized ("I was terrible!"), and preevaluative ("If I do that I'll look silly"), but also apologetic ("I'm sorry about the way I performed"). and inhibiting. It is those aspects of judgment—which might better be called judgmentalism—that in fact block the creative process.

But while one should not throw out the discerning, descriptive, choice-making qualities of judgment along with the generalizing, negative, preevaluative bathwater, one need not keep the baby soaking in dirty bathwater the rest of its life either. There are other choices possible. One can recognize that there is a baby and there is bathwater, and one can make discerning distinctions about the two faces of judgment itself.

We will distinguish between the two faces of judgment in the same way: negative, generalizing preevaluation on one hand, and discerning choice based on clear description on the other. For the performer, the first kind of judgment will be focused on the dualities of good and bad and right and wrong. This will be especially so as they evaluate or preevaluate their use of energy in performances, rehearsals, classes, lessons, and coachings. Judgment in advance of actual experience will tend to prevent us from attempting anything unknown: since we don't know what will happen if we move into the unknown, and can't predict the probability of its success or failure, we will either hesitate or decide not to move—and either way we lose an opportunity for growth.

Judgment is always concerned with the past (judging what we have already done as being good or bad) or the future (trying to anticipate the value of what we may do and therefore make a decision as to whether or not to do it). Awareness of what we have done is vital and inevitable. Awareness of past experience is also vital in making choices for the future, and so is awareness of the direction in which we wish to move, and planning for it—which is also inevitable, whether it is useful planning or not. The power to free ourselves of judgmental blocking in making all these choices is cumulative: the more choices we make freely, the more freely we can make them. The fewer the judgmental predictions about the effects of moving into the unknown, the more freedom we will have to do so. And since all learning and growth is a movement into the unknown, the greater the freedom from pre-evaluation, the greater the learning and growth.

This freedom from judgment demands flexibility. Schaef sees judgmentalism and inflexibility or rigidity as mutually enforcing addictive processes. Rigidity does not allow us the flexibility to flow with process, to move with the constantly changing world around us. Judgmentalism creates such rigidity and does not allow us the flexibility so vital to dealing with ourselves, our processes, and with those around us.

> When we are rigid, we cannot be flexible and "go with the flow";
> when we are judgmental, we become rigid in ourselves, with
> ourselves, and with our way of dealing with the world. (p. 122)

An addiction to a substance or process means we can't get enough of it, even though it has an unpleasant effect on us. To be judged is not pleasant, but the more judgmentally addictive we are, the more we will want to be judged (swinging between loving it and hating it as we do so). And we will not only judge ourselves without ceasing, we will also depend upon others to feed that need. We will come to rely with increasing intensity on authorities to validate or invalidate us through judgment. Any judgment will be preferable to no judgment. A negative judgment allows the judgmental addict to make someone else the issue—the external referent, the outside judge—rather than dealing with the real issue, which is our own judgmental process. Our process is always our own: it belongs to us and to no one else, and regardless of our concern for someone else's opinion about it, neither they nor their judgment is the issue—*we* are. If we give the power—our power—to our teachers, coaches, and directors by making them the issue, we are promoting another characteristic of the addictive system: dependency.

Dependency

Dependency is interconnected with what Schaef calls the process of the external referent, which requires us to develop our concept of self through other people's responses to us. Applying that to singer-actor training, we could also say "a process that requires us to develop our concept of *self as a performer* through external referents." In both cases, in life and in training for performance, we hand ourselves over to external authority figures to do with us whatever needs to be done—and we come to depend upon them to decide just what that is and what it means.

This is a characteristic already touched upon, and one we will return to with some frequency, for it relates to the lack of a personal, private exercise process for the singer-actor. When you are dependent, you assume that you cannnot take care of yourself, and therefore someone or something outside yourself will do it for you. People in a state of dependency rely upon others to provide their emotional, psychological, intellectual, and spiritual needs.

For the performer we can add musical, physical, and dramatic needs to the list. We have not given the singer-actor a description of the singing-acting process (nor ourselves as teachers, directors, and coaches of the singer-actor); lacking that, we also lack a way of exercising that total process which can integrate its many parts into a synergistic whole, and the end result is that the individual singer-actor has no way to take charge of his or her own development. We have created a field that reeks of authority dependency: as a young singer-actor once said in a class (and his words have been echoed countless times since then): "I can't think of anything to do unless someone tells me!" That leads directly to the useful question of who *is* responsible for the singer-actor's process or, more addictively, who is to blame for the situation?

Responsibility and Blame

According to Schaef, "Addicts characteristically avoid taking responsibility for themselves and their lives" (p. 83). They avoid it because they equate responsibility and blame: "If they are responsible for what has happened in their lives, then they must be to blame for it all . . . " (p. 83). And who would want to take the blame for something that has gone wrong in their lives if they can shift it to someone else? So rather than risk taking the blame, addicts give up the responsibility.

The music-theater training situation has also confused the two terms. Without an integrating aesthetic and an exercise process for developing the singer-actor, our training environment has actually prevented us from giving—or singer-actors from taking—responsibility for themselves and the development of their performance process. At the same time, since there is no authority figure to blame for the lack of integration in their total performance, singer-actors receive—or take—the blame for it. Since they have not had a way of taking conscious responsibility for that integration, a vicious circle of powerlessness and guilt is created. The downward spiral of cause and effect goes like this: "If something has happened to me, it is because I made it happen. I believe that I can and should be in control, and therefore I have done this to myself" (p. 83). Schaef regards the individual's movement away from this kind of cause-and-effect perception as one of the most important shifts in recovering from the addictive process.

To make this move away from cause-and-effect blaming in the music-theater training system means two things: (1) providing singer-actors with the means of being responsible for the integration and development of their total performing process; and, (2) dropping the concept of blame altogether. Blame simply helps spawn another characteristic of the addictive system: defensiveness.

Defensiveness

This trait is painfully common in the training, rehearsal, and performance environment of music theater. The very fact that someone is watching the singer-actor so he may tell her what she is doing "wrong" (whether that someone is a teacher, coach, director, conductor, or, worst of all, a critic) simply heightens the potential for defensiveness. And, as Schaef notes, that potential is already immense. "It is interesting—and frightening—to see how much defensiveness is a part of our culture" (p. 80). This defensiveness will be intensified in the music-theater training environment; its challenge to the development of the singer-actor is clear.

For the singer-actor, as for anyone, the greater the defensiveness, the less the learning. "When one cannot respond to feedback or criticism and instead must prove that one is *right*, no real learning or change can occur" (Schaef, p. 80). When we live defensively, "we rob ourselves of the potential to learn. We close ourselves off to information that could move us to new levels of awareness and a new understanding of ourselves. We stop growing" (p. 82). When we are asked to do something (like complete singing-acting) without being told how to do it (how to put all the parts together) and then are blamed for not doing it correctly, defensiveness is the only logical result.

The fortress of defensiveness is further strengthened by the fact that most entanglements are unconscious. Kinesthetic tension, which arises from an unconscious need to control and/or repress the flow of emotion, becomes equated with the expression of that emotion. None of this is part of MIM's conscious process; it was created by our intuitive, right-brain, preconscious resources—the projective modes themselves. However, the only way to discuss it is to use words. But since MIM did not consciously create the entanglement in the first place, it has no *reason* (and no words) to defend it. It must create a seemingly rational argument from an irrational base. Meanwhile the nonverbal modes do what they do, maintaining their tension-controlling entanglements, and leave it to MIM to rationalize and justify them. (Rationalization and justification are two of the principal tools of defensiveness.) Talking cannot get at the reason for the entanglement—since there is no reason, only a conditioned response based on feeling—and so the talk goes on and on and on. This leads directly to another characteristic of the addictive system: negativism.

Negativism

The addictive system promotes negative thinking. Take, for example, the process of analysis. Analysis and synthesis together form a vital spectrum in music-theater. Anything as complex as singing-acting must be carefully analyzed to be understood; and it must also be put back together again intuitively in actual performance—synthesized—to open to the wholeness and power of the full spectrum.

But when the addictive system examines something closely, it concentrates on picking it to pieces and finding out what is wrong with it. Our education is focused on learning to be critical and judgmental. Positive comments in a classroom situation, particularly in college, are regarded as weak and even unintelligent. This attitude translates automatically into the professional singer-actor training process which takes academia as its model however much it may pretend to scorn it.

The difficulty academics find in considering something and responding to it without feeling that they must say something negative recalls the critical one-upmanship I experienced in my own professional drama school training. In a typical directing class, after the performance of a scene directed by a member of the class, it did not feel appropriate to simply "like" the scene, or to have merely enjoyed it. That seldom received reinforcement from either the teacher or the other members of the class. The student who professed to merely enjoy the scene might receive looks or words to the effect, "You *liked* that!? I thought it was totally _____ (fill in the blank, with "implausible," "not convincing," "curiously at odds with itself," "lacking in core or spine," etc., etc.) *Those* comments aroused the interest and the approval of the teacher and the rest of the class—including me, as deeply enmeshed in the overall academic addictive conditioning as anyone. A certain kind of intellectual power was granted to those making a negative critique—*they* weren't fooled, they saw through the sham—while positive reactions seemed potentially naïve, soft-headed, or imperceptive. Perhaps, as in drama itself, opposition is more interesting than accord — villains are more fun than heroes. If so, we made judgmental classroom villains of ourselves, and created a climate of growth-retarding negativism. (For further, horrifying details about destructive addictive behavior in academia, see Judith Kogan's *Nothing but the Best: The Struggle for Perfection at the Juilliard School*. The subtitle points at another characteristic of the addictive system, perfectionism.)

Whatever the reason, critical negativism is listened to more attentively than positive. When I make comments in a class on a singing-acting performance, I notice that all the positive comments tend to be received passively; then, when I say, "There was just one thing" — the ears prick up and there is full attention. That is, of course, a potentially useful sensitivity to the need for changes in one's performance process; unfortunately, it comes from an attitude of critical, judgmental negativism, which has been assimilated and made an internal process by many singer-actors, however well they may disguise it.

Perfectionism

If you are always striving to be perfect and — inevitably — falling short of those expectations, it is difficult to feel good about yourself as you are. Perfectionists carry a terrible burden. They are convinced not only that nothing they do is ever good enough, but, worse, that *they* are not good enough. Further, they know that they never do as much as they should, but that they *could* be perfect if they could just figure out how. They must always know all the answers, always do everything right, always be correct, never make mistakes, and since none of this is possible, they must continually beat up on themselves for their inadequacy.

That is a portrait of many singer-actors. Ironically, the very effort to be perfect contains within it the interference that blocks the movement toward perfection. Or rather, since there is no such thing as perfection in a process, it blocks the movement toward ever more radiant performing — which is always unfolding and in process.

The dynamic of that blocking pattern is simple. We function best when our energies are totally focused in the present (the only reality there is), on the process in question. But perfectionism sets up an overly specific future goal for that present process. Although that goal is both imaginary and impossible, the present process must be constantly compared with it to see if the goal has been attained — or is even any closer. In so doing, however, energy is drained from the present for future comparison. Further, since that comparison will always be negative, it may also arouse regret and self-recrimination, thus wasting additional energy on what has already happened — the past process. And, of course, the past is what is actually being compared with the impossible future — not the present; one can't compare the present until it is past. In all these ways energy is being drained from the present reality to serve the dead past or the imaginary future, and this prevents us from fulfilling our present potential — the only potential there is.

Perfection implies a fixed state; but since no process can be fixed, no process can be perfect. "The Addictive System," on the other hand, according to Schaef, "assumes that it is possible to be perfect" (p. 68). In such a system mistakes are unacceptable. And that means we cannot learn and grow from our mistakes, for we must hide them, cover them up, pretend we never make any, or defend them as "choices."

Perfectionism also intensifies two other addictive qualities: shame and hopelessness. By making us ashamed of our nonperfection, perfectionism robs us of the opportunity to learn from it. And since perfection in a process is an illusion, "whenever we try to be perfect, we end up feeling hopeless" (p. 126). Products are unchanging, and essentially dead; the human being, on the other hand, is a living, ever-changing process. Impose product demands on a human process, and one of the outcomes is frozen feelings, another characteristic of the addictive system.

Frozen Feelings

As performers we may try to produce feeling states as products, as packages of expressivity that are held, fixed, and unmoving. That kind of performance control attempts to produce and communicate inner emotions on demand. In life, on the other hand, there is another kind of conditioning which compels us to control those same inner emotions so they are *not* communicated. This second kind of conditioning is transmitted by the popular media — movies, newspapers, and television programs — which tell us that we must never show our feelings. This applies particularly to men, who learn to conceal their feelings at a very early age (which may explain why they do it better than women). People who show emotion, whether it is sorrow, anger, happiness, hate, contentment, spite or joy, are threatening to the system. The quality of the emotion is not the issue; positive or negative, it must be controlled, and kept from view. These two kinds of control are on a collision course: on one hand, the singer-actor is called upon for free and powerful emotional communication; and on the other, the conditioning of society and life forbids that very thing.

This raises several important questions for the singer-actor training process: What is the conditioning of the human energy system with respect to the communication of emotion? How does emotional communication actually work in that system? How does the communication of emotion work in the context of music-theater performance? How can we exercise the human energy system to allow more powerful emotional communication in music-theater performance? How can we learn to release, replace, or bypass the emotionally repressive conditioning of the human energy system in order to fulfill music-theater performance with freedom and power? The energy is there waiting to be released and transformed into emotional communication. We don't need to create it—only to let it out, to unlock it. Doing that is as simple as turning the key in a door and opening it. But we do have to learn to turn the key and open the door—and that is the subject of this book: finding the keys and opening the gateway of ourselves to more powerful singing-acting communication and to radiant performing.

To answer the preceding questions we must be clear about the conditioning of the human energy system. The concealment inherent in the process of frozen feelings can obscure that clarity, as can another characteristic of the addictive system—dishonesty.

Dishonesty

This is a deceptive issue for the performer. Any good actor or singer-actor must seem to be really doing something, but that something is, in fact, not true. He/she must *seem* to be genuinely angry, joyful, grief-stricken, ecstatic, and the like, whether any of those states are actually part of the real process or not—it is simply part of the art. With the necessity for that *seeming* honesty in singing-acting performance as a background, let us consider the idea of dishonesty as Schaef works with it.

There are three levels of lying in Schaef's view: lying to yourself, lying to people around you, and lying to the world. "Any addiction has as its main goal that of keeping people out of touch with their feelings and thoughts" (p. 51)—thus they cannot be honest with themselves. This in turn makes it impossible to be honest with those around them—the second, family, level. And this virtually ensures that the lying will move to the third level, the rest of the world.

Schaef calls addicts terrific con artists: "They are particularly good at figuring out what is appropriate, expected behavior and behaving that way, even when it has nothing to do with who or what they are" (p. 51). Add authority dependence to the addictive blend, and it produces behavior that is remarkably common among singers: a virtually schizophrenic relationship to those of us they regard as authority figures. I have observed singers who are almost aggressively hostile in their "normal" use of energy turn into fawning sycophants in the presence of authority figures—particularly those who might employ or recommend them. Such dishonesty is not useful for either performer or teacher.

But there are other pertinent questions for the performer. For example, "Am I being honest about my talent?" In answering it, however, we must remember that there is no predicting the speed or outcome of any singer-actor's developmental process. And since confidence is vital in allowing that process to unfold, any prediction which undermines that confidence is not useful, whether it is retrospectively accurate or not. (And it may seem to have been accurate precisely because it served as a self-fulfilling prophecy.) What we might think of as honesty may simply be judgmental negativism, which can destroy the very confidence necessary for fulfillment of hidden potential.

Another significant question is, "Am I being honest about my relationship with my teachers, and they with me?" Here, again, we must remember that confidence and trust are vital ingredients in the developmental process, and what might be called honesty in these situations—particularly from teacher to student—may be more destructive than helpful. Indeed, it may not be truly honest, but simply a reflection of the teacher's subterranean conditionings.

Moving even closer to the core issue is the question, "Am I being honest in my performance?" Here we encounter the true complexity of honesty for the performer. Another way of putting the question would be, "Am I guilty for not thinking or feeling the "right" thoughts or emotions while performing?" We will explore the implications of that question in greater detail later. For the moment, we can say that (1) guilt is never useful in the developmental process—the kind of motivational energy it may seem to provide does more long-range harm than good; (2) thoughts and feelings are invisible, inaudible, and imperceptible in life *and* performance until they are transformed into visual and audible communication by one or more of the three projective modes; and (3) a performer is never being completely "honest," since only a selected portion of his/her thoughts and feelings are being transformed into visible and/or audible communication—and necessarily so. It is not a question of honesty or dishonesty (no one could translate everything in the mind and emotions into visible/audible communications), but a matter of choice.

For the performer, the issue of honesty is more complicated than it might at first appear. Dishonesty in the training-rehearsal-production environment may block the development of the performer, and so may thoughtless honesty. Both concepts become entangled with the question of performance reality: What is real, what is acted, and what is the "correct" relationship between them? Dishonesty is an important characteristic of the addictive system for the performer, but it is definitely not a simple one.

Schaef views dishonesty from another angle in discussing the three ifs of the addict: *if only, what if,* and *as if.* The if-only person is focused on the past, regretting and blaming the past for the present. "If only my accompanist had been better. . . . " "If only I had known what they wanted. . . . " "If only my voice teacher had been better. . . . "

What-if people, on the other hand, are totally focused on the future, worrying and anticipating: "What if this happens? What if that happens?" "What will happen if I try _____ ?" (Fill in the blank with any number of singing-acting exercise possibilities.) The future is always an unpredictable unknown and therefore will frighten the what-if person. If we make that future even less predictable by asking the performer to do something he or she has never done, the resistance can be strong, even in the context of exercise. The what-if person will try to control that future, making it into a "known" by eliminating whatever cannot be predicted. Since all learning, all growth is a move from the known to the unknown, this will scuttle the developmental process. The what-if person will try to keep moving from the known to the known, finding ingeniously disguised reasons to avoid moving into the learning-growth potential of the unknown.

The as-if person is a more complicated challenge. In Schaef's view the as-if person is one who acts as if things are OK when they are not, or disguises from her- or himself and others what is actually going on in the present. The as-if person is "out of touch with the way things are"—and here is a phrase that touches the ambiguity of performance—"They are like actors who are perpetually in character" (p. 52). As-if addictive behavior is to act other than we really feel; yet the magic *as if* of the Stanislavski tradition (as well as common sense) says the performer must do *precisely* that. However, the American acting system has reversed this as-if demand for the actor: acting as if you are feeling thus and so was deemed no longer sufficient, regardless of how seemingly truthful and effective that behavior seemed to be; it was held necessary to be *actually* feeling the way you are acting (ignoring the fact that we can only know what a person is thinking or feeling by what we see or hear in his or her behavior—which is the very acting *as if* we departed from in the first place).

This reversal of emphasis is sometimes so unbalanced that the inner feeling becomes more important than what was actually communicated: one might not have a clue as to what the performer is feeling, but that is OK as long as they are actually feeling it. That kind of absurdity has become less common, but the residue of guilt—"If you're *not* feeling it, you are guilty regardless of whether you are communicating it"—is almost universal among performers.

A case in point: A young singer performed Cunegonde's "Glitter and Be Gay!" from *Candide* for an acting class. The instructor loved the performance until, in questioning the singer about her thought and feeling processes, he found that they did not match what he thought she should have been thinking and feeling. Whereupon he reversed his evaluation of the performance, condemning what he had praised, denying his direct experience in service of the mind-reading fallacy.

Schaef says that in life the external should be true to the internal. Our perversion of the Stanislavski system, while agreeing with that, goes further and says that the external can only be true *if* the internal is true in advance, and that the external must do nothing until the internal arrives at that truth. Both of these faulty derivations are reductions of the complexity of our body-mind energy system, and do not do justice to its potential. Schaef's well-intended rule—be externally true to your inner self—is too general to be useful in specific instances.

We always have choice in how our external resources communicate our interior thoughts and feelings; there are many possible combinations, none of them right or wrong in any absolute sense. Our internal state is generally too complicated to be completely and honestly expressed by our external resources. Moreover, our outer communicating choices influence our inner process, and vice versa; we do not need to be victims of our internal states, nor do we need to cover them up. The interaction of the inner and the outer is far too wonderfully complex to be reduced to an either-or duality. It is also too complex a process to be controlled by MIM, although we may live with the illusion that it can be—which is another major addictive characteristic.

The Illusion of Control

The illusion of control is precisely that: we think we can—and we can't. We can guide processes, but we cannot control them without disempowering them. Our entanglements are concrete examples of the illusion of control. We are conditioned to be afraid of experiencing strong energies—particularly emotional energies. And so we learn to try to control the flow of emotional energy through our system. The physical tensions involved in trying to control our emotions actually put us out of control, both physically and emotionally: the body is rendered partially impotent both by the waste of energy used to repress the emotion, and by the interference with the body's freedom to move, created by the tension itself. The emotion is neither expressed nor completely repressed, but seethes impotently as an ineffective mass of power-draining sludge that will find eventual expression as depression, irrational irritation, and the like.

Efforts to control the energy of any process may appear to succeed, but the repressed energy will inevitably emerge in ineffective or harmful ways. Singers may be obedient and appear to do as they are told, but if they are attempting to control their processes through tension, the cost is enormous: They may be interfering with and damaging their voices, failing to communicate what they think they are and being criticized for it, experiencing unspecified emotional frustration, and, in general, activating many of the addictive characteristics we have examined—especially defensiveness and judgmentalism. They will have been deprived of the true power of their process, which is a loss not only for them, but for their performances and audiences as well.

The more complex the energy demands of a situation, the more it raises the issue of control. Since there is not a more complex task than singing-acting, the addictive need for control within the music-theater training environment is proportionately extreme, for both performers and authority figures. As Schaef writes, "In an addictive system everyone tries to control everyone else" (p. 41). The director tries to control the actor in the singer-actor, the coach-conductor tries to control the singer in the singer-actor, and all the other teachers try to control their own special parts of the whole singer-actor territory.

There is considerable confusion about who is controlling what portion of the turf: each part-teacher can easily become involved with some other part of the whole as well as her own; and in truth, the parts are interconnected in such a way that what is done to one part *does* affect the others. But without knowing how that interrelationship functions, any move into parts of the singer-actor territories in which we have no special expertise may lead us (and the singer-actor) astray.

The addictive need for control also leads to a phenomenon I call *minutia mania*. Each part-teacher may naturally focus more and more intently on the specific details of her expertise. As she does so, those details become increasingly important: the particular openness of a vowel sound, the particular pronunciation of a word, the particular place in which one breathes, the particular shape of one's mouth as one sings, the particular postural set from which one sings, the particular musical interpretation of a role, or the particular emotional quality of a role; these and any number of other musical, physical, or emotional particulars can come to receive an emphasis and attention out of proportion to their actual significance to the whole performance. It is a more detailed version of mistaking the parts—the voice, the body, or the emotions—for the whole performing process. In minutia mania, smaller and smaller parts become more and more important and the forest of the whole is not seen because of overintense focus on branches, twigs, bark, and leaves of the part-trees.

Territorial control is a primary driving force in music theater. It is often referred to in the field as an unacknowledged war. (In *The Shifting Point*, Peter Brook calls the section of the book covering his work in opera, "The Forty Years' War.") That unresolved conflict helps create the confusion and loss of power experienced by singer-actors in the training process. Both the conflict and the confusion are largely created by the lack of an integrating aesthetic with which to approach the singing-acting process. That lack heightens the need for control—no one needs control more than the person who is unclear about what he is doing—which, in turn, intensifies the conflict between rival controllers, thus creating a vicious downward spiral. One of the primary weapons a controller can use—consciously or unconsciously—in controlling others is confusion—another characteristic of the addictive system.

Confusion

Confusion plays a vital role within the addictive system of society, and it plays an even more powerful role in the control-oriented music-theater environment. Schaef connects confusion with control as follows: "First, [confusion] keeps us powerless and controllable. No one is more controllable than a confused person" (p. 65).

Confusion about the singing-acting process, for example, feeds the need for control. As one coach said to me after observing a series of classes, "You're trying to demystify the whole operatic training situation — and how it needs it!" I agreed, and added that the mystification process keeps the power in the hands of the mystifiers and out of reach of the mystified. I want to return to the performers what is rightfully theirs and has been taken from them: their personal and performing power. Not power in the tantrum-throwing, pampered-diva sense of that word — a phenomenon that is usually a delayed reaction to years of repressing feelings in an authoritarian, judgmentally abusive music-theater (or parental) environment. The power I speak of is the power to do freely, fully, and healthily whatever the performer wants to do (or what anyone else may want them to do) with her voice, her emotions, and her physical being in any combination. That is true power, and it serves us all — voice teachers, conductors, musical coaches, directors, acting coaches, and movement instructors alike. But even that kind of power can be threatening to those who want to keep the singer-actor under their control.

Schaef notes other effects of confusion: "It keeps us ignorant. Professionals give their clients confusing information cloaked in intimidating language that lay-people cannot understand" (p. 65). It is only too common to hear of coaches and directors who berate singer-actors for not fulfilling some minor idiosyncrasy (minutia mania) in order to intimidate, confuse, and control them; or who describe the work of the singer-actor they are coaching in negative, judgmental terms, which they don't actually believe, but use for purposes of confusion and emotional manipulation.

"Third, [confusion] keeps us from taking responsibility for our own lives" (p. 66). Or, if we are singer-actors, from taking responsibility for our own total performance process. We become dependent upon others to guide us out of the confusion. It may even be in the interests of the guide to keep us partially confused so that we must keep returning for guidance. That may not be the guide's conscious intent, but it works out that way. And since each guide has a different view of the terrain, a certain amount of confusion is inevitable until we agree on a common map, one that will allow each of us to integrate our mutual efforts with clarity.

"Fourth, [confusion] keeps us busy. When we must spend all our time and energy trying to figure out what is going on, we have none left over for reflecting on the system, challenging it, or exploring alternatives to it" (p. 66). As I often say to my classes, "Every singer-actor does more than he needs to and less than he could." We expend immense amounts of energy straining against our entanglements, and that makes us feel as though we are doing a great deal. If we were clear about what we were actually doing, and were able to release the energy-robbing tension, thus allowing all the blocked energy to flow freely and fully into the performing task, our performances would take a quantum leap in power with considerably less effort.

With that we have a daunting list of addictive characteristics that act to block the potentially unified relationship of human energies and frustrate the flow of radiant performance. But there are two more — self-centeredness, and the scarcity, zero-sum model — which relate to the solo and ensemble demands of music theater. I will treat them as a unit.

Self-Centeredness and Scarcity

The self-centered singer-actor is so common to the music-theater environment as to be the standard. The operatic duet in which the singers hardly look at one another, or the image of the ego-centered diva who is only aware of others as they enhance or interfere with her image are the caricatured norm. It is easy to forget that the addictive system has helped create that stereotype. "In the Addictive System *the self is central*. Everyone and everything else must go through, be related to, and be defined by the self as perceived by the self" (p. 40).

This is the solo situation — the aria in music theater or the soliloquy in theater — which, as such, is not a negative concept. It is only when the star soloist becomes the raison d'etre of music theater and self-centeredness the dominant way of viewing performance that it becomes a critical issue. It need not involve a star, of course, for any soloist can isolate himself in a non-relating way. Or the soloist can be prepared to move into an ensemble relationship with other performers. Together, the solo and ensemble situations form a full spectrum of music-theater performance experience.

While the solo situation is not negative per se, Schaef sees the relationship with others — ensemble in music-theater terms — as the positive pole of a self-centered/relationship duality. Relationship provides a way of living healthily, in process, and of transcending the debilitating conditioning of the addictive system. Schaef calls this the "Living Process System," and goes on to say that "in the Living Process System, *relationships are central*" (p. 40). Yet while ensemble relationship is a rich source of performing opportunity and growth, the conditioning of the addictive system is such that the demands of the self often prevent the singer-actor from drawing upon that source of power, possibly for fear that if one shares the self, the self is diminished. That perception is enforced by the scarcity model.

The scarcity model is "based on the assumption that there is not enough of anything to go around, and that we had better get as much as we can while we can" (p. 74). A corollary to it is the zero-sum model, which "postulates that if someone else gets something, it will not be there for me when I need it. Everything is available in limited, finite quantities" (p. 75). In the performing arts, where performers are evaluated and judged by public reviews and critiques, one often encounters the feeling—usually unspoken—that a performer cannot feel good about herself unless someone else gets a bad review: the envy syndrome and the feeling that "it is not enough that I succeed, my best friend must fail. There is only so much praise to go around, and if my best friend doesn't get any, there may be some left for me." In the teaching situation, if someone is praised for doing something well, there is often a distinct lack of rejoicing by other members of the class: there is only so much praise to go around and one person just got it all.

All the characteristics of the addictive system tend to be mutually reinforcing, and the scarcity and zero-sum models are not exceptions. They heighten the judgmental quotient, increase the comparative, competitive atmosphere, diminish the richness of ensemble interrelationship, and heighten perfectionist guilt. The addictive system—intensified by the music-theater training-rehearsal-production environment—is a closely woven web of negatively synergistic conditioning: the negative whole of addictive characteristics is worse than the sum of its parts.

The first step in dealing with that web of interference in our move toward radiant performing is to become aware of it. However, it is not useful to add judgment or guilt to that awareness—that simply compounds the initial error. Awareness pure and simple, without guilt, judgment, or self-flagellation, will allow us to begin exercising and releasing the conditionings that create the interfering web. We can only do something about those things of which we are aware; and the awareness that Schaef has brought to the addictive conditioning of society as a whole can serve as a guide in exploring, releasing, and replacing their particular manifestations in music theater. Radiant performing is not possible while they stand in its path. Opening that path by transforming them is a key step in creating the conditions for radiant performing—and that is the purpose of the performing power technique.

After our immersion in this distressing and fragmented portrait—the accuracy of which every participant in the music-theater environment can validate—we need to return to the whole for a view of the human energy system that will allow us to begin spiraling up out of the swamp of robotic conditioning. If awareness is the first step, the second is a means of acting upon that awareness in a new way. If we could have done it with our present awarenesses and tools, we would have. We turn, then, to the only place where all the guidance is found: the whole performer.

Chapter 4

Approaching the Whole Performer: Developing a Science of Radiant Performing

A Model for the Investigative Process

In chapter 1 we introduced the expanded list of energy characters that comprise the dramatis personae of the human energy system. The new characters included PIM, the playful intuitive mode; HOBS, the higher consciousness observer; and the Radiant Whole. Each of them involve energy levels and resources that lie beyond the body, the face, the voice, the mind, and the emotions. At this point in our historical development there is no consensus about how to discuss these higher energy levels and their interaction with the more familiar energies. Fortunately, we can turn to the field of transpersonal psychology, which, as the name suggests, investigates energy processes beyond the mental, emotional, and personality levels. Those investigations, while still in process, have begun establishing the basis for such a consensus.

These higher energy levels not only significantly affect life in general, they also interact powerfully with the performance process. They are, in fact, a crucial ingredient in radiant performing, and it would be useful to examine them more fully. In establishing an investigative model with which to pursue this exploration, we will draw upon the work of Ken Wilber, a leading transpersonal psychologist whose research has particular relevance to our own.

Wilber explores the problem of proof with respect to higher energies. Since what we are calling higher energies are not part of the ordinary sense spectrum, it is difficult to establish a scientific basis for them. Wilber addresses that challenge directly. Without recapitulating his efforts in toto, let us examine the basic requirements for consensual proof in any field of investigation (including singing-acting).

In Wilber's analysis, there are always three steps in the process of accumulating and verifying information. I refer to those three steps as the instructional, experiential and interactional steps, or the IEI model. (Note: Wilber calls the three steps instrumental injunction, intuitive apprehension, and communal confirmation.)

Instructional: This is what you must do to investigate the field of information in question: "If you want to know this, do this." There are always instructions that must be followed in pursuing any move into the unknown, skills to be mastered before one can come to know the field by having a direct experience of it. At this point one is still in the knowledge state with respect to the field in question; one does not yet *know* it. Mastering the skills necessary to move to the next step may take years, depending upon the nature of the field.

Experiential: This is the accumulation of data by actually following the instructions, which enables you to directly experience the field of knowledge. In this step knowledge becomes knowing. Again, it may take years of following the instructions before one attains the knowing of direct experience.

Interactional: This step involves communicating the experiential data with others for the purpose of interaction, sharing, support, and guidance. The interactions may confirm the data, or they may reveal differences in the experience of having followed the instructions. If the experiential data is different from that of others, one returns to the instructions with new information. The instructions are followed again, interacting with the new information, and new experiential data is discovered for continuing interaction. (In the field of singing-acting, the step would involve the actual "doing" of the instructions while others watched and then described what had been done.)

These three steps are part of what is called the scientific process in investigating any complex of energies. For example, to investigate the physical-material world — physics, chemistry, biology, etc. — we must first master the necessary techniques — the instructions — for the acquisition of knowledge in those fields. If we wish to learn about the internal workings of the human body, we must follow a long series of instructions before moving to the data-accumulating, experiential step. That done, we are able to experience directly (or with the help of sensory extensions such as microscopes) what we may already have knowledge of — for example, the structure and makeup of a human cell. If we develop our capacities on the experiential level so that we come to know things that others have not experienced, we can share that new information and interact with the community of similarly qualified investigators. They can then follow the same instructions and confirm what we have experienced, or arrive at different experiential data for further interaction.

This sequence of "follow these instructions, experience the results, interact with others" is a fundamental model for the pursuit of knowing on all levels of energy exploration. We will refer to it as the IEI model or process, and it represents the method of science in its simplest form. As Wilber says, "By science, then, we must mean, in the most general sense, any discipline that openly, honestly, and conscientiously opens its knowledge claims to the three strands of valid data accumulation and verification" (*Eye to Eye*, p. 71). Leave out one step (any part of the whole process) and the results will be flawed.

In the case of Galileo — one of the creators of this process — it was a matter of investigating something that seemed logical to the rational mind (MIM) and testing it against actual experience. He created his own set of instructions to see whether objects of different sizes and weights actually did fall at the same speed. He took two different objects and dropped them from a conveniently leaning tower, and experienced the results through observation. He shared the instructions and the experience with others who, if they were so inclined, could follow the instructions, experience the results, and confirm or correct his findings. The concept was so new at the time that a great many were not so inclined and simply argued against the results from a nonexperiential, mental level. But there were those who realized that whatever MIM thought it knew, it could be wrong. The instructions were easy enough to follow, so they did just that. It turned out that the conventional wisdom of MIM had been in error, and the world has never been the same since.

On an everyday level, the same process may involve something as simple as a recipe (a set of instructions) that makes no sense to MIM: "You mean if I mix all those ingredients — most of which I don't care for separately — and put the thin, gooey mess that results into the oven for half an hour at 350 degrees, I may want to devour what comes out instantly?" Had humankind listened only to MIM in such cases, the world would have been a poorer place. But we learned that in order to *know* about the science of cooking, we had to first follow the instructions (which were created by a community of culinary investigators interacting over a period of time), after which we would have a direct experience of the cake recipe for ourselves. If the instructions have been followed accurately, communal interaction with the results by our family and friends may dispose of them rather quickly.

We can apply the IEI model to any level of energy investigation. The previous examples were both from the physical-material level. The word *science* has come to refer only to such investigations of the physical-material world, and only to those aspects of that world that can be apprehended by our senses (or extensions of those senses, such as microscopes and telescopes). But it is clearly possible to apply the IEI process to other levels of energy experience. More than that, it is vital to do so if we are to continue expanding our knowing of what it is to be human.

Because of that limited use of the word *science*, we have sometimes erred by invalidating all investigations that call themselves sciences unless the results of those investigations are available to the five senses or their extensions. If the field of investigation cannot be experienced in sensory terms, we may say the field "is not susceptible to true scientific study" or, worse, the field does not even exist. We have thereby reduced knowing to the level of what we can measure on the physical-material level and have reduced the meaning of ourselves to nothing more than sensory organs hooked up to a computer brain.

In and of themselves, our sensory capacities and the mind-brain are extraordinary processes; through their interaction they reveal and create wonders. But the reductionist view that mistakes those parts for the whole has sometimes prevented us from "scientifically" investigating and experiencing nonmaterially based levels of energy. Such investigations can expand our total human processes in unknown ways, particularly when the experiential data is mutually shared with others who are exploring the same territory. This book is about such an investigation. It is also an invitation to join in the process: follow the instructions (creating new ones of your own in the process), experience the results, and interact with the community of those who are similarly engaged for support, guidance, and expansion (or redirection).

The Human Energy System Seen from the Whole

We are investigating the whole field of energy involved in the singing-acting process. In addition to the mind, the emotions, the body, the face, and the voice, that field includes the previously mentioned resources of HOBS, PIM, and the Radiant Whole. These higher levels of energy interact with MIM, IMP, and the projective modes and supply them with energy that can be either transformed into communication or, depending upon the amount of entanglement-interference, burned up ineffectually within the system.

PIM is a primary creative resource in transforming universal energy into specific communicating concepts. When Albert Einstein said that his most important ideas came not from his rational mind, but from his intuition, he was speaking for creative artists in general as well as for himself. We can exercise our capacity to open our three projective modes more fully and freely to the flow of creative energy from the intuitive mode. Developing the ability to respond to intuitive impulses with our voices, our bodies, and our faces, rather than pre-evaluating them with our minds (thus killing them), is a specific area of exercise we will explore in chapter 12.

HOBS is our awareness gateway to higher consciousness. Awareness begins with MIM, but once we become aware of MIM and of MIM's awareness, we are on another level, which expands as we open to it. Where the awareness of MIM can help guide the vocal, physical, and emotional processes, the higher awareness of HOBS can serve as a guide for MIM and open to expanded levels of consciousness as it does so.

The leading character in our cast of energy resources, the Radiant Whole, provides an infinite supply of universal energy for all the other modes. They, in turn, can open to that unlimited potential (in proportion to their freedom from entanglement), and even draw upon it (if they have the appropriate tools) as they move toward radiant performing.

In *Performing Power* I discussed the well-known fact that everything, from stones to sunbeams, is energy in different vibratory states; and that the human system forms a continuum of these varying energy states. Some of them can be easily sensed and measured (such as the body, the breath, and the sounds we make). Others can be easily sensed but not so easily measured (such as our thoughts, emotions, and imagination). And there are some that can be sensed only under certain circumstances or not at all, and that are not susceptible to our current, limited standards of measurement (such as dreams, our unconscious mind, our higher consciousness, and those fields of energy that scientists such as Rupert Sheldrake are beginning to investigate). One way of visualizing the human energy field in terms of differing frequencies of energy is as follows.

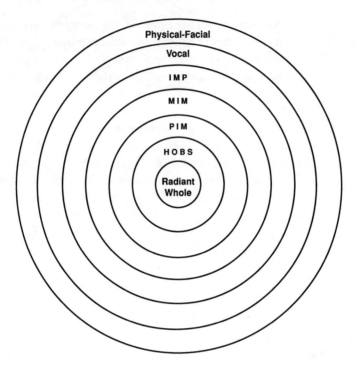

This model shows the projective modes as part of the outer three levels. The physical body is the densest layer of energy, and the only visible one. All the others remain invisible and inaudible unless transformed into communication by the voice and/or the body and/or the face—the three projective modes, individually or in combination. In actuality, of course, all these various levels of energy exist simultaneously in space and time: the body is not simply an outer shell, nor are the mental and emotional energies confined to layers in their physical housing.

Although each succeeding energy level becomes less tangible, lighter, and more refined as we move inward on the model, that does not mean that the power diminishes: the reverse is closer to the truth. For example, the energies of the mind are more refined and subtle than the energies of the body, and clearly have a power that is different from that of the body (without thereby demeaning our physical capacities). In considering the relationship of energy and matter, energy that is vibrating at a higher frequency always has the capacity to direct energies vibrating at a lower frequency, whereas lower or slower energies can never direct higher, faster energies.

Thus while the body can function on its own, it cannot tell the mind what to do; but the mind can give the body instructions, even as it receives information from the body, which guides the instruction-giving process. Instruction flows from above to below: information flows from below to above. And while no individual part can determine the condition of the whole, the more free the interaction within and between the various energy levels of the human system, the more powerfully, effectively, and synergistically the system will function as a whole.

Investigating Higher Energies

We can apply the instructional-experiential-interactional process to any level of the energy model. Beginning with the physical-material level, for example, the biologist follows the instructions for learning about the physical body, using the five senses and the mind in combination. He observes the actual physical processes — say, the growth of cells — and then interacts with the existing information in the field of biology for confirmation or correction.

Moving inward on the energy model, the psychologist investigates the human being on levels different from the purely physical, and in ways that have become increasingly complex during this century. Abraham Maslow — generally regarded as the modern founder of transpersonal psychology — has designated "Four Forces" in the field of psychology: (1) behavioristic, objective-empirical approaches; (2) psychoanalytic approaches; (3) humanistic, mental-intentional approaches; and (4) transpersonal, transcendental approaches. Each approach focuses on a different level of the human energy spectrum. For our purposes, two of them — the behavioral and psychoanalytic approaches — will demonstrate the use of the IEI process in approaching the first invisible energy levels on the energy model.

In attempting to be more traditionally scientific, behavioral psychology approaches the invisible and then retreats from it. As a result, behavioral psychologists confine their efforts to the physical body and to external, measurable behavior. Instead of using this external data to interpret the inner process subjectively, they concentrate on what is visible and objective. This, of course, simplifies both data accumulation and interaction with the rest of the field.

The psychoanalytic approach (of which there are numerous variations) attempts to examine the first two levels of invisible energy: the mind and the emotions. The psychoanalytic form created by Freud involves a dialogue in which one interpretive mind analyzes the workings of another. The empirical scientist may object that such interpretive inquiry leads to subjective data that have no communal objectivity, but the interactional process works with rigor even here. As Wilber points out, some of Freud's theories passed the communal intersubjective screening process and some did not. Those that did have become accepted by virtually all schools of modern psychology, and include the existence of unconscious processes, defensive or repressive mechanisms, narcissism, the importance of development, and the existence of different types of psychological structure. "Other of his theories have not meshed with informed . . . consensus and have thus dropped from the ongoing development of psychological theory" (Wilber, p. 58).

Psychoanalytic data cannot be measured as easily as the physical and sensory data of the behaviorists, "but neither is it 'mere subjectivism,' because there is an external corrective to undue subjective bias": the data must be submitted to the interactional screening process of the field as a whole, which includes all those who are following the IEI process of scientific inquiry (p. 58).

In all cases—whether contributing new concepts or criticizing them—one must become part of the whole process by following the instructions and gathering experiential data from the field of investigation. Only then can one become part of the communal, interactional process. You must develop an understanding adequate to the field in question before you can confirm or correct the experiential data of others.

For example, it is not enough to say, "I don't believe there is an unconscious mind, and even if there was it would not affect the way we act. It does not make sense to me and therefore it is meaningless"; or, in the field of meditation, "You cannot tell me exactly what happens to you when you meditate, therefore it is meaningless." In both these cases (and countless others) you must follow the instructions of the field and experience the resultant data yourself before you can join those capable of confirming or correcting the accumulated experiential data of the field as a whole. Until that is done, one does not have an understanding adequate to the field in question. No lower level of understanding or outer level of energy experience can invalidate the findings of a higher or inner level.

Even on the physical-material level, we would not grant credibility to a layman who said, "I think Einstein was crazy! The idea that everything is energy vibrating at different frequencies is intellectual hogwash!" Such a man-in-the-street critic has not followed the instructions and accumulated the experiential data necessary for his understanding to be adequate to the concept he is criticizing. Anyone who attempts to become part of the interactional process of any field of investigation without having first followed the instructions and having had direct experiences in and of the field itself cannot be given serious attention by those who have.

How does all this apply to the singing-acting process and the performer's approach to it? Two techniques relate powerfully to the whole performance process—the performing power technique and The Radiance Technique. Both of them involve a set of instructions that must be practiced and experienced over a period of time. Instructions for the performing power technique will be clarified in this book (although a hands-on experience with someone who understands the approach is invaluable in developing a personal exercise process). Instructions for The Radiance Technique must be learned in a professional seminar and will not be discussed here (although the principles of energy informing it are fundamental to the concepts of the book).

While the experiential data that emerges from both techniques will vary from individual to individual, there are universal principles of energy informing The Radiance Technique that are transformed into varying specifics in the performing power technique. Both sets of experiential data may be described in widely differing ways; but in both cases we are dealing with relatively new fields of investigation involving the interaction of many different levels of energy: the physical, the facial, the emotional, the vocal, the mental, the intuitive, the higher observational, and other higher levels of energy including that of the Radiant Whole. Until one has begun the investigation, following the IEI process and developing an understanding adequate to the whole field, it is relatively meaningless to make confirming or correcting comments about either the techniques themselves or the field in which they are practiced.

We may note that the more levels of energy are involved in the investigative process, the more complex and seemingly contradictory may be the initial experiential data. Those sciences dealing with only the physical-material level have so gratified the human need for simple answers that we have attempted to impose that simplicity and its methodology on more complex fields of investigation, such as the field of the whole human being. (Although, even on the physical-material level, the data grows increasingly complex in proportion to our capacity for investigative depth: witness the seemingly paradoxical, mystical state of quantum physics—which, it should be emphasized, is still dealing only with the physical-material world.)

Thus, behavioristic psychology reduces the whole field of human psychology—inner and outer—to outer behavior in order to be more consensually scientific. But it may also be a response to the need for control and measurability, and the craving for clearcut, simple answers—which behavioral psychology provides in contrast to the more complex interplay of mind, emotions, *and* behavior that make up the depth psychologies.

Consider, then, the performing power technique—which deals with the exercise and development of physical, facial, vocal, emotional, and mental energies. It also *opens* to higher energy levels—including the intuitive and higher observational energies—but the sheer complexity of dealing with the first five levels is already remarkable. And if we consider The Radiance Technique, which deals with the whole human being and those higher energy levels directly, we have radically increased the experiential complexity.

Again, as the experiential data become increasingly complex, there is a temptation to find simple, cause-and-effect answers to save us from the challenge of dealing with the full spectrum of human energies and possibilities. The part-equals-whole error is a specific manifestation of this conditioned need for duality (another name for oversimplification): we choose one part as *the* answer to spare ourselves from the necessity of dealing with the whole. In the long run, of course, there is no way of avoiding that necessity—nor is there any reason to do so. Interacting with the whole can be a joy. Developing the singing-acting process by disentangling and releasing the blocks to that joy is a major theme of this book.

Even the models we have been using are a concession to our human craving for simplification. (And understandably so in dealing with singing-acting—the most complex single aesthetic task a human being can perform.) So long as we recognize the models for what they are—maps and not the territory itself—they can be useful. Our second pentagon model, for example, narrows the focus of our investigation. Where the pentagon of potentiality dealt with the singer-actor and his/her environment, this one deals only with the singer-actor and his/her performing energies.

If we add HOBS and PIM to the picture, with HOBS in the center and PIM spiraling through the three projective modes, and place it all within the field of the Radiant Whole, we have a more complete model. But the only parts that can be consciously exercised are the five performing energies. This distinction is important when differentiating between the performing power technique and The Radiance Technique. The pentagon of performing energies includes those energies that MIM can identify and for which one can create a direct exercise process. The creative-intuitive energies of PIM and the higher consciousness–observational energies of HOBS (as well as the Radiant Whole itself) are all vital to the performing process—but they must be

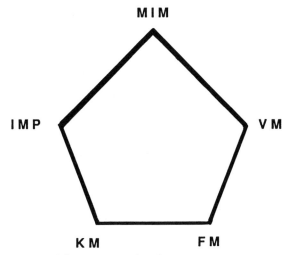

The Pentagon of Performing Energies

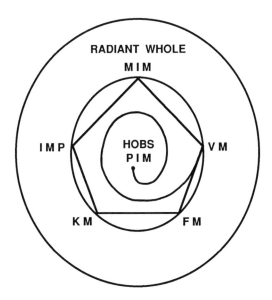

opened to by the performing energies. The freedom to express aspects of those higher energies (especially PIM) kinesthetically, facially, and vocally *can* be exercised, of course, and we will suggest exercises for that purpose in later chapters.

For the moment, let us emphasize the function of the pentagon of performing energies: to specify those parts of the total human energy system that can be exercised and developed by *anyone* using the performing power technique. As we develop the capacity of these parts for greater isolation *and* integration, and fulfilled performing potential, we are also developing their openness to the supporting flow of the higher energies of the human system. The greater freedom each projective mode has to express itself in terms of its own energy, the more it opens to the higher energies that, in turn, further empower that expressive capacity. When the synergy between these processes attains wholeness, radiant performing may occur.

The Performing Power Technique: A Science of Radiant Performing

The performing power technique is a science whose purpose is to create the conditions for radiant performing. It does this by developing and integrating the various parts of our communicating system—the three projective modes, MIM, and IMP—into a better integrated and coordinated whole. In doing this it allows each of those processes to become more responsive to the unlimited, universal energy of the Radiant Whole and thus move in the direction of radiant performing. Our relationship to that infinite potential expands in proportion to the capacity of the external, projective modes to open to it.

As we pointed out in chapter 1, the peak experience phenomenon studied by Maslow is a model for what we call radiant performance. If one were to establish criteria for achieving a peak experience, at least three components would be needed: (1) a field of activity that makes unusual demands on the human energy system, whether they are mental, emotional, physical, artistic, meditational, or some combination of those energies; (2) a person who has the developed capacity to deal with those challenges; and (3) direct experience with the field by actually performing the activity in question. The peak experience occurs when, in actual performance of the whole activity, all the skills involved come together in a synchronized, coordinated relationship with each other and with the demands of the field of activity. When that happens, the human system opens to a new and different state of energy experience, the whole becomes greater than the sum of the parts, and the qualities of the peak experience described in chapter 1—integration, spontaneity, coordination, ease, playful mastery, fearlessness, full expressivity, courage, daring, inner unification, freedom from self-judgment, and wholeness—become one with the performer.

There also seems to be a relationship between the degree of difficulty and/or danger involved in a field and the proportion of peak experiences it provides players. The main motive for playing in such fields is the intrinsic reward they offer their participants. Such activities include dancing, chess, games or contests of various kinds, creative activities of all sorts, mountain climbing, and, of course, singing-acting.

And within each field the choice of challenge offers varying degrees of difficulty: for the singer-actor, the "Everests of performance" include the Figaros, the Lucias, the Rigolettos, the Violettas, the Tristans, and the Isoldes, as well as Othello, in Olivier's radiant performance of that role.

This raises yet another criterion for the peak experience: (4) There must be a balance between the difficulty of the challenge and the capacity of the performer. If the climb or the role is too difficult, there will be no peak experience and no radiant performance—only anxiety and tension. If the challenge is too simple in itself, the climb or performance can be expanded to incorporate other demands: the climber can reach the top by a different route or by imposing special restrictions; the singer-actor by making unusual interpretive choices, or by giving herself personal challenges related to her own energy system.

In singing-acting the element of difficulty, risk, or danger includes the fact that the performance is being watched by an audience, which leads to a special qualification of the peak experience of radiant performing. There can be *inner* radiant performing that is not perceived as such by an audience, although if one could compare it with an ordinary performance by the same performer, it would be obviously "better." Whether that inner radiant performing is generally perceived as such by an audience is interdependent upon (1) the qualities of the performer's instrument—the voice, face, and body—which may not have the inherent power, beauty, or talent to manifest the inner experience clearly; (2) the appropriateness of the role, which may be so at odds with the performer's outer qualities that the inner experience is not perceived; or in some cases (3) the outer circumstances, which may obscure the qualities of radiant performing for the audience because of size of theater, costuming, makeup, orchestral imbalance, or staging.

In my training institutes there have been many instances of peak experience, inner radiant performing that was evident if one was familiar with the performer's work, but was less so to those seeing them for the first time. It is vital to honor both issues: the important growth signaled by inner radiant performing, and the continuing development of the whole singing-acting instrument necessary to fully communicate it.

In a study of a number of activities that lead to the peak experience phe-nomenon (not including singing-acting), psychologist Mihaly Csikszentmi-halyi found that when such activities are fully explored by their members, a kind of personal transcendence is experienced, which he calls "flow."

> Flow refers to the holistic sensation present when we act with total involvement. It is a kind of feeling after which one nostalgically says: "that was fun," or "that was enjoyable." It is the state in which action follows upon action according to an internal logic which seems to need no conscious intervention on our part. We experience it as a unified flowing from one moment to the next in which we are in control of our actions, and in which there is little distinction between self and environment; between stimulus and response; or between past, present, and future. (Cited by Mitchell, *Mountain Experience*, p. 153)

Flow is clearly very close to, if not identical with, Maslow's peak expe-rience. In Richard Mitchell's book *Mountain Experience*, he identifies three elements that constitute and potentiate the flow experience.

> First, for flow to be achieved, it is necessary for freedom of choice among a wide range of uncertain outcomes to be possible. Second, the actor must creatively fashion from these myriad uncertainties some limited task within the limits of his or her perceived abilities. Third, he or she must achieve a level of involvement such that consciousness of the task at hand and the doing of it blend, that action and awareness become indistinguishable. (Mitchell, p. 154)

For the singer-actor, there is an enormous range of possible choices so far as the combination and coordination of his or her own energies is concerned; and this does not take into account the necessity of responding in the mo-ment to the energies of the other performers, the conductor, and the audi-ence. But we will focus on the performer's performing energies—since the others are unpredictable—in creating the field of conditions in which radi-ant performing can take place.

For freedom of choice to exist among those energies, they must be ca-pable of whatever free individual actions may be called for by the singing-acting process, as well as coordinated activity of any kind. The voice, face, body, MIM, and IMP must be available as tools for use separately and in any combination the music-theater score instructions may call for. That will be the major task of this book in defining the science of the performing power technique: clarifying the functioning of those energies with respect to the singing-acting process, in order that they can be exercised individually and together. The performer can then move toward freedom of choice in their use.

That leads to the second criterion for the achievement of flow: creatively putting together the combination of energies that fulfill the score in the uncertain arena of performance. As Mitchell says, "For flow to occur . . . freedom of choice also must exist within the activity itself. This freedom implies an uncertainty of outcomes, defined by the actor as challenge, not necessity; as difficulty, not danger" (p. 158). The very challenge of singing-acting—the most complex aesthetic task a person can attempt—ensures a measure of uncertainty. The risk factor added by the presence of the audience increases the stakes.

As with mountain climbing, the level of the challenge is significant to the potential for the flow—and for radiant performing—so long as the challenge is, in fact, accepted. I say that because it is possible to approach the performance of opera, for example, without actually working with all the performing energies—to reduce it to a concert-in-costume (which does not mean that radiant performing could not occur—although it would be less likely—but simply that it would not engage the whole singing-acting system in the way we are describing). It is also possible to simply practice and never perform, in which case there is no radiant performing as such.

The third criterion—a level of involvement such that awareness and action become indistinguishable—also grows from the combination of complexity and challenge. The task must be complex and demanding enough to require complete involvement in the present moment—no time or energy for future worry or past regret. With the performing power technique, the singing-acting task can always be made sufficiently demanding that the performer—regardlesss of the level of expertise—can maintain the challenge at a level necessary for the flow of radiant performing.

This blending of awareness and action also suggests those moments when the actor or singer-actor *becomes* the character. This increases in difficulty with the level of stylization; i.e., it is more difficult to identify with an operatic character than with a realistic character. That oneness with the character depends to some extent on a great deal of MIM homework, on in-depth study of the character, which is then allowed to simply merge intuitively within the performer.

Combining components of the peak and flow experiences, we have (1) a field of activity with a strong degree of difficulty and an uncertain outcome, (2) a person with a developed capacity to deal with that field, (3) a direct experience of the field by that person, and (4) a blend of the person and the activity into a unity during the experiences. Let us examine Olivier's radiant performance of Othello in light of these general components of the peak-flow experience.

Fulfilled Performing Potential and Radiant Performance: Olivier's Othello

The field of activity we are concerned with here is the field of singing-acting (I include Shakespearean performance as part of it), with the specific part of that field being the play *Othello*. The field as a whole is the most complex and difficult performing challenge a human being can attempt; and of the "Everests" in the field, Othello is one of the most demanding roles. "It has often been said that no English actor in this century has completely succeeded as Othello" (Cottrell, p. 337). Olivier had determined early in his career never to attempt the role, and he finally did so only at the insistence of Kenneth Tynan, who accepted the position as literary manager of the National Theater only on the condition that Olivier perform the role within five years. Among the difficulties for the white actor, of course, is that Othello is black. It is clear that this particular "peak" is not ordinarily susceptible to the peak experience—it is simply too demanding.

In that demand and in the fact that this activity, unlike mountain climbing, is performed for a live audience, lies the element of danger. The presence of hundreds of observers who are assessing not only what you are doing, but how you are doing it compounds the difficulty and increases the necessity of a balance between the challenge of the activity and the capacity of the actor: radiant performing is interdependent upon a balance in that relationship.

Olivier's developed capacity for dealing with the field of Shakespearean performance was extraordinary. His preeminence as an actor-virtuoso in this century is without serious argument. But even with that capacity, Olivier began exercising for the role six months in advance of rehearsals. To change his voice from his own resonant, brass baritone trumpet to the "dark, black, violet, velvet *bass* voice" he felt it must be (Olivier, *On Acting*, p. 155), he exercised hours daily—with a voice teacher as well—until he had lowered it a fifth and more—occasionally a full octave. (It astonished me to hear it in person, by contrast with what I had come to think of as his "natural" voice.)

I was equally amazed by his walk, and his physical way of being, which received the same devoted attention: six months of daily gym work (which he had also done regularly for other roles) and a constant search in the rehearsal process for "the walk [of a] soft black leopard. He should grow from the earth, the rich brown earth, warmed by the sun . . . lithe, dignified and sensual" (*ibid.*, p. 155). Even then, he did not discover the final ingredient until, walking to the stage for the last dress rehearsal, he experimented further with his way of walking.

> I then tried to relax the foot, without placing the heel down first but putting my whole weight on each foot in turn as it touched the ground, thus introducing those swaying hips so generously commented upon, and regarded as the keystone of an elaborate characterization. . . . (*Confessions of an Actor*, p. 254)

Emotionally, Olivier knew that he had to plumb some unusual depths, even for him; and the only place to do that was in actual rehearsal.

> I gave a full-blooded, all-out rendering of the part at the very first rehearsal, and from then on I tried things out extravagantly, way over the top. Hands, eyes, body, a kind of self-flagellation. I have done this most of my acting life, grasping the nettle early on and making a fool of myself.
>
> The company realizes right away how embarrassing it's going to be and I save a hell of a lot of time. I am not doing it for the company. If you are frightened of making a fool of yourself, if you start too subtly, too cozily, giving just little glimpses of what the part might become, you create huge barriers for yourself later on. You must be open, naive, prepared to charge down every alley that presents itself, until you lock into the ones that you and your character need. (*On Acting*, p. 156)

And with that balance between a developed instrumental capacity—mind, voice, body, face, and emotions—and the role itself grew the blend of the activity—the role—and the person.

> I knew I could not play Othello in any detached way; I would have to put every single throb of my tiniest vein right into it. I knew I would not be able to fulfill myself in the part unless I did so.
>
> . . . .
>
> Black . . . I had to *be* black. I had to feel black down to my soul. I had to look out from a black man's world.
>
> . . . .
>
> The play becoming less of a play at times [in rehearsal] and more of a reality. Moments when I think I am Othello, when I am convinced I am black.
>
> . . . .

> The actor breathes into the nostrils of the character and the
> character comes to life. For this moment in my time, Othello is
> my character—he's mine. He belongs to no one else; he belongs
> to me. When I sigh, he sighs. When I laugh, he laughs. When I
> cry, he cries. (*On Acting*, pp. 151, 153, 159)

Olivier's perception of that oneness with the character was shared by the audience (certainly by me), as summed up by one critic: "Sir Laurence has managed, by heaven knows what witchcraft, to capture the very essence of what it must mean to be born with a dark skin. . . . It is a performance full of grace, terror and insolence. I shall dream of its mysteries for years to come" (Cottrell, p. 339).

With that model of a radiant performance, we have some of the particulars that contribute to the flow of unifying wholeness which is our direct apprehension of the Radiant Whole interconnecting our total energy system. There are many gateways through which that flow can enter: the body (opened, perhaps, through the Alexander Technique or simple release of tension); the voice (opened, for example, through a freer singing technique); the face (opened through conscious exercise); IMP (opened through the face, voice, body, or simply intuitively); MIM (opened through analysis, interpretive study, imagination, and greater self-awareness).

But no human endeavor has more gateways available than singing-acting. And this is both its glory and its challenge; for one blocked gateway can set up a sympathetic blocking of others and interfere with the potential flow of radiant performing. For the same reason, the opening of a previously blocked gateway can allow others to open as well. When they all open together, and radiant performing is experienced, it is beyond words, and beyond MIM's power to control or evaluate it; in a word, it is transcendent.

The Radiance Technique:
A Support and Guide for the Investigative Process

The next step, as I put it in *Performing Power*, is to find a technique that complements our work with the performing energies, and allows us to relate directly to our universal source of energy, without having to deny the necessities of our performing art. That technique, of course, is The Radiance Technique, a science of whole, transcendental energy, which continues to expand in its impact upon performers (and the population in general). In using the word *science* in this context, we are referring to the instructional-experiential-interactional model, which, as we have seen, is a paradigm for the scientific investigation of any field of energy.

I have quoted in earlier chapters from the work of Barbara Ray, the world's foremost authority on The Radiance Technique, specifically from *The Expanded Reference Manual of The Radiance Technique®*. As we continue to discuss and refer to The Radiance Technique and the Radiant Whole, I will draw further upon her definitive writings on the subject, which include *The Official Handbook of The Radiance Technique®*.

In exploring the more familiar energies of the mind, the voice, the emotions, the face, and the body, we will model their use upon the free flow of universal energy made available in greater abundance by The Radiance Technique. We will also exercise the capacity of those outer plane energies to open more fully to the qualities of the Radiant Whole.

The Radiance Technique provides a means of accessing directly the Radiant Whole, a source of energy that is innate, that is the luminous factor informing radiant performance, and that creates what we sometimes call "star quality" in a tangible although not easily definable way. The unlimited energy available to us from that source is rarely drawn upon in either life or performance to the full extent of our human potential. While the performing power technique opens the external communicating modes to the flow of energy from the Radiant Whole, The Radiance Technique accesses and amplifies that flow from the source itself. By increasing and balancing the vocal, physical, facial, emotional, mental, intuitive, and higher observational energies, The Radiance Technique "lights up" their relationship and allows them to work together more powerfully and harmoniously. It helps ease the stress of performance and promotes a greater sense of performance health and well-being.

Moreover, with the use of The Radiance Technique, the Radiant Whole can be drawn upon at any time and in any place—even while practicing or performing—with no special mental effort, emotional involvement, physical exercises, or beliefs. In its availability for use at any time—even during the act of performance—The Radiance Technique is unique among those systems that work with higher energies. To my knowledge, it is the only technique in existence that allows the performer to draw upon the support of the Radiant Whole regardless of the physical, mental, emotional, or vocal state of being, and with no external requirement whatsoever.

Together, the performing power technique and The Radiance Technique form a whole, synergistic relationship between the outer communicating process and the inner energizing process. This relationship is the essence of radiant performing.

Summing Up: The IEI Model Applied to Radiant Performing

In the performing power technique, we have instructions to follow in the science of radiant performing. The instructions concern the preparation of the instrument—the whole human energy system—for the process of sing-ing-acting. These instructions for exercising and developing MIM, IMP, the body, the face, and the voice, and opening to HOBS, PIM, and the Radiant Whole are included in chapters 9–14. They are seen as part of a lifelong preparation of the singing-acting instrument for performances of ever-in-creasing radiance—and radiant performing can occur at virtually any point on that journey.

But for radiant performing to occur, we must move to the step of direct experience with the field of activity—which in this case means performing for a live audience. (This is not to say that there cannot be radiant practice sessions. In fact, an increasing number of performers using the performing power technique are bringing back stories of their experiences in exercise sessions that I can only call radiant.) However, in order to move to the step of interaction with others in the field, public performance is important.

That third step of interaction with others also involves interaction with oneself. From the synthesis of actual performance, we move to analysis of what happened: drawing on the observation of others, and on our own level of awareness, we can continue narrowing the gap between what we think we are doing and what we are actually doing. (When that gap no longer exists, it seems possible that radiant performing can become a consistent experi-ence.) We then return to the continuing practice of the instructions and to more performing with the new information provided by the interactional analysis.

Simultaneous with that process is the opportunity to learn The Radiance Technique, and draw upon its unique capacity for support and guidance *at all times*. Since The Radiance Technique provides contact with and expan-sion of what you already are, it can be a faithful companion on the journey to radiant performing, a guide that is always supporting you, whether you know it or not.

Chapter 5

The Seven Lively Entanglements

Entanglement: The Human Condition

Before we go further in using the term *entanglement*, it is important to understand that it is not a dirty word. We are all entangled to some extent — it is the human condition. If we condemn our entanglements, we are continuing the judgmentalism that created the entanglements in the first place: we are preevaluating and trying to control our energies rather than allowing them to flow freely. And allowing them a free flow is the only way we can truly learn how to work with them. Trying to control them prevents that learning from happening.

We may also find ourselves attempting to conceal our entanglements (even from ourselves), which is exactly the opposite of what we must do to develop our performing power. As we will see in discussing the exercise process, we must allow our entanglements free play in order, first, to become fully aware of them and, second, to learn to release them. In any case, the basic rule of *Never judge anything, especially yourself* is particularly true in working with the entanglement process.

Initially I helped enforce the pejorative connotations of the word *entanglements* by what I called them. After selecting seven major entanglements, I looked for a playful, nonacademic name, and arrived at "the seven deadly entanglements." Not being a performer who could feel oppressed by them, I had no problem in taking the name lightly. But it became clear that most performers I worked with thought of entanglements as bad things — and calling them deadly didn't help. I asked a group of performers to find a more

benign title; someone suggested "the seven lively entanglements." And so they are, and so we will refer to them.

In classes I often compare the training of entanglements with the training of puppies: as Barbara Wodehouse, the great English dogtrainer, has demonstrated, the best results are achieved with love. Many of our entanglements were created very early in our lives, and though they are with us still, they remain the puppylike creations of the day they were born: they never age, and like puppies they will respond best to nonjudgmental awareness and love. They are a part of us; we created them in the past for what we believed at the time to be very good reasons. To condemn them now is to deny an important and living part of ourselves. We can train them more effectively by beginning with awareness of what they are (never mind why they were created), and with descriptions of how they function, from which we can derive exercises that allow us to practice releasing them. As I stressed at length in *Performing Power*, one of the most useful ways of avoiding judgment of ourselves or others is with specific, accurate, and nonevaluative descriptions.

Understanding, accepting, and working with one's uniquely entangled condition is a key to increasing performing power in both life and performance. It is also a vital step on the path to radiant performing. But the complexity of the human energy system can so overwhelm us that either we seek out one simple answer, or we resist all attempts at analysis and simply trust our intuition. In the first case, we may focus on a single part of our total process (the voice, the body, the emotions, etc.) and hope that if that part is properly developed, it will take care of the whole. In the second, while it is important to expand trust in our intuition, that trial-and-error method is as limited as our capacity to use it and our opportunities to exercise it in performance. But while both responses are significant aspects of singer-actor development, neither end of the spectrum they form is useful all by itself.

Some performers have been successful in working exclusively from either end of the one-part/intuitive-whole spectrum: at the one-part end are the rare few with voices that, all by themselves, are sufficient to carry their performances; at the intuitive end are those whose intuitive freedom and trust is strong and whose energy systems are usefully responsive to that freedom in producing a powerful emotional performance. But even those few (constituting, at most, 5 percent of the singer-actor population) can benefit by approaching performance in a way that allows them to develop their total performing process; for the other 95 percent it is absolutely vital.

Projective-modes training, which both develops and disentangles the communicating processes, is a way of viewing the human energy system from the perspective of the whole. It allows us to relate to all parts of that system, the guidance modes (MIM, IMP, PIM, and HOBS) as well as the communicating modes (vocal, kinesthetic, and facial modes). This view of the human energy system simplifies and expands our capacity to work with both the whole and the parts, and thus with the full spectrum of performance energies. Entanglements, as we will see, are found in and between all parts of that spectrum, from the inner energies of the intuitive, the mental, and the emotional, to the outer energies of the body, the voice, and the face in communicating the inner processes.

We will simplify the challenge by focusing on only seven entanglements. There are, of course, more (just as there are more than seven deadly sins, lively arts, wonders of the world, and the like); but if the singer-actor is clear about these seven, and learns to work with them, she or he will have taken immense strides in the direction of more radiant performing. However, before investigating those seven, let us review the nature of entanglements in general.

The Origin and Nature of Entanglements

All entanglements are reflections of the essential interconnectedness of the human energy system. As energy moves through the whole human system to communicate, the interconnections between the various parts of that system will be called into play. Those interconnections may be coordinated, mutually supportive, integrated, and open to freedom of choice in how they interact; and all those positive relationships can be enhanced. For anyone interested in performing, this is cause for rejoicing.

But those energy interconnections can also be uncoordinated, mutually interfering, unintegrated, and limited in the ways they interact. We will call any such limitations in their freedom to relate entanglements. Some degree of entanglement is inevitable in everyone, but all entanglements can be transformed into choices through exercise.

Some entanglements are more harmful than others. The most harmful entanglements tend to originate with the judgmentalism of MIM. We are conditioned at a very early age to be careful of the way we use energy: "Be quiet!" "Don't make so much noise!" "Settle down!" "Big boys (or girls) don't cry." "Don't be such a baby!" "Look at the sissy cry!" "Don't you look at me like that, young lady (or man)!!" "Wipe that smirk off your face!" "Is something wrong?" "Don't be such a grouch!" and so on, recalling ad infinitum the "frozen feelings" characteristic of our addictive society.

In his book *What to Say When You Talk to Yourself*, Shad Helmstetter states that "during the first eighteen years of our lives, if we grew up in fairly average, reasonably positive homes, we were told 'No!,' or what we could *not* do, more than *148,000 times!*" and, further, that behavioral research shows "that as much as *seventy-seven percent* of everything we think is negative, counterproductive, and works against us" (pp. 20–21). Most of those "No's!" had to do with our use of strong energy—shouting, crying, running, jumping—which in turn was fueled by strong emotion of some kind—excitement, delight, joy, anger, or fear. Thus our earliest experiences of emotional energy flow became associated with the judgmental nay-saying of MIM.

We learn that it is psychologically dangerous to show too clearly what we are feeling, especially with the face and voice. MIM believes in this danger and tries to control the facial and vocal energies. The only tool it has for this purpose is the body. It calls the body into play to control the energies of the face and the voice with physical tensions of various kinds. This is an unconscious process that gradually becomes a habitual, automatic response to any increase in the flow of energy. Eventually this repressive control comes to be mistaken for the expression itself: the physical tension originally brought into play to control and block the facial or vocal expression of anger comes to be mistaken for the expression itself.

Using the pentagon of performing energies, we can illustrate the process as follows.

IMP experiences emotion that moves for expression through the KM, FM, or VM.

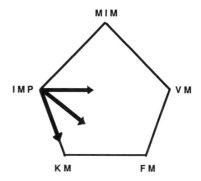

MIM says "No!," but must call on KM to block the flow of energy.

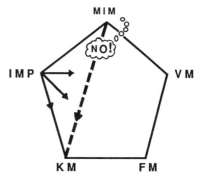

The KM sends out intercepting tensions that repress the expression. Repetition of this process makes it habitual, and the repression comes to be equated with the expression.

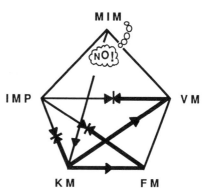

This false repression-equals-expression equation becomes a permanent, unconscious part of our communication system. It interacts with a tightly woven web of three addictive characteristics—judgmentalism, frozen feelings, and the illusion of control—which reinforce and are reinforced by the false equation. The addictive need for control is at the root of most performing entanglements, which can be described as follows.

When a performer changes the quantity or quality of energy through one of the projective modes—say, by singing—and either of the other two modes is compelled to change in some way—for example, the face has to contort in response to the singing—that is an entanglement between them. Such a relationship is neither useful nor necessary. Yet this is precisely what happens much of the time during the process of performing. If such a relationship occurs and the performer can make other choices freely, it is not an entanglement. But when there is no choice in the matter, it is. All entanglements create an energy drain in the human system and/or interfere with the communicating process, both of which rob performers of their maximum performing power.

Entanglements may also be correlated with the concept of mode dominance. The performer may want to use her dominant mode—her favorite means of communication—to communicate in an inappropriate situation. For example, a projective-kinesthetic dominant giving a song recital may attempt to use the kinesthetic mode inappropriately, with tension, overly busy gesturing, or movement: in those cases the kinesthetic mode is not only interfering with the communication—distracting attention from the song being sung—but is also interfering through tension with the singing process itself. In both cases there is an energy loss, either in projective communication or within the system itself.

The Varieties of Entanglements

Let us distinguish between three kinds of entanglements alluded to above. An entanglement can originate as (1) a sympathetic underlining response by one mode to the change of energy in another; (2) an attempt by one mode to control or interfere with the flow of energy in another; or (3) the activating of a preexisting tension link between two modes. The following are specific examples of each (with the reminder that the examples are entanglements only if they are the *sole* choice the performer can make).

(1) *The Sympathetic Entanglement*: When the vocal mode (VM) sings a

lively passage, the kinesthetic mode (KM) may beat out an accompanying rhythm with the body, the gestures, or both.

(2) *The Controlling Entanglement*: When the facial mode (FM) attempts to communicate more emotion, the KM may attempt to control the flow of that emotion with physical tension.

(3) *The Linking Entanglement*: With the KM in a preexisting state of tension, any attempt to gesture will automatically link up with other parts of the body or with the body as a whole, and draw them or it into play.

The following scenario describes all three of those possibilities existing simultaneously. Before the performer does anything at all, his body gets ready for action, tensing up in the process, and establishing the potential for a linking entanglement. When the scene calls for the expression of emotion, the face comes into play to communicate it. As it does so, the body attempts to control that flow of emotion by further increasing the existing state of tension, thus creating a controlling entanglement. Then, as the performer sings, he may gesture in sympathy with the difficulty of the music or the intensity of the emotions. In either case, the preexisting physical tension draws the rest of the body into play via the linking entanglement.

Sympathetic entanglements are relatively benign, and occasionally even intensify the communication. Much of the time, however, they interfere with the clarity of communication, and may also block the flow of energy within the performer. Sympathetic entanglements shape many of our communicating patterns as children; later, MIM attempts to control these immature behavior patterns through additional kinesthetic tension. At that point, the sympathetic entanglement has engendered a controlling entanglement, which becomes an automatic, habitual interference with the flow of energy in the performer's system, on stage as well as in life.

Controlling entanglements of that nature, which interfere with the flow of energy—emotional and otherwise—within the human system, are less benign than sympathetic entanglements. When controlling emotion is the major function of physical tension, it identifies a controlling entanglement. Controlling entanglements are of little use in general, and simply burn up energy within the singer-actor's system to no advantage (and a great deal of disadvantage). They do send messages of powerlessness—which might seem appropriate for some characterizations—but, as we will see, it is never necessary or useful to make such character statements from a condition of entanglement. Like sympathetic entanglements, controlling entanglements may also interfere with the clarity of communication (drawing audience focus to the point of tension); but their most detrimental effect is to rob the performer of energy, flexibility, and freedom, and the performance of its power.

As suggested above, the judgmentalism of MIM is the primary source of controlling entanglements. But MIM cannot control the energy flow in the human system without the aid of the KM (including the facial musculature of the FM.) It should be noted in this respect that MIM can only affect those energies that lie below (or outside) its own realm of the mental: the body, the emotions, and the voice. Those lower/outer energies can *open* to the higher/inner energies of MIM, but the body, the emotions, and the voice cannot draw upon the mental energies directly. Similarly, the body, which is situated below/outside the emotions, can open to the emotional energies, send information to them, and allow the emotions to flow more freely through the kinesthetic system, but it cannot instruct the emotions directly.

The same is true of the relationship between MIM and the emotional process (IMP): information flows from the emotions to MIM; instructions flows from MIM to the emotions. Unfortunately, as we have seen, recent studies indicate that MIM cannot actually instruct IMP, but can only respond through indirect means to an energy flow from IMP with instructions to the body, face, and voice as to how to handle it—usually with some sort of repression-control pattern.

Nonetheless, the flow pattern—information up/in, instruction down/out—holds true for the system as a whole; it's just that IMP won't listen to MIM's instructions. The body, face, and voice are more willing to listen—although occasionally recalcitrant—and much of our exercise will be to find ways of clearing the instructional channels so that we can allow IMP and the projective modes to open more freely to MIM, as well as those energies above MIM.

Similarly with the relationship of MIM and the projective modes to the Radiant Whole: MIM can *open* itself and the lower/outer modes to the Radiant Whole through specific exercises, but cannot draw directly upon it. Opening up/in to the Radiant Whole is complicated by the fact that the lower/outer energies and their entanglements can keep MIM's focus solely on them to the extent that MIM ends up thinking that the body, the voice, the emotions, and the mind are all there is. Thus MIM can be so entangled with the projective modes that its awareness is limited to them. MIM may grudgingly acknowledge the additional presence of the PIM as "merely" a part of the unconscious processes—"dreams and all that." It may also identify with HOBS (equating its own awareness with the higher consciousness of HOBS), but a myopic, entangled, tunnel vision that does not allow MIM to shift its field of perception above/beyond itself is only too common.

Even the invaluable intuitive contributions of PIM and HOBS can be difficult to respond to or even be aware of if MIM is powerfully entangled with the lower/outer energies. MIM's monodirectional entanglement with the projective modes needs exercises to allow MIM to focus up/in at least as much as it focuses down/out. While MIM cannot access the power of the Radiant Whole directly, it can develop openness to the ongoing flow of that power; mentally focusing up/in is a way of doing that. The entanglement that pulls MIM's focus exclusively or primarily down/out blocks, wastes, or at the very least does not open to the incredible energy resource that is the Radiant Whole. We will discuss means of exercising that up/in focus in chapter 13, "The Full-Spectrum Performer."

Another point before we proceed to the entanglements themselves: We are always concerned with expansion, not elimination. We are not trying to get rid of entanglements, but rather to expand the range of choice in our use of energies. Our entanglements are ways of modifying or controlling our energy processes, and as such they represent specific and very often useful ways of communicating. In most cases, however, we will find that other choices, free of entanglement, are much stronger and more useful in both efficiency and actual communicating power. And once we have the choice of communicating without entanglement, we also have the choice of using the entanglement statement—free of its original tension—for the purposes of characterization.

The key word is choice: can you make the choice of communicating that statement without entangled energies? If you can, it is not an entanglement; it is simply another choice. If you cannot, the very lack of choice defines the statement as an entanglement. Our performing power is proportionate to our freedom of choice in using energy; freedom of choice can be developed through exercise; therefore by exercising and expanding our freedom of choice in how we use our energy—by transforming our entanglements—we can increase our performing power.

At this point we will make a brief list of the seven lively entanglements with a more detailed analysis to follow.

The Seven Lively Entanglements

1. *The Judgmental Entanglement*: This is the progenitor of all other en-

tanglements. It is an entanglement between MIM and the three projective modes. MIM calls upon the body to control any changes in the quantity or quality of energy moving through any of the three projective modes. It is a controlling entanglement and also creates the potential for a linking entanglement.

2. *The Anticipatory Entanglement*: This is the creation of a state of tension in the body or face as the singer-actor gets ready to perform. It anticipates a change in the quantity or quality of energy in the projective mode system. It is a controlling entanglement, and also creates the potential for a linking entanglement, which is activated by the change in energy flow. (Both the judgmental and anticipatory entanglements are preparatory entanglements; that is, they are not seen in action. The other five are all in-action entanglements. The change in the quantity or quality of energy is through the first mode or part listed, and the entanglement is with the second.)

3. *The Part/Whole Kinesthetic Entanglement*: When a performer gestures with the arms, the rest of the body often comes into play as well, typically by leaning into the gesture or lifting the shoulders with the gesture. This entanglement is generally the direct result of the anticipatory entanglement, and activates the linking potential already set up. Entanglement 3 can also originate sympathetically as the whole body emphasizes and supports the gestural statement. If the gesture suggests strong emotion, tension may be initiated to control it, thus creating a controlling version of entanglement 3.

4. *The Facial/Kinesthetic Entanglement*: When the face is about to change the quantity or quality of its communicating energies, the body comes into play either to act in sympathy with it or to control the flow of emotional energy.

5. *The Part/Part Facial-Emotional Entanglement*: When the musculature of the face is exercised, or expresses a strong emotional state, the jaw may get tense to control the flow of energy, or move in sympathy with the muscular effort. The eyes may also move sympathetically with that effort.

6. *The Hearing-Vocal/Kinesthetic Entanglement*: When a performer sings or speaks with out-of-the-ordinary energy, the body may move sympathetically (for example, swaying with the music), or try to control the energy (for example, squeezing the throat or partially closing the glottis to make the voice seem to sound more emotional).

7. *The Hearing-Vocal/Facial Entanglement*: When a person sings or speaks with out-of-the-ordinary energy, the face may move sympathetically (for example, the eyebrows may rise as a high note is sung). Moving in re-

verse, from face to voice, when the face expresses a strong emotion, the sound of the voice may be altered to relate to it by the "squeeze" technique mentioned in entanglement 6. Entanglements 6 and 7 involve the voice, which means all three projective modes are functioning simultaneously. This means, in turn, that both 6 and 7 may become three-way entanglements involving all the modes.

That is the list in brief. Now for an in-depth examination of each of them.

Number 1: The Judgmental Entanglement

We discussed the judgmental entanglement in connection with the addictive characteristics that shape the social and performing behavior of the singer-actor. *Performing Power* deals with the judgmental plague that afflicts the singer-actor, a plague intensified by the origin in this century of the stage director and the conductor, the two primary judgmental figures in music and theater.

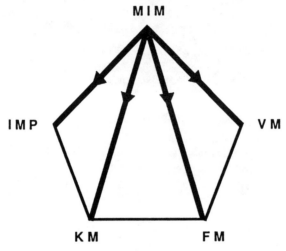

The Judgmental Entanglement

We have also noted the 148,000 no's! that are part of the average person's conditioning in expressing emotional energy. All in all, the singer-actor carries a heavy judgmental burden in doing what her art calls for, i.e., the expression of strong emotional energy with the voice and face.

The judgmental factor is particularly significant in its relation to the concept of entanglement. The premise of the performing power concept is simple: performing power increases as entanglements are transformed into choices. Those new choices expand the field of choice potential from which the performer draws for performance. The power of the performer is proportionate to the number of choices available in that field of choice potential. All other things equal, the performer with the fewest entanglements has the most performing choices and thus the most performing power.

We should emphasize that no one is totally free of entanglement: increase the energy flow sufficiently, and an entanglement will be revealed. A person can counterfeit the entanglement-free condition by reducing the output of energy through the appropriate mode, simultaneously controlling it with the body and concealing the outward evidence of that struggle for control as completely as possible. But this only conceals the entanglement, wastes energy, and diminishes personal power.

There are a great many people (and performers) who do all those things in trying to control both the energy flow *and* the entanglement. A prime example from life is the deeply restrained, nonemoting corporate executive; in performance, the singer singing a high note with an impassive face. Because the entanglement is concealed, however, we may think it is not there; and we grant more power (often confused with control) to the singer who sings a high C with a neutral face than to one whose face reflects the physical effort involved. Neither face is communicating the emotion appropriate to the scene, but of the two we prefer the one that at least makes the high C *look* easier, emotionally connected or not.

We grant power to a seeming lack of entanglement that we withhold from the overtly entangled person. A heavily entangled person who lets his entanglements show may, in fact, be very intelligent, but we tend not to believe it. If we do, we show our lack of regard for revealed entanglements in general by calling those who let them show "nerds."

The nerd is a person whose body, voice, and face reveal their entangled nature freely—or, as a critic would say, a person whose body, voice, and face are out of control. When the nerd is enthusiastic—a suspicious state in itself in our adolescently "cool" society—it shows. Their voices climb in pitch, and may even squeak; their arms and upper bodies bounce along with their voices, and their faces reveal either an innocent openness or an "excessive" emotionality of some kind. The character created by Jerry Lewis—based on what he said was his idea of a nine-year-old—is the archetypical nerd. At the other end of that spectrum is the stone-faced, heavily-controlled, frigid financier who has everything under such control that nothing is allowed to show. He, too, is heavily entangled (as anyone is bound to be who has not actually exercised the release of entanglements), but his particular entanglement complex is carefully monitored and concealed.

The kind of counterfeit control this represents is revealed for what it is by any situation in which strong emotion *is* appropriate. Instead of the emotion, we see the controlling tensions come into play to conceal it, and that concealment, which may have appeared as power and control under other circumstances, becomes weakness, impotence, and even lack of control as it is revealed. The slow burn, the sputtering of blocked energy, the physical rigidity, the sound of the constricted voice, and the obvious inability to allow the emotion to show freely, all reveal energy repressed and entangled; there may be the illusion of control, but as we have seen, the attempts to control our processes actually put us out of control.

When it is not only permissible but appropriate for us to express strong emotion and we do not do so, we are either deeply entangled (and more powerless) or grossly insensitive (another form of powerlessness). Whether we are in a state of extreme entanglement control or not, those repressive, controlling characteristics are to some degree a conditioned part of all of us. The human condition is one of entanglement.

Pour the volatile passions of music theater into that entangled human condition and the entanglements *will* be activated. Our conditioning to suppress crying in public, to avoid creating high energy "scenes," and to monitor and control our display of physical, vocal, and facial energies is in opposition to what we are asked to do on the stage as a matter of course. The process of interfering with those energies begins with MIM and MIM's judgmental conditioning, which is a complex blend of conscious monitoring and unconscious habit.

But while MIM does the monitoring and guidance (whether consciously or not) it cannot attempt to control things without assistance. It must call upon the body to do the actual work of controlling the flow of energy through the communicating channels. Any time MIM senses the energy flow to be in some way endangering, it calls the body into play to modify or block that flow. The sense of danger can involve communication MIM feels is inappropriate: seeming to be too soft, emotional, silly, stupid, weak, or out of control at one end of the spectrum, or seeming to be too strong, pushy, cocky, aggressive, or abrasive at the other, all depending upon the individual's conditioning.

Since the judgmental conditioning responsible for beginning this controlling chain of events is largely unconscious, the person is often unaware that she is doing anything. It all seems totally natural to her—and natural it is, since natural in our terminology means simply that which has been practiced until it is habitual. Since entanglements are by their very nature natural, let us look at the connotations and implications of the word *natural* for the performer.

The concept of being real or natural on stage has hidden traps that are seldom clearly discerned (not unlike Schaef's analysis of honesty when applied to the performer). It helps if we are aware of the following set of principles.

1. The human condition is one of entanglement.

2. Entanglements are unconscious conditionings that interfere with freedom of energy flow in the human system to the detriment of clarity, efficiency, and power in communication.

3. These entanglements not only interfere with the communicating energy flow, they can even damage the voice, putting it out of commission artistically.

4. Every characterization calls for the portrayal of a different set of entanglements.

5. Our personal condition of entanglement is different from that of anyone else — person or dramatic character — in the world of life, theater, or music theater.

6. Our entanglements have been practiced and made habitual so that they are natural to us and remain largely below our threshold of awareness.

7. When we are asked to be "natural" or "real" as performers, we naturally bring on stage with us the entanglements we have practiced all our lives, regardless of their appropriateness, usefulness, or potential harmfulness.

8. Attempting to communicate a strong emotion, or make any kind of energy statement that is opposed by or is simply different from our conditioning will feel "unnatural" to us and will be rejected, especially if we are trying to be "natural" in our performance.

9. As a result we may end up acting both naturally *and* harmfully to our energy system, naturally *and* inappropriately for the character, and naturally *and* non-communicatively as performers.

10. Finally, if we are not aware, on some level, of all of this, we will end up feeling guilty, angry, resentful, judged, and frustrated because our natural selves (with which we identify) are not acceptable for the task at hand, and neither are we if we identify with those natural but rejected selves.

When we understand all this, we also understand the insidiousness of any acting system that asks the performer to be "natural" without having a clear understanding of what that means.

We will clarify this concept further as we proceed. Fundamental to the developmental process of the performing power technique is the understanding that, to paraphrase Polonius, "there is nothing either natural or unnatural, but practice makes it so." What we regard as our natural ways of being and uses of energy are all deeply affected by the habits and conditionings we have practiced diligently, if unconsciously, all our lives. Once we *know* that, we have a new freedom with respect to what we can become. We no longer need to be victims of our history (however benign or even useful some of the conditionings of that history may be); we can begin practicing new patterns *of our own choice*; we can begin transforming our current state in whatever way we choose; we can take charge of the development of our own performing process. All we need is a technique to practice, the ability to actually practice (a greater challenge than it might appear, as we will see), and awareness.

Awareness is a fundamental tool in the growth process and is particularly important in working with the anticipatory entanglement, which is so subtly manifested in many performers that simply bringing it to awareness helps a great deal.

Number 2: The Anticipatory Entanglement

Most singers and actors who take classes are what I call "Good Students." They have been conditioned to do "the right thing" by sixteen or more years of schooling. Schools are by nature judgmentally intensive—grades tell how close (or how far) one is from being OK. This is bad enough for the non-performer who simply passes or fails on a written test; but the performer is both the test and the performance of the test. The performer is on trial, and if he is not passed, it is not just his intelligence or memorizing ability that is at stake: it is his whole being (or so it seems in the conditioning of our academically trained performers). When we stand up in a class to speak or to sing we know (or think we know) we are being judged: we prepare ourselves, we get ready, we get set, and we steel ourselves for the blow. Some version or variation of that seems to be behind the anticipatory entanglement.

As the name suggests, that entanglement anticipates an energy change—in quantity or quality—through one of the projective modes and places the kinesthetic mode in a state of tension to deal with and control the approaching change. But since there is usually nothing for the kinesthetic mode to do—no special physical action of any kind—that state of tension must simply be sustained, burning up useful energy, and creating a block for other, more productive uses of that energy. The singer gets tense before he actually sings, which is not only a waste of power, it also short-circuits to some degree the total performing process. Thus the anticipatory entanglement robs the performer of the full range of his flexibility, his vocal power, his emotional projective capacity, and, perhaps surprisingly, since it is the kinesthetic mode that creates it in the first place, the anticipatory entanglement robs the body itself of the capacity to gesture and move effectively. In addi-

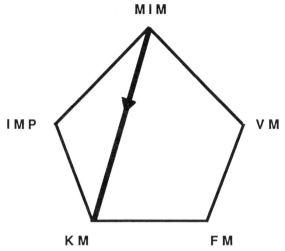

The Anticipatory Entanglement

tion, as we will see, the anticipatory entanglement is linked with entanglement number 3 (the gestures and the whole body), number 4 (the facial expression of emotions and the body), and number 6 (the singing/speaking process and the body).

The highly skilled performer will have developed the capacity to do what he needs to do in spite of the anticipatory entanglement. Even while practicing it, the experienced performer will have modified the overt signals that would tell anyone there is a state of anticipatory tension. The evidence will often be so cleverly disguised that even the performer will be unaware of it. That has been a consistent experience with performers on advanced levels: I have never encountered a performer, no matter how advanced, who did not have some degree of anticipatory entanglement; and the more sophisticated the performer, the more cleverly it will be disguised, from themselves as well as others. But the skilled performer's capacity to perform effectively in spite of his anticipatory entanglements does not change the fact that he is robbing himself of part of his performing capacity and is not fulfilling the rest of his potential. While it can be challenging, even frustrating, to become aware of and drop the anticipatory entanglement, the rewards in increased performing capacity can be great, sometimes startlingly so.

We need to become more aware of *any* alteration we make in our normal (dare I say "natural") state of being for the purposes of performance. It is not that singing-acting uses energy in the same way as we do in everyday life—we have gone on at length to demonstrate the contrary—but that a

useful and supportive state of performance readiness (which can be mis-taken for the anticipatory entanglement) is *also* subverted by the getting-set, tension-holding state of the anticipatory entanglement. Awareness of how we alter our normal state of being in audition or performance is a primary tool in working with the anticipatory entanglement. Exercises that draw upon that awareness will be discussed in later chapters, but, as always, awareness is the first step in transforming entanglements into choices.

The first two entanglements are both preparatory to the actual perfor-mance process; they precede the actual flow of performing energy, and can adversely influence the efficiency, freedom, and power of all performance energies. The judgmental entanglement creates the conditions for most of the other entanglements; and while judgment may not be perceived as a con-scious part of any entanglement, it is always there affecting the process. Per-formers are only too aware that they are being observed and therefore—given their conditioning—judged. The anticipatory entanglement follows directly from that anticipation of judgment, altering the personal environment so that the performer's energies are controlled, blocked, repressed, concealed, or otherwise interfered with. This, in turn, sets up the conditions for the third lively entanglement, the part/whole kinesthetic entanglement.

Number 3: The Part/Whole Kinesthetic Entanglement

The third entanglement, between the part and the whole (the gestures and the body), is also universally common and is most often seen in the alliterative characteristics mentioned above: the lean and the lift. When singer-actors gesture they will typically lean into the gesture without actually taking a step — the lean. And they will often lift their shoulders along with the upper body as they gesture — the lift.

When gestures are functioning naturally in life, neither the lean nor the lift is in evidence unless they are built into the overall gesture itself, as with a shoulder shrug that can say, "I don't know." But even if the lean and the lift were common in everyday life (and, no doubt, there are people who use them habitually just as there are naturally entangled people everywhere), our basic principle holds true: if our natural, conditioned state of being does not support the energy demands of music-theater performance, it is useful to develop new energy patterns that do support that process. We can then practice those new patterns until they become equally natural. By describing our current performing habits, we can devise exercises to change them. We can release blocks in our system and allow a new freedom of energy flow. That

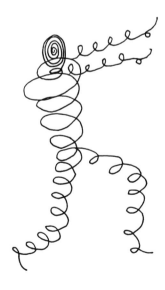

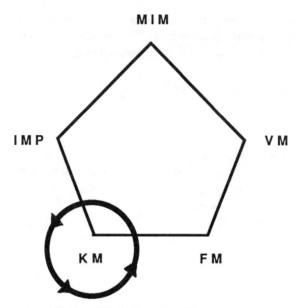

The Part/Whole Kinesthetic Entanglement

new state can become as natural as the old; and when it is, we will be able to fulfill and expand upon the needs of music theater in ways we have not previously experienced.

Let us examine the lean and the lift from that perspective. Since time is extended in music theater, it is important to be able to sustain any gesture for as long as the music and words last. However, the superfluous tension in the lean and the lift makes them uncomfortable and unconvincing. Further, it is truly unnatural: we don't gesture that way in life, simply because it is not effective communication. It is hard work, and it looks odd, as you can see by leaning or lifting into gestures while you are talking with a friend. The confusion lies in mistaking the overall physical tension for the gesture itself. In reality, the gesture is its own, whole statement, and the added tension from the rest of the body diffuses that statement.

This may be one factor inhibiting the free use of gesture by singers. If a performer is aware on a nonintellectual, kinesthetic level that she connects the lean and lift with her gestures, and that the gesture needs to be sustained, she may not initiate gestures in general, knowing intuitively that sustaining them will be very difficult. To lift and hold the shoulders or to lean forward on one leg is fine for a brief moment, but to sustain it for thirty seconds is not only uncomfortable, it will become increasingly artificial as the seconds tick by. In addition, it will interfere with the flow of the performance process. And trying to "sneak" one's way out of a lean or lift calls even more attention to its unusefulness. "With all that inevitable interference," runs the internal monologue, "why even begin the process? Repress the gesture!"

The lean-and-lift entanglement follows directly from the anticipatory entanglement, and is linked to it as an entanglement between entanglements. If the anticipatory entanglement has been engaged so that the performer is in a slight state of get-ready tension, the lean and/or the lift are virtually certain to be triggered into play. The overall tension of the anticipatory entanglement, which can be ever so slight and well disguised, creates a counterfeit interconnectedness of the whole system; thus any energy initiation by one part will bring the total system into play whether or not it is useful or appropriate. The performer is deprived of freedom of choice on two levels: (1) the rest of the body cannot do other things when it is following the lead of one of the parts; and (2) the freedom and flexibility of the initiating part will be limited in turn by the total system's inability to move with the same speed and flexibility. Any gesture can move faster than the whole body entangled with it; and in trying to follow the gesture-part, the body as a whole will force the gesture to slow down.

The anticipatory entanglement is like putting on a subtle body corset: it may feel as though things are more controlled when in fact they are more out of control. This is the illusion of control in a nutshell: we try to control our process through tension, and lose that control in trying to assert it. Not only is the body interfering with its own process by trying to control it; the same tension hampers the body's capacity to assist and support the other two modes.

Entanglement 3 has a sympathetic aspect as well: the whole body coming into vigorous play to enforce, underline, or emphasize the sense of meaning in a gesture. But so long as the performer develops choice in the matter, there is no entanglement; and that same sympathetic involvement can make a useful, even powerful statement once it has been transformed from an entanglement to a free choice. But as long as there is entanglement within the kinesthetic mode as a whole, the potential expressivity of free, sympathetic body work will also be limited.

Number 4: The Facial/Kinesthetic Entanglement

Of all the communicating energies that may feel threatening in our society,

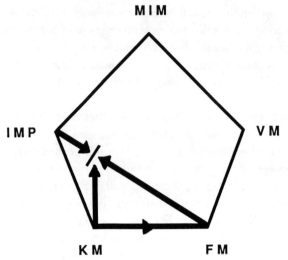

The Facial/Kinesthetic Entanglement

those involving the expression of emotion are primary. I have yet to encounter a performer whose facial-emotional mode is not strongly entangled with the kinesthetic mode. Let us review the way this entanglement works.

First, contrary to body-language theories, the body does not express specific emotions. In discussing the projective-modes concept with a psychologist friend of mine, I made that statement, and he quickly demurred. I responded with a simple and fairly conclusive demonstration: Holding a

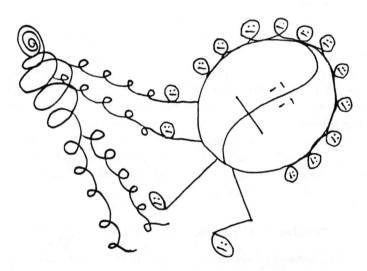

piece of paper in front of my face so that he could not see my expression, I shook my fist violently and asked him what emotion I was expressing. He quickly replied, "You're angry." Lowering the paper, still shaking my fist, I revealed a smiling, joyful expression: the meaning of the shaking fist was transformed by the facial statement into the opposite of its stereotypical potential. "Oh," said my friend, somewhat nonplussed.

If the face can transform the meaning of an obvious physical statement like that, then we can use the facial mode to give any meaning we wish to anything the body can do. (The vocal mode can also assist in this process—a shout of "Hooray!" will also transform the stereotypical meaning of the shaking fist, as will the dramatic situation surrounding the gesture. But our focus here is on the meaning-making relationship of the kinesthetic and facial modes.) Anyone can demonstrate that relationship: simply cover the face, make the kinesthetic statement, have the observers try to guess the emotional statement, do the opposite with the face, and lower the paper. That may sound like a party game—and it has been used as such—but its real function is to allow one to experience and *know* that the body means whatever the face means, and not the reverse.

There is an obvious corollary to the idea that the body is free of emotional meaning until defined by the face or voice. If any physical statement can mean emotionally whatever the face (and voice) is doing, there is no necessary physical statement that *has* to be made as part of any emotion. Therefore, the most useful physical state to accompany any emotion is one that is free, flexible, and responsive to the needs of the singing process, not to an imagined and illusory emotional need. That free, supportive state of being cannot involve rigidity or held tension, yet those are the hallmarks of entanglement number 4. Bodily repression of emotion can become strongly associated with the emotions it is trying to control; but, again, it is not expressing them—it is repressing them. That state of repression makes no specific emotional statement on its own, but acquires its meaning in interaction with other sources. That brings us to our second basic understanding.

The face (along with the voice) is the primary communicating resource for the expression of emotion. It is the most personal, vulnerable, private, endangering, empowering, swift-moving, empathy-creating, communicating resource we have. We learn this very early in life and, depending upon the immediacy and intensity of our conditioning, we learn how to control the facial expression of any emotion that feels threatening to us. There are only two ways for this control to take place, and both involve the body. The first is in the face itself (which is clearly a subsystem of the body, but which can be isolated in its expressive capacity from the body as a whole). The face can learn to be deadpan and not allow strong emotions to show at all. The farmer and wife in Grant Wood's painting *American Gothic* are archetypically deadpan. (In fact, the models are father and daughter, which is a nice example of facial-emotional conditioning being passed from one generation to the next.) I refer to them as illustrations of a level of facial repression that would clearly have to be exercised and released if either one of them wished to become a performer.

Even in such cases, however, the face cannot completely control the flow of strong emotion all by itself. It requires assistance from the rest of the body. Emotional energy felt with sufficient intensity will burst through and be seen in the face unless the body stops it. Even then, the emotion may be facially irrepressible. Since facial expression of emotion is the most personal and psychologically threatening thing our total system can do, the body is automatically called into play whenever we feel strong emotion—it feels like the only "safe" thing to do. When the emotional current begins flowing, the body leaps into any number of tension patterns, all of which are counterproductive to the singing-acting process: we hold our breath, we tighten our stomach muscles, we clench our jaws, we make fists, we lift our shoulders, we tense our necks, we hold our chests rigidly, and, in general, we distort our physical state in service of the illusion of control.

What is worse, we come to believe that all those crippling distortions are not only necessary to the expression of emotion, they *are* the expression of emotion. The idea that they are equivalent to the emotional expression is the intellectual rationalization of the original, nonverbal attempt to control the emotion. We feel threatened by the possibility of revealing something emotionally that would not be in our best interests; the only safe thing we can do is to block it or control it (or so we feel on an unconscious level), and we do just that with our kinesthetic resources.

Thus, there are several stages in the creation of an entanglement and its rationalization: in the beginning, the body comes into play to control the flow of emotional energy; that unconscious control mechanism is activated repeatedly until it becomes a conditioned, robotic response; that response becomes equated with the emotion itself; and when that unconscious, nonverbal process is challenged, MIM begins the process of rationalizing and justifying it.

As we have pointed out, the expression of emotion is one of the most intensely judged aspects of daily life. It is certainly the primary focus of judgment in acting. When we use the word *acting* in America, we are referring primarily to the expression of emotion, regardless of how that may be accomplished. Yet the fact that the face is a primary tool in expressing emotion is seldom referred to or even acknowledged. The next steps—to actually exercise the face to allow it to fulfill its primary function, or to examine its relationship to the other energy resources—do not even exist as possibilities. The layers of resistance and inhibition that block any consideration and development of the facial area as a performing resource are deep. But whatever one's response to the face and the usefulness of exercising it, the entanglement between the face and the body is one that is easily demonstrated and cannot be ignored. The same is true of the fifth lively entanglement, between the jaw and the rest of the face.

Number 5: The Part/Part Facial Entanglement

When we feel a strong emotion, the jaw is the last physical resource we have in controlling its flow before it is expressed by either the voice or the face. For example, when anger or grief are about to be expressed, the jaw may bite down on them, stopping their expression at the last moment. The learning pattern is similar to that described in entanglement 4: initially we control the flow of emotion with jaw tension with no conscious awareness of the

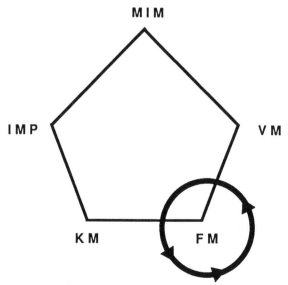

The Part/Part Facial Entanglement

process; then we repeat the pattern until it becomes a habitual response to the emotions that first called it into play; eventually, we come to equate the emotion with the mechanism we created to repress it.

A classic example of this entanglement is the "tight-jawed hero" of novels and films. The actual emotion may be anger, passion, resolute determination, frustration, love, and the like, but the actual expression is confined to the "rippling jaw muscles" seen in film close-ups or described by nineteenth-century novelists. In these cases, the visual effect of the entanglement is the point; but if the hero is about to sing (and it is always the heroes who have this entanglement—heroines are permitted to express their emotions), he—or the performer portraying him—would do well to release the entanglement to allow the singing process the freedom it needs.

The reversal of this entanglement also comes into autonomous play. Since the face is the fundamental means of expressing emotion, any action in the facial musculature sends emotional messages of some kind, whether there is an inner emotional process (IMP) behind them or not. Since those messages are sent to ourselves as well as to those watching us, any movement of the facial musculature will tend to activate the same entanglements that are brought into play by the actual feeling and potential expression of emotion. When the facial musculature is exercised, for example, entanglements 4 and 5 will often be called into play whether IMP is involved or not. As the face exercises its musculature, the jaw will become tense just in case there may be an actual expression of emotion.

In attempting to exercise the facial musculature, the jaw may also come into play in a sympathetic way, for example to support and accompany the movement of the eyebrows. It is useful, initially, to allow the jaw to do that if, in turn, it allows the rest of the face to be exercised more freely. (See the four-step spiral exercise process in chapter 8.) Eventually, of course, it will be important to transform even the sympathetic nature of the entanglement into a choice.

Because exercise of the whole face is so important, the significance of this entanglement was not evident at first. But as I observed the amount of jaw play involved in facial exercise for most performers, it became clear that freedom of the jaw from the whole facial expressive capacity was vital. Jaw movement and tension are not useful in performance; and both are seriously counterproductive to the singing process. No voice teacher in my experience has ever advocated a tight jaw or a chewing motion while singing. (Although, as several of my voice teacher colleagues have pointed out, a tight jaw seems to be the inadvertent result of some vocal techniques.)

At the same time the whole face must be free to express whatever is emotionally appropriate to the song or scene in question. If the jaw must be held in tension or moved as a response to movement in the rest of the face, it will interfere with the vocal process; if keeping the jaw free of tension for the health and well-being of the vocal process means that the rest of the face must be immobilized or passive, that will interfere with emotional expression. Once that negative spectrum of energy use was clarified—sympathetic entanglement at one end, deadpan isolation at the other—entanglement 5 fell into place. Further clarification will be presented in chapter 9, along with exercises to release the entanglement.

The focus process can also be entangled with the rest of the face, particularly in practicing basic facial expansion exercises. For example, as the facial musculature is exercised, the eyes may move about at random in sympathetic response. While this is a less harmful entanglement than with the jaw, exercising its transformation into a choice can be useful for those with a wandering or uncertain focus process.

Number 6: The Vocal/Facial Entanglement

Any necessary alteration of facial expression in response to the act of singing (beyond opening the mouth to do so) is a demonstration of entanglement 6. Some degree of this entanglement is virtually universal among singers. The face and the voice are in such close physical proximity that any alteration of energy through one will naturally demand a response from the other. Thus it

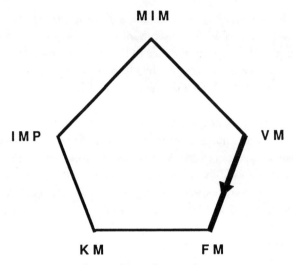

The Vocal/Facial Entanglement

is a rare performer, however skilled, who does not demonstrate this entanglement in some way, for example in raising the eyebrows when singing a high note. The beginning singer's face is often a veritable road map of the vocal route he is taking. This is so obviously a mark of the amateur performer that the voice teacher will quickly train it into submission: after all, who wants singers leaving one's studio looking like amateurs? Thus, it seems, singers in general learn to immobilize the face while they are singing, which eliminates all signs of entanglement 6.

There *is* a sign, of course: holding the face in a neutral mask is as much

a manifestation of entanglement 6 as the hyperactive face. The two form another negative energy spectrum, with facial neutrality at one end and facial hyperactivity at the other. The voice teacher's response to the hyperactive end of that entanglement spectrum is the source of the neutral face accompanying so much "serious" classical singing. Since that kind of face suggests seriousness of purpose and anxiety about the whole process, yet remains essentially and resolutely deadpan, I devised an acronym to describe it: SAD—serious, anxious, deadpan.

This deadpan training (which is not thought of as such by the teacher) may be a necessary first step in learning to isolate the face from the voice while singing; however, the next step of the process—allowing the face to come back into play for the purpose of emotional expression—is rarely taken. If it is, it is an intuitive accident, for there has been no accepted way of exercising and developing the facial capacity in partnership with the voice. As we will see, that capacity can be exercised on a daily basis. Doing so simply means reengaging the facial mode while singing, using both inner and outer exercises.

The reverse of this entanglement—in which the voice responds to a change of energy in the face—may occur as one does facial exercises. The performer may alter the singing process to relate sympathetically to the new facial energies. But this can only be done with the body, by "squeezing" the throat or altering the sound of the voice in other ways. By adding the body, the voice-face entanglement becomes a three-way relationship.

The facial mode and the vocal mode together make up the singing-acting power zone. Because of their closeness to each other, those two modes are strongly entangled in everyone; but that same proximity allows them to work together synergistically with amazing power. Developing the teamwork between the face and voice by first isolating them—exercising their capacity to work alone and releasing their kinesthetically aided interference with each other—and then integrating them—coordinating and synergizing their combined efforts—is vital for every singer-actor.

Number 7: The Vocal/Kinesthetic Entanglement

The seventh entanglement, between the vocal and kinesthetic modes, is one of the trickiest to untangle. Since the full body is necessarily involved with the singing process, the challenge lies in isolating what *needs* to be done from what does *not* need to be done. Can we allow the body to support the vocal and breathing processes on one hand and, on the other, release the

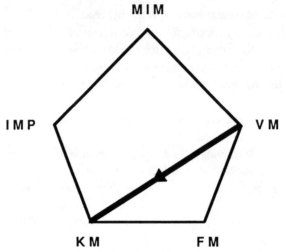

The Vocal/Kinesthetic Entanglement

unnecessary tensions that have become entangled with those processes? Can we first isolate them, and acquire choice as to which of each muscular group should be brought into play? That in itself is a daunting task even without the next step of recoordinating their mutual functions. It might be impossible were it not for the tools of understanding, awareness, and exercise. There are few if any rules about the way this area of entanglement works, how it is activated, and how it is to be exercised and released. What is useful in working with one person's conditionings may be counterproductive for someone else; every person's energy system is unique and must be uniquely approached.

With the trained singing process, conditioning is piled upon conditioning: the voice teacher gives the singer a particular set of techniques with which to approach the process of singing. If the singer is at all diligent, she will turn these techniques into useful conditionings, which will then interact with all the preexisting parental, societal, and educational conditionings (both useful and unuseful) she brings with her to the lessons. The performing power technique provides the tools—a view of the whole process and its interacting parts—to cut through this seemingly impenetrable tangle of mostly unconscious patterns. In using those tools, there is no substitute for a perceptive and capable voice teacher whose awareness moves beyond the hearing mode to a full-spectrum perception of the performing process. In this way both teacher and performer can work with the total energy system of the singer-actor in an integrative, synergistic way.

The seventh entanglement has two parts that we will refer to as the *sway* and the *squeeze*. The sway is a sympathetic entanglement in which the body responds visibly to the pattern of vocal energies. The squeeze is an interfering entanglement in which the body attempts to block, control, and manipulate the flow of energy through the voice by means of glottal constriction, thus creating a sense of emotional intensity. We will discuss the sway first.

It might seem easy to perceive any overt physical tension or unnecessary movement during the singing process. But this entanglement can be easily confused with the facial/kinesthetic entanglement. Lifted shoulders, for example, may be the result of either emotional tension control or a reaction to the singing process. Many manifestations of this entanglement are sympathetic, including conducting hands (which beat time to the music), a swaying body, a tapping foot, a rhythmic head, and the like. Because they are sympathetic (rather than controlling), they have little direct effect on the facial mode.

But there is always some relationship between all three modes in any entanglement. When energy is increased in one mode it will affect one of the other two in some way; that entanglement relationship in turn, whether sympathetic or controlling, will affect the remaining mode: the total energy system is interconnected and what happens between two of them will always affect the third in some way. The vocal energy will increase and as it does so the body will respond to it either sympathetically or in an attempt to control it; the physical tension or movement thus induced will either interfere with the facial *and* the vocal processes, or at least rob energy from a more appropriate use, thus completing the three-way entanglement.

In addition to the overt kinesthetic signals of the sway, entanglement 7 is manifested in another, less visible way. This is the squeeze, which occurs most commonly with the speaking voice. If an actor changes the quantity and/or the quality of vocal energy, the body may come into play to control or modify that change as it passes through the throat. Greater than ordinary vocal energy is commonly associated with increased emotional expressivity of some kind. We are conditioned to control that kind of emotional energy flow in the voice, just as we are with the face: the body comes into play to control the flow whether there is any specific emotional motivation behind it or not. The only way it can do so is to close the glottis partially, slightly blocking the passage of sound, thus creating a harsher, more intense quality. This also necessitates applying more diaphragmatic pressure from below in order to keep the sound coming: closing the glottis without increased abdominal breath pressure will simply stop the sound; increased abdominal pressure without closing the glottis will simply blow the air through the larynx, creating a much breathier, very brief sound. For any sustained speaking, the pressure from below and the glottal interference from above depend upon each other. The increased tension in the sound presumably demonstrates emotional "intensity," "motivation," or "involvement."

In fact, it is another example of a performer's conditioned need to justify emotion through a feeling of internal pressure. We learn, at an early age, to control-repress the expression of strong emotion through both voice and face. When we feel anger or grief (emotions most often repressed) or any other high level of emotional excitement, we learn to control its flow through the voice: we constrict the glottis to some extent, we experiment with vocal repression until we find a level that feels safe (all unconsciously, of course), and then we practice the pattern, still unconsciously, until it is a deeply ingrained habit. As soon as a specific emotion arises, the conditioned pattern of repression-control comes into play and we come to mistake it for the expression. The harsh quality of glottally blocked sound comes to stand for the expression of anger rather than being heard for what it is: the *repression* of that anger.

We go on stage and play a scene in which anger is required. We will "naturally" bring into play the control-repression mechanism that has come to *be* the anger for us whether we are genuinely feeling the anger or not. The body will tense to do the illusory job of controlling, and instead of energy flowing freely through the appropriate mode—the face sending clear emotional messages, the voice expressing the anger through increased musicality of language (by greater volume, pitch variation, intensity, speed, or alteration of rhythms)—the energy will be wasted within the body. The face will remain set and unexpressive (unless the audience guesses that since the words suggest anger, that must be "a face set with anger"); the voice will sound tense and inflexible (with the same stereotypical guessing game going on for the audience). All this will feel natural to us, for we have practiced it most of our lives; yet it will be inefficient, noncommunicative, and damaging to the vocal process. Even though an audience may be able to figure out what is actually intended, it will not be receiving the full power of our performing potential. Once we become aware of the entanglement we can exercise and release it, removing the blocks to our real power, and allowing us to open to our true potential.

I have referred previously to the "squeeze" half of entanglement seven—the blocking of the vocal process by the kinesthetic mode—as vocal indicating, the auditory equivalent of facial mugging. Vocal indicating is more common with actors than with singers and it is easier to detect in the speaking voice. Nonetheless, it is a significant factor in the disappearing diva syndrome (along with the facial/kinesthetic entanglement). Any time a voice teacher works with the concept of emotion, vocal indicating is likely to come into play. The vocal repression-control that has come to *be* the expression of the emotion in life will naturally be triggered by the request for that emotion in the singing process. To begin releasing this entanglement there must be a clear understanding that the expression of emotion is not simply a natural given for everyone—we are all uniquely conditioned in that respect and it affects us all in different ways. However, virtually all of those ways of expressing emotion are counterproductive to the free flow of energy needed for singing. These patterns of interference can and must be altered if the singer's true capacity is to be realized. If not, the existing tension patterns surrounding emotional expression will be reinforced and become permanent, often painful, sometimes dangerous, and always limiting factors in the singer's development.

The next step is to begin exercising and transforming our entanglements. This process has three stages. In the first stage we are unconscious of the conditioning of our entanglements; they are our masters and we act predictably in relation to them. When we become aware of those entanglements we move to stage 2: we become conscious of our unconscious uses or misuses of energy. Becoming conscious of them, however, does not mean that we have also acquired choice with respect to their functioning: they are still out of our control. To move to stage 3 — to become capable of conscious freedom of choice in the uses of our performance energies — we need awareness *and* specific exercises that transform the existing entanglements into alternative choices rather than necessities. At that point, they cease to be entanglements and become part of our field of choice potential.

To create a supportive and nurturing space in which those stages of awareness and exercises can take place and expand our field of choice potential, let us consider some energy qualities to aid the process. These will be qualities to guide us in approaching the seven lively entanglements, and help us in balancing our addictive social and educational conditioning. We will call those qualities "the seven guiding principles for radiant performing."

Chapter 6

Seven Guiding Principles for Radiant Performing

Expanding the Bill of Opposites

In *The Complete Singer-Actor* there is a section called "The Bill of Opposites," dealing with the synthesis of contraries, which is fundamental to the music-theater aesthetic. I have expanded that basic concept, and I would like to return to it from a higher point on the spiral.

The image I used at that time was of a tightrope walker who holds a balancing pole at the center (the opposites at either end), shifting it slightly to maintain balance on the music-theater wire. As I put it, "If the pole is held too near either end, the performer either will be pulled off the tightrope entirely or will panic, drop the pole, and cling to the wire. But if it is balanced properly, there is freedom and security" (p. 37).

F. Scott Fitzgerald once said that the sign of real intelligence was the capacity to hold two opposing thoughts in the mind at the same time. Applying the same concept to performing intelligence would mean the capacity to know that contrary choices exist at every point in performance; and, further, that all these choices need not be "held," but may be accepted as part of a field of choice potential. In Maslow's study of self-actualizing people, he speaks of the capacity of these "artists of living" to fuse either/or dichotomies "not like incompatibles, but rather in a sensible, dynamic unity or synthesis" (p. 162).

Thus the tensions associated with tightrope walking or holding opposing forces together become instead an *acceptance* of all the possibilities in the field with a developed capacity to choose freely and flexibly among them. Rather than finding a balanced place between two opposite choices (which

133

implies that neither of them is acceptable), one can develop a state of readiness to serve any given choice fully, with the awareness and capability of fulfilling any of the other choices as well.

Let us further expand that view with the idea of full-spectrum experiencing. Here, all possibilities between the opposite ends of a spectrum are available to the performer in a broad field rather than on a line. There is no longer the danger of falling off the wire (down, yes, off, no). The balancing pole becomes a weightless magic wand that can be held at any point on its length, and used for a great deal besides balancing. We still exercise with the opposites in question, integrating and playing with them in various ways; but instead of the precarious image of the tightwire (which may remain so for the spectator) we create a safer space for free play with our performing energies. There is greater freedom to make any choice at any time. The choices are parts; the total field of choice potential is the whole.

As Maslow has put it:

> This is precisely what the great artist does. He is able to put together clashing colors, forms that fight each other, dissonances of all kinds, into a unity. And this is also what the great theorist does when he puts puzzling and inconsistent facts together so that we can see that they really belong together. And so also for the great statesman, the great therapist, the great philosopher, the great parent, the great lover, the great inventor. They are all integrators, able to put separate and even opposites together into unity. (p. 162)

Two Kinds of Problems

In *A Guide for the Perplexed*, E. F. Schumacher discusses a confusion in problem-solving, in which all problems are thought of in the same way, that is, as problems to be solved. As he points out, however, not all problems have solutions. This leads to the concept of two kinds of problems: *convergent* problems and *divergent* problems. Convergent problems are the kind that *can* be solved and the various attempts at solution tend to converge into one best answer. An example of this kind of problem would be to make a two-wheeled, man-powered means of transportation. Many possible answers are tested and those solutions gradually *converge* until a solution is found—the bicycle—which proves, with modifications, to be remarkably stable.

However, there is another kind of problem that will yield contradictory answers, no matter how capable the people studying it. The solutions do not converge. On the contrary, as Schumacher says, "The more they are clarified and logically developed, they more they *diverge*, until some of them appear to be the exact *opposites* of the others" (p. 122). For example, in working with the problem of how to educate our children, groups of equally intelligent and dedicated people have come up with two opposing solutions. One group has come to the conclusion that since education involves passing experience and knowledge from one group (the teachers) to another group (the taught), it is vital for this process to be effective that there be *authority* for the teacher and *discipline* and *obedience* from the students.

Another group of equally dedicated educators decides that the best education of the young demands a different concept. "The educator is like a good gardener, whose function is to make available healthy, fertile soil in which a young plant can grow strong roots; through these it will extract the nutrients it requires. The young plant will develop in accordance with its own laws of being, which are far more subtle than any human can fathom, and will develop best when it has the greatest possible freedom to choose exactly the nutrients it needs" (Schumacher, p. 122). Education as seen by this group of advisers, then, calls for the establishment of freedom—the greatest possible freedom—for the child to grow, and not discipline and obedience.

Both groups are correct from their partial point of view. But carry discipline, a "good thing," and a "solution," to its logical, convergent extreme, and schools would become prisons. Similarly with freedom: although it is an equally good thing, taken to its extreme, it could turn schools into chaotic asylums. Thus, with discipline and freedom, we have a perfect pair of opposites, or parts of the whole. Both are partial answers to the same diverging problem: how to educate best? "Logic does not help us because it insists that if a thing is true, its opposite cannot be true at the same time. It also insists that if a thing is good, more of it will be better" (p. 123). It is a divergent problem, or a problem of the whole, which does not yield to linear, partial logic. A divergent problem demonstrates that life seen from the whole is bigger than the partial verbal logic we attempt to impose upon it— and so is performance, or any other human process.

At this point, rather than making a problem of everything, let us use the word *interaction* as our beginning point. As we interact with reality, some interactions will be revealed as actual problems that have solutions, and others will be seen as processes requiring continuing interactions with no final solution possible or desirable. Thus, some interactions will converge to an answer, while others will always diverge as processes with no final answer.

Another way of viewing interactions is to ask whether they relate to the parts or to the whole. Interactions with *parts* of the whole may be convergent, and have solutions; interactions with the *whole* will always be divergent, and will have no single answer. The difference between them is an important one, for any confusion about the kind of interaction one is working with will frustrate either the continuing process or the attainment of a solution, as the case may be.

In a convergent interaction, then, the experiences with it become inceasingly similar — they converge — until there is universal agreement about the most useful response to the interaction. That is the solution or product; and it reveals the interaction to be, in fact, a problem — for problems can be solved. Once they are, they need never be solved again by anyone who knows the solution. A solved problem is a dead problem; it has no more interest.

A divergent interaction, however, can never be turned into a problem; it is always alive; try as we will, we cannot kill it by solving it — for it comes from the whole, and thus embraces many parts of the whole simultaneously. Divergent interactions — or processes — may involve life, performance, consciousness or self-awareness. They also involve spectra formed between polarities such as growth and decay, freedom and order, and life and death. There will always be diverging responses along these spectra, none of which are correct or incorrect, right or wrong. If, in our confusion, we try to solve them, we only kill the solution, not the process. (Although in our attempt to perceive a process as a problem to be solved, we will very likely end up interfering with the process itself.) Divergent interactions (processes) cannot be solved; they can only be transcended.

All the interactions we will examine in this book are of the divergent kind; that is, they are processes that interact with the whole and for which there is no best answer, solution, or product. There is no one perfect interpretation of a role, correct emotion to play, technique for singing, gesture to make, or way to think as we perform. There is a vast range of choices, of possible responses, some of which we may prefer over others, but none of which are final, "correct" product-solutions.

Since such divergent interactions — processes — have no answers or solutions, what is the most useful response to them? We can only respond, of course, by making actual choices — mentally, vocally, physically, facially, or emotionally. But our conditioning will then begin to pose one choice *against* another. The seemingly inevitable opposition can be confusing. Is there a way of viewing the total process that can allow the many choices to become more than their sum, rather than contradictory, mutually canceling energies?

Schumacher suggests that the most useful response to a divergent interaction is to call a higher order of energy into play. On the level of the problem itself, there is not a "most useful" response; on that level, oppositional
duality comes into play, and it will always be either/or, freedom versus discipline, all or nothing, one or the other, etc. Yet some teachers manage this
union of polarities with a minimum of intellectual effort. Their classrooms
embody both freedom and discipline. "If we explained to them our philo-
sophical difficulties, they might show signs of irritation with this intellectual
approach. 'Look here,' they might say, 'all this is far too clever for me. The
point is: you must *love* the little horrors' " (p. 123). Love, in this (and all)
cases, is a higher principle of energy that allows us to transcend, integrate,
and draw fully upon the potential synergy of the lower level parts. Opening
to a higher principle of energy allows us to see things from the whole and
draw upon the power of the whole.

Rising Above It: Transcending Duality

When things seemed impossibly difficult, Sir Tyrone Guthrie was fond of
saying to his actors or colleagues "Rise above it!" This offers another way of
thinking of the higher energy principle: we can literally rise above the spectrum itself. From that vantage point one can see it for what it is: a spectrum
of the whole, a full-field spectrum of choices, with one duality gradually fad-
ing into and becoming its opposite as we move on the spectrum between
them. However, when we are on the level of the spectrum itself we do not
see the trees of choice for the forest of duality. We cling to one dualistic position or another, not perceiving that there are many other possible and
nonthreatening choices; those other possibilities are blocked by the one we
are clinging to. If we rise above that single choice, we see it and our situation
with greater clarity: we are part of a field of choice potential that can expand, and with which we will also expand as we play with its many possibilities.

The diverging interactions of the three-dimensional world of life and
performance will tend to be defined using verbal order and logic, which
means thinking in dualities: freedom and discipline, emotion and logic, art
and life, external and internal, reason and feeling, commitment and indiffer-
ence, repose and energy, natural and stylized, carefulness and recklessness,
and myself and my character. The energy principle that synthesizes such opposites on a higher level, however, often lacks verbal definition. Even if it
does have a word to describe it, such as *love*, that word will be subject to

potential dualistic devaluation by the reductionist nature of language and logic. If there were words to describe how to integrate the diverging ends of a full spectrum of energy choices we would have long since found and used them. A few words like *love, intuition*, and *higher consciousness*, which pertain to higher energy principles, can be drawn upon. (Chapter 14 includes a more extensive discussion of higher energy principles translated into words.)

Beyond the words, we can relate to the idea of higher energies in and of themselves. For example, the Radiant Whole is one way of referring to such a higher, unnamed energy principle. The Radiance Technique is a way of allowing higher energies to support the performance and exercise process more wholly as it aids in the integrating and synthesizing of three-dimensional interactions.

As we discuss the seven guiding principles for radiant performance, each of those principles will point in turn to a higher principle. Because they are words, they cannot *be* the higher energy. We can, however, allow HOBS, our higher observer, to sense intuitively the whole energy behind those words and guide us in that direction. As we discuss each higher principle, we will create a full spectrum of energy choices below it, with the idea of developing freedom of choice over that full spectrum. Each full spectrum defines a field of choice potential—for example, freedom and discipline— and the issue is the capacity of the performer to make any choice on that full spectrum: to blend freedom and discipline in all possible combinations.

The seven guiding principles all begin with the letter *P*. In order, they are purpose, process, practice, play, persistence, patience (in the present), and potential. Each of them arises from a field defined by the following opposites.

Purpose
AIMLESSNESS — — — — — — — — PRODUCT FIXATION
Process
STATUS-QUOISM — — — — — — — — PERFECTIONISM
Practice
PROCRASTINATION— — — — — — — WORKAHOLICISM
Play
IRRESPONSIBILITY — — — — — — HYPERSERIOUSNESS
Persistence
DETACHMENT — — — — — — — — DETERMINATION
Present Patience
PASSIVITY — — — — — — — — — — —PANIC

Potential

PARTIALITY   — — — — — — — — —GRANDIOSITY

The First Guiding Principle: Purpose

Aimlessness and product fixation form a spectrum of energy use made fully available through the higher principle of *purpose*. At one end of that spectrum there is no goal of any kind, no sense of direction, aimlessness; at the other there is an overly intense focus on partial goals that can deviate from the path toward wholeness. Purpose can vitalize and direct all choices along that spectrum.

In navigation there is a phenomenon called the error-correction-error. It works like this: A ship headed in the direction of its destination (its purpose) may go off-course. This error could be the result of lack of guidance or an error in navigation.

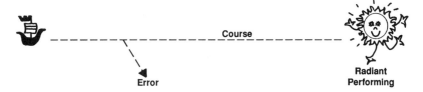

At this point the error is only an error, not a mistake. It can be turned into a mistake in two ways: by continuing on the off-course path, or by the error-correction-error. If that off-course error (or intention) is corrected by trying to return to the original course (rather than realigning to the original destination-purpose) the original error may be magnified.

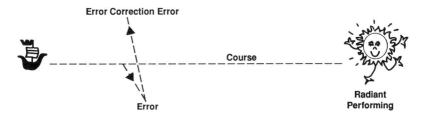

If that error is in turn corrected with the same erroneous logic, the off-course pattern could become a wild series of overreactions, departing further and further from the original destination-purpose. The error has become a mistake.

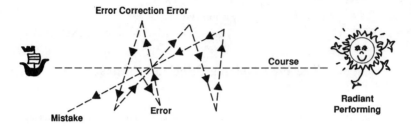

The most useful course of action is always to realign with the original destination-purpose as soon as an error is detected. And this can happen as often as necessary.

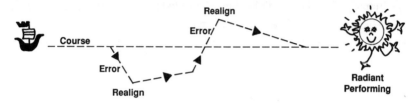

There are numerous examples of this kind of error-correction-error in everyday life. Our purpose may be to become healthier by eating more appropriately. A goal on that path, a diet, can become an off-course fixation in itself (error), leading us to less well-being (mistake); or, we can drop off the diet by eating foods that are not whole (error) and then make up for that binge of bad eating by restricting our diet even more stringently (correction), which drives us to another off-the-wagon binge, driving us in turn back to overrestriction, and so on (mistake.)

Moving closer to the subject of the performer, our purpose may be to practice and develop our performing process fully (a theme we will explore in detail). As we practice, however, we constantly berate ourselves (error), which stops us from enjoying the practice process and from developing as we could; and so, to avoid the unpleasantness (correction), we don't practice (mistake.) Or we decide that the practice must "pay off" with a specific product-goal—say, a good review, or the ability to hit a certain high note. We focus on that product-goal (error) rather than our larger purpose of developing an ever more powerful and integrated total performance process over an indefinite period. When we do not get the good review, or fail to attain the high note on our predetermined schedule, our correction of that error is to quit practicing, or to be harder on ourselves when we do practice, or to get someone else to force us to practice, all of which can become mistakes leading us further and further away from our original purpose.

Let us follow the voyage metaphor a bit further. No voyage is linear, as our illustrations have suggested thus far. The winds of cultural conditioning and the waves of our inherent tendencies push and pull at our vessel so that we must make adjustments, moving now in one direction, now in another, in order to maintain alignment with our destination, our purpose. If we simply aim at the destination with no adjustment for the winds and waves, that will produce an error as surely as will sailing off-course in perfectly calm weather (and the winds and waves on *our* voyage are rarely, if ever, totally calm).

However, if we are not aware of these factors, the necessary adjustments will seem like contradictions: first, we're sailing in one direction, the next minute we reverse course, later we change direction again, reversal follows reversal, and so on. And all this adjusting is vital *if we are to stay aligned to our purpose*. Unaware of this, however, we may obey either the winds of conditioning or the waves of inherent tendency and sail off-course. If we learn to use the energies of the wind and waves, adjusting as necessary to keep in alignment with our destination, our path will resemble a curved zigzag

or, in three-dimensional terms, a spiral.

Thus we have the spiral path to radiant performing, which takes account of where we are (including the traveling conditions and the traveler's conditionings) as well as where we want to go. In Robert Fritz's phrase (and book title) it is *the path of least resistance*.

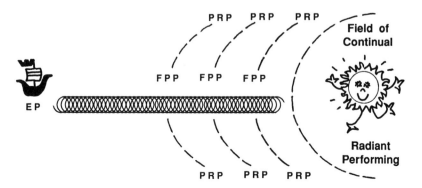

Or, since our path in performance is never acted upon so symetrically, a spiral, which is more in accord with actuality.

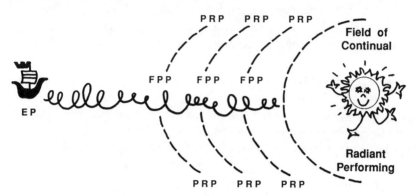

The spiral path gives us both flexibility and power on the journey. It is necessary, however, to be aware and alert, and to acknowledge, accept, respond, and realign whenever the winds and waves affect us (which is most of the time) as we interact with the field. Our response at each moment may seem in opposition to the previous moment: changing voice teachers when necessary, concentrating on the body rather than the voice, the face rather than the emotions, the character rather than ourselves, ourselves rather than the character, and so on. But we can receive and spiral with every bit of wind (our teachers) and wave (ourselves) energy as we move in the direction of our purpose. Part of the skill to be acquired on the journey involves the positive incorporation of all the energies we interact with, including our own— especially those we perceive to be negative.

It is also important to stay clear about the difference between goals— which may require a spiral move that seems different from our purpose— and our fundamental and primary purposes. The higher energy principle of purpose is to remind us that the human being is neither a product nor a goal, and that the various goals and products that may energize our immediate efforts may be useful in themselves so long as they are not mistaken for our purpose. Purpose is a continuing sense of direction rather than a specific goal along the path of that direction; it guides us from a perspective larger than any immediate product-goal can provide.

For the performer, purposes and goals can be easily confused. We have seen some of the goals that can be involved in a performance: getting a good review, pleasing the director, enjoying oneself, making money, keeping busy, making new friends, and so on. If any of those goals are mistaken for our purpose they can seriously interfere with our overall process. A bad review, for example, can draw so much of our energy that we lose sight of our purpose; we may even alter our performance inappropriately in an attempt to answer or satisfy the reviewer, thus contradicting our purpose in the error-correction-error pattern discussed above.

It is another example of mistaking the part for the whole: goals are parts, purpose comes from the whole. In the case of the bad review, it is a double part-equals-whole fallacy: first we mistake the opinion of one part of the audience—the reviewer—for the whole; then we mistake our goal—a good review—for our purpose. We may succeed or fail with any given goal, but there are no failures when working from purpose: only opportunities for awareness, continuing interactions with the whole, and growth.

Some of the goals in working with the performing power technique can also be mistaken for purpose; for example, to become better performers in order to get good reviews, or to get better jobs, or to have something to do to use one's energy between jobs, or to give better performances, and so on. The interesting thing about goals is that once they are accomplished, they are always followed by a "Now what?" Purpose, on the other hand, is never concluded—there is always more. Purpose continues regardless of the fulfillment (or lack of fulfillment) of immediate goals.

Purpose is individual and personal. My own purpose, for example, is not about making money, nor having a job, nor keeping busy, nor getting good reviews. It is simply to understand more clearly and in greater depth how the human energy system functions, to explore the capacities of that system for the fullest, most whole kind of music-theater performance—for radiant performing—and in doing that, to better understand and know myself. In that context, every student (no matter how talented), every rehearsal (no matter how good the piece or how gifted the performer), every performance (no matter what its critical success), is an opportunity for fulfilling my purpose. Which leads us directly to the purpose of this book.

As we have described the fundamental purpose of *The Radiant Performer*, it is to open to and sustain radiant performing with increasing consistency. That fundamental purpose is supported by a primary purpose: to allow the performer to fulfill her performing potential and thus create the conditions under which radiant performing can occur. A secondary purpose—to create an exercise process for the total instrument that will allow the realization of performing potential—emerges from application of the performing power technique and supports the other purposes.

But that trio of synergistic purposes will fulfill many other goals along the way, and any performer may choose to focus on one or more of those goals as a supplementary purpose. Whatever the case, the performer must choose her purpose for herself; if that purpose involves the purposes of this book, that must be a consciously affirmed choice. I cannot and would not choose to impose these purposes on anyone: purpose is only meaningful when it comes from oneself.

Fortunately, the purposes of this book will serve a wide range of practical performing goals. Using the performing power technique, which is the means to realizing those purposes, will give performers a tool for the continual expansion and development of their performing power for as long as they wish. It is not to make them better performers as such—although that is an inevitable by-product and goal; nor is it to give them correct interpretations—although a whole range of new interpretations will become available to them; nor to teach them the correct style of performance—although new stylistic capacities will become possible; nor is it to answer specific questions—although more questions will be answered than they might have thought of asking, and many more will be raised that only they can answer.

All these things will happen in various ways as performers work with the performing power technique: their performing power will increase, they will become more flexible, more capable of making choices of *any* kind relative to interpretation or style, and their performing process will open up in ways they may not have suspected. But a larger, whole purpose makes it more likely that those partial goals will in fact be realized—along with others we hadn't considered. However, if we mistake a part goal for our whole purpose, we will also interfere with the attainment of the goal itself, as well as limit our awareness of alternative possibilities.

If our purpose includes the possibility of opening to radiant performing—with all that that implies—it will include an ongoing expansion of all our performing processes as well. And it will prepare us for the uniqueness of radiant performing when it occurs. In its transcendence of the accustomed performance experience, radiant performing can be threatening—unless it is our purpose. We have seen a possible example of this in Olivier's response to his radiant performance of Othello. If radiant performing in all its wholeness is our conscious purpose, MIM may be better able to open to it and allow it when it occurs, and rejoice in it in retrospect—even if it is beyond MIM's understanding.

At the same time, part goals are useful energizers in moving toward our larger purpose. My own *whole* purpose of preparing, with the performing power technique, the conditions for radiant performing, is energized by a series of part goals as follows. I move in the direction of that larger purpose by describing the nature of the human energy system and the demands singing-acting places on that system, and creating exercises to allow the former to serve the latter more fully. In doing this I allow myself as a performer: to communicate more clearly, completely, and consciously; to create a greater range of possible characterizations; to feel better about performing and communicating; to have more fun in performing and communicating; and to heighten my sense of personal power in performing and communicating. All this will be accomplished in proportion to my acceptance of myself as a *process*, the second guiding principle.

The Second Guiding Principle: Process

The dualities of status-quoism and perfectionism form another spectrum that the higher principle of *process* can energize more fully. At one end of that spectrum is the urge to hold on to the status quo, to resist change, to maintain, to repeat what one already has and what one can already do; at the other end is the urge to discard what we *can* do in favor of some standard of perfection, compared with which anything we have done or will do will suffer.

Process is energy in motion, energy that draws and builds upon what is known, and guides its movement in the direction of a higher purpose. That purpose is not a perfected goal, but is always unfolding as a process. There are positive aspects in both ends of the spectrum: the status quo impulse can be seen as an acceptance of where we are and as a basis for stabilization in the known; the impulse toward perfection can be seen as an urge to expand and develop; both of these aspects are vital, and both are encompassed in the higher principle of process.

For many, the concept of process is an experiential unknown. Barbara Ray speaks of process as follows.

> Process refers to an interrelated series of steps, of interactions; a
> series of natural steps, stages and movements. A "process"
> orientation is one directed towards actually experiencing Life in
> its dynamic spiralling movement and interaction on all planes of
> energy simultaneously, unlimited, non-linearly and without
> boundaries, including all of its cycles. A misconception exists that

> process is only happening when you are noticing it and only
> within the planes of energy which you are aware of. As you
> become a deeper observer of your outer physical, emotional and
> mental planes of energy, you begin to have an awareness of the
> patterns within the process—and that process is *ALWAYS* going
> on beyond the level of awareness on all planes. (*ERM*, p. 86)

Like purpose, process is also to be differentiated from products or problems. A human being is a process (not a product nor a problem); so is life, so is performance. A process is always changing, always unfolding; it is never the same, not a fixed product. A critic's review may create the illusion that a performance or a person is a product, but that kind of imposed product evaluation is simply a measure of someone's response to how a process has been fulfilled at a certain point in time. Every moment of life is always for the first and only time, both for the human being and the performer. The wholeness of our capacity to accept that fact about our process, to draw upon its power and let go of it even while performing a script or score that we have carefully memorized and are supposedly repeating night after night will expand our performing power proportionately.

Our freedom to make other choices is always there, whether we are fully aware of it or not. The more tangible our awareness of that freedom (which is developed by exercising and expanding our field of choice potential), the more powerful will be the choices we actually make from moment to moment. Those actual choices, which may seem remarkably similar night after night, will gain power and spontaneity as our field of choice potential expands.

If we are truly free to make choices other than the one we actually make—a freedom we attain by practicing those other choices—we can make that choice "for the first time" each time. The power of each choice will increase with the sense of spontaneity, which will expand with the capacity to have made other choices. Thus, spontaneity, which is a powerful performance value, is a direct result of two things: full acceptance of performance as a process, and knowing at each point in that process that many other choices are possible.

It is also important to know that there is no necessary opposition between process and product. Like every full spectrum—each of which has the potential for part-polarization—process and product choices are the most powerful when they genuinely interact with one another. The following examples clarify the idea that the best product is a slice of genuine process, and that restricting one's focus to either end of the process-product spectrum loses the power of the whole.

The singer who is overconcerned about the "product" of his singing will be judging what he has just done, thus losing energy in the present by evaluating the past; or he will be worrying about the high C to come, thus wasting present process energy on the future product. In both cases, the singer is robbing energy from the only reality there is—the present—and investing it in the dead past or the imaginary future. In the case of the high C, that note will be best supported, literally and figuratively, by a full investment of energy in every present moment leading to the high C—which is also in, and only in, the present. Rob energy from any point in that process for future worry or past regret, and you are undermining the very thing you are worried about achieving.

On the other hand, if we have no product purpose in mind—the aimlessness end of the spectrum—our process may not be energized to its full potential. For example, to want to perform an aria as well as we can, to realize our best high C, our finest musicality, to do our most powerful and radiant performing are purpose-product goals that energize our process. But to realize them fully, we must honor both ends of the spectrum: the process for its own sake and for the product's sake as well.

Similarly in rehearsal situations. Overconcern with the future product by the director or coach can lead to the same judgmental loss of energy that robs the present process of its full capacity to fulfill the purpose-goal. The director who overemphasizes the gap between the product-goal and the present process of the performer may compel that performer to try to achieve the product immediately (even though there are weeks of rehearsal left in which to achieve it), thus forcing the imaginary future on the present. This may lead, in turn, to comparing what was just done with what "should" have been done, in which case the past will also be draining energy from the present. Again, the pattern is the same: present energy is lost to future and past comparison, and our purpose is undercut.

The aimlessness end of the spectrum is often held up as a danger in rehearsal situations by directors and coaches. "It's all very well to go for process when you've got the time,"—which always seems to be never—"but we've got a show to get up." The implication seems to be that concern for process is pampering, coddling, lazy, self-indulgent, and a threat to product; that if you don't force performers, drive them, judge them, hold the fear of product failure and condemnation in front of and behind them, they won't "produce." But that is the voice of our addictive conditioning speaking. I have never encountered a situation where those dangers actually came to pass. The addictive product orientation in directors, coaches, and performers in general is too strong to allow us to err on the side of a lazy, unenergized process in preparing a piece for public presentation. The errors—or at least the loss of energy and interference with the best possible performance—are almost always on the side of overstress on product and judgment.

Exercising with the performing power technique is a process. That process will do several things: it will develop the power of the performer's communicating components—including both guidance and projective modes; it will allow the performer to become aware of and release the interferences—the entanglements—that block that power; and it will develop the coordination between the three projective modes with specific exercises in isolation, awareness, and integration. However, that process will unfold in its wholeness only if we actually exercise it—if we *practice*.

The Third Guiding Principle: Practice

The spectrum of dualities underlying the higher principle of *practice* are procrastination and workaholism. (Note that Ann Wilson Schaef has followed *When Society Becomes an Addict* with *The Addictive Organization*, which discusses the addiction of workaholism in depth.) At the procrastination end of that spectrum is the urge to avoid practice, to put it off, to find something more important to do; at the workaholic end is the urge toward perpetual practice, to work at it continually through endless repetition, which we believe is necessary in our never-ceasing efforts to grow and become better. This urge is fed by numerous stories of successful performers who practiced endlessly. (The connection of workaholism with perfectionism is evident.)

From one viewpoint, of course, singer-actors *are* always practicing, that is, using the total instrument of themselves; the only question is, how consciously? How aware are we that we are always using our guidance and projective modes, and therefore can always be exercising them? From another viewpoint, and for the same reason, we would never need to make a ritual of practice if we could simply understand how to guide and exercise the flow of energy that is ongoing in our process at all times.

We can learn to understand the principle of practice from both viewpoints simultaneously, resting when we need to and practicing our energy processes in an effortless, resting way even when it is not a defined part of our schedule. While practice is not ordinarily understood as a higher principle of energy, let us regard it in this way as we proceed: as a process that is always available to us interdependent upon our awareness and use of it.

During a coaching session with a class, one performer suddenly stopped and said, with some intensity, "I hope you write a whole chapter on practice in your next book!!" She was reflecting the challenge that all performers seem to experience in becoming aware of the performing power process: since there has been no means of exercising the singer-actor's total performing process, there is no model for doing so. Most performers are so accustomed to authority dependence when they work on the parts of their process—their voice, their body, and their acting—they naturally experience difficulty when given an exercise process to work with on their own. And even if they are able to exercise the *parts* by themselves—having the model of the part-teacher to draw upon—there has been no corresponding authority figure to integrate all the parts, and therefore no model for the whole exercise process.

After taking a performing power seminar, an actor friend told me, "I quit growing about six years ago and now I know why. But there's some good news and some bad news: the good news is that I now have a way of exercising and developing my total performing process; the bad news is that I now have a way of exercising and developing my total performing process." He had an insight about the practice process before he had even begun it (an insight that arose, no doubt, from previous efforts to practice consistently).

That insight might be called the insight-does-not-equal-growth insight. We take classes in which we have insights about life, the world, and ourselves; yet those insights remain in the realm of unactivated awareness unless we do something with them, unless we actually exercise and practice what they have to tell us about ourselves, the world, and life. But, again, we are so habituated to having other people tell us what to do, having them do it for us, or searching for an easy, instant solution—and no insight process has a solution, let alone an instant one—that truly acting upon our insights is profoundly difficult. We can talk about them, write about them, and think about them; but to act upon them and *become* them is another question. As Barbara Ray has said, in discussing this issue, "It's not what you think you're doing, it's not what you feel you're doing, it's not what you say you're doing—it's what you're actually doing." For performers the capacity to actually *do* the exercise process is the very thing that will allow them to become what they can be: performers whose power is always expanding.

What stands in the way of actually doing it? And by doing it, I do not mean simply grinding it out in the manner of nasty calisthenics, treating the body and the self as objects to work with, to get in shape—the workaholic end of the spectrum; I mean working with our performing process with total subjective involvement, and nonjudgmental awareness. Unless we do it in that way, we are perpetuating the very lack of personal process involvement that made it difficult to exercise that process in the first place. When we are treating ourselves as objects, as products that are good or bad, we are automatically judging ourselves. We become geniuses at transforming everything that is said to us by our teachers, our friends, or our parents into criticism and judgment. If exercising our own performing process subjects us to more of that kind of judgment (and we are our own harshest judges, having internalized more stern authority figures than we can possibly remember), then we will always find ways of avoiding it. And avoid it we should—the judgment, that is, not the exercise. But if the two have become inextricably linked in our experience—if the process of exercise and the products of judgment have become entangled—we will avoid them both if we can find any reasonable excuse to do so.

And that is the challenge: to find a way of overcoming our conditioned resistance to practice, which may be simply a resistance to judgment. Those performers who have managed to drop most of the judgment from their practicing have found that practice and exercise can be fun. It should be. Practice means working with your total human energies; it is a joy to be free to do that. While fun and a sense of joy in performing is not a product, your process will develop and expand in proportion to your capacity to exercise with joy. We begin with awareness; as we exercise our process, that awareness will grow; as our accepting, nonjudgmental awareness expands, our joy in performing will expand as well; and that joy will interact synergistically with both the exercise and the awareness. As we expand our capacity for exercise, and cultivate awareness, we can also increase our capacity for joy with our fourth principle, *play*.

The Fourth Guiding Principle: Play

To understand *play* as a higher energy principle, let us look at the spectrum of energies it encompasses. At one end of that spectrum is a frivolous, irresponsible kind of energy use; at the other is an overly responsible hyperseriousness. Both impulses contribute important elements to our growth process. One end allows us to drop overconcern with the future and the past and with product—to play, in the ordinary sense of that word—while the other end keeps us intent (if overly so) upon some sort of goal.

Since we will differentiate between play as a higher principle of energy and play as one end of a duality spectrum with work at the other, let us think of this underlying spectrum, for the moment, as a work-play spectrum. We used the word *workaholic* in discussing the principle of practice, and *work* in referring to the exercise process. To transcend the work-play duality, we could go back and substitute *play* for every use of the latter, or perhaps, *play-work* or *work-play*. The same synergy of interacting opposites holds true for work-play as for all other full spectrums of energy use.

The conditionings we have around those two words affect us deeply. *Work* is filled with connotations of effort, something we must be paid or compelled to do, while *play* has a sense of the frivolous, something that children do that is not appropriate for mature, responsible adult behavior. That neither set of connotations is true does not affect the fact that we tend to "work" in exercising our performing process and, in many cases, we have totally lost our sense of play not only in performing but in life in general. Work is associated with products, goals, and achieving specific ends; play is for its own sake, there is no goal, no end product in mind. The choices available in working are limited—everything is judged in terms of its appropriateness to the job, the goal; the choices available to play are infinite—there is no restriction since there is no goal in mind. In work there is judgment; in play there is acceptance. In work there is effort; in play there is ease. In work there is confinement; in play there is freedom.

Let us now lift play from that duality and experience it as a higher, transcending principle of energy, as *play*. In *Finite and Infinite Games*, James Carse plays philosophically with the word and the concept of play itself. The subtitle of the book says much: *A Vision of Life as Play and Possibility*. The following are selected aphorisms from the book that view the idea of play both in its finite (ordinary) and infinite (higher principle) varieties. Infinite play, for us, will be the higher principle of play, which transcends and enfolds the full spectrum of ordinary play and work.

> A finite game is played for the purpose of winning, an infinite game for the purpose of continuing the play.
>   In one respect, but only one, an infinite game is identical to a finite game: Of infinite players we can also say that if they play they play freely; if they *must* play, they cannot *play*.
>   Infinite players regard their wins and losses in whatever finite games they play as but moments in continuing play.

Finite players play within boundaries; infinite players play with boundaries.

Since finite games can be played within an infinite game, infinite players do not eschew the performed roles of finite play. On the contrary, they enter into finite games with all the appropriate energy . . . but they do so without the seriousness of finite players.

To be playful [in this way] is not to be trivial or frivolous, or to act as though nothing of consequence will happen. On the contrary, when we are playful with each other we relate as free persons, and the relationship is open to surprise; *everything* that happens is of consequence. It is, in fact, seriousnesss that closes itself to consequence, for seriousness is a dread of the unpredictable outcome of open possibility. To be serious is to press for a specified conclusion.

Finite players are serious; infinite players are playful.

Because infinite players prepare themselves to be surprised by the future, they play in complete openness. It is not an openness as in *candor*, but an openness as in *vulnerability*.

The infinite player does not expect only to be amused by surprise, but to be transformed by it . . .

Infinite play is inherently *paradoxical*, just as finite play is inherently *contradictory*.

And finally, to conclude this brief but pithy sampling,

All the limitations of finite play are self-limitations.

Play, as a higher principle of energy, is the infinite play Carse refers to. Similarly, the developmental process of the performer as we are viewing it is the infinite game. In both cases, we are speaking of transcending the ordinary dualities of exercise and performance without in any way losing the energies of commitment to them — to the needs of the finite games that are enfolded within the infinite game: the finite games are the exercise and performance goals that come and go; the infinite game is the purpose that contains them all.

The play space we can create to nurture the development of our process is a place of freedom, a place of no danger, of safety, of freedom from judgment, and a place to explore, expand within, and experience the unknown. Such a space is enhanced by and promotes flexible behavior, which can be viewed as the capacity to rejoice in and interact freely with surprise, a quality emphasized by Carse. Flexibility, as we will see, is one of the primary qualities of the radiant performer. Not surprisingly, flexibility is also a key to the growth of intelligence in children.

In *Grammatical Man*, Jeremy Campbell says,

> The secret of flexible behavior is to have interesting experiences
> in stable conditions as free as possible from serious danger. One
> of the most important of these experiences is play. Play, which is
> the normal activity of children who feel secure, is a symptom of
> versatility that tends to lead to more versatility. [Play] flourishes
> best when the consequences of an action are likely to be of less
> importance than the action itself. . . . In play, it is possible to go
> to extremes, to be daring, to experiment, so that the boundaries
> of the permissible and the practical can be tested to the full. (p.
> 144)

Play and security form a mutually reinforcing relationship: play emerges
from security, and conscious play in a safe and supportive environment can
promote a sense of security.

We could also think of (finite) play and technique as another spectrum
open to the potential synergy of opposites. In discussing the importance of
play in the child's developmental process, Campbell notes the movement
from play to technique as the child grows older.

> Adventurousness wanes in all fields of mental and artistic
> endeavor. Conformity sets in and play is subject to fixed rules,
> strictly observed. [It is] a time for mastering rules, traditions,
> norms, and for understanding the technical aspects of art—style,
> balance, and composition. Very few children can recover the gift
> of original expression [at least under our current educational
> system] and they do so only after attaining conscious mastery of
> technique. They have lost entirely the uninhibited, unrehearsed
> freedom of childhood and instead must learn to be innovative
> again, to break the rules, not innocently, but with full awareness.
> Before they can become artists, they must go through a literal
> stage, and this stage is an essential part of their development.
> (p. 145)

We play, and then we learn the rules and forget how to play; and before we
can become artists, we must learn how to play again, but this time without
the original innocence of that childhood play. But play we must, for it is an
essential of our art, and particularly when the instrument of that art is oneself.

The value of play (finite and infinite) for the performing process is evident. But the conditioning of performers is often such that the concept of
play is totally foreign to the performing process. It has become clear to me
that the first step in exploring the unknown, which is the key to all change

and growth, is to establish an environment in which play is once again possible for the performer. No rules, no judgment, no carefulness or concern with what others may think—just play with your aria, your soliloquy, or your scene as freely as possible while you practice. Until that is possible, the work-product performance ethic will interfere with the kind of growth that could take place. Once the performer is capable of truly *playing*, the practice process unfolds with relative ease and real joy and can even become part of the performing process. Those performers who have begun to play as they exercise and perform have been amazed by what it does to help them achieve a better product; not only is it more fun, but by giving up the work-product orientation, they produce a more useful work product.

And with that, let us also honor the values of the other end of that spectrum, the values of work, technique, and seriousness of intent. In its best sense, work can mean committed, deeply involved effort that is playful even as it unfolds with purpose. Work with purpose is play, just as play with purpose is the highest form of work.

To be able to play with material in practice, rehearsal, or performance means, of course, that the material has been memorized and is technically under control. While this technical "work" needs to be done, it can very usefully interact with the play principle from the very beginning. Often by the time the necessary technical work is accomplished, patterns and attitudes have been established that make it difficult to get back to the profound values offered by play. But play need never be absent from any learning process: from the first time the music (or the voice lesson, or the coaching, or the staging) is approached, the integration of play-work/work-play into the process can begin as well. This is why the irresponsible/frivolity end of the lower spectrum must be allowed.

Every performer takes the *judgment* of her process too seriously—in attempting to make a work product of it—and the process itself not seriously enough as a genuine process of play. When I use the phrase "What we are doing is too important to take seriously," it speaks directly to the integration of those seemingly opposed concepts of irresponsible frivolity and hyperseriousness. We can fulfill our potential most powerfully when we are not concerned about doing so; even while we have a purpose of intense importance, we move in the direction of that purpose with greatest impetus when we are *playfully* involved in our process.

The Fifth Guiding Principle: Persistence

As your process unfolds in the direction of your purpose, practice playfully with *persistence*, the fifth principle. Underlying this higher principle is a spectrum with detachment at one end and determination at the other. Determination can lead to forcing, to tension, to attempts to control; yet a measure of it can be useful, especially when determination is blended with detachment as to the outcome. Detachment by itself might lose the energy necessary for purposeful growth. Together, seen from a higher perspective, the two energy concepts can inform each other and open to the higher principle of persistence.

> In higher consciousness, the Power of Radiant Persistence refers to an Inner energy with the quality of going on, one step at a time, in the direction of Real Light through the process of releasing illusions, of balancing and harmonizing your outer planes with the higher, universal vibration, and of natural transformation. (Ray, *ERM*, p. 84)

It is useful to remember that that process of transformation can always continue, and that we can grow as performers (and as people) for as long as we live. Our growth during that time will be in direct proportion to our capacity to persist in exercising and developing our process. Persistence means regularity; not in guilty spurts, like the weekend exerciser, but consistently; not determined to make everything happen at once, but accepting the capacity for *continual* growth and the for-the-first-time excitement of each day's process. While seeming plateaus may appear in our development, it helps to remember that those plateaus are periods of stabilization, and that we are always changing, whether it appears so on the outer levels or not. Persistence will transform that ongoing change into useful growth.

Persistence has other, potentially negative aspects, such as stubbornness and insistence, both of which will be modified appropriately by the play attitude, as well as by the sixth principle and its faithful companion: *patience* in the *present*.

The Sixth Guiding Principle: Patience in the Present

Underlying the higher principle of *present patience* is a spectrum with passive, habitual inertia at one end and panic for the future at the other. The inert and indifferent aspect of patience (based on the habitual past) balances the aspect that is hyperconcerned for the future outcome (our continuing nemesis, product fixation). The higher principle of patience in the present draws upon and blends all the separate energy choices making up this spectrum.

Patience allows us to focus on our process *now*, in the present. Overintent focus on a goal can make us impatient with where we are and even interfere with our progress toward the goal itself. Another way of saying it is that when we are focused on the imaginary future rather than the real present, we will become impatient with that present. In our discussion of process, we saw how we can lose the immense power of the present moment — the only reality there is — by putting energy into the imagined future or the dead past — worrying on one hand, regretting on the other, comparing, evaluating, and judging in both cases, thus losing energy for what we are actually doing. We lose the patient power of the present in proportion to our passive focus on the past or our impatient focus on the future.

There is a fundamental relationship between accepting ourselves as we are right now, loving ourselves totally in this moment, and being patient with our process in the present. Performer problems in general would largely disappear if we could simply do one thing: accept and love ourselves totally. Learning to sing, to act, and to sing and act would then be a joyful unfolding process, for there would be no judgmentalism to interfere with it, only a heightened awareness and a learning capability that would be astonishing.

Someone will always ask the very logical question, "How can we love ourselves totally right now if we want to become better?" The answer is simple, though not simplistic: "We will be motivated to love ourselves totally in the present moment — which at first may mean simply *acting* as though we do — if we know that our progress and improvement will be in direct proportion to our capacity for love and self-acceptance." A four-year-old is not an imperfect adult; he is whole as he is, and is not inferior in some way because he cannot do as a four-year-old what is possible to an eight-year-old or a twenty-year-old. The best way to ensure that he becomes the most completely fulfilled eight- or twenty-year-old is to accept, love, and nurture him as he is right now, in the present. That acceptance, love, and nurturing will involve discipline, guidance, and firmness (as does the performer and the practice process); and those qualities will allow the most complete, whole unfolding of the process of the child (and the performer) when they are accompanied by patience.

Since we never stop growing (or never *need* to stop growing) we are always in the situation of the child, for a child is within us as long as we live. Like that of the child, our growth as performers will be the most profound and whole if it is nurtured by patience in the present. If we are totally in the present at each moment, it is literally impossible to stunt the growth of our inner child by judgment, condemnation, worry, regret, or any of the other energy-robbing qualities that are so often a part of our personal performing process. All such qualities derive their very existence from being out of the present: we can only judge, condemn, or regret what has already happened — what is past — and we can only worry about that which is to come — the future.

Being in the present, of course, does not mean being amnesiac or losing the power to plan. As we have pointed out, the powers of the mind include remembering and imagining — both of which can be used positively in the present. In discerning rather than judging our past choices, we can learn from them in making present choices. In imagining the future creatively and playfully rather than fearfully, we are able to create a vision of purpose which will also energize and inform the choices of our present process. By letting go of negative approaches to the past and future, we allow the present to make use of the powers of remembering and imagining. And a useful way to exercise letting go of past regret and future worry is by practicing discernment with the past and creative play with the future, both of which will automatically re-focus our energies in the present. It is an exercise process like anything else, and a deeply challenging one. It is made simpler by a clear undestanding of our process as performers, and by knowing the specific physical, facial, emotional, and vocal techniques that allow us to serve the singing-acting process. When we know those requirements in detail, we then have specific processes on which to focus; and since those processes exist only in the present, focusing on them will help us remain in the present. Developing the capacity to do that may be the single most significant thing a performer can do for the expansion and development of his/her performance process. It is the key to realizing the fullness of the performer's potential, our seventh and final principle.

The Seventh Guiding Principle: Potential

Patience in the present with our unfolding process can be further aided and motivated by knowing that we have an unlimited *potential* for increasingly radiant performing. The spectrum underlying this principle has timid partiality at one end and grandiosity at the other.

At the timid partiality end, we underestimate our capacity and are overwhelmed by the fullness of the whole. In reaction we focus on one or more of the parts, which can lead us into the illusion of mistaking them for the whole. This bolsters our ego—a part in itself, and another name for MIM—into thinking it is controlling the whole by commanding one of the parts. This seems to protect the ego from having to do what it thinks is threatening—that is, to accept itself as a part that cannot control the whole. To the ego-MIM, control of the whole (another illusion) seems essential. How useful it would be for ego-MIM to know that not only will accepting itself as a part empower it, but also it will be nurtured by the whole in proportion to its freedom from the illusion that *it* (ego-MIM) is the whole. And even more important, it will move the whole system in the direction of radiant performing.

That twin illusion of the ego-MIM either controlling the whole or being the whole points to the other end of the spectrum—grandiosity. Attaining our infinite potential is seen as an ego-furthering achievement, which is simply another the-part-equals-the-whole error. In this case, the error is in mistaking the product-goal of a smaller part (the ego-MIM) for the larger purpose of the whole. The part arrogates to itself the glory of an attainment that can only come from the whole.

The higher principle of infinite potential integrates the driving, polarizing urges of the two ends of this spectrum—which are also parts of a greater whole. The timid retreat of one part into its separative self is nurtured into a new relationship with the whole, even as the illusions of grandiosity are gently but firmly dispelled. The vision of both parts is realigned with the purpose of integrated wholeness.

While some may bridle at the idea that we have infinite potential, we can look at it in another way: infinite or not, our potential is *always* greater than we think it is. Regardless of your present capacity, your performing power can always be expanded: there is always more—any performance can be more radiant.

The immense challenge of singing-acting is proportionate to its potential power when fulfilled. Because music theater demands both an unusual output of human energies as well as an unnatural combination of those energies, it has the potential of being, as Tyrone Guthrie put it, "the most extraordinary experience one can offer an audience." The experience of performing can also be that extraordinary. Fully and freely realized singing-acting—the realization of radiant performing—is the most complex, challenging, and rewarding aesthetic act there is—its potential is truly infinite.

In every class I teach, I speak to the potential of the singing-acting process by making the statement, "Any singer can become a great singer-actor." I usually receive a few skeptical looks (along with some bemused and hopeful ones). Upon hearing me say that to a new group, a performer with whom I had worked on occasion said, "Do you really mean that, Wes?" Before I could answer, a colleague who had observed that performer's remarkable growth in a relatively short time, said, "Of course he does. Look what's happened to you."

I have since replaced "Can become a great singer-actor" with "Can open to radiant performing." The difference is important: "a great singer-actor" is an evaluation of an implied product; "radiant performing" is a description of a process, and, as we have seen, a process that includes letting go of product control as it opens to greater wholeness.

In either case, I would hesitate to make such a statement if the potential of singing-acting were dependent upon the quality of any single part of the process. But it is not. Radiant performing (and great singing-acting) both involve a free, synergistic relationship of the parts to the whole, and to each other; and they are not solely dependent upon the quality of any individual part. The relationship of the parts to the whole can unfold, expand, and move toward ever-greater potential—the potential of the whole *is* unlimited—for as long as the singer-actor has breath to sustain it.

Every singer-actor is a *whole* system of energy to which all these higher, whole principles apply. The continual unfolding of the singer-actor's potential will be proportionate to her capacity to focus on the whole rather than only on the individual parts. This calls for a simultaneous development of *all* the parts—not just the voice, the body, the face, the emotions, and the mind, but the other energy levels as well, opening to the whole source of all those energies—the Radiant Whole—which supports and guides not only their development, but their interrelationship as well.

This also gives the performer a great many more avenues to approach the expansion of her performing power. Instead of focusing exclusively on one part month after month, for example, hurling oneself at the voice, demanding that it achieve some specific capacity, the performer can continue to exercise the voice even while focusing on one of the other energies of the total performing process. One can move from part to part—from the expressivity of the face to the gestural capacity of the body, to the freedom of the emotional process, to the release of counterproductive mental habits, developing the flow of the intuitive and higher consciousness modes—opening to the nurturing of them all by the Radiant Whole, which supports each of them individually, and nurtures the wholeness of their interrelationship simultaneously.

With these seven principles as a guide, let us examine the exercise process for total—and radiant—performing. Until now there has been no such process for private, individual use. A great many systems and methods have been devised to supply this missing ingredient. Some of them strive for a whole view, but do not relate to all the parts; others resolutely focus on a single part, mistaking it for the whole, and ignore or slight the other parts in the process. Some of these methods are very useful, others are less so, and some are potentially harmful. But they are all parts of the whole, and each of them can make positive contributions when placed in the context of the whole. We will reexamine the singer-actor's relationship to the exercise process with these existing methods in mind, and begin developing an individual practice process that does not deny the existing resources, but enhances each of them and allows them to complement and interact with one another synergistically.

Chapter 7

Why the Singer-Actor Doesn't Practice: Confusion about the Exercise Process

The Missing Process on the Pentagon of Potentiality

At this point we have a sense of destination: we know where we want to go on our journey; the fundamental and primary purposes of radiant performing and fulfilled performing potential are clear. We also have a sense of where we are, of the traveling conditions and our own conditioning. The only thing lacking is a vehicle, an exercise process with which to begin the journey. Lacking an integrating view for the whole act of performance, we also lack a model for the exercise process.

In chapter 1, the pentagon of potentiality was presented as a way of viewing the total interaction between the art, the environment, and the per-

161

former. As illustrated there, the pentagon has never been completed, nor has there been a model for its completion until recently. The art is there, the environment is there, the singer-actor is there—but no exercise process for the total performance has been developed to complete the pentagon at its peak. Instead, it has looked like the accompanying figure.

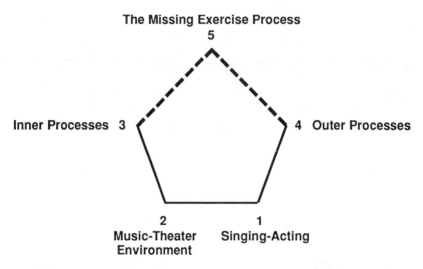

I have asked hundreds of performers, "Do you have a way of exercising your total performance process by yourself, without the aid of outside ears or eyes?" There has never been an affirmative reply. We have had no method for teaching the total performing process, and therefore no way of exercising it. There are many who are capable of teaching the parts, but who is able to teach each of the parts as well as their integration into a whole? And if teachers, directors, and coaches have not agreed upon a way to work with the whole process, we can hardly expect performers to have developed a technique for doing so on their own.

Like their teachers, performers can work with the parts of the process separately: they can do vocal exercises, practice interpretation, do physical exercise, memorize and drill their songs and speeches; but there has been no concept for understanding and working with the interaction and integration of those parts. (It should also be noted that there is no way of working privately with at least one of the parts—the emotional process—since that has come to be dependent upon an outside observer—the director or the coach—to validate it as real or believable.)

The Paradox of Choosing Not to Practice

Assuming for the moment that we will arrive at a clear and specific exercise process for the performer—let us call it a "total-performance nautilus," after the universal exercise machines—what keeps performers (and all of us) from using that nautilus to exercise our processes on our own? We have grown so accustomed to not having such an exercise process that, even when one is made available, the habit of not doing it may persist. If we were aware of that habit, all we would have to do is overcome it. The desire to do that is generally there—at least according to the many performers I have asked.

For a long time I believed that if we knew how to exercise total performance, we would naturally do it. That was an illusion. The performer quoted above who said, "I hope you devote a whole chapter to the practice process in your next book," had a means of exercising her total performance process; she simply found herself unable to use it with consistency. And she was not alone. As I began questioning singer-actors about the personal exercise of their total performance process, her plight appeared to be universal: they all had the means (however partial some of those means may have been), yet somehow they were blocked from being able to actually use them.

If the desire is there, and we choose not to use a nautilus we have been given, *why* do we choose not to? What stops us? Most performers will agree that (1) they want to grow—they have the desire—and (2) they can best do this on their own. All they need is a way to do it. But although we can now give them that total-performance nautilus, experience indicates that they still will not use it. If we receive an actual nautilus machine as a gift, and there is no room for it in our apartment, we can't use it. Similarly with the singer-actor and the metaphorical nautilus for exercising their performance process: it appears that there is no psychological space for it. Performers may agree that it is vital, and may genuinely want to use it, but without clearing a space for it within themselves, they will not be able to do so. What subterranean conditioning blocks us all from clearing that space, and from claiming our freedom of choice with respect to the development of our own process?

This chapter is dedicated to the performer quoted above who confronted that conditioning directly. But while she requested a single chapter, I have gone further: the following chapter will describe ways we can exercise our performance process, while this one will clarify the obstacles that prevent us from doing it once we do know how.

Thus, before we describe and create our total performance nautilus, and before considering the principles to guide our use of it, we will examine the interferences that keep us from taking the nautilus home and exercising with it. Awareness of the conditionings that block us from doing what we need (and want) to do to exercise our total performance processes will give us the choice of clearing the exercise field of its obstacles and actually doing it.

Losing the Personal Power to Grow: Authority Dependency

The most important single purpose of this book is to put performers in charge of their own total performance process (even if they have never been there before). Performers need the information—the instructions—necessary to develop and expand their performing power *on their own*, and to be released from dependency upon external authority figures. Yet all the instructions in the world will be meaningless unless the performer actually follows and practices those instructions consistently. Performers must come to *know* the information and instructions through direct and persistent experience with them.

Having had that direct experience, the next step is interaction with others in the field—including teachers, directors, and colleagues, as well as audiences in general—for support, guidance, and (if appropriate) realignment with purpose. Finally, the capacity to perform consistently using the information and instructions will develop with increasing flexibility and power. Thus, the process of knowing and becoming one with the information depends upon the performer following the three-step IEI process: follow the instructions, experience the energies in question directly, and then interact with others who are involved in the same field.

The initial block, as we have seen, is created by the partial approach to the total process, the lack of an integrative view and the resultant conflicts, and various part-equals-whole errors. This interference is heightened by a related factor: the dependency of the performer upon the authority figures who teach the separate parts. These authorities, consciously or unconsciously, pass on their specific biases about the relationship of the parts they teach to the whole process, particularly with respect to the disproportionate importance they may attribute to their own parts.

But beyond passing on particular biases ("The voice is all that counts," "If you really feel it, that's all that matters," etc.), authority dependency does more to rob the singer-actor of personal power than any other factor. It creates an addictive need to be validated by an outside source, and a corresponding desire to please that external referent, which in turn gratifies the authority figure's control needs. So the external referent tells the singer-actor whether he is good or bad, which is vital to the singer-actor's need to please, since he won't know whether he has done so until his performance is judged. Based on that judgment, the singer-actor will change behavior to please the external referent, and so on.

All this creates a particularly vicious circle, which stops the personal and private exercise process dead in its tracks. We can pick any point in that circle of mutual addiction as a starting point for examination—say, with the addictive need for product on the parts of both teacher and performer. The rub is simple: a product demands a person who judges that product as being good or bad. We need an outside referent to tell us about the worth of what we are attempting to do, and to guide us in our efforts to do it. Since we are already trying to be good at something, we will tend to try to improve what we are already doing. This, of course, eliminates the possibility of working with all the things we might learn to do that we *cannot* already do well.

We develop the habit of confining our efforts to those things we *can* do, understand, justify, or rationalize already. Since we are our own instrument, and may not be aware of what we are *actually* doing and certainly not of how *well* we are doing it, we become increasingly dependent upon that external referent to tell us both of those things. Our sense of self-worth, of self-validation, of self-awareness and self-understanding is largely handed over to an authority figure outside ourselves (or, as in the case of the singer-actor, to several of them). By and by, we lose touch completely with the development and validation of our own process and with how that whole process functions in relation to its parts, or those parts to the whole. We also begin thinking of *ourselves* as a product (which, by definition, is a fixed, noninteracting state of being); that removes us even further from an interacting relationship with and within our process (which, by definition, is always moving, and always changing.)

Carrying this load of conditioning with us, we go home and try to "practice our exercises." But the only thing we have been trained to do is strive for our best product. This is true even when we are doing simple vocal exercises in the presence of our voice teacher. We do some of the exercises better than others, and the teacher tells us which, even while trying to help us realize which is "best" by how it "feels" or how we are "thinking" about it while we are doing it. Again, to turn out a "good product" demands someone outside ourselves to judge the worth of that product. When we are alone we find that we are both product and judge: we are trying to turn out our best product for a judge who is ourselves. Given our conditioning, the judge we have learned to be (by imitation) may be an exacting one, possibly a harsh one.

We are trying to do two contradictory things simultaneously: we are attempting to develop our process by allowing the most free and flowing, in-the-present process possible; but we are also attempting to give the best possible product performance, which requires judgment, judgment that, being past and future oriented, will interfere with the process, and therefore with the product it is judging. Judgment in process is antithetical to our best product. As a corporate slogan might put it, "Process is not only our most important product, it is our best product! (But it can't be judged as such during its process.)" We have a deep need to *please* an external referent-judge; yet the attempt to please by doing something *while* in the act of doing it virtually assures that what we do will *not* please as it could; the judge for whom we are doing it may be gratified by the intensity of our effort to try and please—but that is the double bind for both teacher and student: the secondary gratification of *trying hard* blocks the full unfolding of the primary need to please.

We have been so strongly conditioned to judge ourselves sternly that the addictive characteristics of perfectionism and always doing our best are even thought of as being useful guides to practice behavior. As a result, it is sometimes impossible to please even ourselves. The need to please an external referent is internalized—that internal judge becomes a perfectionist; and since we are *producing ourselves* and have no way of viewing our parts from the perspective of the whole, nor any way of evaluating our total performance process without an external referent, the need to please is starved in proportion to the degree of perfectionism, and howls for judgmental sustenance.

In the end, our practice process will either be experienced as unjudgable and, given our conditioned need for judgment, pointless and frustrating; or we will judge ourselves as we are practicing, interfering with the process as we do so, thus ensuring that the judgment will be negative. We are either frustrated by not being able to judge, or guilty because we do judge. Our practice time will be spent beating up on ourselves, which ensures that we will avoid it whenever we can find an excuse. It is little wonder that there is so little useful practicing being done—the minimal improvement in most performers over a period of time attests to this—and so much frustration around the idea of private exercise time.

Do What Thou Wilt: Balancing Authority Dependency

My experiences with this authority-dependent need to please have led me to say something like the following in all my classes.

> You can do whatever you want to do. If I suggest an exercise and you don't want to do it, that is just as OK as if you want to do it—in fact I would rather drop OK and not OK, and have you simply be aware of and describe whatever choices you make. I may ask you why you made different choices from those suggested, and, again, you have the choice of sharing or not sharing your reasons. Do whatever you want to do. It is not necessary to ask permission to try anything you like with your own process—it is *your* process, not mine. I can't have your experience for you—I can only offer guidance in working with it. Since it is your process, there can be nothing harmful for anyone else in whatever you do with it. Furthermore, any choice you make is not good or bad for you yourself. Whatever you choose to do is simply information for your awareness and growth—and any product judgment of it (yours, mine, or anyone else's) is meaningless in this context. So have MIM leave its judgmental hat at the door, come on in, and play.

And so on, in that vein, attempting to release performers from the timid, careful use of their energies that blocks their growth and keeps them right where they are.

Great performance can be defined by the capacity to use personal energies as powerfully and freely as is appropriate to the performer's system. You learn to work with your power by working with your power, not by being careful. Of course, guidance is helpful and supportive in working with that power, but the first step is to get the blocks to that power out of the way so it can flow. Only then can you find out what you are capable of, and that may be something MIM would never have guessed.

There are two related "rules" that I invoke in order to encourage release from this timidity and carefulness. One is the NBC rule, which means *Never be careful*; the other is the GTF rule, which means *Go too far*. Unless you feel as though you are going too far, you will be working within the limits you already know, and you will not be expanding your conditioning boundaries. I anticipated that both rules might lead to some truly chaotic, performance-endangering behavior; but performers are so deeply conditioned to achieving a good product, and are so concerned about the judgment of others, that no one has even come close to going too far or doing something even vaguely threatening.

Again, this does not mean doing intentional damage of any kind to the voice or body or to another person; it means using your energy with a freedom and power you have never experienced. The fact that you have not experienced it means that it will be surrounded by inhibitions and entanglements of one kind or another. They may block the vocal energy with the glottis, or the facial energy with the body, or the kinesthetic energy may be blocking its own efforts.

Let us repeat the point: in order to learn to work with different energies, you have to work with those different energies—there is no substitute for the direct experience of the energies themselves. In doing so, you will bring into play the entanglements that attempt to control and block them; and at that point the entanglements become part of your conscious awareness in a new way: it becomes possible to work with them rather than being controlled by them, and to transform them into choices by developing other responses to the different uses of energy.

In the teaching-guiding situation, then, I do everything possible to create a free and safe space in which to exercise. I maintain an attitude as free of judgment as possible. That in itself is a challenge, for I am also conditioned in the unconscious use of judgmental patterns. It takes constant alertness and practice to communicate to performers what they have actually done while being clearly descriptive *and* nonjudgmental (even while being nonjudgmental about the judgment that may appear). Aware of all this, I do what I can to convince the performers that I am telling the truth when I say, "Do whatever you want to in class." Sometimes they act as though they believe it, although the conditionings that insist otherwise are strong and largely unconscious. When they do act that way (whether they believe it or not), they make enormous progress. They stop asking permission to do something different with their energies, and actually *do* it. But how much persuasion it takes! And how much weeding out of the judgmental undergrowth from within one's teaching self before that persuasion is more than just words. However, we must begin with words, with descriptive, accurate, nonjudgmental words: the knowing will follow, for both teacher and taught, just as the practice of external technique for the performer often precedes its integration with inner meaning.

But when performers leave the guided situation of a relatively judgment-free class and go home to practice on their own, there is no one to help them maintain that nonjudgmental environment. From countless tales of difficulty with the exercise process, it appears that the momentarily suppressed judgmental demons reassert themselves: the careful cautiousness sneaks back into play. Once performers are aware that they themselves are responsible for those demons and for creating an unpleasant personal exercise space, they can begin creating a nonjudgmental environment of their own, where the demons are not allowed in, and the judgmental hat is left outside. That is the first step in developing a process-oriented, personal exercise process: creating a space in which you are free to do whatever you wish with your energy system; a psychological place where critical evaluation is checked at the door, and you enter with only yourself and the fundamental tool for all growth: awareness.

Spiraling into the Unknown

One model introduced earlier was the spiral of expansion, which represented the movement from the known to the unknown. We learn and grow by making that movement, and yet if we are not secure in the known (what we can already do) we will cling to it and be less likely to move away from it toward the unknown (which we may or may not be able to do). Judgmental fear or apprehension, some measure of which is virtually universal, will also block movement into areas we have not already experienced. Let us recall

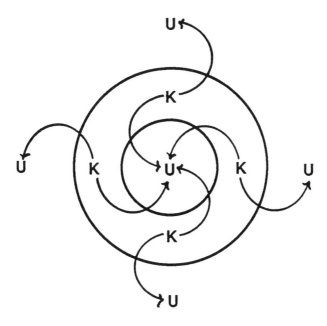

the distinction between judgment as condemnation or criticism (which is how we have been using the term), and judgment as discernment. We will always make discerning choices between what seems useful and what does not. In the exercise process, however, let us make those discerning choices *after* we have worked with them, not before. Preevaluation of experience is a sure way to block our move into the unknown, and thus interfere with new energy choices, block our experience of them, and stop us from realizing their full potential.

If we cannot predict what it is we are about to do, we cannot preevaluate it, and if we cannot preevaluate it, we cannot know whether it is a safe thing to do. Yet the only way to grow is by risking movement into the unknown, wherein lie all the rest of the choices possible to us as performers: it *is* the field of choice potential (unactualized).

Preevaluative judgment keeps us from fully experiencing whatever choice we may preevaluate. By preevaluating experience, we are pulling the unknown into the framework of the known, thereby reducing it, and screening ourselves from experiencing the unknown for what it actually is.

We can recognize that the unknown feels like a risky place to move into, and acknowledge that judgment will keep us from making that move; we can choose, despite that, to practice moving into the unknown as a regular part of our practice process. Performers can make that move a habit by practicing it in as many small ways as possible, using facial expressions, physical gestures, vocal sounds they have never used, and playing with the energies of performance in various ways, even though (and especially if) those ways seem to be "wrong." (This obviously excludes actions harmful to others.) As performers exercise their performance process in this way, movement into the unknown becomes a regular part of it. They learn to create ways of exercise that automatically bring new, unknown choices into play in all three projective modes. Whatever the risks may seem to be, they are illusory; and the benefits have the possibilities of the virtually infinite field of choice potential itself.

The fear that we may lose our sense of discrimination by dropping preevaluative judgment is an illusion that simply keeps us from moving into the unknown. The product orientation of most rehearsals, performances, coachings, classes, and lessons is strong enough to ensure that we will not lose our deeply conditioned concern for product and our need to preevaluate and judge what we do. (Would that we could!) But our deep-seated fear of the unknown will use the rationalization of "losing our sense of judgment" as a key argument to prevent the movement of growth: "Do it wrong once and that will instantly become a habit and corrupt you from then on. Stick to what you know is right." (If only habits were that easy to establish!)

The Paradox of Exercise: Revealing Our Entanglements

There is a paradox in the performer's conditioning about performance and product. As we have pointed out, virtually every point 2, music-theater environment situation — rehearsals, coachings, classes, lessons, and performances — is product oriented, i.e., one in which performers are trying to give their best performance. Showing one's best product means, among other things, the concealment of entanglements (whether consciously or unconsciously), for entanglements are simply more clearly defined descriptions of behavior patterns we have been trained to avoid all our lives. We learn very early in life that overt entanglements are not a good thing (hence the "nerd" image). We don't like to think of entanglement as the universal human condition, certainly not as *our* condition. (A voice teacher who heard me speak on the subject in an afternoon workshop introduced one of her students in recital that evening as being "unentangled." This illusion was quickly dispelled by the student's performance — although possibly not for the teacher: we perceive what we have trained ourselves to perceive.)

Entanglement *is* the universal human condition; it simply depends upon the amount of energy flowing through the system as to whether it is revealed or not. Yet our conditioning leads us to resist revealing our entanglements, even to ourselves. Thus we learn to hide them, treating ourselves as a fixed product — "If I don't show them, that is the way things are" — rather than as a process that we can transform through appropriate exercise.

This life conditioning operates with even greater power in performances and rehearsals. In all these potentially judgmental situations, the performers will be attempting to control their entanglements so that they do not show. For example, increased facial-emotional energy will activate the physical tension necessary to control it; that physical tension will either be felt as physically unattractive or interfere with the voice; to avoid either or both of these things, the facial-emotional energy will be reduced sufficiently so that neither the physical tension nor the vocal interference will be evident. Similarly with the facial response to the singing process, the anticipatory entanglement, or any other obvious manifestation of entanglement: they will all be concealed either by reducing the energy flow or by blocking it in carefully disguised ways.

This, of course, is precisely the reverse of what the exercise process must do. Here is the paradox: To truly exercise we must do the opposite of what we have been carefully (if unconsciously) conditioned to do by life and the music-theater training environment. But since that training tends to be product oriented, it prevents performers (or allows them to prevent themselves) from working with what they cannot already do; this in turn prevents them from growing as they could. To speak to this paradox I devised another spiral of growth, the spiral of Rs.

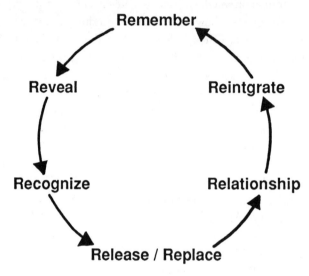

We must *remember* to allow sufficient energy to flow through our projective modes so that we *reveal* our entanglements, so that we may *recognize* them for what they are, and learn to *release* them or *replace* them with new energy *relationships*, thus transforming them to choices that can be *reintegrated* into our field of choice potential. When exercising performers, it is useful to remind them to not only allow the entanglements to come into play, but to encourage them, to play with them, emphasize them, allow them full rein, and get to know them intimately as their "beloved entanglements." Only then can they work freely with the energies involved and acquire true freedom of choice. Entanglements will best become choices if they are brought to full awareness and acknowledged for what they are. If they remain unconscious repressions, they will continue to rob the system of energy.

To play with and exercise your system (rather than trying to do your "best") is one of the most challenging *and* rewarding things the performer can do; challenging, because it goes against the prevailing conditioning of having to achieve our best product each time; and rewarding, because it allows us to grow in specific and tangible ways that are new to our experience. Nothing is more exciting than that.

The spiral path is a universal pattern of growth. "Spirals are more than the timeless symbols of eternity. . . . [they] are the actual 'shape' of fluid energy evolving order from chaos" (Blair, *Rhythms of Vision*, p. 72). Growth is not a linear, ladderlike process of leaving old steps behind forever. Those old steps in human growth are energy interactions to which we will return in a more complex form from a higher point on the spiral. Our voice, our emotions, our thoughts, and our bodies interact in ever-changing ways as our process develops and unfolds. These patterns of interaction are not then discarded, but constitute a known model to draw upon as we learn other new ways. For example, as we use the face and voice to express joy or anger, we learn ways of doing that through actual experience. When we next return to the expression of those emotional combinations, they are supported by our experience of learning them at the earlier stage on the spiral of growth—as well as all the other experiences since then.

Each time we return to a previously experienced interaction of parts in expressing emotion (or anything else), it is always for the first time, no matter how similar it may seem to the earlier event. It is from a point further along on the spiral of development, which means that it *will* be a different experience. That voice-face expression of emotion that MIM may have thought was "figured out" has a whole set of new ingredients, including its own previous experience; the interaction returns in a different way, and we learn that there are no fixed solutions or resolutions, but only a continually unfolding process of change.

We can resist that process of change by trying to fix it in place as a product; or we can become one with it, rejoicing in its flux, allowing the unfolding energies of the process to assist us rather than struggling against them. As an anonymous bit of rhymed wisdom has it:

> Swimming against the flow of the river,
>   We lose its power, and our own.
> With its flow we gain a power,
>   Greater than either and always unknown.

The Power of Awareness

We return again to awareness, which is remembering in another guise. Every time performers sing, it is possible for them to grow through awareness. By remembering to be aware of what happens when the act of singing begins, and even prior to it, the performer can be exercising continually, even if it is no more than the exercise of awareness. Awareness *is* exercise. The exercise nautili of performance are around us all the time—they only need remembering and awareness: not always *doing* something, but simply observing what is happening; not judging it as good or bad, but being aware of what it is. As Richard Carson puts it in *Taming Your Gremlin*, "I change not by trying to be something other than I am; I change by becoming fully aware of how I am" (p. 56). In the case of the performer, that awareness includes the interaction of our projective-mode system as we change the quality and/or quantity of energy moving through it.

The fact that awareness all by itself *does* create change received confirmation from a report in *Science News* (June 1987). In brief, it involved a study of methods of controlling blood pressure. There were three groups of patients: one worked with behavioral, biofeedback methods, one with drugs, and the control group did nothing except have their blood pressure taken at weekly intervals (thus making them regularly aware of it). Of the three groups, this last one, in which awareness was the only altered factor, experienced the greatest change in both systolic and diastolic readings at the conclusion of the study. While this was not the purpose of the experiment (the project director said, "We were surprised by the results"), it is a wonderfully simple demonstration of the power of awareness to create change, surpassing even overt mental and technological efforts to do so.

Before we are aware of it, the conditioning of our projective-mode system is largely unconscious. That sounds redundant, but it is possible to be conscious of something without being fully aware of its implications for one's performing energies. For example, we can be conscious that we get physically tense when experiencing anger, without being aware of how that affects us as performers. We can also be *unconscious* of our physical responses to emotion, and moving from that state to conscious awareness is the first step.

To speak to that issue, I devised another spiral of growth. This one is a spiral of Cs, which addresses the awareness factor from a slightly different perspective: We can develop *consciousness* of our *conditioning*, which then gives us the *choice* of making a *change* in our use of energy, which can then be *coordinated* with our ongoing process as we return to *consciousness* of that process from a higher point on the spiral.

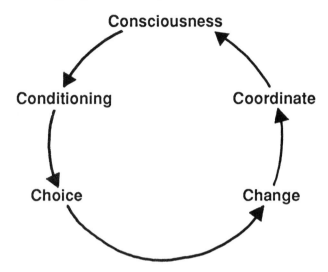

We can best become conscious of the conditioning revealed in our entanglements by changing the quantity or quality of energy we put through our projective system. This leads us back to the spiral of remembering Rs and the necessity of doing what we have been deeply conditioned not to do: exercising our performance energies in a way that does not reflect our best product. As the aphorism goes, "The only exercise worth doing is the one you can't already do." The key to our potential growth is not simply to do such exercises when they are made available to us, but to actively seek them out and rejoice in the opportunity they offer.

The Confusion between Exercise and Performance

We have examined the paradox of the exercise process for performers. It asks them to *do* something that they have been trained all their performing lives *not* to do: to *reveal* the entanglements that limit their performing power, so they can expand that power by transforming the entanglements from necessities into choices. This paradox, which would deny us the right to fulfill our potential, reflects a deep-seated confusion about the difference between exercise and performance—knowing when we are doing one and when the other. Every time I present the performing power technique to a new group, there are questions that reflect that confusion: "Can I use the exercise for performance?" or "What good will it do?" or "Won't it look (or sound) funny in performance?"

The answer is the same in all cases. Exercise is not for singing-acting *performance* any more than it is for athletic performance. A football player who runs in a rope grid or lifts weights will do neither of those things in an actual game, and if he tried to, it would seriously interfere with his performance. Yet both of those things, practiced independently of the game, will expand his capacity to play the game itself.

It is precisely the same for the singer-actor: to be confused about the difference between performance and exercise is to be confused about one's total singing-acting process. An accomplished performer will be aware that there is exercise potential in a performance and will often be able to try things that he has not tried before; but no performer should feel the *necessity* of exercising in performance — that is, in venturing into the unknown in a product-oriented situation. Working in actual performance with the freedom of the performance process is an exercise in itself. Conversely, no performer should feel the need to achieve performance-product standards when he or she is exercising.

This two-part aphorism differentiates between exercise and performance.

> When you exercise, practice what you cannot do;
> When you perform, allow what you can do.

Another way of putting it:

> When you exercise, move into the unknown;
> When you perform, allow the known.

The word *allow* is significant in both cases. It encourages a release of self-conscious monitoring when performing, replacing it with a focus on *doing* instead, allowing the skills and capacities already developed in the exercise process — most of which are beyond MIM's capacity to monitor anyway — to flow with freedom and joy.

This confusion between exercise and performance can also reflect a confusion between purposes: the exercise process is a secondary purpose, which is to serve the primary and fundamental purposes of fulfilled performing potential and radiant performing. If we regard the exercise process as an end in itself, it can become self-reflexive problem solving — e.g., getting rid of entanglements — rather than a means of creating a vision beyond itself. As Robert Fritz points out in *The Path of Least Resistance*, "There is a profound difference between problem solving and creating. Problem solving is taking action to have something go away—the problem. Creating is taking action to have something come into being—the creation" (p. 31). If the exercise process looks beyond itself to the radiant performing it wants to create, it acquires the motivational energy of the creative process.

Fritz relates an experience (with an actual nautilus program, appropriately enough) that clarifies the relationship between what he calls primary choice (our primary and fundamental purposes) and secondary choice (our secondary purpose). He made a primary choice to have a well-toned body, with a three-month nautilus exercise program as a secondary choice. Often during those three months he would wake up in the morning with many reasonable excuses not to do the program that morning—and he would get up and go downstairs. Then he would think, "I'll just go to the bathroom and back to bed"—and he would put on his workout clothes. Then he would think, "I could work around the house and read this morning"—and he would put on his coat and walk out the front door. In his car he would think, "This is great—I can go have breakfast!"—and he would drive to the gym. Halfway through the nautilus program he would think, "I've done a good job—I don't have to finish the whole program"—and he would finish the last few exercises.

This is an example of making a series of secondary choices to support the primary choice. As Fritz says,

> I was easily able to make these secondary choices because I had clearly made my primary choice. . . . At no point did I need to argue with myself. . . . What mattered to me more at each point along the way was my primary choice to have a well-toned body. Each of the secondary choices I made—to get up, to go to the gym, to complete the exercises—was made easily and without hesitation because each directly supported my primary choice. (pp. 181–182)

If we have a clear vision of what we want to create—fulfilled performing potential and radiant performing—the exercise process, rather than being a problem-solving effort for its own sake, becomes a labor of love in moving toward that vision.

Changing Behavior: Four Negative Methods

In the next chapter, which discusses the exercise process itself, we will draw extensively upon Karen Pryor's book, *Don't Shoot the Dog! The New Art of*

Teaching and Training. Pryor lists eight methods of changing behavior, either in others or in oneself. That, of course, is what the exercise process is about: changing our performance behavior. Four of these methods are negative in their approach—Pryor calls them "the bad fairies"—and they have a special connection with the question of why we don't exercise.

Calling these four methods bad fairies does not mean that they are not occasionally useful. As we will see, however, they can contribute additional negative resistance to the exercise process unless one is clear about their use. We need to be aware of what we are actually doing in using these methods (and what is being done to us when someone else uses them on us). Saving the "good fairies" for the following chapter, the first four methods for getting rid of behavior follow.

Method 1.   "Shoot the animal." (As Pryor says, this definitely works. You will never have to deal with that particular behavior in that particular subject again.)

Method 2.   Punishment. (Everybody's favorite, in spite of the fact that it almost never really works.)

Method 3.   Negative reinforcement.

Method 4.   Extinction; letting the behavior go away by itself.

We can dispose of the first bad fairy quickly. As Pryor suggests in the title of the book, *don't* shoot the dog. If this method is used, it means, literally, getting rid of the problem rather than dealing with it. Get divorced if the marriage is a problem, change roommates if the roommate doesn't act as you wish, or give up trying to become a singer-actor. If you do, you will definitely not have to deal with the challenge of singing-acting.

We may note that method 1 can be applied *within* the context of continuing to work in the field. For example, if someone with whom you are working behaves in ways that are, for you, intolerable, and you are unable to change their behavior with any of the other seven methods, you can always sever the relationship: quit the job, change voice teachers/coaches, drop the class, etc. And this is often the wisest thing to do.

Beyond that, bad fairy 1 has little to recommend it for the singing-acting process. As Pryor says, "The vital thing to understand about Method 1 is that it teaches the subject nothing" (p. 112). You learn nothing from it, and since this book is about learning and growth in the specific area of singing-acting, we can be aware of method 1 and move on to method 2.

We all know bad fairy 2 — punishment — perhaps better than we might wish. But because we are deeply conditioned to believe that it is a useful means of changing behavior, it is important to develop greater awareness about it. Pryor suggests that although punishment is humanity's favorite method of motivating learning, it is not as useful as common belief suggests. We berate performers, scold children, fine companies, spank dogs, invade countries and so on. But not only are those clumsy ways of modifying behavior, most of the time they don't work.

Among the reasons that punishment doesn't usually work is that it does not occur at the same time as the behavior one is trying to change; it happens later, and we don't always clearly connect the punishment with what we did wrong. Even if one does relate the punishment to the crime, the trauma of punishment tends to focus our energies on the past and on future avoidance of the same error rather than on the present and on the process of what one *is* attempting to do.

Another mark against punishment as a learning tool is that the subject learns nothing about how to change the behavior, only that it was wrong and that punishment is no fun. The most that one can hope for is increased motivation, but the motivation will be based on avoidance of punishment rather than on learning a new behavior, thus robbing the process of the energy useful to learning the new behavior. It focuses all one's efforts on *not* doing something rather than on learning to do something else.

Pryor expresses surprise that many people have great faith in the effectiveness of punishment. In fact, it is connected closely with the addictive characteristics of our society because it is a simple and direct way of maintaining dominance and control. It does neither of these things, of course, but it creates the illusion that it does. In such cases, it has nothing to do with changing a person's behavior, but rather with dominating and controlling them or asserting one's own status.

For performers working on their own behavior, punishment most often takes the form of self-inflicted guilt and shame (which is reminiscent of David Mamet's remark about most acting training being based on guilt and shame). "Almost no sensation is more disagreeable than the clammy hand of guilt closing around one's heart; it is a punishment that only the human race could have invented" (Pryor, p. 116). And, as with any other punishment, it is not an effective way of learning, growing, and changing behavior. Performers who use guilt and shame to motivate their growth should recognize that it is a Method 2 approach. Since they do not deserve that kind of treatment and it is not the most effective way to change their behavior anyway, they are encouraged to work with some of the other methods or combinations of methods below.

Bad fairy 3, negative reinforcement, is easily confused with punishment. "A negative reinforcement is any unpleasant event or stimulus, no matter how mild, that can be halted or avoided by changing one's behavior" (p. 117). The difference between that and a punishment is that negative reinforcement happens *while* the behavior is going on, not afterward, and the subject can stop the negative reinforcement by changing the behavior. Since there is no gap between behavior and negative reinforcement (as with punishment) it is much more useful than punishment, and is a "perfectly appropriate method of shaping behavior" (p. 119).

This is a particularly challenging concept in theater and music theater, where directors in general give notes *after* the performance, sometimes hours after the behavior itself. The conductor, on the other hand, can often give immediate negative (and positive) reinforcement as the performance proceeds. Similarly, in a coaching situation, it is difficult to give immediate reinforcement of any kind while the person is performing. Their singing is usually too loud for them to hear spoken comments, and it is not useful behavior to have them looking continuously — if at all — at the authority figure at the piano for negative or positive cues. Also, if the coach stops them too often, it can break the flow and block the learning process: interfering anxiety about getting it right may spring up, rather than a flexible adjustment to the new information. We will discuss this issue in further detail when we discuss the good fairies — particularly positive reinforcement — in the following section.

We use spontaneous negative reinforcement all the time: we send negative signals of various kinds while interacting with other people, such as negative sounds or words with the voice, frowns or warning signals with the face, and physical tension signals with the body. We often use too many such signals, particularly as teachers or on ourselves. The important thing about the use of negative reinforcement is to use it until it achieves some behavioral improvement, and then *stop* doing it immediately.

There is one class of subjects for which negative reinforcement is neither effective nor appropriate — human babies. Babies are simply unable to learn easily through unpleasant experience. However, they are capable of rapid learning through positive reinforcement. An obvious question is: when do we ever change in that respect? When do we stop being creatures for whom negative reinforcement is neither effective nor appropriate and turn into beings for whom it is? The answer, I think, is never. The addictive trait of judgmentalism is fueled or created by inappropriate use of negative reinforcement. Performers are like babies all their lives in the positive sense that, unlike the average person, they are always learning new ways of behavior. They can always be growing, can always be moving into the unknown; and for that monumental task, they need what babies need, that is, support and nurturing. They do *not* need what is "not effective nor appropriate" (negative reinforcement) for the ongoing, exhilarating, and formidable task of personal expansion that they share with babies.

The final bad fairy is extinction, a psychological term that refers not to the extinction of a person or animal, but to behavior that dies out for want of reinforcement. Unwanted behavior will sometimes go away of its own accord, just by being ignored or by not providing any response to it. No response, of course, means just that: neither positive nor negative reinforcement. Either kind of response will reinforce behavior we want to change.

For the singer-actor, who is trying to release heavily conditioned entanglements, extinction is unlikely to be a useful approach. With most entanglements, we are either unconscious of the behavior or, if we are conscious of it, we believe it is necessary, natural, or that nothing can be done about it. In any case, ignoring it will do nothing to alter it, except perhaps ingrain it further as a habit. Sometimes a singer will be so judgmental about an entanglement that ignoring it might be the best thing, a useful antidote to a crippling self-monitoring process. But in general, extinction as a technique for changing behavior is less useful to the developmental exercise process itself than it is to the psychological environment *around* that or any other performing process. That brings us to the point touched upon above: the unwitting reinforcement of behavior we wish *would* go away.

The Usefulness of Bad Fairy 4

There is a kind of behavior we all might wish to extinguish, a behavior that is only too well known in the world of theatrical and operatic rehearsal and performance: the resistant, unpleasant, unproductive, defensive, tantrum-throwing, diva-esque variety. It is important to recognize that *any* response to that kind of behavior will reinforce it. Pryor uses the example of whining in children as a behavior we would like to extinguish but end up reinforcing instead. The most persistent whiners are those with parents who have such great self-control they can last for hours until they finally give up in exasperation and let the child have its way—to have an ice cream cone, stop walking, go home, go to the park or whatever. What we forget or do not understand is that any reinforcement—good or bad—maintains behavior. What we are training in the child by maintaining control for long periods before giving in is the power of persistence in whining.

We can apply this fundamental principle to the performer who always comes to rehearsal in a bad mood, and who wants to rehearse what he wants and in the way he wants, with frequent, lengthy breaks. Depending upon the stature of the performer, the worse his mood, the harder the stage-manager, coach, director, or conductor works to accommodate and placate him. What are they actually reinforcing?

Crabbiness, petty tyranny, and bad moods.

On the other hand, being cheerful and pleasant, not accommodating the unreasonable requests, and not showing concern or worry will do a lot to reduce the usefulness of moodiness and bad temper. We must remember, however, that yelling back, withdrawing into a cold silence, or any attempt to punish the malcontent would all be results that might very well reinforce the behavior rather than change it.

If we could learn to ignore the behavior of a person, without ignoring the person, we could do much to allow unpleasant rehearsal displays to extinguish by themselves because they get no response, good or bad. It takes a lot of energy to keep up those kinds of displays, and if they are not productive in any way, they may be abandoned. This, of course, is a side issue so far as this book is concerned. Most of our work will involve becoming aware of *unconscious* resistance or behavior patterns. We are working with ourselves or with other singer-actors, and willingness, in general, is part of the situation—none of us would be doing it if we didn't want to.

However, the technique of extinction can be applied by singers to unpleasant directors, coaches, or teachers—albeit not as easily—with useful results. In addition, we can apply the same principle to ourselves. By not responding to our own bad moods—by neither condemning ourselves nor treating ourselves to some indulgence when we feel bad, but simply continuing to function as we would if the bad mood weren't there—we might find some interesting changes in our own behavior.

With those four bad fairies in mind, and with awareness of the challenge of exercising our performance process on our own, let us consider the singing-acting exercise process itself: What is it? What can it be? And how can we use it most effectively?

Chapter 8

How the Singer-Actor Can Practice:
Clarifying the Exercise Process

Shaping Behavior: Principles, Not Methods

In *Don't Shoot the Dog!* Karen Pryor deals mainly with the principle behind effective shaping—to change behavior in small steps in the direction of a specific goal—rather than the methods of training themselves. However, in the field of singing-acting we must work with the methods as well, for, as we have seen, there has been no method for the whole, only for the parts—hence the potential fragmentation of those parts. Pryor's work is most helpful in clarifying how to practice the methods with maximum effectiveness in changing performance behavior. She distinguishes between the principles of shaping and the methods of training. Training is generally concerned with the methods themselves: how to do something, whether it is singing, acting, or singing-acting. There are specific skills to be learned, habits to master, techniques to acquire: freeing the jaw, opening the rib cage, developing focus, releasing physical tension, singing with projective power, communicating emotion, and so on. All that is a significant part of our purpose in the book, i.e., developing and coordinating the skills that open to radiant performing.

But beyond the methods and the shaping process are the principles, the rules that tell us how best to apply the methods, how to achieve maximum learning as we practice the skills: when to persist, when to let up, when to challenge, when to take it easy; what to do when you are stuck, and even when to quit. While these questions are usually left up to the individual teachers or coaches—and depend upon their intuitive skills and experience—or to chance or luck, Pryor helps clarify the principles underlying good teaching. The use of these principles makes the difference between a learning process that is happy, fast, and successful and one that is frustrating, slow, boring, and disagreeable, between great teaching and adequate teaching. It is not simply methods, but effective shaping principles that make for effective training.

In this section, we will concentrate on the performer who is shaping herself rather than the teacher who is guiding the shaping process. That is a challenge expressed by the performer quoted above and discussed by Pryor. The difficulty is in the reinforcement, which is anything occurring during an act which increases the probability of the act happening again in the same way: a singer sings a high C while communicating intense joy, and the teacher immediately rewards her with praise, which makes it more likely that she will do it again. But the person trying to change her own behavior must reinforce herself; the reward is never a surprise, and all the judgmental factors that stand between the act and its reward are also likely to intrude. The student/teacher always knows what the teacher/student is up to. As Pryor puts it, "This makes it awfully easy to say 'The heck with getting another star on my chart, I'd rather have a cigarette' " (p. 78).

Having discussed in some detail the factors that block the personal exercise process, and ways of bypassing, circumventing, or transcending those blocks, let us turn to the principles underlying effective exercise, or shaping. Shaping performance behavior is to take a small tendency in a useful direction and shift it, one step at a time, toward an ultimate purpose. Any time we practice something, from golf to dancing, from trying to be assertive to trying to eat less, from acting to singing, we are shaping or trying to shape our behavior in various ways.

In the case of the singer-actor the shaping process is remarkably complex, beyond any examples that Pryor gives; but the principles underlying the shaping process hold true for all shaping no matter how complex.

The Ten Laws of Shaping

Pryor has a list of The Ten Laws of Shaping, drawn from psychology laboratory experiments and from her own personal experience as a trainer. Adapted for our purposes, those laws might read as follows. After this brief listing, I will discuss the implications of each law for singer-actor training.

1. Let each new step in the learning process be small enough so that you are likely to succeed, and thus be reinforced.

2. Learn one thing at a time; don't try to take two steps simultaneously. (This will be an important rule for our work since our purpose is the shaping of three separate skills that are already entangled and must be unentangled even as we exercise them in isolation. At the same time that isolating capacity is being developed, we must also integrate them: they must be shaped as an efficient, synergistically working trio.)

3. Before moving to a new step, put the most recently learned step on a variable schedule of reinforcement. (We will clarify this concept later, but for the moment, we can note that simple repetition of what one has already learned—doing one's aria over and over in the same way—will lead to diminishing quality. It is useful instead to bring other elements into play—to make different musical, emotional, and physical choices—returning only occasionally to the well-practiced version. This will

empower and expand that choice beyond the practice of ordinary repetition.)

4. When taking a new step, don't worry about getting the old steps right. (Given the complexity of the singing-acting challenge, this is an important principle. For example, when working on a new exercise with the kinesthetic mode, don't try to simultaneously correct a lapse of behavior in either the facial or vocal modes.)

5. If you are a teacher, stay a step ahead of your student: If a new step is suddenly mastered, always have the next one ready. (Since the singer-actor is his own subject with respect to the exercise of his total process, a clear understanding of the whole process will always allow him to move to a new level of exercise when the current challenge is either mastered or blocked. Without a vision of the whole, however, a specific skill can become an end in itself with nowhere to go.)

6. Don't change teachers in midstep; any new step can have a new teacher, but only one teacher per step. (The singer-actor, by the nature of music-theater training, has several different teachers. Each of them is very likely to intrude upon the behavioral territory of another: the voice teacher may try to deal with the acting process or with musical interpretation; the coach may try to deal with the acting process, and the director may sometimes try to deal with singing or musical interpretation. This rule speaks to the heart of the training challenge; unintentional violation of it has led to the previously noted situation in which the finest professional singing-acting training programs in the country are robbing the young performers of their personal power. The practical effects of this "entangled-trainers" syndrome needs ongoing attention.)

7. If one approach to a new step is not working, try another; there are as many ways to learn a new step as there are teachers. (If one mode is stymied, go to another: draw upon the power of their capacity for synergistic interplay.)

8. Don't casually interrupt a learning session in mid-step; that's a punishment, not reinforcement. (While this is directed more at the trainer-trainee relationship, we will also examine the singer-actor's commitment to his private practice time. For example,

you wouldn't break off a voice lesson for a bite to eat, or to have an extended phone conversation; but does that same commitment apply to your *private* work with your total performing process?)

9. If learned steps fall apart and nothing is working, review all the steps leading up to that point. "Go back to kindergarten" and work your way up, reinforcing all the way. (We will discuss specific suggestions for the application of this law below.)

10. Finish each session with a success, if possible, but in any case quit while you're ahead. (This law is often violated by the performer who wants to get "just one more thing done" or who wants to make certain that he can repeat the breakthrough that just occurred.)

The Laws of Shaping Applied to the Singing-Acting Process

Let us now discuss each of these principles in greater detail, with specific reference to the singer-actor and the total performance process.

Law 1: Let Each New Step in the Learning Process Be Small Enough So That You Are Likely to Succeed

Given the immense complexity of singing-acting, it is easy to violate this principle by attempting to cover the journey of a thousand miles in a single (or several) giant steps. Instead, challenge yourself in ways that offer you a reasonable chance of succeeding (reinforcement). And do not demand that the individual steps be mastered immediately: if you have never worked with a specific exercise before, for example, have no expectations about whether you "should" be able to do it. Be easy on yourself. As a corollary to that, don't demand that you master a particular challenge within a certain time. Anything you do that blocks the possibility of success-reinforcement while exercising is not useful. Such a block may occur in trying to "solve" or master an exercise; but in working with singing-acting performance, no exercise process is ever "solved"—one merely moves to a new level of interaction within the total system.

If we do attempt to make the journey in a few gigantic leaps, we may lose our footing and miss the path altogether. A leap which is out of line will only take us further off course and set up the potential for an error-correction-error. Gradual, constant, persistent progress will move in the direction of our purpose of radiant performing more quickly than impatient leaping which may not only go off course, but may also have to be unlearned.

Law 2: Learn One Thing at a Time; Don't Try to Take Two Steps Simultaneously

This is a principle that, in my experience, is constantly violated in working with ourselves and others. The violation occurs because of the complexity of the singing-acting process. There are so many things to be learned, so many energy relationships involved, that we will often attempt to attend to several of them at the same time.

For example, in my initial work with the entanglement concept, I suggested ways of exercising that promoted the tendency of the performer to try to do two things at once. As we develop one mode — say the facial — by increasing the amount of energy moving through it, that increase will activate any entanglement with another mode — say the kinesthetic. This can lead to confusion as to which is the issue: the expansion of the facial mode, or the release of its entanglement with the kinesthetic mode. I have often said, "both," and it was not until I watched and heard students experiencing frustration at trying to do the two things at once that I understood that while both *are* the ultimate issue, they must be exercised separately. Performers would say, "I'm working so hard *not* to be entangled that I can't do anything more with the face!" Exercised simultaneously, the expansion and the release were canceling each other and heightening the judgmental quotient in the process.

Although I stress the importance of dropping judgment as we use the tool of awareness, judgment will assert itself if we try to do two things at once. You may get one of those two things "right" (the face may express more), but it automatically brings in something "wrong" (tension in the body), and if you are aware of it (and you *will* be if you are focused on the idea of dropping entanglements), the frustration will be inevitable: you will end up judging the whole process, feeling bad about the exercise, and avoiding it on any excuse.

Let us remind ourselves of the three steps in the exercise process: the step of changing the behavioral capacity of a mode (for example, increasing the capacity of the face to communicate); the second step of observing how that change interacts with the rest of the system (what happens to the kinesthetic and vocal modes as the facial behavior changes); and the third step of releasing anything that interferes with that interaction. It became clear that those steps needed to be separated for maximum efficiency of the exercise process and full realization of performer potential.

The Four-Step Spiral Exercise Process

It was out of this interaction between the needs of singer-actor development and Pryor's second law of shaping that I developed the four-step spiral exercise process. It has proved a profoundly useful tool for singer-actor training, and will be the basis for exercising all three modes in succeeding chapters. I introduce it here in its general form in the context of Pryor's second law of shaping. The four steps in the process are as follows.

1. Develop one of the modes by increasing its communicating energy.

2. Repeat the exercise. This time become aware of what happens in either or both of the other two modes as a result.

3. Repeat the exercise. This time select one of the unuseful interactions (entanglements) observed in step 2 for release or replacement.

4. Repeat the exercise. This time become aware of how the energy increase of step 1 is affected by the release of step 3. Return to step 1, adjusting the energy flow as desired, and repeat the sequence.

The spiral aspect of the process is evident: when you complete step 4 you return to step 1 at a higher point on the spiral of growth. Using a specific example, let us say that we are increasing the energy through the vocal mode by singing. That is step 1. Step 2 involves repeating step 1, with an awareness of what happens—for example, in the facial mode—as one does so. Perhaps the eyebrows lift each time one begins to sing regardless of the emotional content of the song. Having become aware of that entanglement, you move to step 3 and sing the passage again. This time you release the newly discovered entanglement, doing something with the eyebrows besides raising them. Step 4 involves repeating step 3, this time with awareness of how releasing the eyebrow entanglement affects the singing of step 1. In each step, it is essential to do only that step—train one thing at a time—with a non-judgmental awareness of the total process *to that point*. Do not, for example, anticipate step 3 as you do step 1.

Having completed the first four steps, one is ready to begin the second spiral of the process. Return to step 1, and make certain you are doing what you want to do with the vocal process. Having been through the process, steps 1 and 2 will start to become simultaneous events: even as you attend to the increased energy needs of the vocal mode, you will be aware of the eyebrow entanglement. As you do step 3, you will be aware of its effect on step 1. The four-step process becomes a two-step process. And finally, as the behavior around that particular entanglement is shaped, the four steps become one step. You have then learned to work with that part of the process and can begin shaping the next piece of behavior. When you have completed one four-step spiral process, the principle you have learned can then be applied to all learning processes—always proceeding one step at a time.

There is no rule as to how much time should be spent on any single step of the four-step spiral process. As you repeat step 1, you may remain on step 2 for several repetitions, each time generating more awareness of its effect on the other modes. Or, you may remain with step 1—for example, until you have learned a particularly difficult passage—before moving to step 2.

Similarly with step 3: you may want to practice releasing the entanglement a number of times (generating step-4 awareness as appropriate) before returning to step 1 at a higher point on the spiral. There is infinite flexibility in the four-step process—it can be adapted to anyone's learning speed. The important principle is to do one thing at a time—don't take on the burden of learning two skills simultaneously, for that simply slows down the growth process.

There are two special challenges involved in the four-step spiral process: (1) to experience the step you are on fully, *in the present*, before moving on to the next step, and (2) to become aware of what is happening in each step without allowing that awareness to turn into judgment. Once we become aware of a problem, there is always the tendency to take care of it immediately: we want it to be solved *right now*. And yet in developing the singing-acting process, trying to prematurely combine learning processes will seriously interfere with the speed, efficiency, and power of our development.

Drawing upon our juggling image, it would be ineffective and depressing to ask a person to juggle three objects at once the very first time he attempted it. That *is* the larger purpose, but the most effective movement toward that purpose may begin with the tossing and catching of only one object at a time. Just so with the singing-acting process. The larger purpose of total mastery and coordination of the three energy streams is always there; we will move with the greatest speed and efficiency in the direction of that purpose by taking the spiral path of adding single and specific additions from the unknown to our process.

The four-step spiral exercise process addresses two aspects of the entanglement condition: while our purpose always involves both the development of individual modes and their disentanglement, we cannnot disentangle them without first putting sufficient energy through one of them. This developmental increase of energy will then activate and reveal the entanglements, making them accessible to the performer. Unless we develop the power of the individual modes, we can't disentangle them; and we can only disentangle them when the entanglements are revealed through developmental exercise.

The corollary is true as well: we can't develop the maximum communicating power of any mode without disentangling it from the other two. The four-step spiral does both: it develops the individual mode in step 1, works with the disentanglement in step 3, and develops awareness of both parts of the total process in steps 2 and 4.

The process can also work within a single mode. If, for example, a particular facial behavior is blocked, one can divide that behavior into separate components, each of which can then be exercised and shaped apart from any interaction with the other two modes. Take the projection of anger: it will often be difficult to allow the face to communicate anger strongly until we isolate the various facial muscle groups that are part of an anger statement. The lowering of an eyebrow, independently of trying to actually feel or communicate anger, has proved to be the muscular twig in the logjam of blocked emotion. That would be step 1 in the four-step spiral process. Step 2 would be the awareness of the effect of that muscle movement on the inner processes and the rest of the facial musculature. Step 1 could then be practiced simultaneously with step 2, until one wished to move to step 3 and allow the inner emotional feeling to be the generator. Then one could add step-4 awareness of how doing that affected the outer musculature in expressing the inner. In the case of the lowered eyebrow, once that twig was removed, the emotion itself could flow more freely; further, removing the twig actually created the feeling of anger—which, in turn, made the person feel queasy for having finally allowed the forbidden external/internal to come into play after God knows how many years.

Until the individual components of the behavior have been isolated in this way, one is trying to learn two things at once: (1) to allow the feeling itself to happen, and (2) to also allow the expression of that feeling by the external musculature. And since inner feeling and outer expression may be entangled, a vicious circle of mutually reinforcing repression may be set up.

This explains the plateau phenomenon, in which we make no seeming progress in a skill no matter how much we practice it: we may be unconsciously working on two mutually canceling things at the same time. In the example just given, the more we feel the anger and try to express it, the more strongly the repression comes into play, blocking not only the expression but also our actual feeling of the emotion. If we divide the task into smaller parts and exercise them separately, it gets easier.

In addition we can ask whether the blocking within the mode is the result of its entanglement with the other modes. I have often seen a performer's face spring to life when an entanglement with the kinesthetic mode was released; in other cases, activating the face mode allowed a release within the kinesthetic mode when that had not been possible in itself. Both of these examples were regular occurrences prior to the development of the four-step spiral process. The understanding of their dynamic could have (and has) unfolded even more rapidly now that that process is available.

As we will see, the four-step spiral process can be applied to any developmental need. Additional applications and examples will be given as we proceed.

Law 3: Before Moving to a New Step, Put the Most Recently Learned Step on a Variable Schedule of Reinforcement

Law 3 is a particularly challenging idea to understand and apply. In Pryor's words, "It seems to be a peculiarly difficult concept for many people to accept intellectually." The concept itself is clear: once you have learned to do something with consistency, it is most useful to reinforce the behavior only occasionally, not a regular basis. Instead, one should reinforce learned behavior on an unpredictable, random basis. Such a variable schedule of reinforcement maintains behavior *far more* effectively than a predictable, everyday pattern.

This means, in practical exercise terms, that you don't go through the same exercise process every single day, exercising in the same way with the same exercises, *once you have learned the behavior involved.* Regular reinforcement—for example, doing the facial flex while singing—is important until you have actually learned that skill. That done, however, you need not, in fact *should not*, do it every day; doing it every so often, with different material, will ensure the retention of the capacity far more than daily repetition. We have discussed the workaholic, perpetual-repetition end of the practice spectrum; Pryor clarifies the nature of the error of being stuck there.

It may be our insecurities around challenging skills, and the judgment we bring to bear on them, that make it difficult for us to accept this principle. But if we know that overrepetition will tend to *diminish* the skill of a behavior once that skill is learned, it may motivate us to practice variable reinforcement. This is not to downgrade the intensity of effort that may be required to learn something even for the most highly skilled—Allan Jay Lerner's recollection of Fred Astaire working on a few bars of music for three or four days is one example among many—but rather to focus on the process of keeping a skill alive and growing once it is learned.

We can also note that repeated praise diminishes in its reinforcing effect over a period of time. If you praise a person continually for the same behavior, what began as reinforcement will become boring repetition; the energy that might have gone into the behavior to elicit the praise may unconsciously diminish when the reinforcement becomes, if not tedious, at least not worth the effort.

To be the most useful and productive, exercise should be as stimulating and interesting as possible; that is part of its reinforcing power. It is often necessary, of course, to do exercises that quickly become tedious, difficult, and distinctly unexciting. Exercises that are fun, stimulating, or playful and that celebrate our process are easier to deal with. But any exercise can offer us that possibility of celebration. Those that are repeated over and over need not be tedious, but *can* be experienced for the first time, *can* be celebratory and therefore more useful to us. It depends upon developing the capacity to transcend the potential boredom of repetition.

If we have learned what a particular exercise has to offer us, then there is an opportunity to lift it (and ourselves) to a higher point on the spiral, adding new and different twists to it from a previously unused part of our total system. For example, a new mental or emotional energy can be added to an existing vocal exercise—transforming the exercise (and ourselves) in doing so. We can then return occasionally to a reexperiencing of the exercise in its simpler form.

We must also distinguish between the two kinds of exercise: there is the exercise of learning to do something—sing a particular passage or master a specific gesture; and there is the exercise whose purpose is the development of our instrument for its own sake. The exercise of learning something tends to fall into the area of product orientation—getting something "right" for someone else's approval; the exercise of personal development, on the other hand, is more difficult for MIM to define in immediate product terms, and can thus be the kind of exercise we neglect. To some extent, of course, we do the two simultaneously, for learning to do something automatically develops our performing capacity in some way—whether positively or negatively—and we generally use material we know in exercising our instrument, and come to know that material more fully in doing so.

We can apply the four-step spiral process to this integration of doing and development. In step 1, for example, we learn a specific song and attempt to fulfill its musical and stylistic potential (with or without the guidance of a coach); in step 2, we become aware of how that song and its demands challenge the other capacities—emotional or physical—of our total instrument; in step 3, we focus on development of one aspect of those capacities; in step 4, we become aware of how that focus affects the musical and stylistic requirements of step 1. We then return to step 1 at a higher point on the spiral of growth: we are newly aware of the interaction of our total instrument with the needs of the song and, using that awareness, can begin the process of coordinating and integrating it into our total performance, spending as much time as needed on any single step.

We could also develop a new four-step spiral with any one of the aspects of step 3 as follows. If in step 3 we chose to work on greater emotional projection, that could be thought of as a new step 1. In that step we would increase the level of facial-emotional communication. As we repeated that increase in step 2, we could become aware of how it affected the body or the voice. In step 3, we would choose one of those relationships to release or alter in some way, and so on, continuing the spiral as desired.

As the spiral process continues, we always obey the basic principle of learning one thing at a time—working on combinations only when one part of the combination has been learned sufficiently to do so. The sufficiency of learning necessary before combining steps will depend upon the individual: any feeling of frustration in working with a problem suggests that it is too early, and it would be useful to stabilize one part of the combination—e.g., make sure you sing the passage with some degree of accuracy before adding a facial or physical challenge.

Law 4: When Taking a New Step,
Don't Worry About Getting the Old Steps Right

This principle interacts with the second law; train one thing at a time. In working with the four-step spiral process we have said, don't try to do steps 1 and 3 at the same time. For example, in step 1, as you increase the facial energy, don't try to simultaneously release the entanglement which that creates with the kinesthetic; and in step 3, don't demand that the face continue the level of emotional communication it had attained in step 1 as you attend to the release of the kinesthetic entanglement.

Once again we see the complexity of the singing-acting exercise process: to work with the entanglement in question (number 4, FM/KM), it must be activated by increasing the energy flow through the face. The facial-emotional capacity, in turn, can only be developed by activating it with sufficient energy to bring the entanglement into awareness. You can't develop one part of the process without involving the other.

Most of us seem to have a deep-seated insecurity that we will forget something we have learned. As Pryor puts it, however, "What is once learned is not forgotten, but under the pressure of assimilating new criteria, old well-learned behavior sometimes falls apart temporarily." She then recounts a situation familiar to anyone who has gone through the music-theater rehearsal and production process.

> I once saw a conductor, during the first dress rehearsal of an
> opera, having a tantrum because the singers in the chorus were
> making one musical mistake after another; they seemed virtually
> to have forgotten all their hard-learned vocal accomplishments.
> But they were, for the first time, wearing heavy costumes,
> standing on ladders, being required to move as they sang: Getting
> used to new criteria temporarily interfered with previously learned
> behavior. By the end of the rehearsal, the musical learning
> reappeared, without coaching. (p. 59)

This syndrome is another factor in the loss of personal power in singer-actor training programs. The singer learns something—say, in an acting class—that is to be incorporated into her singing performance; at the next singing lesson or musical coaching she attempts to integrate that bit of acting behavior with what she is being told to do with the music. She cannot do it the first time—how illogical to expect that she *should* be able to. But the teacher or coach, who has no way of knowing what the singer is trying to do, focuses on the negative effect the behavior has on the music, and corrects the singer from that partial view. Without a total perspective from which to work, the singer then throws out the integrative baby with the acting-lesson bath—and does similarly when returning to the acting process. This time, however, the integrative baby, being somewhat bruised from the previous dumping, may suffer mortal injury when being dumped out with the musical bath.

Even if the singer attempts to explain, the concept of integrating a new behavior into the total process through practice — with some kind of modified four-step spiral process — is generally foreign to the teaching process. Instead, the teacher will often say, in effect, "That's fine, but don't work on it now — just get the music (or the acting, or the vocal technique, or the posture, or movement, or whatever) right." And the same reinforcement of fragmentation — and death of the integrating process — will take place.

To repeat: this is not to blame anyone for this well-documented sequence of teaching and behavioral events. Without a clear awareness of the whole performing process, and an aesthetic with which to integrate its parts, it is only logical that each part-specialist will ask the performer to dump any new piece of unintegrated and seemingly harmful behavior.

However, in the case of the conductor in Pryor's story, there is far less rationale. All of us involved in music-theater production know — or can at least accept the fact — that everything always seems to go to hell when a new element is added to the rehearsal process. We also know that that hellish condition is not permanent — nohing has really been forgotten. After the new challenge has been assimilated — whether it be costumes, sets, choreography, a new environment of any kind, new blocking, or the addition of the orchestra itself — the old learning will reassert itself. In our eagerness or anxiety about the final product, those of us guiding the process may interfere with that assimilative, reassertive sequence. We may try to force it to unfold more quickly with judgmental intensity or harsh criticism. But, as Pryor suggests, to beat up on yourself or anyone else for making mistakes in already learned skills while performing under new circumstances is simply bad training. The mistakes will usually clear up of their own accord without further attention, but calling attention to them through berating tactics will often make them more difficult to correct.

The more harshly we judge ourselves in trying to prematurely combine steps 1 and 3 in the four-step spiral processs, the less likely that we will be able to accomplish what it is we are trying to do. Even though we have learned step 1, that behavior will probably deteriorate momentarily as we focus on step 3; the same is true of step 3 as we focus on step 1. Awareness will create the change in behavior, and full acceptance of our process, whatever its level of attainment, will allow awareness to accomplish its purpose with maximum power.

Law 5: If You Are a Teacher, Stay a Step Ahead of Your Student

While this law of shaping is specifically directed at teachers, it also has application to the singer-actor who is shaping himself. Without denying the
first law of shaping—which says, in effect, don't overchallenge yourself beyond the possibility of reinforcement—it is occasionaly useful to give yourself the opportunity to perform in a way that is beyond what you imagine
you can do. Singing-acting is so complex a task, and so difficult to define,
that you cannot always know what you can accomplish by moving into the
unknown. You may think you are doing all you can do with your song, and
yet you are not getting the response—either from yourself or others—that
you feel is possible. And you (or MIM) may literally not know what to do
next. In other words, you feel in the position of not being ahead of yourself
as a subject.

The anxiety energy of not knowing what to do next may then be focused
on sheer repetition, thus putting the third law of shaping at risk. You may in
fact be reducing the effectiveness of your performance by simply repeating
it. So, what *does* one do next?

While there is *always* something to do next, it may be unknown to us—
and we will tend to resist moving into the unknown. And that is an important part of our exercise process: to develop our intuitive freedom to do
something different—something unknown—without MIM knowing in advance what it will mean. We can develop our capacity to open to PIM (our
playful, imaginative, intuitive mode) and come to know that the whole (including PIM and HOBS) always has answers the individual parts would not
have thought of; we only need to open to the whole to allow our process to
unfold when we get to "stuck" places. For example, simply playing with
your song—physically, emotionally, or musically—can open up new possibilities.

The total view of the performance process provided by the projective-
modes concept allows anyone any time to find new approaches, new opportunities for expansion with any song, soliloquy, or scene, no matter how often they may have performed it. In the chapters dealing with the exercise of
the three modes, as well as in chapter 13 and 14, we will explore these approaches in greater detail. They are there to allow you to be ahead of and
with yourself simultaneously at all times, and to provide you with a view of
your purpose that allows you continual expansion of your process.

Such opportunities for expansion also allow you to overcome one of the
deepest conditionings of our educational system, which says: do just enough

to get by. As Pryor puts it, "Our whole school system seems to be set up to prevent children from learning at their own rate—to penalize not only the slow learners, who don't get the time to learn, but the fast learners, who don't get additional reinforcement when quick thinking moves them ahead" (p. 60).

In *The C Zone*, Robert and Marilyn Kriegel point out the importance in achieving peak performance of finding the "comfort zone" in which to challenge oneself. Above the comfort zone is the panic zone, where one is overchallenged, and peak performance is stifled; beneath it is the drone zone, where underchallenging fails to stimulate the greatest possible development. To paraphrase Polonius: Neither an overchallenger nor an underchallenger be, but this above all, to your own process be true, and it must follow as the night the day, you cannot be false to any performing circumstance. By being aware of both ends of the spectrum of challenge and opportunity, we can move about on it according to the needs of our own processes.

Law 6: Don't Change Trainers in Midstream

Since, as suggested above, singer-actors have little control over the number of trainers interacting with their total process, the importance of having a view of that process that allows them to do the integrating on their own becomes increasingly important. This book is about some universal principles that, if clearly understood, can help us guide our total process. If they are understood, we can amend the sixth law of shaping to read: Don't change principles in midstream. Once you have an understanding of the whole performing process, and the way in which the parts of that process are developed and interrelate in the context of the whole, you may use that understanding as a guide. Follow the instructions, experience the process, and interact with yourself and others in doing so. The principles that support and guide that process will allow you to develop in the direction of a larger purpose—whether it is fulfilled performing potential or radiant performing. Purpose, as we have seen, is one of those principles in itself, freeing one from overstress on short-term goals and the judgment potential surrounding them.

Law 7: If One Shaping Procedure Is Not Eliciting Progress, Try Another

Rather than hurling oneself against the same issue over and over, shift tactics. If there is a stuck place involving the voice, go to the facial or kinesthetic mode. This can be a valuable tool for performers working with themselves, as well as for teachers and coaches. One or two examples will clarify the process.

A coach who was familiar with the performing power technique told me of a singer with whom we both had worked who seemed to be simply unmusical. No matter how clearly the coach described what she wanted, the singer was unresponsive. Since both the coach and I knew the singer was a kinesthetic dominant who loved working with her body, this offered a way of communicating more fully with her. I suggested that the coach ask the singer to translate the musicality requests into kinesthetic terms and do them with her body first. The next step would be to ask her to translate back again, from the kinesthetic to the musical. The next time I saw the coach I asked her how this approach worked. "Perfectly," she replied. "She could do exactly what I asked her for musically once she had physicalized it. She's more musical than I would have guessed."

This approach was used consistently by the late Eloise Ristad (although not in the context of the projective-modes system as a whole). It is a useful approach for those whose kinesthetic needs are strong and who understand best through physical experience. It is not the only approach, however, and may be as ineffectual for singers of a different dominance as the hearing-mode approach was for the kinesthetic singer in our example.

I am a kinesthetic dominant and like very much to demonstrate physically concepts I want singers to work with. But I have become increasingly alert to the necessity for the use of the other modes in communicating. In working on a scene with a young tenor, I found myself demonstrating physically the sort of thing I was after (I never ask for exact duplication—it is simply the clearest and most efficient nonverbal way for me to communicate a complicated piece of action). The other singer in the scene was very responsive to this approach, but the tenor seemed unable to understand what I was trying to communicate and was unable to do it in several attempts. Moreover, he did not watch me as I was demonstrating. He was not being rude; he was very cooperative and willing, he just wasn't watching. Realizing in the moment that he was a hearing-mode dominant, I went to my table, sat down with the score and began to *tell* him, as clearly and precisely as I could, without any physical accompaniment, what I wanted him to do. He not only listened, he followed me to the table and *watched me intently* as I told him what to do. And, sure enough, he was able to do it without a flaw the first time after *hearing* about it.

This is reminiscent of those grade-schoolers who are dunces in third grade and geniuses in fourth, all on the basis of appropriate or inappropriate mode match-ups. The point here is that we may be practicing mode mismatches on ourselves. We may be using the same kind of mode communication over and over without success, rather than using the mode we favor. However, we can learn to take other approaches with our own system, just as in the preceding examples. When we experience a vocal block, we can try a new emotional approach, or a new kinesthetic approach, or both. We can focus on the face as well as the body; or, if the block is emotional, focus on the voice or the body; or, if the block is kinesthetic, focus on the face or the voice, or on shifting the energy within the kinesthetic mode itself.

Similarly, if one four-step spiral process is jammed, try another one. As we will see, there are a remarkable number of branches this process can take. The important thing is that we take one branch, work on one opportunity for expansion at a time, generating awareness with respect to that single issue before moving to combinations.

Law 8: Don't Interrupt a Training Session Gratuitously; That Constitutes a Punishment

Stopping *any* process is a negative act, even though it may be to realign a negative use of energy. A process is always unfolding, and to stop it to analyze it is a way of momentarily killing it. For performers working with themselves, this law translates as follows: Don't interrupt the positive support of your own process with judgmental recriminations; maintain the most supportive energy field possible for the duration of your exercise session. If you constantly judge yourself during an exercise session, it is not a punishment to interrupt the session — it is a reward, thus turning the eighth law of shaping on its head. If we create an unpleasant context for our exercise process, it is a sufficient reason to avoid exercising in the first place. Don't interrupt the generation of awareness by turning it into judgment. Awareness ceases when judgment comes into play. Awareness is in the present, judgment can only live in the past and the future.

A positive way of using the "punishment" aspect of this law is to remove attention from a recalcitrant part of the process. Pryor points out that one of the few ways one can say no! or wrong! to a dolphin is to remove one's attention by, for example, picking up the fish bucket and walking away for a minute. Similarly, in working with an entanglement that will not release, or a technique that will not stabilize, or a coordination that will not come together, it can be useful to simply remove attention from it for a while. Whether it is the learning-to-skate-in-the-summer principle, or whether the part-problem in question actually feels neglected and wants to regain attention, removal of attention will often be helpful in releasing the blockage. In any case, "removal of attention is a powerful tool, so don't use it carelessly or unfairly" (Pryor, p. 64). And do not make removal of attention a judgmental reprimand of yourself—simply remove the attention.

Law 9: If Learned Steps Fall Apart and Nothing Is Working, Review All the Steps Leading Up to That Point

Return to the basics, proceeding one step at a time. Apply the four-step spiral process, taking care that each step is a separate one. You may have begun adding unconscious and unnecessary complications to the process, or you may have omitted some essential ingredient. Give special attention to the awareness of steps 2 and 4: allow them to be simple observations of what is happening without judgment.

Law 10: Quit While You're Ahead

It isn't how long you work, or when you stop: the important thing is the quality of the last thing that happened when you stopped. You will tend to pick up in the next session where you left off in the last. So you should *always* stop on a high point or at the very least, quit while you are ahead. This applies to the parts of a practice session as well as the whole. In moving from a vocal step to an emotional step to a physical step, make the moves after a successful effort in each step. Similarly when working with relationships between the modes: move from practicing a release from a facial/physical entanglement at a moment of success.

We may have an intuitive sense that the last behavior is the one that will stick with us, so we often keep trying to make it just a little bit better. But what often happens is that we make a breakthrough—perhaps we can suddenly sing a passage that has eluded us—and we are so excited we want to do it again and again. We repeat it, and, inevitably, one of the repetitions won't be as good, which will make us anxious; the next repetition will be worse, the downward spiral continues and the practice session has not only been wasted, it may even have been counterproductive.

An important point here is that what psychologists call "latent learning" (what we have called learning to skate in the summer) is facilitated by the last behavior prior to the latent learning period. If you end on a good response, the first attempt in the next session will be "not only as good as the last one of the previous session but noticeably better" (p. 65). If our anxiety about whether we really have the behavior under control drives us to try it just one more time to make sure, and that one more time leads to deterioration of the behavior, our mistrust will turn into a self-fulfilling prophecy: it wasn't as good and it *won't* be as good next time around.

While all of the ten laws of shaping have significance for the singing-acting process, laws 2 and 4—learn one thing at a time, and relax old standards when incorporating new behavior—are the most telling. They address most directly the complexity of the singing-acting process, and are the basis for the four-step spiral exercise process. There are so many interrelated skills involved in singing-acting that no single approach can answer all its needs; yet each of them must be served fully. At the same time, the variety of needs can easily interfere with each other. Thus the importance of both ends of the spectrum: do one thing at a time, *and* attend to the interrelationship of those things.

The 25-Positions Concept: Training for Flexibility

There is a related exercise process, developed prior to the four-step spiral, which I call the 25-positions concept. It is a way of systematically approaching the exercise process for teachers as well as for performers exercising privately. I first presented that concept to a NATS (National Association of Teachers of Singing) convention and have since expanded it to cover all phases of the exercise process.

As I said then, most singers learn to sing while maintaining some sort of "correct" postural set—a habit sometimes encouraged by the teacher, sometimes learned unconsciously as a form of the anticipatory entanglement. This stance—which is remarkably similar from singer to singer—is relatively formal and is used virtually every time they perform in a recital context. And while it is only appropriate for a limited number of singing-acting situations, it is a physical set that the singer most commonly associates with the act of singing. But it is not so much the careful, held nature of the stance that is significant; it is the fact that it tends to be the singer's only choice—at least the only choice he practices with his teachers. Yet when performers go on stage they will be asked to adopt many other physical ways of being, and will have to learn a whole new coordination of the singing process with those new and varied physical characterizations. In many cases singers will be unconsciously (or consciously) resistant to those requests for changes in the habit-conditionings they have learned so well in the voice lessons.

Having often experienced this unconscious and generally unintentional resistance in working with singers, it occurred to me that it would be very useful if, during voice lessons, the teachers were to have the singers adopt a different sort of stance, posture, or character set every ten minutes or so — now in a slump, now with one foot up on a chair, now leaning against the piano, now seated casually, now standing in the usual way. The teachers would be fulfilling a vital aspect of their basic function, which is to help the singer sing efficiently, powerfully, effectively, and freely from *whatever* posture may be called for by the dramatic situation.

The number 25 is, of course, arbitrary — it could be 5 or 125 positions; the important thing is to expand the singer's freedom and capacity for choice. With that newly acquired freedom of choice, the singer would be equipped to go into any rehearsal and fulfill both musical and dramatic requirements in a coordinated and synergistic fashion. The power of the performer expands proportionately to the scope of the field of choice potential, and the voice teacher can help the performer expand that field with respect to the body (or the face — see below), as well as the voice. The truly significant thing is that with the 25-positions concept this can be done without special knowledge of or expertise in the other modes: the voice teacher need not be an expert in acting or movement or even in musical interpretation.

The same is true of all other aspects of the exercise process. Anyone teaching any part of the total performance process can apply the 25-positions concept to their own or to other parts of that process. For example, the 25 emotions: here the singer-actor would sing the aria several times with a different set of emotional combinations each time. The 25 gestures would involve aria repetition with a different set of gestures each time. For the coaching process it would mean 25 interpretations.

The coaching process, in fact, seems the most pragmatic of all the 25-positions applications. It has always seemed odd to me that while every conductor will have a different interpretation, the singer is usually trained very carefully in only one (the one the coach in question happens to favor). When the singer goes to work with Conductor X (who happens to have an interpretation totally at odds with the singer's preparation), a radical adjustment of some kind will have to be made, thus wasting energy (or worse) for the singer, the conductor, or both. All sorts of judgmental, defensive, power-draining interactions can (and do) result from such situations.

How much more useful it would be, it seemed to me, if coaches were to train singers in several different interpretations—a Muti version, a Mehta version, a Marriner version, an Ozawa version, and so on—helping the singer fulfill each of those versions completely with a sense of total commitment and understanding. The singer would then be prepared to go to any conductor with the flexibility to do whatever was asked with full freedom and power. The singer would also come to a deeper understanding of what interpretation can be when one's personal worth is not associated with a single, "correct" interpretation.

It was only in July of 1987 that the application of the 25 positions to the vocal mode in the coaching process become an exciting reality. In chapter 12, "Exercising the Vocal Mode," I will describe in detail the workings of that process. For the moment, let us examine the interaction of the 25-positions concept with the four-step spiral process.

Combining the Four-Step Spiral Exercise Process and the 25-Positions Concept

Each time one takes a new "position"—whether that means an unusual physical state, an unaccustomed emotional state, or a new musical interpretation—one is taking step 1 on the four-step spiral process: one is changing the energy output through some part of the projective mode system. That change will interact with the total system in new ways, some of which will be useful, others not. It is a move into the unknown. And that is the point at which one can either grow or return to the known. If one demands that the new energy statement "work" the first time, without making any adjustments or working with the process, then one will return to the known and remain there. But if one proceeds to step 2, and becomes aware of what happens to the rest of the system as step 1 is initiated, one has choice. One can then move to step 3 and select one of the unuseful changes that accompanied the new choice and release it, even while reinitiating the new choice.

Perhaps the new position is to slump down in a chair while singing the aria; that posture may have created an unuseful constriction in the breathing process and some lack of body in the vocal sound. In step 3 the slump would then be repeated, but this time one would make adjustments within the slumped posture to free the breathing process without giving up the basic statement of the slump itself. It might be necessary to repeat step 3 several times to attain what one desired with the vocal and breathing processes. Step 4 would generate the awareness of how much had been lost from the physical characterization of the slump itself. One could then return to step 1 and renew the "power" of the slump statement, only this time from a higher point on the spiral of growth. The adjustments necessary to an effective breathing and vocal process would then be on a new level of awareness — and step 3 would begin to be integrated with step 1 through the awareness generated by steps 2 and 4.

The same process can be followed with every one of the "25" positions — physical, emotional, or musical. The important thing is to create the new circumstances to be learned by moving into the unknown in the first place.

We can also consider the 25-positions approach to exercise within the context of full-spectrum experience. Any process — vocal, physical, facial, mental, or emotional — takes place within a spectrum defined by the extremes involving that process. For example, the process of speaking a text can be fast or slow, high or low, loud or soft, legato or staccato, or anywhere along the various spectra defined by any of those extremes. However, the range of actual, practiced choices available to performers along any given spectrum is likely to be limited. Along the spectrum of tension and relaxation, for example, most singers select a point somewhere between the two (usually closer to the tension end) and tend to remain in a relatively narrow zone of choice. That is the voice lesson position, discussed above. All the other choices along that spectrum are unknown. Since, as we have seen, all learning and growth involves movement into the unknown, the singer needs to exercise and develop other choices along that spectrum (as well as many other spectrums of energy use).

Let us call this the 25 *choices* concept — the number continuing to be arbitrary — with every spectrum seen as enfolding 25 choices of styles or states of being. The capacity to make any of the 25 choices depends upon moving into the unknown — into the field of choice potential — and exercising there with some of the infinite number of possibilities.

Further Combinations: Adding the Full-Spectrum Concept and the Spiral of Expansion

If we combine the ideas of the full-spectrum 25 positions with the spiral of expansion, and the four-step spiral process, we have the circle of the known with the unknown lying outside it, and the spiral of expansion moving from one to the other.

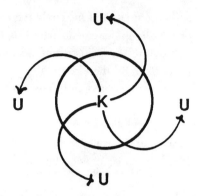

We also have the 25-positions, full-spectrum concept. We will use a style spectrum—realistic to abstract—for the purpose of illustration.

REALISTIC   ABSTRACT

And we have the four-step spiral exercise process:

1. Increased energy statement and reinforcement of process

2. Awareness of entanglement and reinforcement of process

3. Release of entanglement and/or modification of energy as statement is repeated, and reinforcement of process

4. Awareness of the effect of step 3 on step 1 and reinforcement

If we lay the spectrum on the known-unknown circle, part of the spectrum will be in the known, part in the unknown.

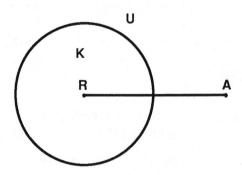

Add the spiral of expansion as the performer moves from the known province of the realistic to something more abstract or unusual in its style. That will constitute step 1 and step 2 of the four-step spiral process.

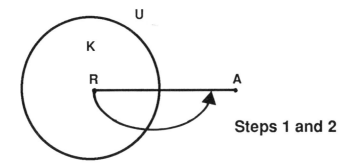

Steps 1 and 2

Step 2 could involve awareness of tensions or holds that often accompany moves into stylization or abstraction, and that keep such statements from seeming *areba*. Step 3 would then be a move back toward the realistic known in releasing the tension holds that block it.

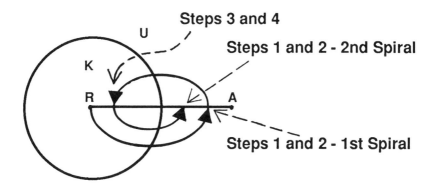

Steps 3 and 4
Steps 1 and 2 - 2nd Spiral
Steps 1 and 2 - 1st Spiral

Step 4 would occur at the same point and involve awareness of how much stylized energy was lost from the original step 1. The spiral would then continue to step 1 on a higher level, repeating the total process until a new integration of the two ends of the spectrum was achieved.

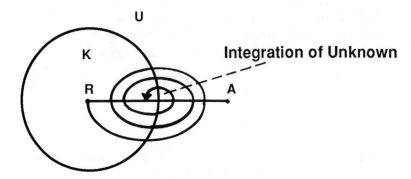

If this process is repeated with a series of spectra, the circle of the known expands in turn.

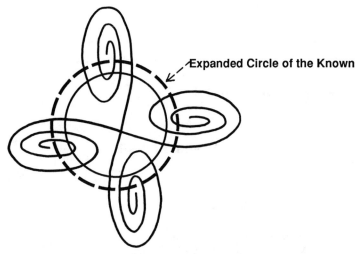

At this point we are ready to begin applying this universal exercise concept to the projective modes themselves. We only need to bring Pryor's four "good fairies" into the process to create an exercise environment as supportive as possible.

The Good Fairies: Four Positive Methods of Reinforcement

In the last chapter we examined Pryor's "bad fairies," the negative methods of reinforcement. While some of those techniques are useful on occasion, I separate them from the "good fairies" to place even greater emphasis on the importance of working with positive methods of reinforcement. In continuing order, the good fairy methods for changing unwanted behavior are as follows.

> Method 5. Train an incompatible behavior. (This method, Pryor says, is especially useful for performers.)
>
> Method 6. Put the behavior on cue. (Then never give the cue.)
>
> Method 7. "Shape the absence"; reinforce anything and everything that is *not* the undesired behavior.
>
> Method 8. Change the motivation. (Pryor calls this "the fundamental and most kindly method of all.")

Method 5: The First Good Fairy

This method simply means learning to do something else that doesn't allow simultaneous performance of the unwanted behavior. The 25-positions approach is a version of this method. For example, if every time you get up to sing, you induce a state of slight tension of which you are unaware (the anticipatory entanglement), that is the behavior to be changed. Slumping, sitting, kneeling, leaning back against the piano, having one leg up on a chair, and so on, are all incompatible with the anticipatory holding pattern. Thus each of those positions presents not a new "position" to be learned, but rather a way of releasing an unwanted learned behavior. Instead of replacing one behavior with another—a slump as such may not be preferable to an anticipatory entanglement—we are altering and freeing the state of being that underlies them all. This will allow all the behaviors involved to function more freely.

There is a striking example of the use of incompatible behavior by pianist Glenn Gould to solve a technical challenge in preparing for a concert. It was his practice not to re-work pieces he had already learned until a week or so before the performance. On this occasion, however, one of the pieces he was to play had a technical problem in a passage for the right hand, which he had never solved. He had forgotten this when he scheduled the piece, and now, with less than a week to go, the problem got worse the more he worked on it. He finally hit upon a solution: since the left hand was simultaneously playing a very simple arpeggio pattern, he concentrated on playing that simple pattern *unmusically*. For an intuitive musician of his genius, that took every bit of his concentration. And as he did so, the right hand accomplished its hitherto impossible task with consummate ease!

There are many lessons here, including the concept that removing *mental* involvement from a problem will often allow it to be solved by the intuitive knowing of the non-mental parts — in this case, the pianist's kinesthetic mode, specifically the right hand. The incompatible behavior in this case was practiced by the left hand, a part of the whole process, and also involved Gould's innate musicianship. Gould might also have used the technique with the right hand, playing the passage even more incorrectly, playing with a full spectrum of possible choices, all incompatible with the existing technical error. One of these choices would become the right one — or at least one which was preferable to the habitual error.

This particular method will be used extensively as we exercise the individual modes. It is one of the fundamental means of replacing inappropriate, unuseful behavior — and entanglements are certainly that. Training an incompatible behavior is also useful in modifying one's personal behavior, which is the essence of actually doing the performance practice process. It is useful as well in working with emotions, particularly the negative spectrum. Find a behavior that is incompatible with your emotional state, and throw yourself into it. Feeling self-pity, anxiety, grief, loneliness? Go for a run, sing in a choir, do some volunteer work with people who are truly burdened, join a support group (there is now one for virtually any emotional malady), clean house (literally and figuratively), or play any kind of game you can. Method 5 may hold an antidote for whatever ails you emotionally as a person or as a performer.

Method 6: The Second Good Fairy

Method 6 is seldom used in the singer-actor training context. If a specific behavior comes into play only on a specific cue, that behavior will tend to extinguish if the cue is never given. Thus, if there is a behavior you want to get rid of, put the behavior under the control of a cue, and then never give the cue.

A version of this method that I have found useful is to increase the intensity of the entanglement rather than trying to get rid of it: get familiar with it, bring it to a more conscious level of awareness, play with it, create a full spectrum of choices around it, thus transforming the entanglement itself into one of those choices; then never make that choice.

Part of the challenge in dealing with entanglements is that we are not conscious of how they function. In many cases, we have subtly disguised them, albeit unconsciously, so that they are unobtrusive. We unconsciously modify the amount of emotion we show on the face so that the tension entanglement with the body is not noticed or is unconsciously incorporated as an essential part of the statement. It is very difficult to drop or eliminate something of which you are not aware. Increasing the level of the entanglement—the tension in the body—or increasing the energy through the mode—in this case, the face—which brings the entanglement into play, is a way of recognizing that the entanglement behavior *is* on cue. The next step is to become aware of what the cue is. In the case of entanglement 4 it is the inappropriate relationship between the face—which is actually sending the message—and the body, which insists on coming into play regardless of the performer's wishes. The cuing of this behavior is usually on an unconscious level: it is a conditioning that long ago became an unconscious habit. By raising it to the level of awareness, and not only allowing it, but encouraging it, we begin to replace the original unconscious cuing with conscious cuing. Once we have done that, we need never cue it unless we wish to.

As another example, suppose you have a problem singing flat. No singer that I know of *tries* to sing flat—it happens for unconscious reasons (which may include physical tension or faulty technique). But instead of trying *not* to sing flat, do so intentionally, varying the pitch consciously—more flat, less flat, sharp, and so on—until you acquire genuine choice in the matter, and have replaced the unconscious cuing with conscious choice. (In the process you may also get in touch with the physical tension or faulty technique that was the original unconscious cause.)

Working with entanglements in this manner is also a way of accepting them, of honoring their origin, which was probably something the system thought necessary at the time: "I mustn't cry or Daddy will get angry"—ergo, I repress the crying impulse with physical tension. By allowing them to come into play, encouraging them and playing with them in various ways, they lose their guilt-making identity as nasty habits that you want to conceal, and become available for release.

Method 7: The Third Good Fairy

Method 7, shaping the absence of the behavior, has very direct application to the exercise process. It is specifically oriented to not-doing rather than doing. In this respect it is part of step 3 of the four-step spiral process. Step 1 is the doing step, step 2 is the awareness of what you add to that doing that you wish you didn't, and step 3 is the not-doing of the unwanted addition (even while continuing the doing of step 1).

Using method 7 sometimes "takes some conscious effort over a period of time, but is often the best way to change deeply ingrained behavior" (Pryor, p. 142). One of the most significant aspects of method 7 for us is to focus on praising anything that replaces the unwanted behavior rather than condemning the unuseful habit. One of the reasons for the four-step spiral process was the recognition that almost all the performers working with the entanglement concept were judging their entanglements. They were trying to do steps 1 and 3 simultaneously, and as a result were doing neither. With the emphasis of method 7, we do step 1 all by itself; we then praise the new energy of the process, and do not condemn any entanglements that may appear. When, in steps 2 and 3, we turn our awareness to the entanglements activated by the step-1 process, we continue our nonjudgmental approach. Rather than criticize any entanglement tension that may remain—and there will probably be some—we praise any release at all, no matter how small, concentrating on positive reinforcement rather than focusing on what was not accomplished.

We can make praise a significant part of steps 2 and 4 as well. After completing step 1, the awareness of step 2 can include self-praise for whatever energy increase was accomplished in the first step. Similarly with step 4. Along with the awareness of what was released and what remains, a few words spoken out loud in praise of your release can be as important as anything else you may do.

Method 8: The Fourth Good Fairy

The final positive method is to change the behavior by changing the motivation for the behavior. This "is often the kindliest and most effective method of all. The person who has enough to eat is not going to steal a loaf of bread" (Pryor, p. 145).

In the case of entanglement behavior, we often don't know what the motivation is: it is an unconsciously conditioned program that we simply act out. This is one reason for our extended analysis of the human energy system and the demands the singing-acting process places upon it: unless we understand that our human energies are conditioned in ways that put it at odds with the demands of singing-acting, we have little motivation for changing it. Once we learn that the reasons for our entanglements have to do with repressing energy, with creating a "good impression," with controlling ourselves, with being "nice," with being approved by an outside authority, and myriad other repressive and controlling functions, we can replace those motivations with more appropriate ones. We can find a more useful and expansive purpose for singing-acting. We can do it as play, for fun, for the expansion of our self-awareness, for its own sake, for no reason at all.

We can also draw upon methods 5 and 7. We can practice not acting in conditioned ways that are no longer appropriate to present circumstances. As we sing and act, we can behave as though we don't care, as though we are having fun, as though we are playing, as though we feel good about ourselves (by self-praising), as though we are enthusiastic about our skills, as though we love ourselves, as though performing is a joy, as though we enjoy receiving comments on our performance, and, even, as though we are unentangled. We can create a feedback loop between our outer behavior and our inner motivation. We can work on the motivation, the behavior, or both, allowing each of them to reinforce the other in the ways we choose. We will pursue this topic at greater length in the next chapter, exercising the facial mode. And with these exercise guidelines, we are prepared to do just that.

Chapter 9

The Facial-Emotional Complex I: Exercising the Outer

The Continuing Expansion of the Facial-Emotional Complex

When I was writing *Performing Power*, the concept of the facial-emotional mode (now seen in three parts as the facial-emotional complex) was in process. The flood of new discoveries about its functioning and how it interacted with the other two modes was remarkable. Not a class or coaching situation went by that didn't reveal some new facet of the concept. As I rewrote the final manuscript copy at that time I said, "Because (the facial-emotional mode) has been the most sacrosanct mode, it has the greatest potential for exploration and discovery. It is virgin territory that has never been

214

adequately examined from the performing point of view. As a result, new findings continue to emerge . . . [and] . . . this discussion is necessarily open-ended in its conclusions. It will reflect most clearly the process orientation of the search" (p. 142). Since that process of discovery continues to unfold, I will refer to the original findings in *Performing Power* in order to clarify and expand upon concepts that were then in embryonic form, as well as to view them from a higher point on the spiral of development.

An immediate example of this development is an expanded view of the entire complex of facial and emotional energies. That complex is now seen from three different perspectives: the facial mode itself, the outer communicating resources; the inner emotional process, IMP, which is invisible until communicated by the facial mode; and the synergistic interplay between them—the facial-emotional complex. The exercise of this complex will also proceed in three stages: the outer, the inner, and the connecting process. In this chapter we will emphasize the outer aspects of the complex, and in the next chapter, the inner and connecting parts.

In working with the whole facial-emotional complex, we are realigning a polarizing, part = whole error that has been part of the acting process from the beginning. The error was to mistake parts of the inner or outer facial-emotional complex for the whole spectrum. Since the Greeks—and thus from the beginnings of music-theater—actors and theorists have been choosing sides. One group, the emotionalists (devotees of the inner), cries out, "You *must* identify personally with the emotions of the character or you'll be false and artificial, and you won't move the audience!" The other group, the anti-emotionalists (devotees of the outer), coolly responds, "You *can't* identify personally with your character's emotions unless you want to lose control of yourself and your art, and play all the characters in the same way."

That polarizing, out-of-balance arguing continues today—British technique versus American feeling being an obvious example. But once we have recognized the limiting partiality of such debate, we can choose to embrace the whole spectrum and drop the need to cling to any single choice along it as the best (or only) way to deal with the art of communicating emotion. We can read of the Greek actor Polus, who brought an urn containing the ashes of his own dead son onstage as he portrayed Electra in order to arouse his personal emotions, without setting his action in opposition to the outer facility and power of the great English actor David Garrick, who, revealing only his face between two folding doors, could run a gamut of emotions—"from wild delight to temperate pleasure . . . to tranquility . . . to surprise

... to blank astonishment ... to sorrow ... to fright ... to horror ... to despair, and thence ... to the point from which he started" in "five or six seconds" (Cole and Chinoy, p. 168). When Marlon Brando talks of the importance of outer technique to convey emotion, while Laurence Olivier talks like a method actor, we can rejoice in the new freedom we have to accept great acting and singing-acting as such, and not as proof of the supremacy of any single approach to the emotional process. As with all full-spectrum work, those choosing sides and defending positions have only their true power to gain by embracing the whole. We can all develop new choices— not in opposition to the previous choices, but in synergistic partnership with them. Those previously unknown choices can draw upon the power of the full spectrum, and work with the connecting process between the inner and outer ends of that spectrum.

Expanding Interest in a Neglected Mode

In chapter 1 I referred to research by Dr. Ledoux of the NYU Center for Neural Science which suggests that in many cases emotion originates in the old brain before its recognition by the mid- and new brain. Thus, emotion occurs *before* thought, not in response to thought as conventional psychological wisdom had supposed. This means that MIM becomes aware of the emotion *after* it has begun affecting the system, and at that point begins to try to control it (the origin of entanglements). If the emotion is strong enough (the "scared shitless" level), a higher imperative than MIM's control takes over, the emotion flows, and the system prepares for action. Otherwise, the body holds itself, the voice, and the face in check in various entangled ways.

That has significant implications for our work. Since emotion is premental to begin with, MIM has no way of making emotion happen for the acting process by acting directly upon IMP. Stanislavski's intuition was correct: we can't make emotion happen—it must be allowed. It is as though IMP lives in a walled city and will only emerge when conditions are to its liking. It is similar to a lower energy version of radiant performing, of which a free emotional flow is a vital ingredient: we can only prepare the conditions for it. MIM can concentrate on releasing the control patterns; the voice, the body, and the face can exercise their capacity to open the gates to the free flow of emotion; we can create a free, intuitive play space for it; and we can relate with awareness to our own experiences of free emotional flow. If we do all this, IMP may come out to play. But that is the subject of the next chapter. I mention it only as part of the unfolding research around the facial-emotional complex.

Public and professional interest in the face has also intensified since the publication of *Performing Power*, particularly with psychologist Paul Ekman's important work on a scholarly level. On a popular level the impact is seen and often commented upon in television — a seeing-mode medium — and many references to the use of the face are made in cinematic critiques and reviews. There have also been a number of books discussing aspects of facial meaning and communication — including an *Atlas of Facial Expression* (Peck), which is directly concerned with the physiognomy of the face as an expressive medium, and *About Faces* (Landau), an examination of the evolution and functions of the face.

In *Performing Power*, I emphasized the importance of the face in opera from several points of view. The most important was the powerful effect the facial mode has on the performer both positively and negatively, depending upon the degree of entanglement conditioning: "For this reason alone, it deserves to rank as an equal partner with the other two modes, even though it has received less attention as an independent entity." The word *equal* needs qualification in this context. In discussing the parts of any whole system the concept of equality is not as significant as the freedom of any part, both to fullfill its own unique purpose within the context of the whole, and to contribute to the purpose of the whole to its full capacity. It is less meaningful to speak of the equality of the heart and the stomach than of the capacity of each to fulfill its own purpose, as well as that of the whole, with maximum power, ease, and efficiency. The relative importance of the parts of any system is constantly changing: the stomach is very important during the digestive process, the heart is very important during heavy exercise, and both of them are always there, contributing to the whole. If either of them is malfunctioning, it affects the other and the whole in any number of ways; thus the purpose of the whole is interdependent with both of them and equality is not the issue.

The same is true of the projective modes. They each have specific functions to serve, and their relative importance at any point will depend upon the needs of the situation — needs that will always involve the purpose of the whole. For maximum performing power, each mode must be free to fulfill its individual purpose; simultaneously, all three modes need the capacity to interact in a flexible and coordinated way that fulfills a purpose greater than any of them individually: they are not equal, but interdependent; they are not independent, but interconnected; and all three are vital to the total process of performance.

Having said that, it is also true that if any part in a system has been neglected for whatever reason — lack of awareness, exercise, or interest — that deficiency must be made up. Special energy must be given to empowering the neglected part in order that the system as a whole may function more effectively. If the heart has been abused/neglected so that a heart attack occurs, special attention must be given to its functioning beyond the ordinary course of events; similarly with the stomach if an ulcer has developed.

The same is true of the facial mode. We must give it special consideration in order to redress a long-standing imbalance of attention to the face as a communicating instrument and to achieve greater clarity about its functioning. The importance of a part of a system becomes more evident when it is not functioning up to capacity or is interfering in some way with the purpose of the whole system. In that sense the facial mode requires continuing attention, beyond what would be required if it were functioning freely within the system and the relationship between each of the parts and the whole were clearly understood.

The neglect of the facial mode stems to some extent from confusion about its function. Until it is differentiated as a distinct and separate communicating channel, its purpose cannot be clearly defined. Having clarified its role in the communicating process, we can also specify its primary function, which is the communication of emotion and thought process. It shares this function with the vocal mode — although the two may reinforce or contradict each other. But if the voice is singing rather than speaking, the face becomes more crucial in realistically comunicating specific thought process and emotion. (The singing voice is a glorious communicating tool, but it does not communicate emotion naturalistically, the vocal-*emotional* process having more to do with speaking than singing.)

The communication of emotion with the face, in turn, is more prone to entanglement interference than the communication of thought process. As we have seen, this is because there is a deep-seated confusion as to the relationship of the body and the face in expressing emotion. In order to clarify this confusion, we must isolate and concentrate on the development of the facial mode (even while isolating and developing the kinesthetic and vocal modes as well).

This necessity for emphasis and isolation initially kept me searching for new ways of exercising the facial mode to the relative neglect of developing kinesthetic and vocal mode exercises. While I worked with both of the latter two (particularly with the spoken vocal mode) it was not until I had fully explored the exercise process of the facial-emotional complex that I gave the other two the same depth of attention. But once a full spectrum of exercise possibilities had been developed for the facial mode, similar exercises for the kinesthetic and vocal modes began to suggest themselves (and are discussed in their respective chapters).

Erroneous Assumptions about the Facial Mode

Another factor that caused me to spend more time exploring the facial mode involved the number of assumptions, many unconscious, that relate to the face and the emotions. These assumptions interfered with the development of the facial mode exercise process.

For example, when I first asked performers to exercise the facial mode, it was evident that the capacity to *sustain* a given emotional statement longer than was "natural" was vital to the singing-acting process. One of the principal conventions of the music-theater form is the extension of time: three seconds of real time becomes thirty seconds or three minutes of music-theater and singing-acting time. That is the main challenge to the performer in appearing to be *areba* on stage.

Thus I focused on the capacity of the performer to sustain time in exercising the body and the face, choosing a spectrum with sustaining at one end and holding at the other. This was to distinguish between *sustaining*—a dynamic unfolding process, which is vital—and *holding*—a frozen, rigid, product-oriented control pattern, which is not only unnecessary but distinctly unuseful to the human process. From that spectrum grew the no-hold-is-healthy rule. All this seemed logical, and for a long time the concept of sustaining was a primary motive in exercising the facial mode.

Simultaneously, I was exploring the facial capacity to shift rapidly from one state to another—but *only* as an exercise. In exercising the face with performers I would stress that each exercise was simply that: a means of expanding the capacity of the facial mode, and not a performance product. Our purpose is to be able to do with our face whatever is desired as an exercise so that in actual performance we can simply allow that new capacity to function freely and intuitively.

I was aware at the time that I was to some extent hedging my bets, that I was a bit uneasy about "violating" all the rules about acting I had consciously and unconsciously absorbed, rules that said in effect, "Do *not* fool around with the face! Get self-conscious about it and you will kill the natural acting process!" But so long as I treated my efforts with the face as "merely" exercises, they were permissible.

Then one day, while coaching a singer, I devised an exercise called "rapid-fire attitudes." This involves the performer going through a series of facial-emotional changes in quick succession. The coach can either call out a sequence of attitudes or hold up cards with attitudes written on them, changing them rapidly as the singer communicates them with her face. (I will discuss the exercise in greater detail below.) To my surprise, the singer's face seemed to be consistently *areba* during the exercise. I suggested that she continue to do the exercise and sing at the same time. I held up the attitude cards, changing them rapidly as she sang so she could see and project the emotions. She did so, and I was stunned. It was clearly the most exciting performance I had experienced from her (and she was a very good performer to start with). What I had expected to see was a case of massive mugging; what I actually experienced was a powerful demonstration of the facial capacity to communicate a wide range of emotions rapidly and believably. The exercise "should" have led to mugging, but it didn't. It was another case of the human system transcending the limitations our minds place on it.

I needed to test the exercise further, for the capacity of a single face does not a theory prove. I took the same exercise to a class that included a broad range of performers—from mature singers with considerable experience to relative beginners. I had them all do the exercise and the viewer response was consistent: it was "the most exciting," "the most interesting," "the most believable" work each of them had done in the class (they had been together long enough to be familiar with each other's performance levels). And while that did not prove anything either—for there is no proof of anything concerning the effect of an exercise on the human energy system— it was obvious that the exercise was useful and deserved further exploration. As I have worked with it, the rapid-fire attitude exercise has become increasingly useful for expanding the power of emotional communication. It is also a useful demonstration that the facial-emotional complex can function effectively without MIM's constant control—for there is no way MIM can keep up with rapid-fire attitudes. It creates for many performers what I have dubbed "the Callas effect" (after the opera singer): an ongoing, continuously unfolding emotional flow of intense and compelling power.

The point of this is not to discuss the exercise—that will be done in the next chapter—but to encourage all of us to shed assumptions and expectations about the nature of the singing-acting process. In this case, my exploration of the facial-emotional process was blocked by the assumption that one would never want to have rapid facial change in performance, regardless of context or execution. Once freed of the inhibitions of that assumption by the "just an exercise" approach, I discovered that it is false.

It also became clear that the sustaining-holding spectrum was not a true continuum. The two terms are actually at one end of a true full spectrum of energy play, with *changing* at the other. Holding is merely an unuseful, tension-locked version of sustaining.

Once that particular assumption-interference had been removed for the facial mode, it opened up exercise processes for the vocal and kinesthetic modes as well. Just as a block in one projective mode will thwart projection in another, a perceptual block in one mode can impede one's perceptions of the other two. Only when an idea is put into practice can we come to know what will actually happen. The mind can theorize about it endlessly, but without the direct experience there is no knowing. (This is not to suggest I have uncovered all my own unuseful assumptions about the face; there are, no doubt, many more waiting to be exposed as inadequate to the expressive possibilities of the face and how it relates to the total human energy system.)

Reconnecting the Inner and the Outer

Now that there is a three-way view of the total facial mode, we will give increased attention to the relationship of the outer and the inner. As I pointed out in *Performing Power*, the inner emotional process (IMP) is a constant in human experience—we all have the same potential range of human emotion. The vast potential of the inner energy processes are greater than we can imagine or realize with our outer resources. Even MIM, *especially* MIM, can have no grasp of the extent of that power. Those innner energies await release but are interdependent on the capacity of outer resources to do so. In itself IMP does not need exercise. What does require both exercise and development is (1) the relationship between IMP and the FM (the facial-emotional process), and (2) the capacity of that process to express and communicate IMP. If the facial mode (FM) cannot interact with IMP and express it, that inner emotional process does not get expressed.

What I did not discuss in *Performing Power* is the connection between the two—the facial-emotional process—which varies enormously from person to person. Singer A will create an external mask and it will connect with his interior both for himself and for the observers; singer B, on the other hand, may develop a very flexible and facile facial capacity and yet it will not seem to connect on an interior level. It will not feel *areba* for himself nor appear so to viewers. Whatever causes the lack of connection is visible, of course; we are not mind readers — we can only read faces. What is occurring in the FM is a more subtle masking of the facial-emotional connecting process and requires approaches beyond working with the facial mode alone.

The specific signs in the FM that betray the lack of connection with IMP are often too subtle to detect easily, even for the person making them. And without falling into the old trap of telling them to feel it in order to connect (if they could have they would have) we can ask them to allow the interconnection to happen with the same inner and outer relationship as they experience with other, more accessible emotions. In my experience thus far, a lack of connection between inner and outer parts of the whole process indicates a strong conditioning about the emotion in question: it is not "nice," and may be a "forbidden" area of expression. It may also be entangled with an overt holding pattern in another part of the kinesthetic mode. For example, anger that is "forbidden" to the face may be controlled by a tension in the shoulders. In either case, the lack of inner-outer connection and the possible blocking factor between the two can be detected with sufficiently keen observation.

Another, full-spectrum, way of viewing the facial-emotional connecting process clarifies how the outer and inner parts of the total process link up or connect. My initial work with the facial mode did not involve the full complex of facial-emotional energies. It focused on the outer in order to redress the imbalance created by our partial appropriation of the Stanislavksi system. American acting practice in general had mistaken the inner part of that system (IMP) for the whole, and had concentrated on that part to the neglect of the outer parts, and of their relationships to each other and to the whole. Thus I gave more attention to those neglected parts — the facial mode and its interaction with the kinesthetic and vocal modes — which, taken together, are the outer tools for expressing the inner process.

Having done that, it is critical to reaffirm the importance of the inner processes, especially as they relate to the whole facial mode; at the same time we will continue to emphasize the significance of the still-neglected outer parts. We can do that with a full-spectrum view of the inner-outer thought and emotional processes.

Full-Spectrum Emotional Choice

We begin with the reiterated principle: Whatever a person feels or thinks is invisible (and inaudible) until it is given expression by the face (or the voice).

As those feelings and thoughts move toward facial expression, the person has a full spectrum of choice potential as to what he will actually express. At one end of the spectrum is free and open communication—call it *allowing*; at the other end is total *concealment*. Between those ends are all the emotional modifications one can make. Since there will always be some kind of modification, or blending, of processes with regard to the expression of thoughts and feelings, we will call it a modification spectrum. Thus all the expressive choices one has lie between *allowing* at one end and *concealing* at the other.

ALLOWING — — — — — — — — — —CONCEALING

Allowing refers to the capacity to allow whatever emotional feeling is being experienced to be fully and freely communicated. We can speak of being transparent to that emotion. If the emotion is hurt, that feeling of being hurt moves from the inner to the outer with perfect transparency and communication. There are no blocks to the process, no smudging, misting over, or opacity. The reality is that total transparency is virtually impossible given (1) the nature of the human face, (2) the nonexistence of a "pure" emotion, and (3) the tendency of viewers to interpret whatever is perceived in ways that may be at odds with what is actually happening. But the concept of transparency defines a range of choice that is vital in exercising our facial-emotional communicating capacity.

Modifying, which includes all the choices between the extreme possibilities of allowing and concealing, means either to blend another emotion with the originating emotion, to control its flow, or to substitute another emotion for it. The hurt is blended with anger, or it is controlled so that it is only modestly communicated, or a substitution is made, with surprise or bewilderment replacing the hurt.

Concealing means the capacity to hide the originating emotion with no external manifestation whatsoever. Concealment in this context requires freedom from entanglement, so that the total instrument, including the face itself, is left free to communicate anything else appropriate to the circumstances.

Concealing is an ambiguous capacity for several reasons. First, it is what we are already conditioned to do by society—to *not* show what we are feeling—and since that kind of concealing is almost always accomplished with entanglement, it is difficult to differentiate between concealment with and without subtle entanglement.

Second, it is difficult to differentiate between concealment and simple nonresponse; concealment can simply look like bad acting. Dramatically, it is important that the audience know the actual situation and what the emotional communication *would have been* so that the concealment or lack of response makes a significant statement. For example, if the feeling of being hurt is not expressed by the character, but the audience *knows* that hurt is being felt, then that concealment makes a powerful statement. Iago hides the hurt he may have experienced on being passed over for promotion; that concealment acquires increasing power and destructiveness as the drama proceeds. One can, of course, interpret his malignancy as motiveless—but if the interpretive choice is to make Iago's hurt his motive, then keeping that from the other characters is as important as its revelation to the audience. Both the concealment and revelation should be as free of entanglement as possible so the character is free to substitute anything he desires.

A third ambiguity of concealment as an acting tool is that there is no such thing as a nonstatement by the face. Viewers will always interpret some sort of emotional statement, and that statement becomes a modifying substitution rather than concealment. The significance of concealing, in short, lies in the capacity to do so without entanglement so that any other statement can be made by the other two modes or by the face itself.

Along with Iago, the other two leading characters from *Othello* create a full range of choice on the concealing-allowing spectrum. Desdemona is hurt by Othello's actions and she is relatively *transparent* to the expression of that hurt (or she *can* be if the performer is capable of such transparency). Othello is hurt by the suggestion of Desdemona's infidelity, but he *modifies* the hurt, substituting rage instead. Iago is hurt by being passed over for promotion and, as said before, he *conceals* the hurt. Later he substitutes a series of manipulative actions that take advantage of Othello's incapacity for transparency to the hurt. Othello's jealousy prevents him from investigating the situation more rationally, which leads to the tragic conclusion. Since Iago's concealment is free from entanglement, the hurt is not modified as disgruntlement, pouting, annoyance, or overt resentment, and he is able to express himself in whatever way is useful to his needs, despite what he is actually feeling. Thus he is seen as "honest Iago" by the other characters in the play (with the exception of his wife, Emilia, and she conceals what she knows from the others).

The primary focus for exercise of the facial mode is at the allowing end of the spectrum, and ranges over all the modifications between that and concealing. Allowing is characteristic of aria or soliloquy situations, where the character is alone and under no societal restraints about what she can express, and therefore can and should be as transparent as possible. In our oft-cited example, hurt can be expresssed with total vulnerability, without fear of being hurt even further by having revealed it to someone else.

Ensemble situations will always involve some degree of modification: the hurt may be blended with anger, or controlled in its level, or one may substitute surprise or bewilderment for the hurt.

As we proceed, let us bear in mind the importance of developing all the following capacities: (1) to be able to allow the inner to flow with perfect transparency through the facial "lens" of the outer; (2) to be able to modify the actual emotion in any way we choose; and (3) to be able to conceal the actual emotion without entanglement and, from that place of unentangled freedom, to be able to substitute any other kind of facial-emotional statement we wish.

At this point I would like to proceed systematically through the exercise process for the facial-emotional complex, beginning in this chapter with the outer—the facial mode—summarizing material from *Performing Power* when appropriate. The next chapter will cover the inner emotional process (IMP) and the connecting process between the inner and outer—the facial-emotional process. This reflects the expansion of the exercise process for the face—from three exercises to eighteen—since *Performing Power*.

Exercising the Facial Mode: FOCUS and FAMUS

The Focus Process

Once we have clarified the precise function of the facial mode (FM)—the communication of thought process and emotion—we are ready to examine the tools with which it does that, and create exercises to develop those tools. As we do so, I ask the readers—performers and teachers—to work with the actual energies being discussed. Without a direct experience of the process, any exercise can be intellectually written off *or* endorsed; logical arguments and conclusions can be created for or against any of them with no relevance beyond mind games. The purpose is to learn how the energies function *in action*, and that can only happen through direct experience. The three-step IEI process—follow the instructions, have the experience, and interact with others in the field—holds here as well: one can only reach the interactive stage of confirming or correcting the exercises and concepts by following the preceding steps of instruction and experience.

The FM has two basic components: the eyes and the musculature of the face surrounding the eyes (including the eyelids). We will refer to these two components as the focus process and the facial musculature process respectively, or, as they were named in one of my institutes, FOCUS and FAMUS.

FOCUS sends messages concerning the structure of the thought process, and FAMUS sends the messages that clarify how one feels about the thoughts in that structure. "I am thinking a thought (FOCUS) and this is how I feel about that thought (FAMUS)." FOCUS by itself—the eyes alone—communicates very little emotion over a distance. For example, the narrowing of the pupils cannot be perceived more than a few feet away, which leaves the actual communication of emotion to the musculature *around* the eyes, that is, to FAMUS.

At the same time the eyes are truly "the windows of the soul" and the establishment of their power through the focus process is an essential step in activating the facial mode as a whole. I have had many singers who have worked with the performing power technique for years come to a sudden realization of the power of FOCUS. With great enthusiasm they will tell me that, in retrospect, the foundation of the technique as a whole is in understanding, trusting, and developing the focus process.

While the effect of FOCUS on the performer himself is sufficient reason to develop it, there are also countless instances validating its effect on audiences as well. And if the eyes seem too tiny for concern as a part of the performance process, research has shown that eye movement can be detected over a much greater distance than one would think: half the length of a football field, according to one study.

The reasoning behind the concept of FOCUS is simple: as I put it in *Performing Power*:

> There is a parallel between the movement of the eyes and the movement of the mind behind those eyes. When the eyes are focused on a point, the mind is also focused on a single idea; when the eyes wander, the mind is wandering; when the eyes search, the mind is searching; when the eyes make a sudden shift of focus, the mind has made a sudden shift of thought or attention. (p. 164)

The use of FOCUS thus creates the initial connection between external and internal energies, in this case between the eyes and the mind. Most important, it does this for the performer as well as the spectator, creating an outer environment that allows the realization of inner potential.

For performers who have difficulty in concentrating, FOCUS can actually create inner concentration from the outside. Dozens of singer-actors have validated the experience of a performer who found the focus process helpful in that respect. Initially he had great difficulty sustaining any sort of outer focus. Finally, I told him, "Simply look at that lamp for one phrase, shift to the picture on the wall for the next, the fire alarm for the third and the exit sign for the fourth." He did so, and the class was unanimously enthusiastic about the result. When I asked the performer how it affected him (for it was the first time we had experienced him performing with a specific and controlled focus sequence), he said, "I felt concentrated in a way I never have before."

For all performers, there will be areas of emotional expression that have never been inner-outer connected and expressed. In all such cases the outer communicating resources — the facial mode — must be exercised first. Then attention can be given to the inner emotional connection. In many cases this connection will occur automatically in response to the new availability of the outer resources. But we will approach the exercise of those external means in three ways: (1) from the outer to the inner (FM to IMP); (2) from the inner to the outer (IMP to FM); and (3) blending and integrating both those approaches (the FEM process). We will exercise the outer capacity of the facial musculature to receive and project thought and emotion from the interior; the capacity of the mental and emotional inner processes to allow and nurture the flow of a wide range of thoughts and emotions; and, from that inner understanding, we will combine and connect all three phases in various ways as we expand the capacity of our FM to communicate emotion and thought with freedom and power.

The Functions of FOCUS: What the Eyes Can Do

In keeping with my fancy for alliterative mnemonic devices, I have a list of five S's to describe what FOCUS can do in conveying thought structure: search, select, sustain, shift, and (with an assist from FAMUS) shut. A brief description of these functions follows.

Search: The eyes can search the communicative thought space with a series of minifocuses. These are simply focus points of shorter duration, most often used during introductions, interludes, and postludes (or any other time when one is not singing). The communicative thought space is located between the performer and the audience. It consists of all the space a performer can focus on and be seen by the audience in doing so. It encompasses the full width and height of any proscenium or audience space and is the imaginary canvas on which the facial-emotional mode paints with its two tools: FOCUS and FAMUS.

On that space FOCUS provides the line drawing of the picture—the *structure* of the thought process—and FAMUS colors it in with emotion— which tells how the character *feels* about the various components of the thought process structured by FOCUS. The search is to be differentiated from simple wandering focus, and this is clarified by FAMUS.

The search, then, is a series of briefly sustained focus points that can be, variously, worried ("Where is the solution?"), fearful ("Where is the danger?"), bored ("What can I think of to do?"), joyful ("What can I do to share this happiness?"), contemplative ("What should I think about?"), or any variation or combination of these, depending upon circumstances.

Select: As the search (the introduction or interlude) concludes, the eyes select the focus-thought that motivates the singing itself. This happens a beat or two before the singing itself begins, and is simply the selection of another focus point. This one, however, will last longer and have more emotional weight behind it. It is the culmination of the search scenario created by FO-CUS and FAMUS combined. When that major focus selection point is reached, the performer should be prepared to sustain it.

Sustain: This is the most important single function of FOCUS: it gives the performer mastery over the alteration-extension of time. Since a moment of focus-thought time lasts as long as the focus itself is sustained, this is a specific technique for extending time. The longer the sustaining, of course, the greater the pressure on FAMUS to give that continuing focus a sense-making emotional life. A long focus phrase can easily become emotionally neutral (if it did not begin that way) and the only way to transform that neutrality is with FAMUS.

There is also an increasing pressure on the kinesthetic tension entanglements that exist in us all. If the body is in a state of tension of any kind, it can be challenging to sustain FOCUS—for in that case it will automatically mean prolonging the physical state as well. At the same time, sustaining FO-CUS can also help the performer become more *aware* of the specific nature of the tension entanglements, which might otherwise go unnoticed, being masked by random, extraneous movements of the eyes and body that release the tension, but also diffuse and distract from the power of the performance.

Shift: This is the movement from one thought to another (speaking from the inner view) or from one focus point to another (externally speaking).

There are two kinds of focus shift: the thought-process shift, and the kinesthetic shift. This distinction is between a focus in the mind's eye, where a performer is thinking *about* something but is not actually looking at something, and a focus in which the performer *is* looking at something in the environment around her (or wants the audience to *believe* she is looking at something that is actually there).

Most arias are largely concerned with thought process: the performer is thinking about the beloved, the battle to come, the enemy, the challenge, etc., but is not actually looking at any of these things even though the individual focus-thoughts are sustained as though they were. In some arias, on the other hand, it should seem as though the character is seeing things that *are* there in the environment of the drama. For example, Nedda in *Pagliacci* seeing the birds as she sings the Balatella, Susanna in Carlisle Floyd's *Susanna* seeing the stars, the valley, and the lights of the town as she sings, "Ain't it a pretty night?" If they seem to see things that are *not* actually there, they are in states of madness or hallucination. For example, Lucia seeing her dead mother, or Macbeth seeing the nonexistent dagger—both of which are appropriate to the circumstances.

The key factor in seeming to actually see something, as opposed to thinking about something, is determined by the nature of the focus shift. If the whole head turns to "look" at something, that creates an external kinesthetic space between the observer and the person or thing observed. If only the eyes move, that suggests an internal space with no outer referent, a thought process. (Even when someone actually comes into a situation, if the performer looks at them out of the corner of his eyes without moving his head, it suggests that he does not want the person entering to know that he has been noticed.)

In a thought-process focus shift, then, the actual shift is made without moving the head, with the head following slowly and easily if desired. If the head *has* to move when a focus shift is made, this is part of the overall entanglement between the FM and the kinesthetic mode. While this is not an uncommon entanglement, it is not in the critical category and can generally be transformed by exercise into a choice with relative ease.

In a kinesthetic focus shift, the head moves swiftly and softly to look (or to seem to look) at the person, thing, or event in question. In recital, concert, oratorio, and symphonic performances, thought-process shifts are the norm, while kinesthetic focus shifts are relatively rare. (Kinesthetic focus shifts are not to be confused with a performer relating to or focusing on the audience—a technique to be discussed later.) However, judicious use of kinesthetic focus shifts in a song recital can convey a marvelous sense of an imagined environment that need not suggest hallucination or madness. It can create the effect of having an impassioned, imaginary dialogue with someone or something, kinesthetically shifting away from and back to the subject of the focus-thought.

In opera/music-theater performance, kinesthetic shifts are more common, though still outnumbered by thought-process shifts. In ensembles, of course, one *is* looking at something real and present—other characters—a good share of the time, and kinesthetic shifts predominate, except for those moments when all the members of the ensemble are in moments of private thought, and are not focused on each other.

Shut: During moments of extreme emotion, shutting the eyes (with the help of FAMUS) can convey an intensity that is greater than anything they could say while open, short of the character breaking down totally. Shutting one's eyes to contain or control emotion is actually a kind of entanglement: if one didn't shut one's eyes the emotions would flood through and overwhelm the situation (or so our conditioning would have us believe). It is a control device, not unlike the deadpan face, only here the controlling barrier is thrown up almost too late, which is what makes it a powerful emotional signal. The deadpan face simply asserts control earlier, and while it can also be a signal of overcontrolled emotional turmoil, the emotion under it all has been so deeply buried that we cannot guess what it is. The eye shutting, on the other hand, being a last-minute, last-ditch attempt to control the emotion, communicates the intensity of the emotion by the very need to control it in that way. Since eye shutting under stress is commonly understood to communicate this (whether intellectually or not), it is a useful choice for the performer to have available. This suggests, of course, that the performer should also have developed the capacity to allow the emotion to flow freely without the eye-shutting control. In recital situations it is sometimes easier to shut the eyes, "go inside," when playing strong emotion, whether the emotional level is of eye-shutting intensity or not. (The videotapes of Maria Callas in recital demonstrate this propensity.) The reader is referred to *Performing Power* (pp. 151-56) for further details about the use of the eye shutter.

There is a special distinction between thought-process shifts and kinesthetic shifts, between what we will call experiential focus and narrative focus. In narrative focus, one is relating an event to another character on stage (or to the audience) and looking at the character or the audience in telling it. One may be recalling an event from the past or anticipating one in the future and looking at the person to whom one is speaking. This a straightforward, everyday way to communicate information—you look at a person and tell them something.

In experiential focus, on the other hand, one would be relating an event to another character or the audience (it could be the same event as in the narrative focus above) *without* looking at them. In this case, one is focused on the thought-image of the event itself, and is, in fact, experiencing (or re-experiencing) that event *in the present* with all the emotions that were (and therefore are) a part of it. If you relive such an event in the present while looking at the person who is *actually* present, he/she becomes a part of the reexperienced event itself. Past and future become entangled with the present: the person being told the story becomes "the mean mother," "the beautiful seductress," "the threatening opponent," and the like. Experiential focus can have tremendous power, since there is nothing that cannnot be reexperienced *in the present* in the mind's eye. But if that relived past becomes confused with the actual present by drawing the other person into it, the situation becomes potentially psychotic—the rapist who locks the door and then tells the woman he has trapped the story of his life, making her the cause of his distress and therefore to be punished for it—or it can simply be embarrassing for the listener.

In experiential focus, then, we are not looking at the person to whom we are speaking; instead, we are focused elsewhere, in the mind's eye, and can allow any expresssion of emotion whatsoever. It is in our mind only, and there is no barrier to that expression, nor any way that anyone else can judge it—that is, to think that it should be otherwise. It is our mind and the object of focus is known only to us, which means that the appropriateness of our response to that focus is also known only to us. When we look back at the person with whom we are speaking, we return to narrative focus: we are concentrating on something in our environment—in this case, the other person—and societal restraints enter in; we modify the level of emotional intensity (unless the character we are playing is on very intimate terms with the person), or we risk seeming psychotic (which may be dramatically appropriate).

One can have the experiential focus-cake and the listener too, of course, by simply moving back and forth between the two—filling the experiential focus with all the power of the reexperienced past brought into the present, and shifting to a "this is what happened" (not "this is happening") narrative mode when looking at the person. In short, in narrative focus one is telling someone about an experience; in experiential focus one is reexperiencing the original event.

Those are some of the functions and techniques of the FOCUS process, which will guide us in exercising it. But since FOCUS can be most effectively exercised in partnership with FAMUS, let us first examine the techniques and functions of FAMUS.

The Functions of FAMUS: What the Musculature Can Do

FAMUS has the major responsibility for the communication of inner emotional states, how the performer *feels* about things. As suggested above, FOCUS communicates the structure of thought (or lack thereof)—the line drawing, as suggested earlier—which says, "This thought is being sustained for this long, then (with a focus shift) this thought for this long," and so on. Meanwhile, FAMUS colors in the outlined structure, specifying how one feels about each thought by alterating the facial musculature. There is an amazing range of emotionally expressive potential available to FAMUS. Sometimes the muscular changes are subtle, sometimes strong—eyelids opening or closing, eyebrows rising or lowering, the forehead knotting or releasing, the nose and cheek muscles contracting or opening, the mouth and lips exploring their wide repertoire of devices—but they are all parts of the singer-actor's total performing potential, to be exercised, developed, and integrated for expanded performing power.

However, the expressive potential of FAMUS has been strongly and restrictively conditioned in virtually everyone. Because FAMUS can send messages of an extremely personal and revealing nature, it has been taught to be careful of the size and power of those messages. This was covered in some detail in the discussion of the seven lively entanglements, particularly with reference to number 4, the FM/KM entanglement. At this point, we are preparing to develop and expand that message-sending capacity with specific exercises. In the process of doing so, we will also activate the entanglement between the face and the body that blocks the expression, thus making it accessible for transformation into a choice.

We begin the process with a simple question: Can the performer allow FOCUS and FAMUS (the eyes and the facial musculature around those eyes) to do whatever is desired, *independently* of mental/emotional meaning? If she cannot accomplish such a seemingly unthreatening task, it is unlikely that those two FM players will suddenly spring into free communicative play when strong and potentially revealing emotions are called for in the presence of an audience. If the facial muscles are inflexible and cannot move freely in private, they will not instantly acquire mobility and expressivity in front of hundreds of observers. Our first task, then, is to exercise the capacity of performers to do whatever they wish with their external communicating resources. That process begun, they will become increasingly capable of allowing those resources to open freely to as large a range of inner emotional expression as possible. The first step in that process is FOCUS PLAY.

Exercising FOCUS PLAY

FOCUS PLAY develops the capacity for choice with the five S's, using both thought-process and kinesthetic focus shifts. This step also involves FAMUS, since FOCUS by itself conveys no emotional content. Further, since there are no emotionally neutral situations in music theater, each moment of FOCUS PLAY should involve FAMUS, however modestly. (If there are such neutral situations, they are rare enough to ignore for the moment and, in any case, probably don't require exercise.) Thus, each sustained focus-thought should convey some sort of feeling—positive or negative—about that thought.

FOCUS PLAY develops the capacity to fill those moments in solo performance when the performer is not singing—the introductions, interludes, and postludes. During those moments, the level of feeling called for will not be as strong as during the singing itself, but some degree of emotional communication is vital. A sample FOCUS PLAY exercise sequence is as follows.

Search: Five to eight mini-focus-thoughts, each sustained for two seconds or so, with FAMUS shifting gently from positive to negative emotional statements for each separate focus point in the search.

Select/Sustain: The final focus point in the search is sustained, with a negative attitude, for six to ten seconds. The length of time here, as with the search, is arbitrary—the point is to be able to hold for whatever length is desired. It is sometimes useful to sustain a focus much longer than would ever be necessary—say, for two minutes—to find out (1) what makes it difficult, what blocks the choice, and (2) what one must do to keep the focus alive, both for the viewers and for oneself.

Shift/Sustain: A kinesthetic focus shift is made to a new focus point, thus implying that one is actually seeing something in the environment. When the focus point is reached, an attitude is allowed from the positive end of the spectrum—pleased, happy, amused, etc.

In choosing points of focus, use the full range of the proscenium-audience space, far left and right, and up and down across that range. In general, it is most useful to work with eye-level and higher points of focus. I call this the anti-Rodin principle, after the famous figure of *The Thinker*, in which the focus is down and in. That head-down posture is a natural physical adjustment to the thinking process, for it shuts out external stimuli that might interfere with concentration. The "navel-watching" school of acting, which was a direct response to the need to show that one was thinking, drew upon this natural response to the needs of the thinking-concentrating process in actual life. Yet one of the primary functions of the performer is to share thought process with an audience as clearly as possible, and the head-down posture interferes with that purpose by partially hiding the face. As performers, then, we need to develop the capacity to "think" in a shared way. This will mean that the performer will use relatively few head-down, contemplative focus points—thus practicing anti-Rodin techniques—despite the motivation of the Rodin pose. Singing-acting, to reiterate, is an unnatural (and glorious) art; through exercise we must reshape, develop, and make natural those uses of our human energy system that are conditioned contrarily to the needs of singing-acting.

Shift/Sustain: Make a thought-process shift (eyes only, following gently with the head once the shift is accomplished if desired). Sustain the positive attitude of the previous focus until the new focus point is reached, then allow that attitude to transform to a negative state—worried, annoyed, disturbed, etc. To sustain the attitude until the new focus point is reached is important to both the outer and (especially for the performer) inner sense of reality in the thought and emotional processes. This coordination between FOCUS and FAMUS is vital; when the shift of attitude occurs simultaneously with the shift of focus, I call it the "Hi, how are you?" syndrome.

That anticipatory pattern gets its name from the following example. Suppose I am an actor on stage with my back to a door. Someone comes in the door. I have no way of knowing, as a character, who the person is. Despite this, I smile and react *as I turn* before seeing who it is, saying, "Hi, how are you?" In doing this, I would be anticipating. As an actor, of course I know who is coming through the door—it wouldn't take four weeks of rehearsal to learn that. But as a character, I can't *know* that until I actually see the person. And therefore I would not alter my existing emotional state until I *do* see who it is; if I am laughing, for example, I don't go into neutral as I turn, but rather sustain the laughing or sense of amusement until *the sight of the person* gives me reason to change (or sustain) that state.

Similarly with the focus process. Until the new thought "walks into my mind" via the shift of focus, I cannot respond emotionally to that thought. Yet it is one of the most common reality-dispelling habits many singer-actors develop. The basic energy principle violated in cases of anticipation is that thought precedes energy use—whether emotionally, physically, or vocally. And since focus structure delineates thought process, that structure must precede the emotional (or physical or vocal) response within that structure: the line drawing must be there before it can be colored in.

Logically enough, anticipation of this kind is strongly related to the anticipatory entanglement. Since that entanglement places the whole system in a state of tension, any movement of any part of the system—the arms, the head, or even the eyes—will tend to bring all or part of the rest of the system into play in reaction or adjustment. Thus, if the anticipatory entanglement is already established when FOCUS moves, so will FAMUS. This, in turn, creates a subtle but powerful dissonance with the performer's sense of the thought-energy relationship. He may be unaware of it at first, but once the "rightness" of this principle has been experienced—that focus-thought precedes energy use—he becomes strongly aware without being told when he violates it.

Shift/Sustain: The overall sequence can go on as long as desired, working with thought-process and kinesthetic focus shifts, and with positive and negative attitudes. An occasional eye shutter can also be added to the sequence: the positive or negative statement is intensified as the eyes close; then, after a few seconds, they can be gently opened to the same focus point, and then shifted to a new focus point while sustaining the emotion. And, not to be completely anti-Rodin, one can include an occasional lowered focus. In fact, the eye shutter and the lowered focus can both be used to convey similar kinds of controlling or turning-within messages. Since the eye shutter tends to communicate such statements more powerfully, it is useful if the musical-dramatic statement is proportionately intense and powerful.

To this basic FOCUS PLAY exercise process, we can begin adding FAMUS exercises. It is well to have the focus process in a state of choice before the addition of FAMUS, so that we adhere to the principle of learning one thing at a time. But so long as one does not feel overloaded, and is not trying to do steps 1 and 3 simultaneously—which in this case would be to exercise

the unassimilated focus process and the equally unpracticed facial musculature at the same time—it is not only appropriate but useful to add FAMUS
exercises to those for the rapidly developing FOCUS.

Exercises for FAMUS: The Facial Flex

The first and most basic of the exercises for FAMUS is the facial flex. Doing
the facial flex means moving the facial musculature continuously: raising the
eyebrows, wrinkling the nose, widening the eyes, moving the cheeks, the
lips, symmetrically and asymmetrically, one side, then the other, together,
independently. As with all other exercises, the question is not "Is this useful
as a product?" but rather, "Will this expand my communicating capacity?
Can I do whatever I want to do with my facial musculature, independently
of meaning, and therefore allow it to be more open to actual meaning and
emotion?"

The facial flex is a pure, nonproduct, process-oriented exercise. It is
highly unlikely that one would ever be asked to do a facial flex in actual performance, except perhaps in a highly stylized, experimental production.
Thus MIM has no reason to judge it in terms of product or performance. As
a pure exercise, however, it develops the freedom and flexibility of FAMUS
to do anything imaginable, and therefore places that capacity in the service
of the inner expression.

In discussing entanglement number 6, VM/FM, we referred to one of
the most common characteristics of the trained singer: a facial expression of
anxious neutrality. In one of my classes we created an acronym for that virtually universal singer-face: SAD—serious (singing is serious business), anxious (I hope I don't do it wrong), deadpan (whatever I don't show can't hurt
me). In giving workshops at NATS conventions, whenever I mention the
passive, nonexpressive, vaguely anxious face of the average young singer,
there is a unanimous nodding of heads and rolling of eyes. Somehow, the
young singer learns the habitual SAD expression simultaneously and in coordination with the process of singing. The act of singing and the serious,
anxious deadpan are deeply entangled in a majority of singers.

The reason for that entanglement is obvious once one understands the
dynamics of entanglement. Before learning to sing, the voice and the face of
the average person will be strongly and naturally entangled—entanglement
number 6. She will open her mouth to sing and her face will begin its accompanying dance. When voice teachers see that obvious sign of the untrained amateur, they immediately begin training the student (consciously or

not) to immobilize the facial muscles while singing so that, whatever she may sound like, she doesn't *look* like a total beginner. This is a logical step to take, and I have great sympathy for the many voice teachers who have asked me, "But what do we do? We don't want them to look like agonized amateurs." I also have an answer for that question, which, as the reader may have guessed, lies in exploring the 25 positions along another spectrum of energy use, that between facial *immobility* and facial *mobility*.

IMMOBILITY   — — — — — — — — — —MOBILITY

The facial-immobility end of the spectrum involves the capacity to isolate the face in stillness from the act of singing. The facial-mobility end is the capacity of the face to move freely and continuously while singing. The singer who only practices at the immobile end of that spectrum is training in inflexibility, lack of freedom, a holding pattern, and power-robbing tension habits. It is true that deadpan immobility is one way of eliminating the agonized forehead, but it also eliminates the appropriate expressivity of that same forehead. I have worked with many singers who, because their teachers told them not to lift their eyebrows while singing, were unable to use the eyebrow-forehead area at all. Such training is, of course, a logical response to the fact that raising the eyebrows while singing a high note is one of the most common demonstrations of entanglement number 6—an entanglement everyone is aware of, whether they have a way of defining it or not—but it simply locks an equally unuseful, expressivity-robbing tension hold into place. With exercise, however, these same singers were able to bring that part of the face back into expressive play, and begin reopening that blocked channel to receive and express thoughts and emotions appropriate to its use.

While the singer will want to practice the facial flex while singing, it is useful at first to isolate it from the singing process, concentrating on awareness of the face as an expressive instrument by itself. When first attempting the facial flex, there is often little actual movement of the facial musculature. When I ask new groups to do the facial flex en masse, I sometimes think they are purposely not doing it. When I ask them that, however, their laughter tells me that they thought they *were* doing it; but the inhibitory patterns governing their faces are so strong that nothing appears to be happening.

It becomes the function of someone watching to provide this information; performers exercising by themselves can use a mirror (yes, I said a mirror). However, rather than watching oneself continuously, one can stand at right angles to the mirror, do a facial flex, and in midflex turn the head to look in the mirror to learn how much one is actually flexing. This will also release head-neck tensions that are often activated by the facial flex. (This is also a useful exercise technique in combination with extreme masks—see below.)

As I say to my classes, becoming an artist means getting what you *think* you're doing and what you are *actually* doing to be the same thing. Once aware of that gap of illusion (I call it "the thinktuality gap"), one can begin closing it with exercise. Since the face is the part of our total instrument of which we are the least conscious, we can begin closing the gap with the facial flex. It is the most fundamental of facial exercises and can be the first step in opening the emotional process to greater expressivity.

As we raise our conscious awareness, of course, the specter of self-consciousness about the face may rear its threatening head. That threat is also an illusion through which one must pass on the way to technical mastery. Technical mastery for the singer-actor means being *areba* and not merely going through the outer form. The facial flex is an outer exercise, of course, and simply doing that outer process is the exercise. But even here there will be stages of growth. We can call upon the Zen image: First there isn't a mountain—one is unconscious of technique; then there is a mountain—one becomes strongly conscious of and even self-conscious about technique; then there isn't a mountain—the technique is integrated and functions without conscious attention. But first one must become aware of one's total instrument on as many levels as possible—practicing what one cannot do while exercising, and allowing whatever has become integrated to simply *be* while performing, with a minimum of monitoring.

One can assist this process of awareness by isolating parts of the face and moving them independently. In the spirit of play, one of my classes gave the parts of the face supertechnical names: the superorbital (forehead) plane, the ocular plane, the nasal-pharyngeal plane, and the labial (mouth) plane. One can work with these parts separately or in various combinations: lips and forehead, eyes and nasal-pharyngeal, forehead and eyes, lips and nasal-pharyngeal. The two sides of the face can be exercised symmetrically or asymmetrically. One can heighten awareness of the amount of movement by touching the face as one is working with it (as well as by using a mirror or a video camera).

The part/part facial entanglement (number 5), is the primary exercise focus in the facial flex. The eyes and the jaw are the two parts of the face that may become entangled with the rest of the face as it exercises. For example, the eyes may move about at random in sympathy with the facial flex. This relatively harmless entanglement is worth exercising for the freedom of interrelationship—especially for the benefit of the focus process.

The jaw is a more significant factor, for in its sympathy with the rest of the facial musculature it can seriously interfere with the vocal process. The jaw is also a primary means of blocking and controlling the emotional process through the voice. Thus the sympathetic involvement of the jaw is often a controlling entanglement as well: the facial musculature moves, the jaw comes into play sympathetically and/or repressively—alert for the control of any threatening emotional flow through the face; and given the deeply interconnected relationship of the voice and the face, that flow would probably give rise to a vocal utterance as well. But, for the singing process, it is vital that the jaw remain free *in all circumstances*—regardless of the emotional communication.

As a secondary point of attention one can also be aware of the amount of head-neck and upper-body breath-holding tension that may also come into play via entanglement number 4—between the face and the body.

Let us examine a four-step spiral process as applied to the facial flex. The exercise can be practiced with the face alone, or in combination with singing or speaking.

A Facial Flex Four-Step Spiral Process

Step 1. *Increase/Nurture.* Do the facial flex (with or without singing or speaking). Reinforce the energy given with praise.

Step 2. *Awareness/Nurture.* Repeat step 1, becoming aware of such entanglements as jaw tension, dancing eyes, head-neck tension, breath holding, or any other kinesthetic tensions. Be aware as well of any missing facial ingredients—those parts of the face not involved in the flexing process, which, by definition, should include the entire face. If you are flexing while singing or speaking, be aware of how the voice is affected. Reinforce the energy given with praise.

Step 3. *Release-Replace/Nurture.* Repeat step 1, this time selecting one, and only one, of the step 2 awarenesses to work with. Release the jaw tension, take charge of the focus process, release a selected kinesthetic tension, add an unused part of the face, or adjust the singing or speaking process as you choose. Reinforce the energy given with praise.

Step 4. *Awareness/Nurture*: Repeat step 3, becoming aware of how the facial flex of step 1 is affected by the attention to step 3. Is there less flexing, more, or is it about the same? Return to step 1, this time at a higher point on the spiral of growth, again concentrating on the flex itself. Make any appropriate adjustments for the purposes of that step. Continue the four-step process as desired. Remain on any single step as long as it is useful.

A gifted performer with whom I work is also a teacher, and uses the performing power technique with her students. She and her husband have devised a group facial warmup for the music-theater choruses with which they work. They call it "our ballet bar exercises for the face," and their experience is that the exercise "transforms the energies of the choruses." It works like this.

Open everything:		Top open, bottom closed:	
Close everything:		Top closed, bottom open:	
Mask to the left:		Top right, bottom left:	
Mask to the right:		Top left, bottom right:	
Everything up:		Top up, bottom down:	
Everything down:		Top down, bottom up:	

Facial Expansion: The Importance of Persistence

While dramatic new facial capacities often emerge in a relatively short time, expanding the capacity of the face to communicate does not happen overnight. It is always a long-term process, however immediate some of the initial improvement. We have spent most of our lives practicing the repressive conditionings that control and limit our current capacity for facial expressivity. It is unreasonable to assume that we will drop all those conditionings and become facially free simply because MIM understands the concept of entanglement and sees how useful it would be to allow greater facial freedom. Yet we often think that if MIM grasps the concept, that is all it takes. An experience I had early in working with the process made this clear.

A performer who had been in my studio before I had developed the projective-modes concept contacted me years later to do further work. I was not particularly eager to do so because my memories of the person's performing capacity were of a repressed, noncommunicative, seemingly defensive rigidity. But I agreed—I needed to learn something, and such situations always have growth potential.

The problem was immediately apparent: the performer's face was almost totally noncommunicative. I remembered how hard I had worked with her kinesthetic skills in trying to allow a communicative performance to emerge. With the new information, I shifted attention to what had been the missing mode, and began the exercise of the facial-emotional mode with the facial flex. At the time I called it facial "brushing" and advised performers to "brush your face every morning just as you brush your teeth." The results in this case were immediate and gratifying: the face began to release some of its long-held patterns and new kinds of emotional communication began to flow, which was a surprise to both of us. After working with the process for a week, during which it continued to unfold, I had to be out of town and did not see the performer for six weeks. When I did, I was disappointed to note that the facial communication was, if anything, slightly diminished from the last time I had seen it. Without mentioning that, I casually asked the performer if she had been doing her facial brushing every day. She replied, "Why, no. I thought once I understood the idea, that would take care of it."

It was at that point that I created the Integrative Pledge of Awareness. I asked the performer if she wished to take the pledge and improvised a rough version of it. In slightly more polished form, it reads as follows.

The Integrative Pledge of Awareness

Recognizing that all three projective modes are always present and
sending messages whenever I am singing or speaking, I will always
be aware, without judgment, of their interconnected,
interdependent relationship when warming up, learning music or
lines, practicing, rehearsing, being coached or directed,
improvising, or taking a voice lesson. Whenever possible in these
situations I will exercise with new energy choices, loving and
letting go of conditioned entanglements between the modes,
allowing each mode to develop its own unique communicating
capacity, thus increasing the synergy between them.

Purposefully practicing my process playfully, persistently, and
patiently will expand my range of artistic choice, my freedom of
expression, my total performing power, and allow me to open to
my unlimited potential.

The point of the pledge, and the exercise process as a whole, is this: As
performers, we are always exercising our projective modes, whether we
think so or not, and the more awareness we can bring to that process regularly, the more our projective capacity will expand. Again, awareness does
not mean simply MIM's understanding of the process—although in many
cases, that will do a great deal—but an actual energy interaction by the total
projective-modes system. MIM may understand the concept to be a good
and useful one, but in most cases that understanding will not create the degree of change desired—only the motivation for it. If it took twenty-five
years of careful, albeit unconscious, conditioning to achieve our current
state of facial control, a week or two of sporadic exercise is not going to
release that control and replace it with new patterns. To create the maximal
change in our capacity for choice, we must exercise it as well as be aware of
it—for we only learn to skate in the summer if we've actually tried to skate
during the previous winter. MIM's understanding that skating is a good
thing will do nothing to change our ability to skate unless we allow the body
to actually exercise with the process of skating.

The principle of variable reinforcement is the other end of that exercise
spectrum. The idea of constant exercise is balanced by the understanding
that once you have developed the facial-flexing capacity, it does not need
daily repetition—only occasional practice. At the same time, there are many
ways of working with the facial flex, and one can easily drop the exercise at
a superficial level without exploring its expanding possibilities. (For example, the facial flex can be combined with arbitrary attitudes; see the following chapter.) By using the four-step spiral process with special attention

to different choices for step-3 releasing, the facial flex can be kept fresh, alive, and free from the negative effects of humdrum repetition for even the most advanced performer.

More Exercises for FAMUS: Extreme Masks

The second step in exercising the outer facial-emotional process is the extreme mask. While the facial flex is at the change-variety end of the facial mobility spectrum, the extreme mask is at the sustaining end. The idea of the extreme mask is to allow the face to make as large and strong a statement as possible—a Halloween mask in scale—and then sustain it for six to ten seconds (or as long as one wishes—the length of a musical phrase in an aria, for example). The challenge with extreme masks is to sustain them with as little superfluous or held tension as possible, so that one does not reinforce the association of large-scale statements, whether emotional or physical, with controlling physical tensions.

The scale and intensity of energy in extreme masks will bring ordinarily hidden entanglements into perceptible view, where the performer can experience them more directly. This allows an awareness of entanglements with a clarity not available at more normal levels of energy. As with all projective-mode exercises, the point of the extreme mask exercise is twofold: (1) to develop the capacity of the FM to communicate more powerfully and freely; and (2) to bring into awareness the entanglements that limit that freedom and power, thus allowing the performer to begin transforming those entanglements into choices rather than necessities. We are expanding the known boundaries of the facial communicating capacity by moving into the unknown with the facial musculature, even though this is purely on an outer level, with no concern for inner meaning at this point in the exercise process. The entanglements that created the boundaries of the known in the first place, and that remain largely unactivated so long as those boundaries are not threatened, will spring into play when the unknown is approached. They will effectively interfere with and block the acquisition and taming of new facial-emotional territory—outer though it may be. However, once the performer becomes aware of them and exercises the capacity for releasing them and making that move, the newly explored unknown can become a free communicating potential that can in turn be linked up with an inner sense of meaning. That inner-to-outer connection completes the transformation of the unknown to the known on all levels of technique and meaning.

Contrary to what I thought when I began working with this exercise, it is a rare performer who can create an extreme mask that is too much *so long as it is not entangled.* I had supposed that everyone would be able to make gigantic, weird masks, all of which would be totally inappropriate for performance. What I found was that remarkably few people can make masks of any size without activating and demonstrating a deep level of entanglement; and it is precisely those entanglements that make the mask feel and appear to be too much for performer and observer.

The entanglements that create that feeling and perception of too-muchness are the face-jaw (number 5) and the face-body (number 4). If, however, a performer creates an extreme mask, and then releases the jaw and the physical tension brought into play with it, one of two things occurs: (1) the mask either goes away—along with any sign of the entanglement itself, which is simply the entanglement operating in reverse—or (2) the extreme mask becomes a strong and, given the appropriate context, useful facial-emotional statement. That is where the exercise process enters: releasing the entanglements—even while sustaining the mask itself—allows the facial statement to feel more *areba* to the performer and the observers. Until this is done, the unknown extremity of the statement will feel threatening and too much—because of the entanglements—and the performer will be blocked from the potential power of that expression, and dozens like it, in appropriate situations. Consistent exercise with extreme masks can make available to the performer emotional communicating resources that would otherwise remain dormant and, in an everyday metaphor, turn pinching new shoes into comfortable and useful old shoes that can be worn whenever appropriate.

Because of its large scale, the extreme mask is also a useful way to exercise the coordination with the focus process. For example, when using extreme masks, any violations of the "Hi, how are you?" principle by anticipation are immediately obvious to performer and viewers alike. And since extreme masks tend to bring entanglements into play, it is even more likely that such anticipations will occur. When the body is in a state of tension, movement by one part will tend to compel movement by another: as the eyes shift from one thought-process focus to another, the whole head will tend to move, and the facial mask will tend to change simultaneously. For those who might otherwise find it difficult to detect an anticipatory change of expression as the focus shifts, the use of extreme masks will make it clear.

In working with extreme masks, it is tempting for the performer to combine steps 1 and 3. The entanglements are made so obvious by the extremity of the masks that the performer will want to leap to step 3 and attend to the entanglements. This, of course, neglects the purpose of step 1, which is to expand the capacity of the face, not to deal with entanglements. Thus the first part of step 2—the praise aspect—is vital in reinforcing the move toward greater facial expression. The second part of the step is to become aware of the entanglements generated by step 1, but without any judgment or attempt to correct them at that point. That is the function of step 3.

This also means that since the primary point of doing step 1 is the expansion of the facial capacity, one should do *anything* to allow that to happen, entanglements be damned! If throwing the body into a spasm helps allow the face to expand its expressive capacity, then one should do that; we can deal with the body spasm entanglement in step 3, but meanwhile the face has been allowed to move further into the unknown. That is the function of step 1, and we grow most fully and quickly by doing one step at a time. Let us examine the four-step spiral process applied to the extreme mask.

The Extreme Mask Four-Step Spiral Process

Step 1. *Increase/Nurture*: Focus, and allow an extreme mask. (If desired, do step 1 as a focus sequence, shifting focus several times, sustaining each extreme mask as the focus shifts are made, changing to a new extreme mask after the new focus point is reached.) Reinforce the energy given with praise.

Step 2. *Awareness/Nurture*: Repeat step 1, becoming aware of any of the following entanglements: jaw tension, head-neck tension, shoulder-upper-body tension, breath holding, or any other aspect of the body that feels held or uncomfortable. This includes the face, for within an extreme mask there can be more tension than is necessary to sustain the mask. If you have chosen to use a focus-shifting sequence, be aware of any anticipatory changes in the masks before the new focus point is reached. Reinforce the energy given with praise.

Step 3. *Release-Replace/Nurture*: Repeat step 1, choosing one and only one of the awarenesses generated in step 2 to release. It is possible, of course, to repeat step 3 several times, dealing with one entanglement after the other, before moving to step 4. Thus, on one repetition, one could allow the breath to flow, the head-neck tension to release on the next, then the jaw tension, and so on, before moving to step 4 and focusing one's awareness on how those releases affected the purpose of step 1. Reinforce the energy given with praise.

Step 4. *Awareness/Nurture*: Repeat step 3, becoming aware in the process of any reduction or change in the energies of step 1. Reinforce the energy given with praise. Return to step 1 with the cumulative awareness and continue the process as desired.

It is sometimes useful as a warmup to do rapid-fire masks and even rapid-fire extreme masks. This last is a cross between the facial flex and extreme masks: the extreme masks are changed rapidly, say, every second, but sustained for that brief moment instead of being in a state of continual flux like the facial flex. One can use a metronome, snapping fingers, or a drum to set the beat. The beat can also be irregular, which requires a continual readiness within each of the extremes. Because of the increased speed, it is more difficult for the accompanying entanglements to keep up with the process of the face alone; accordingly, the performer can become more aware of the entanglements as they attempt to do so.

Together with the focus process, the facial flex and the extreme mask form the basis for exercising the facial mode—the outer aspects of the whole facial-emotional complex. In the next chapter, we will examine the inner emotional process—IMP—and the facial-emotional process connecting IMP and the facial mode.

Chapter 10

The Facial-Emotional Complex II: Exercising and Connecting the Inner with the Outer

Persuading IMP to Come Out and Play

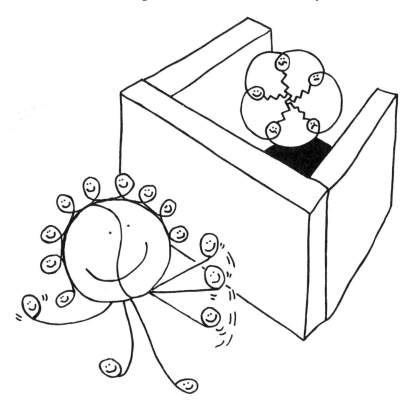

Earlier we suggested that if one had to define the acting process in a single phrase it might be something like "showing how a character feels"—the passion of the briefest definition of theater, "planks and a passion." While both are vast oversimplifications, there is a great deal of truth in the idea that a fundamental task in acting is getting IMP to come out and play, freely and openly. However, as we saw in the last chapter, recent scientific evidence indicates that that is not an easy thing. The emotional process *precedes* the rational thought process—MIM—and therefore is not responding to one's thoughts about what is happening, but is a direct response by IMP itself. This means, in turn, that MIM cannot cause emotion directly—a truth that Stanislavski intuited almost a century earlier. But since the arousing or activating of IMP is central to, if not the core of, the acting process, how do we do that?

Let us pursue that question by taking a closer look at what happened in the 1930s in our maladaptation of the Stanislavski teachings. The Group Theater was the main conduit for those teachings in America, and the first person to create a specific methodological approach to them was Lee Strasberg. Without attempting to reduce "The Method" to a phrase, we can say that it was a MIM-based effort to get IMP to come out and play through the use of sense memories about actual emotional situations. It is a kind of self-hypnotic technique in which the mind focuses on what the five senses experienced in that situation—not on the emotion itself, for Stanislavski's insight about our inability to make emotion happen was also part of this technique. If the attempt is successful, IMP responds to the sensory recreation of the original settings and joins it as well: IMP comes out to play. IMP is then available for other kinds of emotional input into the dramatic scene being played.

But one only knew if the attempt was "successful" if Strasberg validated it by "believing it." (This also contributed to the origin of the mind-reading school of directing—a subject dealt with at length earlier and in *Performing Power*.) Some actors in the Group Theater loved it, but some—notably, Stella Adler—resented the controlling aspects of it: this man tells you what you must do with your mind, then judges the result, and if it is not what he wants, *you* are guilty, not he.

As it happened, Stella Adler had the opportunity when she was in Paris to have three weeks of daily conversations—in French—with Stanislavski (who was recovering from an illness). She learned—so she reported—that Strasberg was working with a technique long since discarded by Stanislavski. She brought this information back to the Group Theater, where it naturally created a furor. Strasberg said, in effect, he didn't care what Stanislavski said now, and that what he, Strasberg, had developed got at the real truth of the emotional process. And he continued to develop and work with that process for the rest of his life.

Stella Adler, on the other hand, created her own approach to the acting process—a freer, more intuitively based way of arousing the emotional system in the present—which she still uses in her acting classes. She will go to almost any length to arouse IMP in coaching a scene—it has been said that if you can survive an acting class with Stella Adler, you can survive anything. Cajoling, threatening, manhandling, attacking, screaming—anything to bypass the societal conditioning that keeps IMP from coming out to play, and to put the performer in a state of emotional flow. The insight here is similar to that of the sense-memory approach: once IMP is aroused, by whatever means, all emotions will be more available for stage use: deep grief can be followed by hysterical laughter, as in Agee's *A Death in the Family*.

Together, the Strasberg and Adler approaches form a teaching spectrum: MIM control through the use of sense memory at one end and intuitive-emotional arousal by any means at the other. We have already suggested the limitations of the sense-memory approach—that the arousal of a previously experienced emotion will also arouse the entanglements inevitably connected with that experience. It is also a very complicated approach—hence all the control required—and an increasing number of acting teachers (including Strasberg's son, John) are dropping the sense-memory approach from their work. (See *A New Generation of Acting Teachers*.) But it is, at the least, a specific technique that can be used and applied by others.

Adler's intuitive arousal approach, on the other hand, is strongly authority dependent. Without Stella Adler—or someone of comparable teaching charisma—to model the free flow of emotion or to badger or beat you into an emotional state, there is no technique to draw upon. The devotion of many of her students is extreme—and this, in itself, is an indication of the authority dependency inherent in the approach.

And in the wrong hands that kind of approach can be destructive. Certain directors picked up on the idea of emotional manipulation, sometimes literally beating up on actors (usually women), then thrusting them on stage to play a scene for which the emotion thus created was appropriate; or, in acting classes or rehearsals, they would humiliate the performer to the point of tears or anger, then say, "Now use it in the scene."

These are extreme and perverted examples of an aesthetic that tolerates any means to achieve "real" emotion, as well as an unhealthy dependency on authority. And it is not that a certain amount of emotional modeling—the teacher "demonstrating" the free flow of emotion while interacting with a student—or purposeful arousal of an actor's present and real emotions are not useful techniques. They are. But they are limited by the necessary presence of a gifted, principled, charismatic teacher.

We need another approach in getting IMP to come out to play—an approach based on actor control rather than on authority control. There are two steps in the process of getting IMP to come out and play: activating and allowing. We need first to arouse IMP, then remove all interference from her path: get her involved, and then open the gates (or open the gates, which may get her involved). The performer has four basic tools with which to activate IMP: MIM, the body, the face, and the voice. We have seen how one of MIM's three principal powers—remembering—is used in the sense memory approach. The second power—imagining—may be even more useful.

Imagining, or pretending you are someone else, has been fundamental to the acting process since it began (it may have *been* the beginning). Remembering actual events to activate emotion rather than imagining events that will do so (two sides of the same coin) is simply part of our century-long addiction to the aesthetic security of realism. In *The Complete Singer-Actor*, imagining was included as the fourth of six basic skills of singing-acting (the others being energizing, concentrating, structuring, stylizing, and coordinating): "Imagination is a personal adventure which cannot be confined by rules, dictated by the experience of others, or compelled by any outside force" (p. 82). Then as now, the emphasis is on the creative, playful, fantasizing aspects of imagining, free of the inhibiting effects of judgmental criticism. The imagined events are the activators; the freedom from the judgmental entanglement is the allowing factor. (For further information, the reader is referred to the list of questions to energize the imagination in *The Complete Singer-Actor*, pp. 138–39.)

The other three tools for activating and allowing are the projective modes: the actions of the body, the expressions of the face, and the sounds of the voice are the activators; the freedom from entanglements 2–7 is the allowing factor. As with MIM's use of imagination, external actions may activate IMP after which she must be allowed; alternatively, allowing can be an activating factor in itself if musical and dramatic circumstances are appropriate.

In this context, many things can activate IMP, including information about the psychology of the character, exercises such as facial extreme masks, physical statements and actions, vocal musicality statements, and arbitrary attitude requests—the first exercise we will deal with. Every performer will have preferred activators, but in all cases the creation of a free, allowing, nonjudgmental space is vital in coaxing IMP to come out and play.

Exercises to Activate IMP

Arbitrary Attitudes

In the previous chapter we concentrated almost exclusively on the outer processes. As we will see, all outer-oriented exercises are also opportunities to activate IMP and thus create a connection between the outer and the inner. The outer and inner processes are part of a full spectrum, an interconnected continuum with no real break between the two ends. Entanglements in fact are a counterfeit demonstration of that full spectrum of uninterrupted interconnection: the inner expression is automatically accompanied by an outer manifestation—which, when it is an entanglement, is for the purpose of control, which makes it counterfeit. For the moment, however, we will continue to speak of outer and inner exercising as though they were actually isolated ends of a spectrum.

One of the most useful ways of activating inner emotional states is with an exercise I first developed in *The Complete Singer-Actor*. It is called the arbitrary attitude exercise, and many variations have developed from it. It works with emotional attitudes in a direct manner—for example, calling out attitudes—anger, joy, fear, etc.—while performers communicate them facially (or vocally or physically) and noticing what happens to the whole energy system as one does so. This kind of exercise goes strongly against the grain of standard American acting tradition ("You can't play attitudes"), but having dealt with those issues in both *The Complete Singer-Actor* and *Performing Power*, I refer the reader to those volumes. At this point in my own work, the concept has been so useful for so long and contributed so significantly to the *areba* factor in performance, I can only say, try it: follow the instructional-experiential-interactional sequence and find out for yourself that performance energies can and do expand with the use of arbitrary attitude exercises.

To facilitate the use of arbitrary attitudes, I have had a pack of ninety attitudes printed on cards. Anyone could make their own set of cards, of course, but it has been surprising how many more performers use them once they have been made available through modern technology. (To facilitate the process of making one's own set of cards a list of attitudes is included in appendix C.) For private use, these cards can be set up on a mantel or music stand, flipped through, or drawn at random for use with an aria or song. Some performers record them on a cassette, and play them back. For use in large group situations and in communicating with performers while they are singing, I have also had the cards enlarged. In exercising with the cards, then, the attitudes may be communicated either aurally or visually. *Performing Power* recounts examples of performers using arbitrary attitude cards in audition and performance situations, but here our concern is mainly with the exercise process.

If the attitudes are spoken, there can be a focus shift between each attitude, the previous attitude being sustained until the new focus point is reached. The pattern might go like this: "Focus, joyful (brief pause), shift focus, sustaining joyful, then angry (pause), shift focus, sustaining angry, then rapturous" . . . and so on.

In this stage of the exercise process, it is useful to express the attitudes as one would normally. Intensification of that expressivity is a later step. As always, there are two aspects of the exercise process: (1) developing the facial capacity to communicate the emotion; and (2) releasing/replacing the entanglements that come into play as the facial emotion is expressed.

Let us look at the arbitrary attitude approach with the activating-allowing sequence and the pentagon of performing energies—voice, body, face, IMP, and MIM—in mind. Whether called out or displayed, an attitude— say, anger—is a message to MIM (as is any scene MIM reads that calls for anger). But it is also a message to the other parts of the system—if we are aware of those parts and how they function. It is a message to IMP as well (and to the body, the face, and the voice—all of which have intuitive understandings of how that emotion is expressed). From that point, the performer who is aware of those parts *and* their interactions (whether entangled or free) can begin to exercise the process of allowing the emotion to flow freely, to arouse IMP in the present. It may mean activating the intuitive knowing of the face in expressing the emotion; it may mean releasing the body's conditioned need to control that flow of emotion with tension applied to the voice, the face, or the body itself; it may mean using MIM's power of imagining to encourage the flow of emotion; it may mean releasing—or acting despite—MIM's chatter about "what should be done" or "how it isn't working"; it may mean doing something physically to allow the flow; and it will mean allowing IMP as much freedom of flow through all or some of the foregoing to express itself in its own, nonintellectual, preverbal way.

With all these possibilities for activating and allowing the flow of IMP's process in mind, one could go through a sequence of attitudes several times, playing with a different approach each time until one has found the most immediately useful ones (and identified those that are more difficult and are therefore useful to exercise). One could also go through the same sequence of attitudes several times and use the four-step spiral process as follows.

An Arbitrary Attitude Four-Step Spiral Process

Step 1. *Increase/Nurture*: Lead the group (or oneself) through a brief sequence of attitudes in coordination with the focus process. Reinforce the energy given with praise.

Step 2. *Awareness/Nurture*: Repeat step 1, becoming aware of entanglements or energy uses you wish to release or replace: jaw tension, head-neck tension, breathing holds, kinesthetic tensions of any kind, "Hi, how are you?" anticipations, releasing the facial statement before the focus shift, or anything else you may notice that is connected with but not contributory to the facial expression of the emotional attitudes. Reinforce the energy given with praise.

Step 3. *Release-Replace/Nurture*: Repeat step 1, this time choosing one and only one of the awarenesses to work with for each attitude. It is possible to pick a different release/replace factor for each attitude: for example, if *anger* creates jaw tension, and *joyful* does not but instead creates upper body tension, release the jaw in the former and the upper body tension in the latter, and so on with each attitude. Reinforce the energy given with praise.

Step 4. *Awareness/Nurture*: Repeat step 3, becoming aware of how the attention to releasing/replacing may have modified the original purpose of step 1. Return to step 1 at a higher point on the spiral of growth, and continue the entire process as desired.

Rapid-Fire Attitudes

The facial-emotional mode is, at least potentially, much quicker and more flexible than the kinesthetic mode. But if there is a strong entanglement between them, the kinesthetic mode can slow down the facial mode and rob it of its true capacity for expression. To help release the facial mode from the kinesthetic mode and thus realize its true speed and flexibility of expression, one can use the rapid-fire attitudes exercise. This is simply an accelerated version of the standard arbitrary attitude exercise. The rapid-fire attitude exercise is discussed at the beginning of this chapter in connection with the expansion of my own conditioning around exercising the face. It progressed from being "just an exercise that expanded capacity" to an exercise that has a strong and useful relationship to performance. It works as follows.

Rapid-fire attitudes can be done aurally or visually, either reading the attitudes aloud or flashing the cards in sequence. The focus-shifting process is not used in either case because the attitudes go by too quickly to allow normal focus shifts. The performers select a single focus—if it is done visually, the focus is on the attitude cards themselves—while the cards are read aloud or flashed. The shifting rate can vary from one per second to one every few seconds. At first the performers will have difficulty in keeping up—"I was five cards behind when we finished!"—but each time the FM gets quicker and more flexible in its response as it frees itself from the slow-down constraints of its kinesthetic entanglement, or from the needs of MIM to "think up" a situation in which the emotion would "make sense." The exercise is fun to do, and is a clear demonstration of the capacity of the FM to be isolated from the KM in its emotional expression. Indeed, the performer has little option when doing it *but* to practice that isolation, for the body can't possibly keep up the pace in its slower, overall efforts to communicate the emotion through repression.

The four-step spiral process can also be used with rapid-fire attitudes. While it is not necessary to repeat the four-step sequence in detail, step 1 would involve a sequence of five to fifteen attitudes, which would then be repeated for each successive step. The main entanglements to be released in step 3 would be between the facial and kinesthetic modes, and the judgmental entanglement with MIM. Repetition of the rapid-fire exercise is useful in making performers more aware of those entanglements, as well as in demonstrating immediate progress in allowing the face to carry out its primary function with increasing speed and flexibility.

One basic idea that allows arbitrary attitudes to work in auditioning and performing situations is that there are no pure attitudes; there are always blends of various kinds: there is not simply pure anger, but anger tinged with sarcasm, bitterness, self-righteousness, annoyance, joy, exuberance, etc. Any emotion can be combined or blended with any other emotion. Even seemingly opposite emotions are commonly blended in life, the integration of joy and grief as we smile through tears being a typical example. And that is why virtually any arbitrarily selected emotion can work with any given aria: one simply blends the arbitrary emotion with the existing emotion of the aria. All that is required to develop that capacity is to exercise the imagination and then the facial capacity to *express* that expanded imaginative range. To do both those things, we can use the attitude-combination exercise.

Attitude Combining and Linking

Attitude combining can also be practiced either visually or aurally, with two attitudes being read or flashed in sequence and the performer putting them together. If done aurally, the focus-shift process can be used, just as with the regular arbitrary attitude exercise: "Amused-frightened (pause), shift focus, sustaining that combination, then haughty-joyful," etc. If the cards are flashed in combination, it is possible to also use focus shifting with this added complication: the performer glances at the new combination, then returns to the previous focus point before shifting to the next focus point and making the transition to the new attitude combination. While this sounds complicated, it is a very useful coordination exercise for advanced practice.

Combinations can include three or four attitudes. Performers will often look disbelieving when such a thing is suggested. Even with only two combinations, our MIMs will often say, "That combination doesn't make any sense—it can't be done!" But when one actually puts the combination together with the face without MIM "thinking" about it, it makes perfect sense. After doing an unusual combination, performers will often say, "It's like those times when you are . . . " (then describe an actual life situation in which those emotions *were* blended). This demonstrates again that MIM is not capable of "knowing" all the experiential possibilities of the total human system.

One can progress to the pile-on game as a conclusion to exercising with combinations. This refers to the piling on of the attitudes themselves as an extended sequence is read aloud. The performers then incorporate each successive attitude into the previous total blend. After three or four attitudes, of course, the actual communication of the specific blend becomes improbable. Nor should that goal be made an issue—the exercise is to develop capacity, not attain a performance product.

Attitude combinations lead directly to blending attitudes with specific arias, and expanding one's range of emotional choice with traditional material. Most arias or songs have what we may call a prevailing emotional tonality (PET): they have a general sense of grief, anger, joy, worry, or rapture, all combined with various modifying emotional specifics. To that PET (which is not unlike the idea of finding a one-phrase description of the emotional situation of the aria), we can then add a sequence of arbitrary attitudes to be successively blended with it. This is not a pile-on, but one attitude after the other, with the PET serving as the factor that strings them together. Because singing is involved, it is necessary to communicate the attitudes to the performer visually rather than reading the cards aloud.

One can also blend attitudes in rapid-fire sequence, or even complicate things further by making the PET a combination to start with; for example, the PET can be "angry grief," and then new attitudes can be added, one by one, to that existing combination.

One can also practice varying kinds of transition between attitudes with the linking development exercise. (1) "Focus, begin with inspired and make a transition to pitying, remaining in the same focus." (2) After that linking transition is made, "Shift focus and sustain pitying until the new focus is reached, then make a transition to desperate, and from that to loving, remaining in the same focus." (3) After the linking transition is made, "Shift focus," and so on. One can link two, three, four, or more attitudes in each focus, as well as link from combination to combination: cynical-horrified to tender-hurt to elated-disgusted, etc. The exercise combinations in this area are virtually unlimited.

Viewing IMP from a New Perspective

Having inveighed at length against the mind-reading school of directing, and the illusionary assumption that if we are thinking and feeling the right thoughts they will automatically be expressed by our outer resources, it is important here to do some full-spectrum rebalancing of my own as follows.

The very reason that the arbitrary attitude exercise works is that we *know* (not just have knowledge of) each of those emotional states from personal experience (or observation). Our biocomputer is filled with inner, personal, experiential information that allows us to know how to express the emotional states as well as feel them. The confusion arises, as we have pointed out repeatedly, because we also *know* (unconsciously) the control conditionings connected with all emotions that are personally threatening in any way. Those control conditionings are manifested as tension-entanglements in our system. While those entanglements are often mistaken for the emotional expression itself, they actually interfere with and block the expression, as well as interfering with other parts of the communicating system. Unless we release/replace those entanglements through exercise, our expressive capabilities will be confined within the boundaries erected by our control conditioning. Since that conditioning was not a choice in the first place—we simply acted intuitively and unconsciously to do what we felt needed to be done—we are the victims of our history until we become aware of our conditioning, take charge of it, and develop other choices through specific exercises.

Some performers will seize the outer process with a great sense of relief, having come from exclusively inner-oriented training, and the results will be spectacular. The rebalancing of their total process will give them a performing power they have never experienced. Others, who have not gone through the inner search, will grasp at the outer exercises with equal enthusiasm. In some cases, the outer will activate the inner and allow it to flow more freely and fully; in others that inner activation will continue to be blocked, and the outer flexibility and mask-making capacity will remain just that: an external statement that is not quite *areba*. But that "not quite *areba*" state is *visible*—we do not know its nonarebability from reading minds—it is not an inner guessing game. To reaffirm a basic principle, the lack of arebability can be *seen*, even though it may defy description in its subtlety.

I have experienced both kinds of process in working with performers. In the case of continued inner blocking, the resistance can be deep and intense, for it means allowing something to flow from within that has been very carefully locked off in unconscious controlling patterns. The outer resources may have developed the capacity to project that emotional process freely, but even before it can reach that point it is locked off on a deeper level. The newly developed external capacities assist in the disguising, counterfeiting process with masks that are ever so close to arebability—but not quite there. And the more intense the resistance, the more closely the performer may have learned to approximate the emotion in question. It takes keen observation, and patient, persistent nurturing by the performer and the coach-instructor to break through that resistance. It helps greatly, of course, if one has a clear understanding of what is actually happening in one's energy system.

Sometimes one can help performers break through that barrier by spotting and helping them release some tiny blocking factor in the outer facial musculature. Those almost imperceptible facial holding patterns are sometimes like a twig in the logjam of emotional flow. One very talented performer simply needed to do less, and the only question was, what did *less*

mean? In her case, releasing the entanglement tension in her otherwise powerful kinesthetic performance decreased the overt diffusing activity and allowed the face to become "radiant" (in the words of one observer who knew
nothing about the developmental process being exercised).

In other cases, one will need to nurture the inner processes in ways that
may seem contradictory to anyone who has worked with the performing
power technique from the outer only. As one of my performers said to me at
a point of frustration in dealing with this very issue, "Now you're asking me
for all that 'method' garbage you say is so worthless!" I then pointed out that
to work with the inner processes is not garbage; that some fine acting teachers have helped performers in using that approach; that the only *real* error is
in confining one's work to one end of the inner-outer full spectrum—
mistaking the part for the whole; and that we could make the same error by
clinging to the outer end of the spectrum. I then suggested to her that we
work with the inner processes using the same principles we have applied to
the outer. That made sense to her, and allowed her to readdress the issue
with new energies. Her emotional process began to unfold in new ways.
That kind of clarification may have to be repeated in different ways, but
once understood, it will allow the *whole* process to expand.

Nurturing that revelation of the inner is vital in order for the performer
to feel safe in allowing it to be seen. It was the violation of that process
through bumbling, amateur psychosleuthing that made me leery of using exercises that probe the inner processes. A common example of this kind of
exercise is the personal experience. Until developing the four-step spiral exercise process, I had left those complication-fraught exercises to what to me
seemed to be their unwise use by others. A story I heard at a NATS convention workshop gave me the impetus to make such exercises more useful.

One of the teachers had attended a workshop in which a well-known
young director (who shall remain nameless) was working with a group of
young singers in front of an audience. He asked the singers to go through the
following sequence: (1) to arrive at a one-phrase statement of the emotional
situation of the aria they were singing; (2) to find in their own past the personal experience that most closely matched that of the aria, and then to reexperience the emotions of that past event; and finally (3) to sing their aria as
they went through those personal reexperiences. (He also asked the audience to rate each singer on a scale of one to ten as to how much they were
able to "stay in it." This is an extraordinarily unuseful thing to do, but since
it has nothing to do with the exercise itself—only with increasing the judg-

mental environment around the exercise—I will concentrate on the confusions about the exercise.)

The primary confusion lies in two unarticulated assumptions: (1) that our past personal experiences with emotion were free-flowing, open processes and that our conditioning in the expression of emotion is healthy and unentangled; and (2) that those past personal experiences are therefore suitable as they are to combine with the singing-acting process. For low-key emotional states this may be true. For the high-intensity emotions that are automatically a part of most arias and songs, those twin assumptions are rarely if ever accurate. We are all deeply and unconsciously conditioned in our expression of powerful emotion, and those conditionings manifest themselves in opposition to the needs of the singing-acting process. While I have stated this repeatedly, it bears repetition in this instance. If we ask a young singer to reexperience an intense emotional event, it is inevitable that he will do so in an entangled manner—particularly in front of a group of people, where the repression-control aspects of the original experience will be intensified. And then, with no adjustment, we compound that error in direction by asking him to drag that experience, with all those interfering entanglements, into the singing-acting process. (To top this off by asking an audience to rate the singer as to how strongly he is able to sustain the entangled condition simply intensifies the confusion and potential harm of the situation.) It is the disappearing diva syndrome used as a teaching technique, and given the imprimatur of an authority in the field.

I make this point strongly because I have made the same kinds of erroneous assumptions in the past. Now, with more clarity, the confused logic that led me and my colleagues into this kind of amateur psychotherapeutic destructiveness is both evident and demonstrable for what it is. The sooner we stop doing that kind of thing to singer-actors (and to ourselves), the better. As one way of doing that, let us examine the use of the personal experience exercise in relation to the four-step spiral process.

The Personal Experience Four-Step Spiral Process

Step 1. *Increase/Nurture*: Draw upon a personal experience of sufficient emotional intensity to match or relate to that of your aria, as you perform it. Give full attention to the reexperiencing of the emotional event, using sensory recall of the sights, smells, tastes, sounds, and kinesthetic feelings surrounding the event. Reinforce the energy given with praise.

Step 2. *Awareness/Nurture*: Repeat step 1, becoming aware without judging or trying to change it, how the emotional recall affected your performance process. Note any tension entanglements: head-neck tension, throat tension, altered breathing patterns, upper body or arm tension, tension in any other part of the kinesthetic system, alteration of any kind in the singing process, facial tension, etc. Reinforce the energy given with praise.

Step 3. *Release-Replace/Nurture*: Repeat step 1, this time choosing one and only one entanglement or interference to release or replace as you do so. In other words, continue the experiential recall, but release one of the entanglements that accompanied that experience in real life. If you are working with a whole aria or song, you can release different individual interferences at different points, depending upon what is most prominent; but only work on one thing at a time. Reinforce the energy given with praise.

Step 4. *Awareness/Nurture*: Repeat step 3, becoming aware of how the release of the entanglement/interference modified the intensity of the emotional experience, which was the purpose of step 1. Reinforce the energy given with praise. Return to step 1 with the awarenesses generated by the four steps and continue the entire process beginning from a higher point on the spiral of growth.

One can also combine the use of arbitrary attitudes with the personal experience exercise in the following way. After summoning up the energies of the personal experience, let them feed into new emotional choices as indicated by an arbitrary selection of attitude cards. This, of course, is precisely what one must do when drawing upon a personal experience for use with an aria, for no personal experience will match the musical-dramatic situation and character exactly. A blending exercise of this kind also lets performers know that they always have choice in transforming the emotional nature of the inner energies: they may not have realized that at the time of the original personal experience, but in the reexperiencing they can discover their true power of choice (and, by extension, that same power of discovery and choice about every personal and dramatic situation they experience from then on).

Exercising the Facial-Emotional Process:
Connecting the Inner and the Outer

The Illusion of Separateness: Resistance to Oneness

We often proceed on the false assumption that the inner and outer emotional processes are two separate things. They are not, of course; they are inseparably interconnected and are, as we have indicated, parts of a full spectrum of interaction. Nonetheless, since we often separate them in our minds, to this point we have also exercised them separately, concentrating first on isolating them, beginning with the outer facial mode, then proceeding to IMP. A basic principle here is that one cannot integrate energies fully until one can isolate them freely. Let us proceed to the process of integration and examine exercises that connect the inner and the outer and strengthen their already existing interconnection.

Every exercise—inner, outer, or both—is an opportunity to work with that interconnection. Any change in FAMUS sends a message in, as well as out, providing the performer with an opportunity to expand the inner response to outer potential. Similarly, every inner-oriented exercise is an opportunity to develop the outer response to and communication of that interior experience. The inner-outer resources form one spectrum, and there is a varying blend of inner and outer energies as one moves from choice to choice along that spectrum. Integrating the inner and the outer with each new choice along that spectrum—not simply doing one or the other—is the function of the exercise process in achieving maximum performing power.

The inner-to-outer route is the familiar one. It is the basis of the American acting tradition, and for many people that one-way route is the only viable and legitimate one. But opening, developing, and using the reverse route—from outer to inner—is not only possible, but necessary if one is to develop one's full potential. The outer resources can stimulate and enliven the inner in ways that MIM would never have imagined, as witness the following experience, which is one among many.

An outstanding performer came to me to work with him on a solo piece for which he had written the words. He felt that sections of the piece (which he had performed many times with great critical and audience success) were not as exciting as they could be and he didn't know why. He performed the piece for me and the reason for the slightly diminished interest was evident. The performer was an outstanding singer and a kinesthetic dominant to boot: he sang brilliantly, even while moving and dancing with tremendous skill and vitality. When he was using those two modes in combination, the performance was spectacular. But there were places where the kinesthetic was stilled—he simply sat down and sang. Nothing was added to sustain the complexity of performance information in those sections. When he was singing and dancing, there was more than enough information—one did not need or desire anything from the facial mode, nor was additional facial information possible given the fact that he wore sunglasses during those portions. But when he took off the sunglasses and sat down, the only additional source of information was the face, and it was left in a relatively neutral state.

Recognizing that, I introduced him to the arbitrary attitudes concept. Being a highly skilled performer, he picked up the idea quickly. We exercised a bit, and then I asked him to perform the piece again. This time, however, I spread attitude cards all over the living room floor and asked him to use them at random as he did the sit-down, nonkinesthetic sections. He did so, and sure enough, those sections no longer seemed less compelling. They were equally if not more involving, for him as well as for me. In some ways those sections now seemed more interesting, certainly more personal. And all the attitudes "worked." No matter how odd they might have seemed in advance, in the actual doing, they made total and fascinating sense.

But the most interesting aspect of all was his response to the attitudes: although he had written the words of the piece and performed it many times, the new, arbitrary but specific attitudes he drew upon as a result of the exercise gave him, in his own words, "ideas about the very words I wrote that I had never thought of before." It was a fascinating if inadvertent demonstration of the limitation of MIM in knowing all that can be known, even in the realm of words—which is, after all, MIM's speciality. Nonverbal information from either the FM or the KM can trigger the release of ideas that might otherwise be unavailable to MIM.

In the case of this performer, and any performer who has a flexible and free outer instrument, the inner-to-outer emotional connection triggers the free release of new mental concepts. Since the performer is able to allow the inner energies suggested by the cards to be translated into clear, outer emotional messages, with little or no resistance to the free flow of emotion between inner and outer, there is no interference with the mental processes in understanding the new meanings suggested by the nonverbal emotional energies.

Using the outer-to-inner route, there have been cases where performers playing freely with external masks while singing were startled by their emotional responses. As one singer described it, "I was singing my aria using external masks as an exercise, when suddenly I found that I was in tears—but not choked-off, out-of-control tears. They were free-flowing and did not interfere with my singing—I had total control of them. And they were not only totally appropriate to the aria, I understood and experienced the aria in a way I never had."

This two-way interconnecting process can also arouse resistance. When the opening is not free and accessible, as in the cases cited above, the resistance can be reflected in entanglements, which block the flow of energy between the inner and the outer. When such entanglements are overt and physically evident, one can become aware of them and exercise their release. But such interference with energy flow can also be concealed and may remain unconscious. If those entanglements are allowed to continue in their unconscious state, MIM will often defend their existence with rationalizations that argue against even *attempting* the energy choice in question, let alone exercising it repeatedly. In such cases, MIM is given the responsibility for defending a position of which it is not even conscious: it is asked to argue against an energy use without knowing the real reason for not doing it or what would happen if the choice were made to do it. This is essentially a resistance to moving into the unknown. But that kind of disguised resistance is itself overt; MIM is churning out arguments at a rapid pace, and one can recognize *that* and work with it. More subtle yet are blocks that interfere with the interconnecting process but are totally unconscious and remain concealed on all levels. MIM doesn't even argue about them: it doesn't recognize either the source or the manifestation of the resistance, and therefore, instead of arguing, is simply puzzled—there is no idea of what is actually happening within the system. The following instance is a demonstration of this process.

A singer with whom I had worked frequently but sporadically brought in a song I did not know, in a language I was not fluent in. She sang it, and I remarked that it must be a happy song. She replied that, on the contrary, it was an angry song. I realized (and shared with her) that I had never seen her express anger with her face and that perhaps we should explore that possibility. She agreed and we decided to work on external masks that might reflect anger. (The inner approach obviously didn't work; if it could have, it would have, for she was very bright and knew the song was about anger.)

I had her mirror some masks I made that reflected anger. She was able to do that with some accuracy, but something was still missing: instead of a sense of anger, there was more a sense of hurt. I mirrored her in turn, and noticed that the communication of hurt (and the noncommunication of anger) had to do with the eyebrows. So I asked her to lower one eyebrow (which had been raised slightly); as she did so, there it was: I experienced a sense of anger from her for the first time. It was not fully connected, but it was clear in intention. Simultaneously, and this is the point, she felt sick to her stomach.

Somewhere in her past, she had expressed anger and had received strong negative reinforcement for doing so. It may have been a parental response to an angry look — "Don't you look at me like that, young lady!" But the cause is not important, only the conditioning that results from it. Whatever the initial experience that set the conditioning in motion, it was probably repeated in various ways until it was no longer possible for her face to express anger. And the subtle twig in the logjam of that emotional expression happened to be a tiny difference in one eyebrow: when it was up, even in combination with the rest of the face seemingly expressing anger, she knew unconsciously that it was not doing so, that the lifted eyebrow turned it into an expression of feeling hurt, which was permissible. But move those tiny muscles down, change the outer mask in that minimal way, and the expression entered the forbidden zone. She had to be punished, and the body did so by making her sick to her stomach. And through all this, there was no conscious resistance, no awareness, and, therefore, no arguing.

The good news is that through practice the sick feeling diminished, and has disappeared. That performer can now work freely with the outer state of anger, and is developing the capacity to connect it with the inner process. This has also given her access to other related emotions that were part of the forbidden zone as well. She was, in fact, the same performer, described previously, who resisted working with the inner "garbage." But that work with the inner end of the spectrum was as necessary to the whole process as exercising and expanding the outer capacity. While she still prefers the outer approach, she has begun to recognize that the connecting process is not automatic, and she is overcoming her resistance to work with the inner. When she does so, the effect is emotionally moving in a new and different way. But the process moves step by step: one cannot suddenly leap to levels of powerfully connected emotional expression that have been repressed and controlled for decades; the expression of connected annoyance precedes the expression of connected anger, connected worry precedes terror, connected happiness precedes joy, and so on. It is an unfolding process in which each step is full and complete in itself, and there are always steps to come.

This resonates with an experience related by another fine performer. Given her facially repressed upbringing (in the best Lake Wobegon tradition), she knows her face is not projecting sufficiently until she feels she is doing something bad, naughty, and forbidden. Whenever she feels that way, the response she receives from others is strongly positive about the clarity and power of her facial communication; if, on the other hand, she feels OK about what is happening facially, the face is never doing enough. As with the previous case, access to her forbidden zone is becoming easier: less effort is needed to fight her way into it and she is less dependent upon that "naughty" feeling for reassurance. (She is a former "Bach singer" who has developed into a powerfully expressive performer through the use of the performing power technique.)

Connecting Exercises: Extreme Masks and Arbitrary Attitudes

The first connecting exercise combines the extreme mask exercise (outer) with the arbitrary attitude exercise (inner). The performer makes an extreme mask; then an arbitrary attitude is read aloud or shown visually while the mask is sustained. Without radically altering the extreme mask, the performer allows the arbitrary attitude to be seen through it by whatever slight facial muscular alterations are necessary. I call this exercise "The hunchback of Notre Dame has feelings, too." The extreme mask (if it is truly extreme) will be a bit grotesque, and yet the character it suggests will have feelings (the arbitrary emotion), which can always be communicated through the character mask. It is a very useful exercise for experiencing the interaction of the inner and the outer while simultaneously exercising them both.

More Connectors: The Extreme Mask Release and Return

An extreme mask is, by definition, an unknown for the performer: it will have no meaning outside of those momentary ugly faces we make in derision or anger. The performer will not have used and sustained extreme masks in her daily life, and thus will have no sense of learned meaning with which to invest them. In the extreme mask release and return, the performer makes an extreme mask, then slowly releases it bit by bit until it touches the known, contacts meaning, or connects with a sense of emotional understanding. At that point, the performer reverses field and returns gradually to the extreme mask state, only this time she brings along the new emotional meaning. When she reaches the original extreme mask state, it will then be connected to the inner emotional feeling that was contacted and carried back out to it. It is a movement from the known to the unknown (extreme mask), then back toward the known (release) until it touches the boundaries, then expands those boundaries back out to the previous unknown (return). One can visualize the process with the help of the accompanying illustration.

Move into the facial unknown with an extreme mask.

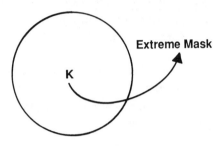

Release the mask gradually until the known is touched.

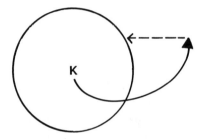

Return to the extreme mask, stretching the boundaries of the known as you do so.

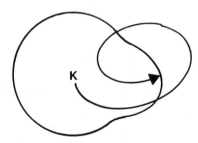

Another Connector: Attitude Expansion

Another useful inner-outer connecting exercise for the facial/emotional mode is the attitude expansion. Beginning with an attitude expressed at a comfortable, normal level, the performer expands that attitude, letting it grow in scale and intensity until it moves beyond his known realm of expression. The attitude will change in the process, of course, with *happy* becoming *insane with glee*, *sarcastic* becoming *enraged*, and the like. The performer should not try to hold onto the original verbal definition, but let the face expand and move to whatever areas of expression may arise. Since any latent entanglements underlying the normal expression of emotion will also be intensified, the attitude expansion is also a useful exercise for awareness of those entanglements. A visualization of the attitude expansion is as follows.

Beginning in the facial known, move toward the unknown.

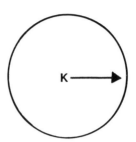

Continue the move even though the direction may change, expanding the boundaries of the known as you do so.

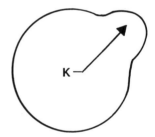

The Attitude Expansion Four-Step Spiral Process

A four-step spiral process with this exercise is as follows.

Step 1. *Increase/Nurture*: Beginning with the normal level attitude, expand it to an extreme. Reinforce the energy given with praise.

Step 2. *Awareness/Nurture*: Repeat step 1, becoming aware of entanglements that may also be a part of the process: breath holding, upper body or head-neck tension, and the like. Reinforce the energy given with praise.

Step 3. *Release-Replace/Nurture*: Repeat step 1, releasing or replacing one and only one of the entanglements noted in step 2. Reinforce the energy given with praise.

Step 4. *Awareness/Nurture*: Repeat step 3, becoming aware of any

alteration in the energy of step 1 as a result of step 3.
Reinforce the energy given with praise. Return to step 1 from
a higher point on the spiral of growth and continue the
entire process as desired.

One can also do a rapid-fire version of this attitude expansion, thus
shortening the transition between the normal and extreme levels. The performer would hear or see the attitude, and move to an expanded version
immediately, uniting the inner known and the outer unknown in an instant.
To warm up for this exercise, rapid-fire extreme masks are useful (described
earlier in the outer exercises).

Connecting Play: One-to-Ten Attitude Spectra

This exercise develops an awareness of the capacity for choice in the intensity of expression, as well as exercising the inner and outer spectrum. Using
one arbitrary attitude at a time, the leader calls out numbers from one to ten
(ten being the strongest). The performers then project the emotion in question at the suggested level of intensity. Moving quickly between high and low
numbers soon acquaints the performer with the amount of actual change
and encourages expansion. The exercise developed as I worked with arbitrary attitudes and asked performers what level of intensity they felt they
were projecting. In most cases, their own subjective estimate matched my
perception: they would estimate a five, which is about what I perceived.
However, since they had been asked to project as strongly as possible and, in
fact, acknowledged that they wished to do so, there was a gap between their
awareness and their capacity to make change based on that awareness. One
of our guiding purposes is to get what we *think* we're doing and what we're
actually doing to be the same thing. But in this case, what they thought they
were doing was accurate, only it was not what they *wanted* to be doing. By
playing with the one-to-ten attitude spectrum, they developed the capacity
to move, for example, from a five to a six. The five may have seemed at first
to be the limit, but once there, one can always move a single point higher,
and from a six to a seven, and so on. (I often moved to eleven, twelve, and
thirteen as well—there is always more than a ten, although that is presumably the maximum.) By moving around (five . . . six . . . seven . . . two . . .
eight . . . one . . . nine . . .), one can also achieve a sort of rebounding boost.

Outer-Inner Rebounding Play

Here, an exercise expansion is called into play and then allowed to affect one's normal level of expression. Using one phrase of an aria, do it normally. Then do the same phrase again, this time making an extreme mask out of the attitude. On the third repetition, allow the normal level of expression again: invariably there will be a noticeable change in the level of normal expresion. The third repetition will be not only stronger but also more *areba*.

This exercise can be done in many different ways: a totally arbitrary extreme mask or a different attitude can be used for the second step. The important thing is that it involve an expansion of the facial mode capacities so that the energies of IMP can flow through it more freely. It is also a very useful way to demonstrate the exercise process in action with immediate results.

The facial mode is the least exercised and the least consciously developed mode of the three. It is the only one that can function by itself, and for that reason deserves an exercise chapter all to itself. In exercising the kinesthetic mode, the facial mode is automatically included (the kinesthetic, in fact, depends upon it for specific emotional meaning—especially when the voice is not being used). The vocal mode includes the other two whenever the performer is visible while singing or speaking. Thus, exercises combining the modes will be included in the following chapters—"Exercising the Kinesthetic Mode" and "Exercising the Vocal Mode."

And exercising is the point—not simply finding things to do for use in actual performance. The exercise/performance aphorism is especially important in developing the communicating power of the facial mode: when you exercise, practice what you cannot do; when you perform, allow and rejoice in what you can do. Develop the instrument capacity through exercise, then let it do what it is newly capable of in the joyful process of performance.

Chapter 11

Exercising the Kinesthetic Mode

The First Kinesthetic Confusion: Communicating Emotion

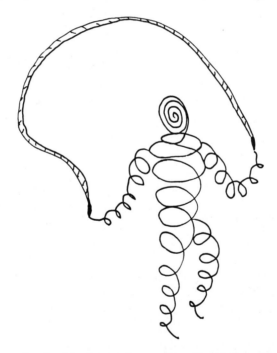

I would like to begin this chapter by recalling David Bohm's comment on the confusion caused by fragmentary thinking in life in general and performance in particular. Here the confusion concerns the kinesthetic mode:

what it can do, what it cannot do, and the differences between those two things. As Bohm put it, "To be confused about what is different and what is not, is to be confused about everything" (p. 16). There is much confusion about the functions of the kinesthetic mode in relationship to the rest of the human energy system, not only between what it can and cannot do, but also in how it can share communicating responsibilities in the total system of the three projective modes.

Two of the crucial issues surrounding the singing-acting process are (1) the need to "do something" to fulfill that process, and (2) the need to communicate emotion. The kinesthetic mode is deeply entangled in fulfilling both of those functions. Let us deal first with the confusion around the projection of emotion. To encounter this confusion, bring up the communication of emotion with any group of performers. Their discussion of the issue will demonstrate a deep conceptual entanglement between the communication of emotion and the use of tension in the body in order to "feel" that emotion.

The following comment, from an otherwise useful book on bodywork and massage techniques by someone who is an expert in the field, is only one of many written examples of this confusion. The subject is the Alexander Technique.

> Various psychosomatic and emotional disorders respond positively
> to the [Alexander] technique. Because the psychological and
> physical are not separate aspects of the individual, we tend to
> *reinforce our feelings with our bodies.* When we experience anger,
> for example, our jaws tighten, our fists clench, and our muscles
> tend to tense. As we learn to balance our bodies, to employ the
> principles of use and inhibition, we release the muscular tensions
> associated with anger and can then *redirect our energy to deal with
> the angry feelings in a productive way.*" (D. Baloti Lawrence,
> *Massage Techniques*, p. 104; my italics)

This does not reflect in any way upon the value of the Alexander Technique. I hold it in high esteem and regard it as one of the most useful body-mind adjunct techniques to the total performing process. But the information in that quote lays bare several misconceptions about the body-emotion relationship.

One is the mistaken idea that tension reinforces emotion. In fact, tension is the greatest single factor in blocking and repressing emotion. The confusion for the performer may lie in the question: reinforcing it for whom, the performer or the audience? The performer may "feel" it more intensely as a result of physical tension, but he is actually feeling the repression of the emotion rather than its expression. And the more powerful the emotion, the harder the performer will have to work in order to suppress it. That, of course, could make the performer aware of the power of what *could* have been expressed. But what is actually being reinforced is an illusion: that the effort of repression is proportionate to the power of its communication.

Another confusion in the quote is the idea that the experience of anger requires and is in fact expressed by various tensions in the body and, further, that this is the natural way of things. In truth, the interplay of emotional experience and physical reaction is a learned conditioning that begins, as we have seen, with sympathetic entanglements. Those sympathetic entanglements are gradually transformed into controlling entanglements through repeated and finally habituated repression. The blocked energy of repression gradually becomes identified with the experience and communication of the emotion itself.

We should stress the fact that the Alexander Technique *can* and does help the performer release that physical blocking; but unless the performer also understands the working of the false expression-equals-repression equation—and is able to release it through specific exercise in connection with, but apart from, the Alexander Technique, all the Alexander lessons in the world may have little effect on his performance when a strong communication of emotion is called for. When that happens, the same emotion-associated tension is likely to return, with as much intensity and potential for damage as ever.

A related vagueness in that brief paragraph lies in the idea of redirecting "our energy to deal with the angry feelings in a productive way." Where are we to redirect them? And how? Unless he is aware of the facial mode as the appropriate and specific channel for the expression of emotion, the performer will not know what redirection means except in a generalized and misleading sense. Feeling that what he has already done is not acceptable, the performer will increase the tension—which he equates with the emotion itself—and try to "redirect it" without understanding how to do so. If redirection is interpreted as releasing the tension, the process can reverse: without an understanding of the entanglement relationship between the face and the body in expressing emotion, and without the means to exercise its release, the performer may release the facial energies along with the kinesthetic, and give a boring total performance.

As one very accomplished performer said to me, "I'm taking your class because at this point in my career, I have two choices: I can give an exciting performance and lose my voice, or I can sing beautifully and be bland." She was a strongly kinesthetic performer who was experiencing the effects of the confusion between emotional expression and physical tension. Her "exciting" performances were "feasts of kinesthetic entanglement" and they *were* exciting; they were also creating so much interference with her vocal process that she would lose her voice. However, when she relaxed the tension, all the emotion she had associated with it also departed: her face, which under the physical stress of tension communicated strongly, also relaxed and became "bland" along with the body. And while that allowed her to sing well, no performer should be forced to choose between the Scylla of bland performance/beautiful voice, and the Charybdis of exciting performance/vocal damage.

What is needed to avoid both those possibilities is (1) a clear understanding of how the human energy system works, (2) an accurate description of the singing-acting process, and (3) a way to exercise and develop the first so that it can serve the second. An important part of achieving the first step—understanding the human energy system—is dispelling the confusion between physical tension and emotional expression.

The Second Kinesthetic Confusion: Getting Set to Do Something

The second confusion—the need to "do something" to fulfill the singing-acting process—is also a result of effort by the kinesthetic mode in taking unnecessary responsibility for doing that something. The body ends up doing more than is needed by "getting set"—the anticipatory entanglement in action—which, as we have seen, is virtually universal among singers.

There is a basic principle guiding our work with the kinesthetic mode and emotional expression. It goes beyond our societal conditionings, and it might be phrased as follows: Whatever the conditioning of your life process, it is vital for the singer-actor that no expression of emotion radically alter the physical state of being, interfere with the breathing, or in any way block the free, vital readiness of the body. To fully realize the act of singing, the body must be free to support it in whatever way is necessary; if the communication of emotion interferes *in any way* with the body's capacity to do that we must find new ways of communicating emotion that do not interfere. Since the facial mode can do precisely that, we can relieve the body of the responsibility it has very logically but unnecessarily assumed.

That misplaced responsibility originates with the judgmental and anticipatory entanglements, both of which involve the relationship of MIM and the kinesthetic mode. Since MIM is powerless to act without the kinesthetic mode to carry out its judgmental control needs, the two of them become the cocreators of all the other entanglements. They do this most specifically in the case of the anticipatory entanglement.

Having discussed the universality of the anticipatory entanglement, we can proceed with the process of exercising it. Since everybody does it—that is, gets set when it is time to perform—the anticipatory entanglement is readily available for exercise. Many performers are initially unaware of their anticipatory preparation, but when it is called to their attention, MIM immediately comes into play to justify and rationalize it. After all, MIM originated the anticipatory entanglement in the first place (albeit unconsciously) and will generally put up some sort of fuss if it is questioned: "Well, isn't that OK? You have to get ready, you can't just sing without preparing, etc., etc."

There are many ways for coaches and teachers to address that resistance to dropping the getting-set habit. A useful approach is to address the question of choice: "Can you try performing *without* getting set? Can you exercise varying *degrees* of getting set? Have you actually *experienced* what it means to not get set in your habitual way? Have you experienced what happens when you perform *without* getting set? Until you have choice in the matter, you are limited by your conditioning. Since we know that any held tension interferes with your total process—for no hold is healthy—and that the anticipatory entanglement is a held tension, let's try performing without initiating it."

One can introduce the full-spectrum, 25-positions view as well. The getting-set/not-getting-set spectrum is part of a larger spectrum—that of tension/relaxation.

	Getting	Not Getting	
TENSION — — — — — — — — — —	Set	Set	RELAXATION

However much tension may be involved in the anticipatory entanglement, it will not reach the total-tension end of the spectrum, nor will not getting set be completely relaxed. This allows exploration beyond the gettting-set point, as well as the "25 positions" between. Performers can and should be encouraged to explore this spectrum on their own—it is surprising how few have done so—in learning from direct experience what they need to do and what they do not need to do in approaching the singing-acting process.

The Three Stages of Kinesthetic Awareness

Most performers are responsive to the idea of expanding choice in their process. When they are, it allows the three stages of awareness to unfold. In the first stage, the performer becomes aware that she is in a state of tension—the anticipatory entanglement. In the second stage, she becomes aware of entering that state: she is *becoming* tense. And in the third stage, she becomes aware that she is *about* to become tense. At that point she has a choice: to consciously inhibit the old habit of getting set by simply not altering her normal state of being; or to put herself in a pysical state of being that does not allow, or discourages by its very nature, the getting-set process.

These two choices represent the two approaches to releasing any conditioning pattern: (1) don't allow the old habit to come into play, or (2) replace it with something different. In *Performing Power* I referred to this as the don't-think-about-elephants challenge. It is possible to not think about elephants; but in *trying* not to, we sometimes end up doing it in spite of ourselves. When that happens we can think about roses instead; for in thinking of roses, we are not thinking of elephants. Not thinking about elephants is Pryor's "good fairy" method number 7—shape the absence of the behavior; thinking about roses is number 5—training an incompatible behavior.

The 25-positions concept is an adaptation of the think-about-roses concept. Applying it to the release of the anticipatory entanglement would mean taking many different physical positions when beginning the performance process. In taking a voice lesson, most performers learn to sing using one basic physical stance or way of being. That way may be one that is thought to be the most supportive of the singing process, or it may come from the ideal way for the body to be set for singing or performance.

Whether there is such an ideal physical way of being or not, the idea that there is tends to encourage the habit of what I call the good-student stance—a practiced form of careful posture unconsciously designed to send a message to the teacher that "I am interested in what you are teaching—I am alert, cooperative and enthusiastic—I am a good student." It also tends to be a subtle form of the anticipatory entanglement. By practicing this teacher-pleasing set in private lessons, performers (1) develop specific ways of setting themselves for performance in general that (2) create holding patterns counterproductive to their own best use of energy. In actual rehearsal and performance, performers will be asked to adopt many different physical ways of being, most of which may run counter to the good-student stance they have practiced so carefully. The anticipatory entanglement created by that unconscious practice of stance taking ends by interfering with the total process—including the voice.

One can often allow performers to experience the usefulness of not adopting the anticipatory stance by catching them off guard while discussing the process with them. While the singers are standing, casually listening, you can suddenly ask one of them to begin singing, "without changing anything." If he does so (and even if he does adjust, it heightens his awareness of it), he invariably sings and performs with greater life and presence. One group called it "coming from the living-it space"—singing from their own, unobstructed way of being rather than from a maladjusted attempt to "be better."

Instructor Awareness: Unconscious Reinforcement of the Getting-Set Habit

Teachers in general often enforce this habit of getting set in unconscious ways. I once asked a class not to make any adjustments in their physical being when they did an exercise. I was interested in what *my* response would be, even though I was consciously asking them to make that choice. The habitual reaction of every group I have worked with, when they are asked to do an exercise of any kind, whether it involves the kinesthetic mode or not, is to adjust themselves, "get set." I point this out whenever it happens (which is repeatedly), but I treat it lightly, playing with the concept so that judgmentalism does not further pollute the already deeply conditioned exercise environment.

I became aware, however, that when certain members of a group would learn *not* to get set when I asked them to do an exercise, *my* judgmental conditioning would come into play with a series of almost unconscious defensive thoughts: "They aren't listening, they don't care, they're being arrogant, they are defying me, they don't believe me, they're judging what I am saying, they are out of control, etc., etc." My MIM was negatively chattering away, echoing the defensive, judgmental, addictive conditioning patterned in so well by society, education, and life. If I reacted unconsciously to those thoughts, it would tend to pull the students into doing something to make me feel better—letting me know by getting set that they did care, they did agree with me, they *were* interested in what I was asking them to do, and that they were "good students."

But I had never had a whole class "not get set" at once. So we acted it out: I introduced an exercise and then asked them to do it. Not a single person got set or made any physical adjustment (the exercise was one that could be done without having to do so). The impact was amazing, even in full consciousness of the setup: I felt all the defensive, paranoid energies mentioned above even while being fully aware that they came from a conditioning pattern, an illusion, that had nothing to do with the reality of the situation.

On another occasion a voice teacher asked me to work with her as she gave one of her students a voice lesson. The first thing that happened was an unconscious message from the teacher to the performer. As the performer was about to sing, the teacher did what I have seen dozens of voice teachers do: sitting at the piano, with the singer watching her intently, the teacher lifted her shoulders and eyebrows—which I suspect is our attempt to encourage our students. The singer naturally imitated the model she was given and created a nicely crafted anticipatory entanglement. Having worked privately with the singer, I was aware of the strength of her anticipatory entanglement: it was not only deeply seated, it also blocked her performance process in significant ways. It was fascinating and disturbing to see where it came from, at least in part, and how easily and unconsciously it was taught.

Another fine performer-teacher with whom I had worked, but for whom I had never clarified the anticipatory entanglement, suddenly realized why a performance she had recently judged as part of a vocal competition was so compelling. In retrospect, she realized that it was the only performance in which there was no anticipatory entanglement. As a result it drew her and the other judges into the experience totally—and it won the competition. With this new awareness of the significance of the anticipatory entanglement (and in this case, the lack thereof), the performer-teacher now had a teaching and performing technique to draw upon. Rather than simply generalizing about the importance of believability or involvement, or whatever (as she and the other judges had done in discussing the winning performance), she could work specifically with the process.

Since the anticipatory entanglement is as unconscious for most performers as the teaching of it is for the teacher, the first step for both performers and instructors is to become aware of it. An aspect of that awareness is the psychological implications of inducing a state of anticipatory tension. If something tells us we have to alter our state of being in order to perform, it means we do not feel OK as we are for performance. In trying to feel OK we alter ourselves in some way: we try to be bigger than life, more noble, more grand, more imposing, or more filled with energy. We try to accomplish all that by changing ourselves, which usually amounts to creating tension in our body. It is a subtle but significant nonacceptance of ourselves as the powerful beings we are. In that nonacceptance we block or short-circuit a part of the power that is available to us in our unobstructed state.

Conversely, *not* getting set for a coach, director, or teacher carries the conditioning connotation that *they're* not OK—they aren't worth getting set for. It is another vicious circle: I'm not OK, so I get set, which actually makes me feel less OK. The teacher, on the other hand, doesn't feel OK unless I act as though I'm not OK by getting set, which means that one of us *has* to be in the not-OK position. Since the teacher generally has the power in teaching circumstances, the performer remains in the one-down position unless the teacher is aware and can allow them both to be OK. Like the mind-reading game (of which this is a subtle variation), the process is mind numbing and debilitating.

The Isolation-Integration Spectrum

Another important spectrum of the kinesthetic mode has *isolation* at one end and *integration* (or interconnection) at the other.

ISOLATION —   —   —   —   —   —   —   — INTEGRATION/
                                                                         INTERCONNECTION

The anticipatory entanglement is a counterfeit interconnection within the kinesthetic system. It is an interconnection that is tense and entangled rather than integrated and free. In order to correct the anticipatory imbalance along that spectrum, it is vital to exercise isolation: to sing with no overt physical adjustment, to gesture with no overt full-body response, or to make no change in the energy flow through the mode system, while allowing the body to remain in isolated readiness. Otherwise the power-robbing entanglement will be continually reinforced and yet will remain outside the performer's awareness.

When the capacity to isolate is established, it will be equally important to exercise integration as well. For example, when we are free to do what we wish with gestures with no full-body response, we can develop the capacity of the body and gestures to work together efficiently and effectively. (And both integrating and isolating can and should be exercised concurrently, for awareness and development of one promotes it in the other.)

There is a series of pure exercises—never to be used in actual performance—that develop the kinesthetic isolating capacity, and that stem directly from the facial exercise sequence: the body flex, the gesture flex, body masks, extreme body masks, and body masks and gesture flex combined.

This sequence was only recently added to the performing power exercise process and has already proved invaluable to a number of performers. Early in my work with the singing-acting process, I included a kind of kinesthetic warmup; but I did not stress it and eventually dropped it from the exercise sequence, reasoning that no singer was going to pull a muscle gesturing. Later it became apparent that it wasn't a physical warmup that was needed, but an isolating psychological-physical release from the universal tension of the anticipatory entanglement.

The Body Flex

The body flex is best exercised at first in isolation, adding the voice and face later. As with the facial flex, its purpose is to develop the performer's capacity to allow the body to do whatever is desired in isolation from the singing, speaking, or gesturing process. The exercise puts the body in continuous motion without the arms being involved. The head, the shoulders, the rib cage, the pelvis, and the legs are all moved separately and in various combinations, freely in any pattern desired.

As a pure exercise—like the facial flex—there is often an unconscious resistance to doing the body flex. The prevailing product orientation of training and performance ("If I'm not going to do it in actual performance, why should I practice it?") encourages such resistance. Several singers to whom I recommended the exercise told me later that they thought it would be of little benefit: "After all," said one, "I'm a kinesthetic dominant anyway, so why should I need a kinesthetic exercise to make it stronger?"

However, when they actually did the exercise they were amazed. One singer called me long distance following a class to say that it was the most important breakthrough in her singing process in fifteen years. Another performer—who only tried the exercise on the insistence of her coach, who had been present when the exercise was explained—said it opened up her sound in a way that astonished her, and made her aware of tensions she had been holding unconsciously for as long as she had been singing. While not everyone will have such striking experiences, it is a useful exercise and warmup, based as it is on the universal need among singers for free isolation within their systems.

Resistance to the body flex when actually singing also relates to the way the singer has learned to sing. As we have seen, that often involves a certain body stance, which is felt to be the "best" way for the body to be while singing and which often turns into a holding pattern. That pattern—which says in effect, "This is the way my body must be held in order to sing properly"—will create the resistance to any change the singer might try to make while singing. The body flex, then, becomes the 25-positions exercise in motion. By definition, no hold is healthy—that is, no holding pattern can possibly be useful in working with the always-changing flow of the performance process. When singers do the body flex while singing, the resistance they feel puts them in direct contact with unconscious holding patterns, which allows them to become aware and change them if they choose.

The Gesture Flex

Where the body flex puts the body in action without the gestures, gesture flex puts the arms in constant motion without the body. Here, again, the exercise is best practiced in isolation before being combined with singing. The arms are moved continually through all the possibilities available: touching the head all over, the body all over, and moving through space all around the body. Since the anticipatory entanglement will slow down the gestures, it is useful to do the gesture flex rapidly, although changing speed in the process is also helpful in developing coordination.

Extreme Body Masks

Extreme body masks, like facial masks, are sustained physical statements involving one or more parts of the body—the head, the shoulders, the rib cage, the pelvis, the legs—with as little held tension as possible. Here the isolation is within the body proper—only one body part being activated—as well as being in isolation from the gestural process. For example, whatever body mask one might choose to make with the head-neck area, one attempts to maintain the freedom of the rest of the body, as well as the freedom of the head-neck to remain in a state of readiness, capable of moving as freely, swiftly, and softly as desired.

Here again, resistance will be encountered: "I can't sing from that position," a statement that usually means: "I don't think I will make my best possible sound if I do that." There are operatic characters like Rigoletto, of course, for whom the extreme body mask is a necessity, and the singers who perform such roles often sing better when they have to make such physical adjustments than when they can use themselves in habitual ways. It may be that the sheer exercise of isolating such physical statements also frees the rest of the body in ways that enhance the singing process.

Extreme Gesture Masks and Combinations

One can also do extreme gesture masks, which are sustained but extreme or unusual gestural statements. These are also isolated from bodily involvement, and should be initiated with the same ease and freedom of our natural use of gesture. (After doing this exercise a short time, performers become quickly aware that there are very few impossible gestures, or gestures that feel unknown or unusual, so long as the naturalistic dynamic informs them.)

We can also combine extreme body masks with the gesture flex, or the body flex with extreme gesture masks. In the first case, the gesture flex heightens the awareness of any superfluous tension created by the extreme body mask. The gesture flex will require that any extra tension around the specific extreme body mask be released. In addition, the ordinary level of the anticipatory entanglement is potentially heightened, allowing greater awareness and access to exercising its release.

In combining body flex and extreme gesture masks, the movement of the body ensures the freedom and isolation of the extreme gestures — which might ordinarily tend to increase the physical tension.

The Four-Step Spiral Exercise Process and the Kinesthetic Mode

The four-step spiral exercise process can be applied to each of these exercises. Although they should also be practiced while singing, as suggested above, we will include combinations involving the kinesthetic mode and the hearing-vocal in chapter 12. While we are prepared to apply this process to combinations of the kinesthetic mode and the facial mode — a process begun in chapters 9 and 10 in working with entanglement 4, between the face and body — let us focus for the moment on the kinesthetic mode by itself. The four-step spiral exercise process would work (as follows) with the body flex, the gesture flex, extreme body mask, or extreme gesture mask exercises.

Step 1. *Increase/Nurture*: Do the body flex, gesture flex, extreme body masks, or extreme gesture masks. Reinforce the energy given with praise.

Step 2. *Awareness/Nurture*: Repeat step 1, becoming aware in the process of how the other parts of the kinesthetic system were affected by the specific exercise. If you did the body flex, did the gestural process want to come into play? Were you able to isolate the parts of the body flex? Could you work with the shoulders independently of the rest of the kinesthetic system? The head? The hips? The legs? The rib cage? If you did the gesture flex, did the rest of the body want to come into play? Did any area of the gesture flex feel especially uncomfortable or create tension? If you did extreme body masks, how much unnecessary tension was necessary to sustain the mask itself? If you did extreme gesture masks, how much superfluous tension was in the gesture? How much in the rest of the body? In all cases, reinforce the energy given with praise.

Step 3. *Release/Nurture*: Repeat step 1, selecting one and only one awareness to work with as you do so. Reinforce the energy given with praise.

Step 4. *Awareness/Nurture*: Repeat step 3, becoming aware of how the energy of step 1 was affected by the new choices made for step 3. Reinforce the energy given with praise. Return to step 1—with the new awareness generated by the first four-step spiral—at a higher point on the spiral.

Each of these kinesthetic exercises can also be combined with facial exercises from the previous chapter. As each succeeding mode is added to the total process, the possible exercise combinations increase dramatically. To list all the possible three-mode, four-step spiral combinations would take a book in itself. Let us examine one of these combinations as a model. With that as a guide, every performer and/or instructor can create combinations that are specific to the needs of the individual situation.

Combining the Kinesthetic Mode and the Facial-Emotional Complex in the Four-Step Spiral Exercise Process

One could combine any of these facial exercises—the facial flex, extreme masks, arbitrary attitudes, extreme arbitrary attitudes, rapid-fire masks or attitudes, and others—with any kinesthetic exercise, including body flex, gesture flex, extreme body masks, or extreme gesture masks.

The assumption is, of course, that one can already do with some degree of skill one of the two exercises to be combined, and has an understanding of the other. It is not necessary to have mastered either of them—one might never move on to new exercises if total mastery were a criterion. And while we want to honor the rule of learning one thing at a time, one can learn a skill well enough to practice it in combination with another without absolute command of either one.

There can even be an unexpected bonus in combining in-process exercises: a skill in which one has been blocked will often fall into place automatically when another challenge is added to it. For example, a difficult facial exercise will sometimes open up when a kinesthetic challenge is added to it. Take attention off trying to do one thing by focusing on something else, and the rest of the system, freed of MIM's control efforts, will accomplish it with ease.

Let us examine one of the suggested combinations as a model: the gesture flex and arbitrary attitudes.

Step 1. *Increase/Nurture*: Do the gesture flex and arbitrary attitudes simultaneously. The arbitrary attitudes can either be called out or displayed. (Note that the focus process can also be given attention.) Reinforce the energy given with praise.

Step 2. *Awareness/Nurture*: Repeat step 1, becoming aware of how the two exercises interacted. For example, was the gesture flex inhibited by the arbitrary attitude process? Did the arbitrary attitudes activate entanglement 4 (FM/KM) so that body tension blocked the flow of the gesture flex? Or was it the other way around? Did attention to the gesture flex inhibit or interfere with the expression of emotion through the face? Reinforce the energy given with praise.

Step 3. *Replace/Nurture*: Repeat step 1, selecting only one interaction to give attention to. For example, if the expression of emotion through the face was inhibited, one could choose to increase that flow of energy. Reinforce the energy given with praise.

Step 4. *Awareness/Nurture*: Repeat step 3, becoming aware of how the part of the exercise not focused upon was affected by the shift in emphasis. Reinforce the energy given with praise. Return to step 1 from a higher point on the growth spiral, shifting the balance in the combination. Repeat the sequence as desired, until a useful and balanced coordination is attained.

With that as a model, individual performers and instructors can create other such combinations as needed. An example of that occurred with a director who attended one of my institutes, and became acquainted with the four-step spiral exercise process. Three months later she told me the following experience.

She was helping an outstanding young singer in her school release kinesthetic tension that was interfering with his total performance. As he did so, he experienced obvious improvement in his performance and in his overall process, which delighted them both. A week or so later, however, he seemed depressed. When the director asked him why, he said it was because he was singing flat and couldn't seem to do anything about it. The director commiserated, but the "ah ha!" experience did not come until later as she remembered the four-step spiral process.

She went to the singer's voice teacher and asked him if he could pinpoint the time when the singing flat began. Sure enough, it was the day after the release of the kinesthetic tension. What had happened was obvious in retrospect: in releasing the tension, the young singer had also released a part of his vocal support process, which was entangled with the tension. As a result, he began singing flat.

The director told the singer what she suspected, and explained the four-step spiral process. As they began going through it, things began clearing up. Part of the step-2 awareness had already occurred: the singer had released some unnecessary tension in the body (as well as a necessary part of the support system); and he had also noticed—without being aware of the relationship—that his singing was adversely affected. Accordingly they moved to step 3 and replaced the necessary vocal support. From there they moved to step 4 and became aware that some of the unnecessary tension had been reactivated through its entanglement with the support process. They returned to step 1 to release, with a new awareness of the total process, the reactivated, but unnecessary tension. And so on, through as many cycles of the four-step spiral process as necessary.

The young singer understood the process, and was able to make significant progress immediately. As the director said, however, "It takes time and practice to release something as drilled in as that; the initial, quick, easy answer got at it superficially, but with long-term results that are not only unacceptable, but dangerous in their own way! The young singer may no longer have been doing vocal damage—thus avoiding the disappearing diva syndrome—but singing flat would have stopped his career just as effectively." In a postscript written with obvious enthusiasm, the director reported that the young singer had just won the regional NATS (National Association of Teachers of Singing) competition—and his voice *and* total performance process had expanded remarkably.

The Three-Phase Gestural Process

In *Performing Power* I described the three-step gestural process that grew from a spectrum created by *naturalism* (real time) at one end, and *music-theater* stylization (extended time) at the other. The performer must seem to be natural—*areba*—in her use of gesture; at the same time, that seeming naturalism must obey the time extension required by music theater. Slow-motion gestures are sometimes justified as an attempt to extend time. In fact, their real source is the anticipatory entanglement in which full-body tension necessarily slows down the individual gestures. In either case, the slow-motion gesture is an unnatural, much parodied, and unnecessary part of music-theater (mainly operatic) tradition.

On the other hand, of course, if there are too many gestures in a given period of time, it denies the necessary extension of time, however believable and free the gestures may be. The three-part gestural process works with both ends of that spectrum as follows.

Phase 1. The naturalistic, impulse phase, in which gestures are initiated as naturalistically—swiftly and softly—as possible. There are exceptions to the swift-soft rule, but they are rare. The reader is referred to *Performing Power* for discussion of these.

Phase 2. The gesture is sustained for as long as the music-theater extension of time requires—which will be the length of the phrase or phrases chosen.

Phase 3. There are always two choices in phase three: (1) a new gesture is initiated—again, swiftly and softly (with the occasional exceptions mentioned above), or (2) the gesture is released. The concept of the release, particularly the floppy release, deserves expansion at this point.

The Letting-Go Principle in Action: The Floppy Release

The floppy release refers to the complete letting go of a gesture, that is, letting it "flop." If this release is total, there will also be a release of residual body tension along with the interfering tension between the body and the

gestures. For this reason, some performers will find the floppy release difficult to accomplish. It means giving up tension control—however briefly—
and that need for control can be very deep-seated. Precisely because the
floppy release brings that control behavior to awareness, it is an extremely
useful exercise.

As babies we learn to hold on to things before we learn to let go of them
(probably for the evolutionary reason that babies who let go of the limb
didn't survive, and babies who held on did—at least for that moment—to
pass on their genetic heritage, which included the urge to hold on). In adult
life that tendency is the basis of habit formation and attachment behavior: it
is easier to hold on, to stay attached to something, than it is to let go. Since
the process of habituating attachment behavior is largely unconscious, we
will hold on to many things that are of no benefit to us unless we give conscious attention to the letting-go capacity. Physical tension to control energy
flow in the system is one of those unuseful things; the floppy release is a
specific, tangible and doable way of getting at it and letting go of controlling
physical tensions in general.

Once the concept is grasped, the floppy release can be applied in many
ways besides with gestures. One can do an overall floppy release of the body
even while sustaining a gesture; one can also do an *inner* floppy release to get
at internally felt tensions that are not overtly evident. Many singers use an
inner floppy release every so often as a spot check on their "ecological system," whether they notice any overt tension or not, for the subtle onset of
tension can be a subliminal process.

The floppy release can also be used as one of the exceptions to the principle of learning one thing at a time. Since music-theater exercise will always
involve the sustaining of time, one can sustain a gesture and also become
aware of entanglement tension that is part of that gesture. At that point—
while doing step 1 with the gesture—one can simultaneously become aware
of the tension connected with it (step 2), and let go of it with a floppy release, thus combining steps 1 and 3 with no contradiction of effort or interference with the learning process.

I have had much positive response from performers about the use of the
floppy release in performance as well as in exercising. In performance it can
be very useful without anyone knowing that a technique is being employed.
The performer may fear that "if I release the tension I am holding, everyone
will know, and it will be a denial of everything I have been doing to this
point, so I must hold on to it." In fact, the floppy release is a gift to the
audience as well as the performer. Any tension in the performer is commu-

nicated to the audience, and any release of that unnecessary tension by the performer also releases it in the audience.

The audience, however, will not know that the floppy release is a tension adjustment—they simply see it as the character making a common and logical statement. I have watched performers in productions I directed doing floppy releases (as I had suggested) and *I* was not aware they were doing it until later. At the moment I saw it, I was simply grateful on some level for the release of the tension, and integrated that into my overall perception of the performance. If I had not been aware of the process from our work together, I would never have realized that it was anything apart from the performance.

Among the many reports I have received from performers about the value of the performing power principles in general, and the floppy release in particular, is the following.

> I have been a musical-theatre performer on a professional basis
> for fourteen years now. There has always been a level of
> underlying physical tension and vocal fear when I've been on
> stage, but since I assumed that was part of the whole experience,
> I never questioned it. The looming high note, the overly
> kinesthetic response to emotion, the guilt over not feeling or
> thinking the "right thing" (I'm "Method" trained as an actress)
> always seemed to keep me from fully enjoying myself onstage,
> even though my raw talent and hard work combined with training
> have enabled me to push through a lot. After working playfully
> for over six months on the exercises I approached the challenge
> of playing Lilli Vannessi/Kate in *Kiss Me, Kate* with a sense of
> excitement I haven't felt in a long time. All during rehearsals I
> kept working on releasing my entanglements and kept a playful
> attitude most of the time. Numbers seemed to "stage themselves."
> The more "operatic" parts of the singing were a breeze. Then
> when I finally got on stage I felt a sense of lightness, freedom and
> ease that I had never known before. Everyone commented that it
> was my finest performance ever and I was able to perform the
> entire second week of shows with a killer cold that had me laid
> up in bed whenever I wasn't actually on stage or teaching my
> morning class in Musical Theatre for Teenagers. Floppy releasing
> during the physical and vocal highlights of the show released
> incredible power into my being. My face never stopped (I was
> doing what felt like rather extreme facial masks that no one
> thought were "too much") and I had an absolute ball! I even
> took a very "deep" emotional moment and chose to use familiar
> facial masks to reach my "inner" and it worked!

That is the point, of course: to gain performing power, a better product, and have more fun all at the same time.

I have incorporated the floppy release into an exercise sequence that is like bar work for the singer-actor. It is an expansion on the face-space-bod exercise sequence in *Performing Power*, which I call the head-flop sequence.

Bar Work for the Singer-Actor: Head-Flop-Space-Flop-Bod-Flop

In addition to isolating and integrating the kinesthetic capacities, we also want to increase the vocabulary available to the kinesthetic mode. The head-flop sequence does this as well as providing a general integrating exercise. It is based on the following approach. Gestures can touch the head (and neck) with one or both hands; gestures can move into the space around one with one or both hands; and gestures can touch the body with one or both hands. In addition, gestures can be released completely or allowed to "flop," hence the name: "floppy release."

The head-flop sequence, as called out, would be as follows:

1. "Head" — one or both hands touch the head;

2. "Flop" — floppy release;

3. "Space" — one or both hands work in the space around the performer;

4. "Flop" — floppy release;

5. "Bod" — one or both hands touch the body;

6. "Flop" — floppy release.

    Repeat total sequence as desired.

The sequence is arbitrary, of course, and any other pattern can be chosen: bod — head — flop — bod — flop — space — flop — head — space, etc. The alternation of floppy releases with head, body, or space gestures was chosen to begin the process because it releases after each gesture any tension that may have crept into them.

It is also important to note that the head-flop sequence should always be coordinated with the focus process. As we pointed out in discussing the facial-emotional complex, focus is the delineator of thought structure, and thought precedes all energy use, including gestures.

A description of a head-flop sequence including focus shifts, as called out, would be as follows. (Initially one could call out all the instructions until they are understood, finally calling out only the part in quotations.)

1. "Focus, Head"—sustain focus and gesture;

2. "Shift focus"—sustain gesture until new focus is reached;

3. "Flop"—sustain focus;

4. "Shift focus, space"—sustain focus and gesture;

5. "Shift focus"—sustain gesture until new focus is reached;

6. "Flop"—sustain focus;

7. "Shift focus, bod"—sustain focus and gesture;

8. "Shift focus"—sustain gesture until new focus is reached;

9. "Flop"—sustain focus.

Repeat total sequence as desired.

Let us also note that arbitrary attitudes can also be added to the head-flop sequence as follows.

1. "Focus, attitude (anger, joy, etc.), head"—sustain focus, attitude, and gesture;

2. "Shift focus"—sustain attitude and gesture until new focus is reached;

3. "New attitude, flop"—sustain focus and attitude;

4. "Shift focus"—sustain attitude and gesture until new focus is reached;

5. "New attitude, space"—sustain focus, attitude, and gesture;

6. "Shift focus"—sustain attitude and gesture until new focus is reached;

7. "New attitude, flop"—sustain focus and attitude;

8. "Shift focus"—sustain attitude and gesture until new focus is reached;

9. "New attitude, bod"—sustain focus, attitude, and gesture;

10. "Shift focus"—sustain attitude and gesture until new focus is reached;

11. "New attitude, flop."

Repeat sequence as desired.

All these sequences can be practiced individually or in a group, with the instructor calling out the shifts, attitudes, and gestures. Calling the sequence out allows the instructor to vary the sequence in any way desired. To facilitate this process, arbitrary attitude cards can be used (a list is included in appendix A). To work with singers as they are singing, the arbitrary attitude cards can also be reproduced in a larger size, the instructor simply holding them up so they can be seen.

In addition to the individual head-space-bod gestures, combinations are also possible. For example, head-bod (one hand on the head, one on the body), head-space, and space-bod. And if the instructor notices that the same gestures are always repeated (e.g., only one hand to the head), the calling-out process can break patterns by saying, "Head-head" (meaning both hands to the head, with "head" meaning only one hand); "Space-space," and "Bod-bod."

Exercising with Arbitrary Gestures

In appendix B there is a list of arbitrary gestures that covers most kinds of things one can do with gestures. These can also be written out on cards and used in the head-flop sequences above. For individuals working alone, these cards (along with the attitude cards) can be set up on a mantel or pinned to a bulletin board and used with arias. The exercise potential is obvious: If singers would work with five cards a day from both the arbitrary attitude and arbitrary gesture lists (the number of possible combinations is enormous), their performing power would expand tremendously over a period of months.

Because of entanglement 3 — the tension lock between the full body and the arms — expansion of the gestural capacity is a great challenge. As we have seen, any trace of the ubiquitous anticipatory entanglement places the whole body in a state of tension that — however slight — will automatically bring into play the lean and/or the lift. Either the lean or the lift will make the gestures feel uncomfortable and unnatural and therefore — unconsciously — something to be avoided.

And gesturing *is* an uncomfortable process for most singers. I have never encountered a singer who felt free and easy about gesturing in whatever way he/she wished. This is not to say that such singers do not exist, but they appear to be rare exceptions. For all the rest, a clear awareness and understanding of the anticipatory entanglement, its effect on the use of gesture, and the dynamics of gesture itself (see the three-phase sequence discussed earlier) is a vital first step. The next step is to actually practice the gestural process, regardless of how it feels at first, so that one can get in touch with the entanglements that interfere with that process and begin to release them. Actual exercise with gestures (not just thinking about them) is facilitated by the head-flop sequences as well as by the arbitrary gesture cards.

Because gesturing is made so difficult by the universal but unidentified anticipatory entanglement, teachers may simply avoid the process of working with them. Singers, particularly in recital situations, are often told that gestures are not appropriate in those circumstances—that tradition does not permit it. Those kinds of traditions, of course, are often created by default: it is difficult to do something (to gesture while singing), yet no one knows why; but instead of finding out, the thing itself is discarded—the gestural baby is thrown out with the tension bath. Thus the real creator of that tradition is the anticipatory entanglement that makes gestures difficult, and therefore uncomfortable, for singers and audiences alike. Because of this, a great many singers—some of whom are famous—don't use gesture in recital, and that establishes a "tradition," but a tradition based on incapacity rather than artistic choice.

The truth is, gestures are *always* appropriate—it depends totally upon the capacity to use them freely and naturally. And, contrary to what is often counseled, that capacity can be developed through practice, but only if one understands the dynamics of natural gesturing and the complex of unconscious entanglement that interferes with that process, and then develops a way of exercising the gestures and releasing the interferences.

An Annotated Paragraph of Confusion about Gesture

In an otherwise useful book, *The Art of the Song Recital* (Emmons and Sonntag), there is a remarkable paragraph on gesture (the only reference to gesture in the book's 571 pages) that demonstrates both a lack of understanding about the gestural process in the field as a whole, and the gun-shy reactions that result from that lack. Because it is a long paragraph, and is filled with so many misconceptions, I will present an annotated version of it, taking one or two sentences at a time with my own comments following them.

> What about gestures? Whether or not permitted by tradition in
> recital, a gesture is never successful unless it begins with a true,
> sincere intention. (p. 320)

Comment: We have discussed the possible origin of that supposed tradition, but the second half of the sentence is a mine field of mind reading.

The fact is—and I have seen it demonstrated repeatedly—the success of a gesture has to do with *how it is done* and with what is happening on the face simultaneously, and not with the inner and invisible thought processes and intentions.

It is the same inner-to-outer fallacy we have discussed several times: If we get it right on the inside, it will automatically be expressed appropriately by the outer tools—in this case by the gestural process. That is simply not true. If there are entanglements, the inner processes must work through them, and the outer expression will be uncomfortable, tense, awkward, or limited, and will therefore seem to be inappropriate. This will be interpreted to mean—and this is the killer—that we did not have "a true, sincere intention." Once again, we are guilty for not thinking the right thoughts or feeling the right feelings.

Actually, we have been unconsciously conditioned on the physical level to control the expression of energy in a way that does not allow the appearance of a "true and sincere" gesture. But we can become aware of that conditioning, exercise it, and release it, and *that* can allow us to appear true and sincere *regardless* of what we are thinking or feeling.

> Only a consummately skilled actor can *plan* to use the same
> gesture in the same place and repeat it without looking faked and
> staged. Laurence Olivier managed to do this superbly in each of
> many performances as Oedipus putting his eye out; the late,
> distinguished recital singer Jennie Tourel magnificently repeated
> the exact drunken movements each time she sang the aria from
> *La Perichole*. This practice, however, is not for everyone to try.
> (Emmons and Sonntag, p. 320)

Comment: The first question is, how did those consummately skilled actors get to be consummately skilled? It recalls a question I often ask singer-actors in jest: How many of you have learned to juggle by accident? We have recounted the immense amount of intense practice time Laurence Olivier put in to acquire his consummate skill, which recalls the old saw about the relationship between genius, perspiration, and inspiration. The six months he spent lowering his speaking tessitura for the role of Othello is just one example. If this much time was taken by someone who is generally acknowledged as the century's greatest actor, at the peak of his performing capacity, how much time might the rest of us want to spend in developing the individual parts of our processes? Olivier's greatness was in direct proportion to his willingness to practice and develop skills he did not already possess.

One of those skills, and a skill of any artist, is the capacity to *plan*: to be able to say the same words in much the same way (precise duplication, as we have seen, is not possible nor is it even a useful goal), to sing the same notes in much the same way, to project the same emotional messages, *and* to send the same physical and gestural messages in each performance, *rediscovering* them as though for the first time, rather than simply *repeating* them.

A director who worked with Maria Callas on one of her first performances of *Tosca* told me this story of her gestural planning and practice. At the moment Tosca picks up the knife with which she will stab Scarpia, Callas stopped the rehearsal. She wished to explore the gesture of picking up the knife. After she had done it several different ways, my friend decided to keep count. Before Callas was satisfied with the gesture, she had done it fifty-four times!

Again, if an accomplished, intuitive artist will devote that much time and energy to the practice and planning of a gesture, what does that say to the rest of us?

The artist should also be able to make different choices on the spot when it is appropriate: not changing the words themselves or the music, but making new choices in interpreting the words, the music, the emotional content behind them, or in the use of gesture—this is a vital freedom to draw upon when appropriate, one that can be exercised *and* planned. But to accept implicitly that everything should be planned—that is, the music, the interpretation, the language, the diction, etc., should be practiced, rehearsed, and memorized—with the single exception of the gestures is a remarkable and irrational isolation of something so basic. In this remarkable view, gestures should presumably be left up to spontaneous creation or improvisation on the spot. And that seems to be the intent of the following passage.

> We suggest the following rule to solve the dilemma of the gesture in recital: If in this song it is traditionally and stylistically feasible to use a gesture, and if in the moment of performance it seems natural to gesture, *allow it to happen*. In addition, the less formal second half of the program, if anywhere, is traditionally and logically the more likely place for gestures. (Emmons and Sonntag, p. 320)

Comment: That is another mine field of restrictions through which only the boldest performer would tread. Who and what has determined what is "traditionally and stylistically feasible"? We have discussed the nature of tradition in such things, but feasibility is even more ambiguous, depending as it does upon the capability of the artist as well as the conditioning of the audience with respect to gesture.

But suppose the artist has somehow determined—without actually practicing them—that gestures of some sort are traditional, feasible, and logical at given points in the song. (That ominous "if anywhere" has, of course, driven him to the second half of the program.) Then, at those selected points where, on the spot, it suddenly seems natural to gesture—natural, let us note, to do something he has never done before in a profoundly unnatural context—the singer should simply *let it happen.* I will guarantee that any singer following that rule will avoid gesturing like the plague. Even if he has applied the litmus tests of tradition, feasibility, and logic and received the go-ahead sign, by the time he notices that it seems natural to gesture, it will be too late. That capability can only come through planning and practice. As if to counter just that kind of thinking, the next sentence reiterates the antiplanning/antipractice theme.

> Planning and/or practicing a gesture for a specific place is almost
> never successful. (Emmons and Sonntag, p. 320)

Comment: A gesture attempted through an entangled condition will not feel good nor will it be effective—and lacking both qualities, it will naturally not be successful. However, the problem is not with the gesture itself—it is with the entanglement that interferes with it. If we assume that our entangled condition is permanent and unchangeable, then yes, we will have eliminated the possibility of successful gesture. But exercise and release of the entanglement *and* the capacity to gesture successfully are not only possible, they are exciting opportunities. We can make choices out of those entanglements, develop our gestural capability, and expand our total performing process in doing so. But that depends upon bringing those entanglements into awareness through exercise—and that means practicing gestures that, by definition, will be "unsuccessful" when they are first practiced.

The exercise of those gestures will not seem natural or appropriate at first; that is not the function of the exercise. Following the four-step spiral exercise process, we increase the energy through the gestural process; in the second step we become aware of what else is happening besides the gesture; in the third step we release that superfluous, interfering energy; and in the fourth step we become aware of how that release has affected the original gesture. We then return to step 1 from a higher point on the spiral of growth. A concept of success that is based on the limitations of our societal and music-theater conditioning, and that demands that step 1 be an immediate, finished product, will ensure a severely restricted growth process. The sentence following that warning makes certain that maximal judgmental strictures will be applied to any attempt to work with gesture

> The end result of many motions and gesturing is random and trashy. Restraint is utterly necessary. (Emmons and Sonntag, p. 320)

Comment: If you were hesitant about working with the gestural process before, this clinches it. It seems to connect planning/practice with random/ trashy (whatever those last two interpretive judgments may mean in describing gesture). If the face is in the SAD condition of passive neutrality, *any* gesture will seem to be without meaning and therefore random. What kind of gestures might seem trashy (outside of something sexually explicit) is less clear, but perhaps it was thrown in just to drive the warning home, and to set up the idea of restraint. However, if there is any quality young singers have an abundance of, it is restraint. Restraint—also known as carefulness or caution, which both manifest as hesitancy—is an effective antidote to whatever sense of freedom and play the singer might still possess. To wrap up this paragraph of confusion, the magic name of Stanislavski is invoked.

> Most important, there is no beauty in a gesture or pose done for its own sake; there must be a compelling reason behind it. Stanislavski referred to beautiful poses that lacked all inner meaning as "ballet," an uncomplimentary description. (Emmons and Sonntag, p. 320)

Obviously there *is* beauty in a gesture or pose done for its own sake— the ballet remark simply underscores that. What seems to be the point is that, unless we also perceive an intention behind the gesture, we will not know what it means, and without a compelling *inner* reason for being, it will be neither believable nor beautiful, whatever its abstract qualities.

By and large we can agree: the singer is portraying characters in whom we want to believe as people; the singer is not a dancer, and does not have the skill for the display of balletic gesture, nor is singing the appropriate vehicle for it if he did. But the reiteration of the mind-reading fallacy—that if the inner meaning is there, the gestural process will automatically reflect it— avoids the central issue, which is this: We can only know the intentionality and inner meaning in a gesture through what we see; attending to what is actually seen and practicing with that information is what the exercise process is about. Without the planning/practice of exercise, gestures will not be beautiful, believable, or compelling. With appropriate exercise, they can be all three.

Motivating Gesture

The attempt to motivate gesture, to give it intentionality, can, in fact, subvert the very thing one is trying to accomplish. The body, face, and voice, when they are functioning freely, all work faster than the mind can monitor and control. Attempts by the mind to assert control over those processes *in process* inevitably end up interfering with them. I have found it useful for many performers in the initial phase of gestural exercise to give up the idea of motivating a gesture, and simply do it without being concerned with what it means. A gesture, after all, acquires meaning from several sources besides itself: from the face, from the circumstances around it, the kind of character one is portraying, the statement made by the rest of the body, and the music accompanying it. Attempts to give it meaning almost always involve tension of some kind, and that tension becomes built in to the meaning process. It is similar to the fallacious repression-equals-expression equation. In this case the equally erroneous equation reads, "Tension equals meaning/ motivation."

This leads to another spectrum to explore with the exercise process: *nonmotivation* at one end and *motivated* at the other.

NONMOTIVATION — — — — — — — — MOTIVATED

It isn't that we are after *lack* of motivation, but in exploring that spectrum, the performer can become aware of what she actually does to "motivate" gesture and can then explore other options. The instructor and observers can then tell her which of the other choices communicate clearly and which do not. Putting the attempt to motivate together with what is actually communicated, the performer can learn what she truly needs to do to communicate the invisible inner motivation behind the gesture. It may be that what is needed is more facial communication, or less tension, or more swift-softness in the gesture itself, or some combination of the three. Just as in exploring the tension-relaxation spectrum, our purpose is not to find a single, perfect place on that spectrum, but to develop the capacity for choice over the whole spectrum and to expand one's field of performing choice potential in the process.

The anticipatory entanglement also contributes to the tensions of showing motivation. The subtle, overall anticipatory set creates a tension linkup which ensures that any movement made by one part of the body will tend to pull the entire body into play—as it does in the lean and lift, and as it will do in contributing to the already unuseful tensions of motivation showing. The attempt to motivate a gesture—to give it "a true, sincere intention"—will have increased the existing tension of the body, thus fixing the lean/lift counterfeit interconnection in place. And again, that entanglement of gesture and body will come to be felt as equivalent to the motivation.

To release this particular complex of tensions, the device discussed above—the literal dropping of motivation as a factor in the performer's mind—can also be useful for the purposes of exercise (and even for performance itself). Working from the inner, we can tell ourselves as performers to practice gesturing without motivation, that is, to gesture without doing what we think is necessary for motivation, until we have a clear-felt sense of how the gestures can function without it.

Simultaneously, we can work from the outer to release the externals of the lean/lift phenomena. The gesture flex is a useful lead-in to this process. One can also lean back against a wall or sit down while gesturing, to ensure that the body cannot be involved in its usual way. In working with conductors with the performing power technique, this has proved to be a very useful way of allowing gestures to develop their own expressive power, free of the body as a whole.

We can apply the four-step spiral exercise process to the gesture-motivation/lean-and-lift complex as follows.

Step 1. *Increase/Nurture*: Exercise with gesture, using arbitrary gesture cards or a head-flop sequence, and try to motivate the gestures. Reinforce the energy given with praise.

Step 2. *Awareness/Nurture*: Repeat step 1, becoming aware of how the lean/lift comes into play with the gesture. Reinforce the energy given with praise.

Step 3. *Release-Replace/Nurture*: Repeat step 1, selecting one (and only one) aspect of the motivation-plus-lean/lift tension complex to work with. For example, do the gestures without trying to motivate them, or place the body in a position in which the anticipatory entanglement and/or the lean/lift phenomenon is not possible. Reinforce the energy given with praise.

Step 4. *Awareness/Nurture*: Repeat step 3, becoming aware of how the original gestural (or mental) energy of step 1 was affected by the energy change. Reinforce the energy given with praise. Return to step 1 from a higher point on the spiral of growth. Continue the process as desired.

Another part of this false tension-equals-motivation equation may come, inadvertently, from movement classes. Performers are often told in such circumstances that the gesture must come from the floor, the feet, the legs, the buttocks, the center of the back, or some other imagistic concept that the movement instructor is using to get a sense of interconnection in the body as a whole. The intention is laudable, for the average young performer badly needs to experience and learn how to work with her whole physical being in an integrated and interconnected way. But when the concept of interconnection is translated into gesturing, it almost always comes down to the performer trying to "show" that the gesture comes from one of the places it "should" come from — floor, buttocks, back, etc. — and that showing is done with held tension. When that is the case, it truly looks as though the singer is trying to be balletic.

In fact, the last thing singers want is for the audience to focus on the quality of their gestures. Dancers *do* want that; it is their art and skill, along with the movement of the body within and through space. But the singer is representing a human being who must seem to be as natural as possible, and dancelike gestures will betray that purpose.

Here, then, is another full spectrum for gestural exercise: *balletic* at one end, *naturalistic* at the other. Again, it is not a matter of finding the one correct approach, but of learning how to make any choice along the spectrum. Balletic gestures are occasionally useful — witness the Sills-Treigle performance of Handel's *Julius Caesar* in the early seventies. Learning what one needs to do (and both Sills and Treigle had to learn and practice that balletic style extensively) and what *not* to do are both necessary in accomplishing one's performing intentions and expanding one's performing capabilities.

Gestural Connection with the Inner

Once the performer is partially free of this complex of motivational tensions, she can begin the process of reconnecting the gesture with the total process in a free way. Very often, that connecting process takes place automatically — the release of tension allows gestures to make a connection with the

whole process in a way that flows naturally when there is no tension interference by the parts of the process.

In other cases, the performer will practice and achieve a "motivation-
less" gestural capacity that looks that way, and is not useful as a performance
process. The long-conditioned habit of motivating gestures through the generalized tension of the lean/lift has not allowed those gestures to develop the
subtle modeling and detailing that gives them life in themselves. That diffi-
cult-to-define, but ever-so-tangible quality is what "true" motivation of gesture is all about (along with the contribution of the face). And the challenge
of *describing* those subtle, life-giving characteristics deepens as the performer releases the overt, more easily described entanglements, yet still does
not seem to be *areba* with the overall gestural process. The description of
what makes for arebability in gesturing requires increasing specificity and
detail.

In one revealing instance, I asked a performer to do some sensual body-
caressing with her gestures (for the character of Carmen). She had long since
freed herself of the lean/lift phenomenon, or at least was aware of it and was
able to release it when it occurred. Yet the body-caressing somehow lacked
a sense of motivation — it was not *areba*. Closer observation, and some ex-
perimentation of my own in making the gesture, revealed that the caresses
were made with the fingers rather than the full palm. When the hand was
relaxed and the full palm as well as the fingers was allowed to come into
contact with the body, the gestures immediately became *areba*. Even more
interesting, the performer suddenly felt "naughty" — as though she were doing something that was a little too revealingly sensual; in short, the gestures
became *areba* for her as well. Like the performer mentioned previously, who
knew she was using enough facial energy when she felt like a "bad girl," this
performer had a clue as to how to connect the outer to the inner with her
gestural process: when it felt threatening or too revealing — at least in the
case of sensual gestures — she was connecting.

We bring the same basic trust in the whole human energy system in all
instances: if we get the parts out of the way of that whole system, it has an
innate capacity for powerful communication. Entanglements block that capacity and drain that power; releasing or replacing them will allow clearer
and more powerful communication.

In exploring new, previously unexperienced gestures, we should always
be aware of what the face is doing, as well as the dynamic of the gesture
itself. A blank face will make a gesture look meaningless to the audience and

feel meaningless to the performer. If the face *is* communicating clearly, we may return to examine the gesture and its dynamic: does it function with the same freedom and flow as an accustomed gesture? We can ask the performer to initiate the gesture as though it were one he commonly used, and then sustain it for as long as the musical-dramatic time extension requires.

Another Look at Emotional Expression and the Body

A very useful exercise in connecting the outer and inner processes physically involves the expression of IMP with the body. Although we have stressed the fact that the body does not express emotions specifically—depending for that specificity on the face, the voice, and the situation—that does not mean that the body makes no response to the experience of emotion. It does have a response, of course, and the condition of entanglement is a direct result of that response. The purpose of this exercise is to explore and develop the body's communicating power in responding to emotion. We do this by disentangling those responses from other parts of the body that are not necessary to the communication, and then expanding the range of expression of those responses.

The exercise uses arbitrary attitude cards, and will involve interaction with the facial mode. (You can isolate the face from the body, but not the body from the face.) As the emotions are called out or displayed, one can express them in three possible ways: (1) with gestures only, (2) with the body only, or (3) with the body and gestures in combination. We will assume that the face will express the emotions in all cases. As we apply the four-step spiral exercise process, we have choice in the second step: we can choose either the facial or the kinesthetic branch of the process, selecting from either mode what it is we wish to release or replace.

Step 1. *Increase/Nurture*: Express an arbitrary emotion with a gesture, with the body, or with both (with the face automatically preceding that gestural expression by an instant). Reinforce the energy given with praise.

Step 2. *Awareness/Nurture*: Repeat step 1, becoming aware of the interaction of the body, the gesture, and the face: If the gesture was to be isolated, was the body entangled with it? If the body was to do the expressing, was the gesture entangled with it? If the two were being done in partnership, was it a free relationship or was the lean/lift involved? Was the face sending the emotional message clearly, simultaneously with the energies of the body and/or gesture? Reinforce the energy given with praise.

Step 3. *Release-Replace/Nurture*: Repeat step 1, selecting only one of the awareness observations to release as you do so. Reinforce the energy given with praise.

Step 4. *Awareness/Nurture*: Repeat step 3, becoming aware of how the energy of step 1 was affected by the energy of release. Reinforce the energy given with praise. Return to step 1 from a higher point on the spiral — or begin a new spiral with another emotion.

Working with this interplay of IMP and the kinesthetic and facial modes provides an opportunity for both performers and observers to experience the fact that any gesture can accompany any emotion and vice versa. I will often stop a head-flop sequence, and ask the performers to repeat the gesture they have just done (or ask them all to repeat the gesture of another member of the group) while I give them a series of strongly contrasting attitudes to integrate with that single gesture. This was a response on my part to comments from performers to the effect that "the emotions and the gestures don't go together." The answer is: "*Any* combination of gestural and emotional statements can go together. At the same time, yes, there is a conditioned kinesthetic reaction to many emotions, leading to similar kinds of gestures for those emotions — and, yes, we are interested in allowing that kinesthetic impulse to flow freely. But any gesture can accompany any emotion, and make perfect sense; and since our performing power rises as we add new possibilities to our field of choice potential, we will be aided in that expansion by coming to *know* that we have a much broader range of choice in combining gestures and emotions than our conditionings allow us to think. However, we cannot know all that with the MIM alone, but only by doing it; by taking one gesture, and combining it with many different emotions, we can come to know with our whole system that that is not only possible, it also expands and empowers our performing process."

The allowing-modifying-concealing spectrum with which we approached the facial mode can also be applied to the kinesthetic mode. There are three general possibilities: (1) Emotional energy can be allowed to flow through the kinesthetic mode with transparent freedom, expressing as clearly as possible for that mode the meaning of IMP (always being assisted in this process by the facial mode); (2) the energy of IMP can be expressed but modified in some way; or (3) it can be completely concealed. In all three cases, it is understood that the statement is to be made without entanglement. The concealing end of the spectrum, for example, could very easily involve some sort of entanglement repression; but it need not do so, for one can simply choose to remain in a state of readiness to act, without expressing the inner process through either the body or the face.

Energy Transformations: From One Mode to Another

We have been exercising the capacity of the kinesthetic mode to tranform emotional energy into kinesthetic energy. We can also ask the reverse: to make a kinesthetic statement (without facial involvement) and then ask the face to translate that statement into its own terms. This is different from the ability to accompany any physical statement with any facial statement. Such an exercise accepts each mode as possessing a unique language of its own, and develops the capacity for intermodal understanding and translation. It is also a recognition that the Radiant Whole—prior to the transformation of part of our universal energy into communication—has infinite potential and flexibility.

That infinite potential can be drawn upon to make facial statements, and/or vocal statements, and/or kinesthetic statements; or it can be burned up and wasted in entanglement tension. Since the kinesthetic mode is the fundamental tool MIM uses in controlling the flow of communicating energy, it is also the key to opening the communicating process. It is vital that the performer understand what the body can and cannot communicate, and how it can assist the other two modes in doing what they do best. That understanding can be heightened by the intermode translation process.

Here is a simple example of that kind of exercise in energy transformation: One performer sings a phrase with the other performers listening but not watching. Each of them then translates that musical phrase into a kinesthetic statement with gestures, the full body, or both. Alternatively, they translate the vocal energies into facial terms. A second step would involve one performer making a kinesthetic statement, which would then be translated into vocal or facial terms. A third step would translate one performer's facial statement into vocal or kinesthetic terms. Further complexities are possible: A vocal statement could be translated into a combined physical-facial statement; a facial statement into combined physical and vocal terms; and a kinesthetic statement into a vocal-facial combination.

As we approach the exercise of the vocal mode, we will be able to draw more and more fully upon the three modes in combination. In doing so, we will continue to work with the basic principle of developing the maximum potential of each mode individually, even as we exercise their capacity for synergistic interaction. The better each mode knows the qualities of its own power and is not confused about what it can and cannot do, and knows as well what the other members of the mode team are best allowed to do for themselves, the more powerfully they will be able to interact as a whole system—a whole that is greater than the sum of its individual parts.

Chapter 12

Exercising the Vocal Mode

Vocal Play: Overcoming Resistance to Working with the Singing Voice

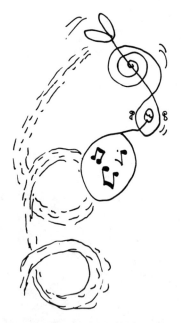

In *Performing Power* I devoted a considerable amount of time to the vocal mode (then called the hearing-vocal mode), exploring its implications and defining its vocabulary. It was the first mode I treated, reasoning that the singer-actor could not actually perform—except for brief interludes—without a speech or a song. It was the necessary, preexisting base for the exercise of the other two modes.

One can also look at the three-mode system in another way. The facial mode can communicate without the body or voice (as in a recital interlude), the facial and kinesthetic modes can communicate without the voice (as in a music-theater interlude), and both of them are always there whether or not the voice is in play. In developing an exercise sequence for total performance, it makes equal sense to begin with the only mode that can function solo—the face—adding the kinesthetic to form a duet, and finally bringing in the vocal mode to form the total performance trio.

After completing *Performing Power*, I concentrated on developing the facial mode. It was the "new" mode, the unexplored mode, and since there were no preexisting models for its exercise and development, it was open to new ways of working. At a certain point in developing the facial-emotional complex, however, I realized that I had created exercises that had no parallel for the voice and the body. I set about rectifying that, developing exercises for the kinesthetic mode that have been described. But it was not until I was halfway through the writing of this book that I finally focused in the same way on the vocal mode and also turned my attention to the *singing* half of the singer-actor, as distinct from the speaking voice—which I had dealt with in *Performing Power*. I began applying the same exercise logic to the vocal mode and the singing voice. In *Performing Power* I made the following brief nod toward the singer-actor.

> Let us distinguish between the speaking voice and the singing voice. The singer works from a score in which a great share of the musicality is already defined. Speed, rhythm, volume and pitch are specified, and the singer works within a far more restricted range of choices than the speaker. But choice is there, and more use can be made of it than is usually the case
>
> . . . .
>
> As we discuss language musicality, I assume that the same changes on a more modest scale can be exercised by the singer and coach: songs can be sung faster and slower, louder and softer, more legato or more staccato, more intensely or more relaxed, along with attention to the other aspects of language musicality. (pp. 104–5)

Exploring Vocal-Musical Play:
Discovering the Spectrum of Musicality

Despite that note to others (and to myself), it was not until April 1987 that I began pursuing the issue directly. Although I have always had good relations with the coaches with whom I work, I had left that province to their discretion (since I knew that some of them used related concepts in their private coaching sessions). But in a working session with a group of singer-actors who were familiar with the performing power concept, I asked one of them (a particularly gifted performer) to play with the vocal mode as we had been playing with the kinesthetic and facial modes—to do anything interpretively she pleased. (This was facilitated by the presence of a particularly open-to-process coach who not only went along with the idea, but was actively enthusiastic and supportive of it.) She began to play, and it was not only an amazing experience—it was revelatory on several levels.

First, there were a number of very expressive and useful musical changes—choices she would never ordinarily make, but that, according to the coach, were "the kind of thing you sweat blood in trying to get singers to do." But more important, there was also a remarkable change in her total performance. She was personally engaged in the performing process unlike anything I had previously experienced from her—or from most singers; her personal power seemed to be unleashed; and there was a sense of commitment and involvement that was electrifying. The other singers in the group subsequently had similarly energizing experiences with vocal play. Why was this so? What allowed such a remarkable change in her freedom of energy flow?

There are many possible reasons, but one thing seems clear. All classically trained singers spend a lot of time doing what someone else tells them to do with their voice, both in singing and interpreting—setting up the potential for authority dependence we have discussed. That concern about what external authorities may think tends to produce singers who are careful and cautious with their performance; it activates their judgmental sensitivities so that they monitor and try to control not just their voice, but everything they do, which is a sure prescription for a loss of performing power. For better or worse, that anxiety about the judgment of others stems to a large extent from their musical training. The training of the singer—musical, vocal, and musicological—tends to create a control-interference pattern that affects everything else they do, physically and emotionally. Generally it becomes a twig in the logjam of blocked energies. Remove that twig, and not only will the musical logs flow more freely, so will all the others jammed up behind them.

In short, it seemed clear that in trying to be "correct," in trying to do it "right" for the many musical authorities for whom they had worked, those young singers—and they were typical in training and background of young singers everywhere—had built up judgmental walls within themselves that blocked everything to some extent, including their personal power. And since music and the voice are fundamental issues for singers, those two parts of the whole, however important they are, can easily be mistaken for the whole itself; if there is repression, overcontrol, or inhibitory cautiousness interfering with those musical and vocal parts, there will be interference with the other parts as well.

The controlling conditionings that are released by such play are present in all of us—coaches and teachers alike—or they wouldn't be enforced with such consistency. Speaking at a gathering of eminent voice teachers and music-theater practitioners in general, I related these and similar experiences I had had in developing performers with play exercises. I emphasized the importance of playing with the score in order to contact and unleash the true potential in both the performer and the score. It was a forward-looking group of teachers and performers, and no one took overt issue with the concept. But one of the voice teachers present (for whom I have enormous respect) found it necessary to emphasize the importance of young singers "knowing what they are doing musically, and having a deep and liberal understanding of the score, of its style, of its cultural characteristics, and of the culture from which it emerged."

One can hardly quarrel with that: it is *True*, a *Good Thing*, and a looming, monolithic description of the kind of student "product" we want to emerge from our institutions of higher cultural learning. I respect the intentions behind such efforts, but if the curricula devised to produce such liberally educated paragons do not contain a good measure of genuine play with the music and with one's capacities, and a balancing sense of irreverence, that "sacredness of the score" imagery will continue to inhibit and limit not only the personal power of performers, but their interpretive and performing power as well.

Clinging to the idea of the "one correct interpretation of the inviolable score" (although few would put it that bluntly) is another example of choosing one position on a full spectrum and losing the potential of the whole. I hope it is clear by this time that I do not advocate depriving young singers, who have had no opportunity to develop an in-depth understanding of musical style and culture, of the expert guidance of teachers in their musical interpretation; nor am I suggesting that they be encouraged to simply do whatever they feel like with the music, or violate the score—although giving them permission to do that very thing is often a useful approach to the exploratory process. But I am suggesting that we must investigate in depth the spectrum of performance possibilities, especially the forbidden end: let us call it the personal, free exploration-of-both-the-score-and-the-performer-with-no-holds-barred end. Unless we do that, we sap the potential power of the other end of that spectrum: let us call it the traditional-disciplined-stylistically-appropriate-true-to-the-intentions-of-the-score end.

No score is sacred: as a colleague of mine likes to put it, a score is simply a set of instructions that can, will, and in fact *must* be carried out in many different ways. Some instructions have more inherent power in them than others, but if we approach any of them with a sense of the sacred, we risk missing what is truly sacred: our capacity to interact fully and completely with those instructions in a living way that transcends both the performer and the instructions.

All this is still and always will be very much in process. I ask every coach I work with to interact with me in exploring it, and I ask the reader— whether performer, teacher, coach, conductor, or director—to do the same. As we examine exercises for the singing and speaking voice, exploring new musicality and interpretive choices with the four-step process, I urge us all to pursue the issue as freely as possible during a part of our work-play process with each other. There is no danger—one can always return to old patterns—and the potential for growth is immense.

The power in playing with musical interpretation has been borne out by ongoing experiences with other singers for whom it has also been an exhilirating and expanding experience. The case of the cautionary voice teacher was noted to increase our awareness of the hidden resistance we may encounter as we venture into the area of interpretive play (my own unconscious resistances will be recounted below). That area will be the origin of our first full-spectrum approach to vocal-musical exercise: the spectra of musicality play.

Full-spectrum musicality involves the exploration of as many musical interpretive choices as possible. The accompanying spectra can serve as a guide for this process (without intending to be all-inclusive).

Full-Spectrum Musicality Play

Movement

HOLDING BACK — — — — — — — MOVING FORWARD

Dynamics

SOFT — — — — — — — — — — — — LOUD

Rhythm

STACCATO — — — — — — — — — — LEGATO

Pitch

SUSTAINING — — — — — — — — — CHANGING

Diction-Articulation

LOOSE, RELAXED — — — — — — PRECISE, CONTROLLED

Tone Color

BRIGHT — — — — — — — — — — — DARK

Discovering the Vocal-Quality Spectrum

The same kind of resistance to full-spectrum play was an impediment to other explorations. Just as the sense of the "sacred score" blocks the interpretive play process, the feeling that there is one kind of perfect, pear-shaped vocal sound that must be found and held onto at all costs blocks the exploration of the next spectrum: the vocal-quality spectrum. On this spectrum we play with vocal sound, or even with the vocal production itself. For just as there is no one true interpretation, there is no one true sound. There is, in fact, a tremendous range of possible useful sounds, some of which may be more "attractive" on some abstract, ideal level, but which become potentially boring if that is the only sound there is. Beverly Sills once said (and I paraphrase), "I will make the kind of sound appropriate to the character — and if that means a scream rather than a pear-shaped tone — so be it." Not only that, but playing with a freer range of vocal expression also enhances the beauty of the pear-shaped tones both by contrast and by the same release of inhibitory tensions that occur with the sacred-score violations.

I first encountered this spectrum in depth as I worked with a group of singers with whom I had had previous contact. We had planned two three-hour sessions over two days. To begin the first session, I suggested a round of vocal play. Six hours later we were still playing with the voice with increasing excitement. It all began with this new exercise: After the singers had begun singing in their normal fashion, I would signal them to use a different kind of sound of their choice: it could be strongly nasal, breathy, open, "blatty"—whatever they wished, so long as they dropped their usual way of singing and made sounds they would not ordinarily make. After they had sung a few measures in that way, I would signal them to move back to normal singing. The results were amazing: every singer's normal use of the voice sounded noticeably better—richer, freer, fuller—*after* they moved back from producing the unaccustomed sounds. Not only could we all hear it, the singers themselves felt better in producing the sound: it was direct experience of vocal empowerment for both listener and singer. That is what kept us enthusiastically occupied for six hours—and it has been a continuing breakthrough for many of them in their vocal and performing processes ever since.

During the second three hours, one singer had an insight that resonated with all the others: she became aware that for years she had been in constant search of the "one perfect sound." And in trying to find it and hold on to it, she was not only judging and eliminating a host of other very useful sounds—she was also interfering with the potential richness and wholeness of the one sound itself. Apparently the attempt to control her way into the one and only sound had also been depriving the system as a whole of its flexibility and freedom, as well as diminishing the sound itself.

Vocal quality, then, became the second full spectrum of vocal-musical play. This spectrum ranges between two acronyms devised for the purpose: at one end is *OOPS* (the one and only perfect sound), which relates to one's normal "best" use of the voice; at the other end is *UBU*—all the "ugly but useful" sounds one can make.

Vocal-Quality Spectrum

OOPS— — — — — — — — — — — — —UBU

(The one and only perfect sound)   (Ugly but useful)

Normal, "beautiful" use of the voice   All possible kinds of sounds

Discovering the Vocal-Emotional Spectrum

I discovered this spectrum in an entirely different way—unwillingly. In retrospect, I am very grateful for the experience. Having spoken of the unconscious resistance of others, it is only fair to recount my own. It involved a series of interactions with the coaches with whom I work, which led to a remarkable and expanding growth process.

Readers of *The Complete Singer-Actor* and *Performing Power* know that many of my realizations about the singing-acting process grew from a constant alternation and interaction between the fields of acting and singing-acting: I teach and direct professionally and educationally in both areas concurrently and often simultaneously. During the fall of 1987, I was doing just that—teaching in a new professional actor-training program at the University of Minnesota, and directing an advanced singer-actor institute in New York City with one of my coach-colleagues. It was an intense and fruitful interaction, both between acting and singing-acting, and between me and my colleague—and from it grew a number of insights.

It was only much later, however, during the writing of this chapter, that I realized the true nature of one of those interactions. In working with my coach-colleague, I recognized that I had had my own agenda for the way I wanted him (and coaches in general) to work with the vocal process—particularly with respect to the expression of emotion with the voice. I have always tried to remain open and encouraging to whatever process any of my coach-colleagues might evolve, but in that area I had an unconscious block.

I had confined my thinking about the emotional process to the facial mode for what seemed to me to be undeniably logical reasons: any attempt to express emotion with the voice would tend to activate the repression-equals-expression error, create interference with the voice, and lead to the disappearing diva syndrome. Yet this coach, whom I respect greatly, was insistent on pursuing the emotional process into the vocal area in ways that seemed to me to be potentially harmful. This naturally led to extended discussions of the issue and of the concepts—emotional, vocal, and musical—around it. As a result, we were able, as we team-coached the singers, to mutually disentangle and expand their performance processes. He approached it from the vocal perspective, while I focused on the physical-facial (as well as the vocal). It was an expanding experience in itself for both of us, but it covered a deeper process. I didn't understand at the time why he needed to pursue the emotional issue in what seemed to me a potentially dangerous way.

The light dawned when I isolated the inner and outer aspects of the vocal emotional process (IMP and the vocal mode). I realized that my coach-colleague, like most of us in this century, wanted to be involved in the total, whole process of the human being. The real message was his need to cover a full spectrum of energy in working with the vocal process, not simply a part of it. Without full awareness, I had been placing unspoken limits on what it was appropriate for him to work with on that spectrum.

And those limits made partial sense, for there *were* risks involved in the process he was attempting—but those risks became opportunities for mutual growth when we interacted fully with the process and with each other. It was expanding to become aware of that situation from a more whole perspective (a kind of four-step spiral process in itself, which I have since shared with him). The process continues to be a full one for both of us.

Any coach with integrity will want to work with the complete performer, to develop and expand the inner processes, and not be confined to dealing only with the technical externals. Such coaches will want to help a singer do more than just get it technically correct: they will want the singer to "feel it," or to seem to be expressing the music from within, from their inner, organic understanding of it. And those coaches will want to *hear* it — naturally enough — not just see it. (Since they are playing the piano simultaneously with the singing, it is unlikely that they could see clearly what was happening anyway.)

But what is the nature of that information they want to hear? It is not *merely* technical accuracy (even in music, the word *technique* has been given a pejorative connotation); two singers can seem to be equally accurate technically, yet one seems to be more expressive than the other. That expressivity may be the result of two things: the facial expression of one singer may be stronger, thus making her total performance more expressive than another's even though the musicality is the same; or it may be an inaccurate description of what is being heard: the vocal characteristics that define the inner qualities have no agreed-upon vocabulary — and therefore one cannot describe them or even know what they are.

Let us grant that something is being expressed that is not only difficult to describe but, even if one could, would be too subtle and complex for any singer — let alone the less expressive one — to be able to control and put into actual practice. That wonderfully complex shimmer of inner essence seems to be triggered by some internal process, and it makes the difference between a good performance and a great one. What is the nature of that inner process? How can we get at it? How can a coach help the performer release the special qualities that emerge when that interior process is tapped? To paraphrase a more passionate statement of the same thing: "Anyone can call for interpretive techniques — accelerando, then a gradual diminuendo, rallentando, subito piano, etc. — but what about the heart and soul of the music? That comes from the inner process, and without it the rest is a lot of external trappings!"

That sounds remarkably similar to the American approach to acting since our fragmentary appropriation of Stanislavski. And in both cases the response is partially true—but no more so than to say that "technique is everything!"—a polarization of the other end of the inner-outer spectrum.

But the musical coaches' questions are virtually identical to those an acting coach might ask. And the partial answer gleaned from Stanislavski has also come to be applied by many musical coaches. The nature of that inner process seems to involve emotion. It is not an intellectual process, but has to do with deep feeling of some kind. Moreover, it is feeling that tends to interest us most as audience members: an actor's ideas may be sound, his thinking clear, and his intellect powerful, but unless he also feels deeply, and projects it as well, we will not be intensely compelled by what he has to communicate.

Thus emotion and feeling it become the issues for the dedicated coach—in singing as well as acting. However, the difference in their respective tasks is that the musical coach is working with a highly trained vocal technique that is not realistically expressive and can be threatened by any confusion in the approach to IMP. The acting coach, on the other hand, is working—in most cases—with an untrained vocal technique that is far more easily responsive to an inner approach and is less obviously endangered by that approach. In both cases, the coaches are working with people who have been heavily and unconsciously conditioned about the expression of emotion, and who share with those coaches in general a certain amount of confusion about the human energy system and how it functions in expressing emotion.

There were two full spectra of vocal-emotional expression that evolved from the extended interaction with my coach-colleague and the insights that followed: an inner spectrum and an outer spectrum. In order to clarify their functioning for exercise application, let us consider the integration of inner and outer in the vocal mode.

Integrating Inner and Outer in the Vocal Mode

Every outer technique has a potential inner meaning. Every movement of the facial musculature, no matter how extreme, has a potential meaning for that person. She may not yet have created the connecting link between inner and outer that will allow her to know that meaning, but it is there to be activated. Observers may even see the meaning before the person herself does, but in order to make that external technique useful for herelf, the person, too, must feel the meaning.

The same thing is true of the gestural process. Every gesture has a potential meaning link with the inner, and that link must come alive for the performer in order for the gesture itself to be useful (the performer won't use it if she doesn't experience it as meaningful). Activating that outer-to-inner connection for the face and body is an important part of their expansion as performing tools.

A further point: While every outer technique has a potential inner meaning, not every inner meaning has an outer means of expression. Our inner process is far too complex and powerful to be totally expressed by the outer. Developing the capability of the outer to express more and more completely the fullness of the inner processes is a primary purpose of the exercise process. And it is important not to place predictive limitations on what *can* be expressed: it is always possible to open the outer more fully to the inner; the inner is infinite in its potential, and the outer, while not infinite, has potential beyond MIM's power to conceive.

The two processes—outer to inner, and inner to outer—are powerfully interrelated. As we work with one—expanding the outer technical capacities and then coming to know what they can mean—we are also promoting the other, for as the outer capacities expand in that way, they also become available for the expression of inner energies as yet unexperienced.

Let us apply this inner-outer connecting process to the voice. Any and every sound the voice can make has a potential meaning for the performer; and while not every inner meaning can be expressed with the voice, we have yet to reach the limits as to what is possible. For all practical purposes (and idealistic ones as well), we can exercise and expand our outer capabilities with the idea that there are no boundaries to our possibilities.

In working from outer to inner, the instructions are to work with technique in an extreme way. By definition, an extreme technique will have no known meaning for the performer. From that unknown extreme the performer moves back toward the known with the technique, creating a link of understanding with the same technique at a less extreme level. Once that meaning link has been activated, one can again move toward the unknown, this time expanding the meaning link into the unknown, thus making it the known. If one stretches the meaning link too far to make the new unknown a known, one can return to the known to reestablish it, and then move toward the unknown once again. (This also relates to the arebacizing spiral that we will discuss later.)

The inner-to-outer process has a similar dynamic. One expresses the chosen emotion as fully and powerfully as the singing voice will allow. If the instructions are followed, this expression will be one that the performer has never experienced — the level of expression will be unknown, even though the emotion itself is known. My experience in working with the inner-to-outer process indicates that the outer expression of that inner understanding is hardly ever too much. It *feels* like it is to the performer, but to the observer it is just fine — one is often grateful that there is finally a useful and communicative level of expression. This means that the move back into the known is unnecessary in moving from inner to outer: the performer already knows what the emotion means; it is only a matter of expanding the capacities of the outer to express it; the integration will take place automatically as the outer gets comfortable with the new level of expression. Let us now consider the expression of emotion with the voice in greater detail.

Expressing Emotion with the Vocal Mode

When we speak of singing-acting, we know the meaning of the singing part better than that of the acting part. As we suggested, the communication of emotion — how a person *feels* about what he is experiencing — is probably as close to a one-phrase definition of acting as one could find: planks and a passion. While the facial mode is the most specific channel for expressing emotion, the speaking voice is also a powerful emotional communicator. But for the voice, that process is far more complex than it is for the face, largely because the voice deals with both the meaning and the music of the words.

The face is either saying something or it isn't; it can give blended messages, but that blend *is* the message. The voice, on the other hand, is always sending two messages, which may be in agreement, contradictory, or different but neutral with respect to each other. The words are the outer part of the vocal blend — they are specific, agreed upon, and can be written down — while the musicality with which those words are spoken or sung relates to the inner process — which is either transformed or not into the outer expression of musicality. The fact that the words can mean one thing and the music another creates opportunities for extreme vocal complexity as well as harmful double binds: "Of course I love you!" snarls the manipulative parent to the confused child.

The distinction between emotion repressed/expressed via entanglement and emotion communicated freely through the musicality itself is a crucial one for all actors — speaking or singing. The snarl of the parent in the previous example usually involves an interference with the vocal flow — a repression-equals-expression error (which the child nonetheless understands as anger, and will probably learn to do herself when she expresses anger). That entanglement—the number-7 throat squeeze—*does* communicate by stereotypical consensus, but it is hard on the voice and, if practiced with intensity over a period of time, can destroy it. That, of course, is the disappearing diva syndrome.

Expression of that same anger through a free but intense use of language musicality is not only more powerfully expressive, it is also vocally healthier. But it is also far more rare. Our conditioning with respect to the vocal expression of strong emotion is deep, virtually universal, and will act to control and block a free flow of vocal-emotional energy. Since a free flow is both healthier and more powerfully communicative, we need to develop the capacity to first allow the free flow, and then to shape it into effective communication.

But since we have learned to *understand* the emotions we express by repressing them, we have come to know the emotion almost solely through its conditioned repression. Now we must reverse the process: we must allow a free-flowing expressive capacity, which is new and unknown, to be connected with IMP—the emotional source. For the singer this connection of IMP with an unfamiliar use of the voice is an obvious necessity, since singing is not a realistic way of expressing emotion. This, in turn, underlines the importance of the facial mode for the singer: the speaking voice as a realistic expresser of emotion has been replaced by the singing voice; and since the body does not express emotion specifically, the face is left as the primary expresser of realistic emotion for the singer-actor.

For the actor it is more complicated, at least initially, because the actor who is trying to be "real" will naturally call upon the real way he has been conditioned to express that emotion in life. If he has learned to express those life emotions freely and healthily, all is well; if not, he is dragging onstage the entanglements of his unconscious conditioning—a point we have discussed above and in *Performing Power*. That same entanglement conditioning affects the singer as well, but in a different way, particularly as it interacts with the singing process.

When a performer is singing, it is easy for him or her to seem less involved with the emotional process, both because of the conditioned facial neutrality acquired in learning to sing, and because singing is not a real way for most people to express emotion. Since I am a director, and not a coach—and can therefore watch the singer-actor performance more easily than a coach—I focus on what I can see to determine the level of emotional involvement. That means, in turn, that I give special attention to the facial mode as a principal means of communicating emotion — with a simultaneous awareness of its relationship to the body. Since the face is such a powerful and indispensable resource in the communication of emotion, I was being pulled into a part-equals-whole error. The fact that the singer does not use the voice realistically in expressing emotion, and must rely upon the face to do so, led me toward the unconscious assumption that the face was the *only* part that expressed emotion.

If I had said that in words, the error would have been clear. As it was, however, the presence of the coaches I work with brought that unconscious assumption to light and renewed my awareness of the emotional process of the singing voice. Coaches in general, no matter how gifted, will be hard-pressed to observe the faces of the singers they are coaching in any detailed way — they simply can't give them that kind of attention while they are playing a complex score. But even if they could watch the face closely, the fact that coaches are necessarily hearing dominants means that they will want to *hear* the emotion as well. It isn't enough to understand the emotion visually, it must also be heard in the voice itself. This is where the interaction of voice and emotion comes into play in a necessary, but very tricky way.

If a coach asks a singer to work with a specific emotion, the singer will logically bring the entanglement around that emotion into play to do so, and the coach may even come to like the resultant emotional "edge" in the voice — and risk, inadvertently, the disappearing diva syndrome. I point this out to the coaches I work with, even while acknowledging their need and the needs of the art to be emotionally expressive with the voice. But that expressivity must be healthy, and that is the challenge: to find a way of drawing upon IMP without bringing into play the vocally destructive entanglements that are universally involved with strong emotion.

Sometimes the facial energies will assist that process, but just as often — especially in the intitial stages of the exercise process — to call upon the facial energies through the use of arbitrary attitude cards will activate entanglement 4 (FM/KM). Since any tension in the body affects the voice, that two-way entanglement between face and body will immediately become a three-way interference that includes the vocal process as well.

In developing a vocal exercise process, one of the primary insights concerned some of the parallels between the facial and vocal modes. An important spectrum in working with the facial-emotional complex was that formed by its inner and outer parts. There were exercises that dealt strictly with the outer (facial flex and extreme masks), exercises for the inner (arbitrary attitudes), and exercises to connect the two (arbitrary-attitude expansion and extreme masks plus arbitrary attitudes). It became clear as I developed this chapter that while the vocal mode has inner and outer components as well, they had not been properly clarified; in fact, they had been confused by the use of musical terminology.

In communicating with the face, we must be able to actually see it: we only know the inner from what we see on the outer. The same principle applies to the vocal mode: knowing the inner depends upon the capacity of the outer to communicate it through sounds we can actually hear; everything else is interpretive guesswork. With the face, every move that FAMUS makes has a potential inner meaning; similarly with the voice: every bit of language musicality also has a potential inner meaning. In developing facial capacity, we expanded its potential to express the inner by the use of extreme exercises for the outer resources. For the fullest realization of that potential, it was important not to demand product sense from those outer exercises.

However, as we approach the singing process, there is a shift in the way the voice is trained. For the actor (in this country, at least) there is relatively little training for the speaking voice. Acting, as we have seen, has focused so exclusively on the inner—on IMP and MIM—that outer exercises for facial and vocal techniques are either non-existent, or are playing catch-up. But for the singing voice, that approach is necessarily reversed: technique is the first and foremost consideration. It is only in the past few decades that we have begun to examine the relationship of IMP to the singing process. Among the results of this unfortunately confused examination is the entangled field called singing-acting. Much of this book is devoted to clarifying the confusions that infest the field and that interfere with the training of the singer-actor. One of these confusions involves the relationship of the inner and the outer in the singing-acting process.

As we continue to traverse this entangled territory, let us review some of the basic principles involved in working with the inner (MIM and IMP) and the outer (the projective modes).

1. The inner and the outer together form a full spectrum of emotional energy flow; it is not an either/or situation.

2. The purpose of exercising both ends of the spectrum is to heighten their capacity to interact, to connect, so that they are always in mutual play on some level.

3. The inner cannot be perceived unless it is given expression by the outer.

4. We can only know the inner by what we actually perceive on the outer.

5. If we do not perceive a desired and agreed-upon inner communication, there is a missing link in the connection between the inner and the outer.

6. That missing link may be an outer incapacity, or a missing connection between the inner and the outer, but since the inner emotion is agreed upon, the lack is not within. (If anger or joy is the agreed-upon intention, its lack of communication lies not in that understanding, but in the movement from that point to its outer expression.)

7. While it is useful to work with the inner, to activate it, and to call upon it in various ways, we must not place upon the inner the responsibility for communicating its messages. That responsibility belongs to the outer, just as the responsibility for the delivery of a letter is not placed upon the person who mailed it, but upon the postal service, which does or does not deliver it.

8. If we do focus responsibility on the inner, it may create harmful reactions within the system as the outer overcompensates for the missing message and tries to make it happen through tension, thus reinforcing the repression-equals-expression fallacy.

As we work with vocal mode, we are dealing with an energy of enormous complexity. The intense, often parental, even quasi-religious relationship between voice teachers and students attests to the challenge of dealing with it. The vocal energies are also the intersecting point between singing and acting, between conductors and directors, and between musical coaches, voice teachers, and acting instructors. The distinction between the inner and outer will continue to guide us as we explore and clarify the exercise of the singing process.

We have two spectrums to relate to in working with the vocal expression of emotion: an inner spectrum and an outer spectrum.

Inner Vocal-Emotional Spectrum

NORMAL VOCAL   ALL POSSIBLE
EXPRESSION —   —   —   —   —   —   —EMOTIONAL CHOICES
                                               (See arbitrary attitudes list.)

From the outer perspective, the voice is used in a variety of ways to express emotion: groans, sighs, laughter, weeping, moaning, crying, etc. If a sigh is the choice for exploration, for example, one would begin with a full, nonsinging sigh; then that sigh would be blended with the singing process at many points along the spectrum, from a sigh that is simply "thought" while singing—and may not be heard as such by the listener—to a sigh that can be audibly identified as part of the singing process.

Outer Vocal-Emotional Expression

NORMAL VOCAL   ALL POSSIBLE OUTER
EXPRESSION   —   —   —   —   —   —   — VOCAL CHOICES

At this point, then, we have three full spectra—each with an outer and an inner component—on which to base our development of an exercise process for the vocal mode: (1) the vocal-musicality spectrum, (2) the vocal-quality spectrum, and (3) the vocal-emotional spectrum.

Exercising the Vocal Mode: The Spoken Vocal Flex

Now that we have established the vocal spectra along which to exercise the vocal mode, we can create specific exercises to do so. In chapter 10 we began filling in the missing parts of the exercise process for the kinesthetic mode, drawing parallels with those for the facial mode; for example, body flex, gesture flex, and extreme body and extreme gesture masks. Let us do the same for the vocal mode—exploring the possibility of vocal flexes and extreme masks—beginning with the speaking voice.

The vocal flex originated as a response to what I call the "rut principle" in the learning of lines. At the first few rehearsals of a play in which everyone reads their lines for the first time for each other, it is not uncommon for line readings to be "set," consciously or unconsciously; those set readings are then heard in essentially the same form weeks later in performance. This can also happen in memorizing the lines of a soliloquy for classroom or audition. In both cases, line-reading decisions are being made long before the performer knows enough about the character, the situation, or his personal interaction with the character and situation to make such decisions. Yet those lines are being set in a way that can be almost impossible to change. Drive a car in the same set of muddy ruts two or three times, and you will not be able to get out of those ruts.

This may be why many actors memorize their lines with neutral readings: so that they will not set an interpretation too early. But there is no such thing as a neutral reading: a neutral reading is a reading with as much if not more meaning than a flamboyant reading. It is not unlike the singer learning to sing with a facial deadpan in order to avoid the overt signs of entanglement 6 (between voice and face). The difference is that with the spoken vocal mode, the purpose of the neutral reading is, presumably, to avoid making a premature commitment to interpretation. (It may also be a way of avoiding making a strong and judgable statement before MIM has figured out what that statement should be. The problem is that MIM can only learn which reading it prefers by testing various options, and only the voice in action can do that.)

We have seen the limitations of the deadpan approach with the face: it confines the face to one kind of emotional statement. We released it from that confinement by making the deadpan approach one end of a spectrum, with the facial flex at the other, thus opening all the choices in between. The unentangled deadpan also becomes a choice and acquires power in the process. In approaching that exercise process, we focused on the facial-flex end of the spectrum, since it is more developmental for the facial process as a whole, allows greater flexibility, and encourages a greater flow of energy.

The same principles apply to the spoken vocal flex. Like the deadpan face, musical-vocal neutrality can be seen as a delimiting factor in and of itself. However, allow the neutral voice to be one end of a full spectrum, and we begin opening up the process, developing flexibility and power. As with our approach to the facial exercise process, we will emphasize vocal flexing rather than neutrality, since increased flexibility, power, and a greater flow of energy are all a part of our larger purpose.

For the speaking actor, the vocal flex means reading one's lines with as great a range of musicality as possible with no concern for meaning. It is a play process, but that does not mean that meaning will never be a part of it. It is simply that finding the meaning is not the primary purpose of the exercise. The vocal flex can and should be used to find the musical meaning structure of the text, but at this stage its primary purpose is developing vocal capacity—instrument expansion, not interpretive expansion—and only secondarily to arrive at a meaningful reading.

In doing the vocal flex, the performer is to explore the various language musicalities as freely and fully as possible—high and low, fast and slow, loud and soft, intense and relaxed, connected and disconnected, staccato and legato—moving from one extreme to another in exploring those spectra. It is not possible, of course, to do them all at once: one can select one or two primary categories each time. (They are all continually present, of course, for one cannot speak at all without using all of the in-time categories — see *Performing Power*, p. 105.)

One can also have at it spontaneously, noting those categories that remain unexplored each time. The basic question the vocal flex asks of the performer and the voice is, "Can I do this with my voice? Independently of meaning, can my instrument choose to speak lines in any conceivable way? And if I can't, what is stopping me?"

The exercise principle behind it is precisely the same as for the facial mode. If the instrument — in that case, the facial musculature, in this, the vocal music-making capacity — is not capable of making a complete range of moves or sounds when exercising abstractly, it is unlikely that it will suddenly acquire the capacity in the more inhibiting circumstances of performance. The outer instrument must be made adequate to the most wide-ranging demands that the inner expressive needs may place upon it.

Vocal-flexing play can also be a way of learning lines that leaves them totally free to interpretive choice. Ideally, the vocal field of choice potential is totally open and free before one has actually read some specific lines; there is no meaning limitation in what can be done with pitch, speed, volume, and rhythm. Practically speaking, however, very few performers have total vocal freedom of this kind; their instrumental capacity is confined within certain kinds of patterns and limitations. Those confining patterns form the individual's personal field of vocal choice potential; it is limited in various ways, and can be expanded through exercise.

That field of *personal* vocal possibility is then imposed upon a given text, which has a field of *performing* vocal possibility. For example, there are a great many ways to read Hamlet's "To be or not to be" soliloquy: the personal vocal possibilities are far greater than the field of performance possibility. The absolute field of personal vocal possibility will always be greater than the specific performance needs of any given speech (and the exercise question is whether all those possibilities are available to the performer). But the vocal flex approaches the personal field and the performance field with the same purpose: expansion of the choice potential of them both.

Using the rut principle image, if one drives across a clean muddy field many times, and drives in the same ruts each time, they will soon become so deep, steering isn't necessary — the ruts (conditionings) take over. Moreover, it becomes increasingly difficult to leave the ruts without considerable resistance. If, however, you drive across the field over a different path each time, you will retain the power of choice as to the path you take; the whole field remains available.

The same principle applies to the exercise process in general, with one difference: our performance "field" is already heavily rutted, and it will take persistent practice to begin establishing new paths. The old rutted paths will pull at us, and MIM will rationalize and justify their importance—calling them "choices" when in fact they are conditioned patterns—in finding ways of avoiding the effort of creating new, genuine choices. The practiced ruts (entanglements) can be transformed into choices by acquiring other choices. As with other entanglements, they are to be accepted and not judgmentally rejected; we simply want to make available for use the area around the ruts so that the ruts can become free choices as well.

This process of rut transformation is particularly challenging in working with the spoken vocal mode. When using words, the vocal mode intersects with MIM and is entangled with all of MIM's addictive judgmental qualities. For this reason, genuine play with the vocal mode is more challenging than with the body or face. Since the vocal flex is really another name for vocal play, the flexing exercise is particularly important. The ruts in the vocal field are far more quickly formed and hardened—often in the course of one rehearsal—than the other two modes. This may be largely because of the intimate relationship between words and judgment.

This is also why the reinforcing, nurturing step of the spiral exercise process is so important. The weight of judgment can assert itself so quickly that we need constant alertness to reinforce *any* move that is made in a useful direction by the vocal mode. Affirming and supporting our exercise process becomes important in proportion to the potential for judgment.

Exercising the Vocal Mode: Spoken Vocal Extreme Masks

The hearing-vocal extreme mask has the same relationship to the hearing-vocal flex as has the facial flex to facial extreme masks: the mask sustains a moment of flex. The performer selects one of the in-time categories (those without which one cannot speak at all, such as pitch, rhythm, volume, speed, intensity, continuity) and works with the lines in question using the extremes of those various musical spectrums. Again, the purpose is not to achieve an appropriate product, but rather to expand the instrument through exercise.

This expansion is also part of an inner-outer spectrum: the external capabilities of the vocal instrument at one end, and the intuitive, sense-making capacities of MIM and PIM at the other. If the outer instrument cannot make the necessary musical statement, the inner sense cannot be translated into musical meaning; and without that musical capacity to draw upon,

MIM and PIM have nothing to exercise with and develop their own sense-making interaction with that musical capacity.

As with all our other exercise efforts, this one involves a move into the unknown: the performer must use the language in a way different from anything she has experienced. As she does so, some of it will make sense immediately, some of it will take practice, and some of it may lie beyond the sense-making capacity—at least for the time being. The essential things are: first, to get the vocal energy out there into the unknown, and, second, to shape it in various ways so its potential meaning is allowed to become *areba*.

I have sometimes referred to this as the vocal seasoning process. To allow the unfolding of meaning—*arebability*—from any language-musicality demands an interplay of all the in-time categories. They are all always present when one is speaking (or singing) and it is their interaction that allows a vocal statement to be *areba*. As with any good recipe, it takes the right blend of the various ingredients—flour, salt, spices, sugar, shortening, liquids—to make it palatable: leave one out and you may have a disaster. Similarly with the vocal recipe: leave one language musicality out of the preparation and you may have, if not a disaster, at the least a lack of arebability and communication.

Two common controlling patterns come into play when performers are exercising with language musicality: (1) a generalized emphasis on one musical category, creating a whitewash over the actual complexity; (2) a breaking of the language into phrase chunks, separated by pauses during which MIM can think about what comes next and how to control it. In the first instance, there is a tendency to flow on in one in-time category (say, speed) without allowing the other categories to interplay with it and enrich the language meaning; in the second, each of the controlled chunks also has a sameness that is intensified by the pauses. Both come from a similar effort to control through oversimplification.

The Continuing Triumph of Play: The Arebacizing Factor

When I began devising this exercise parallel to the facial exercise process, the idea of having a step that dealt with a normal, useful, performance-oriented line reading seemed important. Vocal flex—a pure play step that focused on expanding vocal capacity—would be followed by meaning-play. In that step, the performer searches for the operative structure—the way to speak a line to make its meaning as clear as possible—by playing with all the possible combinations. In *Performing Power* I discussed the importance of finding an operative structure within which to play with language musicality. The operative structure is still vital in finding out how a line works, but the ways of getting at it have changed from a frontal assault to a freer, more allowing approach in which the meaning emerges from playing with the lines. Let me explain.

Whenever I approached the exercise of having performers play with the operatives to find the meaning structure of a line, a sort of invisible barrier would rise; everyone would get hung up on right and wrong, good and bad readings, and it would be reflected in the voice. We were, in fact, searching for an appropriate reading of the line, and in trying to find that "correct" reading, the performers would get tied up in control entanglements. It seemed clear that when we left the area of play and got down to the "serious" business of getting the verbal meaning right, we lost far more than we gained.

This was emphasized during final "celebrations" of one of my classes. (I never give final tests in my classes; we only celebrate the process of performance—usually by playing—and those celebrations surpass in product and performance quality any "tests" I have ever given). I had assigned two versions of all soliloquies and scenes: a play version in each of the three modes (that is, a kinesthetic, vocal, and facial version of each scene and soliloquy), and a "normal" or traditional version in each mode. The idea was to exercise along the full spectrum created by *free play* at one end, and *normal product* at the other: stretch yourself with a play version, then arebacize those energies in making an actual product out of it, as discussed in chapter 8.

That seemed to be a logical approach, and I told the class that I might ask for a play or normal version in each of the three modes, and that they should be prepared to present either one. As it turned out, the normal versions were never presented. I asked the first performer for his play version, and that set the standard: the play versions in every case were the most interesting, useful, and energy-rich work they had done *and* they were also perfectly appropriate for actual performance. Only occasionally was there a need to arebacize them further—and even then, prior to arebacizing, the performance was far more powerful than customary for each performer.

It appears that the human system has an "arebacizing factor" built into it for performance situations. Perhaps it is the judgmental conditioning—almost impossible to release completely—that asserts itself in any performance or quasi-performance situation, and insists on making as much sense as possible out of whatever is performed, arebacizing the play elements regardless of our intentions.

In any event, it seems clear that the problem is not to understand the meaning of something; in most cases we have knowledge of the verbal meaning of the material we are performing. The challenge is in allowing our energies to flow freely and fully into that material, and trusting our system to make projective, communicating sense of it without the over-monitoring that kills so much performance and destroys so much meaning in its very attempt to be meaningful. Creating a play space is the most useful way to allow that free flow of projective energy, and when the playing is brought into a performing context, the inherent arebacizing factor will generally take care of the rest. (The concept of operative play is covered in vocal extreme masks, in which it becomes very clear whether the operative structure of the line is understood or not.)

In connection with this play process, let us remember the arebacizing spiral that leaps into the unknown to create an extreme energy statement, then spirals back into the known with that same statement, arebacizing it even while continuing to work with it. From there one can spiral back out to the unknown, even further than before if desired, then back to the known and so on. This combining of play and product shaping gives the performer permission to move into the unknown in the first place, since there will always be an arebacizing step.

We can combine the arebacizing spiral, the vocal flex, and vocal extreme masks with the three vocal spectra of musicality, quality, and emotion. We can also expand our use of the four-step spiral exercise process to include all three modes at once.

Expanding the Four-Step Spiral Exercise Process

As we apply the four-step spiral exercise process to the vocal mode, the possible choices for step-2 awareness expand: we can choose to focus within the vocal mode itself, or on either of the other two modes. Using the spoken vocal flex combined with the musicality spectrum as an example, the step-2 possibilities include the following.

Step 1. *Increase/Nurture*: Do the vocal flex with a given speech. Reinforce the energy given with praise.

Step 2. *Awareness/Nurture*: Repeat step 1, becoming aware of one of the following areas:

a. What happened in the vocal mode itself? What language musicality categories were not used? What categories were used repeatedly? What patterns emerged? What vocal tensions or limitations emerged in connection with which categories? (For example, high pitch may create vocal tension.) Which categories consistently seemed to work together? (For example, fast might always be connected [entangled] with loud, staccato with high, etc.) Did certain categories seem to connect with specific emotions in the vocal mode? (For example, did loud and high connect with anger?)

b. What happened in the facial mode? Was entanglement 6 (VM/FM) in strong evidence? What language musicalities caused particular facial change? Did certain language musicalities relate to certain facial statements? (For example, was loud and high—if connected with vocal anger—also reflected by an angry facial expression?)

c. What happened in the kinesthetic mode? Was entanglement 7 (VM/KM) in strong evidence? How active was the body in connection with specific language musicalities? (For example, did high pitch create shoulder tension? Was there a strong need to gesture? Was the breathing interfered with in any way?) Was there any squeezing of the throat in connection with any of the language musicalities? Was there any held tension in any other parts of the body in connection with specific language musicalities?
Reinforce the energy given with praise.

Step 3. *Release-Replace/Nurture*: Repeat step 1, choosing only one of those many possibilities to release or replace. Reinforce the energy given with praise.

Step 4. *Awareness/Nurture*: Repeat step 3, becoming aware of how the energies of releasing-replacing affected the original energies of step 1. Reinforce the energy given with praise. Return to step 1 from a higher point on the spiral of growth, and continue the process as desired.

There is tremendous flexibility in the four-step spiral exercise process. For example, the step-2 awareness could initiate a whole new spiral process from that point. Having noticed that the face had certain habitual emotional connections with certain musicalities, one could begin a new four-step process, exercising with arbitrary attitudes while doing the vocal flex. In that case, the new step 1 would be an arbitrary attitude sequence with the addition of the vocal flex. Step 2 would then be the awareness of how the vocal flex affected the energy of the arbitrary attitudes.

We have seen the spiral process with combinations in chapter 11. Step 2 of a kinesthetic spiral exercise process can focus on awareness of the intra-kinesthetic effect *or* on the effect it has on the facial mode. In choosing the latter, we saw that one could then initiate a new kinesthetic-facial spiral process.

As an example of new combinations branching off from an original four-step spiral, one could become aware in step 2 of a vocal flex spiral that the gestures did unuseful things. At that point one could begin a new spiral, combining, for example, arbitrary gestures or a head-flop sequence with the vocal flex. The full range of possibilities might be illustrated as follows.

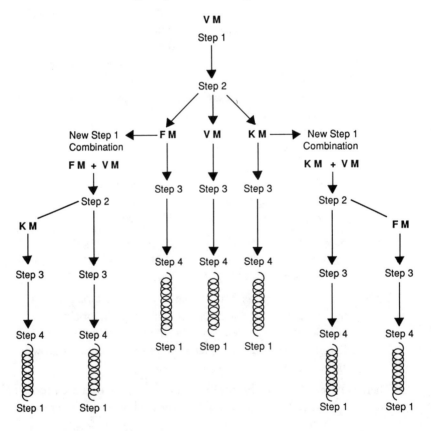

The important thing is to know what one is doing at each step of the process. In moving to steps 2 and 3 it is tempting to deal with all the awarenesses at once, thus violating the learn-one-thing-at-a-time principle. One always has choice, and it is vital to make one choice at a time.

A Trimode Four-Step Spiral Exercise Process

The only combination left is a three-mode spiral process, which involves a coordination so complex that anyone able to attempt it may not need to. For clarity, an example of such a process would be as follows, using the vocal flex as a basis.

Step 1. *Increase/Nurture*: Do a vocal flex, an arbitrary attitude sequence, and a head-flop sequence. Reinforce the energy given with praise.

Step 2. *Awareness/Nurture*: Repeat step 1, becoming aware of the interaction and coordination of the three modes. Notice any entanglements that come into play between them. The possibilities involve all of the in-action entanglements (3–7) from both directions: that is, the facial-mode increase may change the voice and/or the body; the kinesthetic increase may change the face and/or the voice; and the vocal increase may change the body and/or the face.

Step 3. *Release-Replace/Nurture*: Repeat step 1, choosing only one of the interactions noticed in step 2 to release, replace, or otherwise alter.

Step 4. *Awareness/Nurture*: Repeat step 3, becoming aware of the alteration in any of the other mode interrelationships as the result of attention to the one selected for alteration. Return to the original intention of the trimode combination, and continue the process as desired.

Since performers are always giving a total performance (all three projective modes are always involved in some way), the trimode combination is not an unknown concept. The challenge, of course, is in giving specific attention to choices in all three modes simultaneously: the nonplanned choices ensure the specificity of that attention. In the example given, the vocal flex is the only one of the three that might be put on automatic pilot. And if one wanted to specify the assignment in that mode as well, arbitrary language musicality assignments could be used.

Vocal Extreme Masks and the Spiral Exercise Process

The spiral exercise process is particularly useful with vocal extreme masks (as it is with any exercise that requires a move into the unknown). In this case, the first step necessitates a use of language musicality that the performer cannot yet *arebacize*. A complete sequence would be as follows.

Step 1. *Increase/Nurture*: Choosing an extreme from one of the in-time spectrums (pitch, speed, rhythm, continuity, intensity, volume), read a sequence using that extreme as the dominant characteristic. For example, fast, high, relaxed, or discontinuous. Do not be concerned about making sense of the line as you do so—the purpose of the first step is to work with one thing only. Here it is to get one kind of extreme vocal energy into experiential play. For this very reason, the nurturing step is vital: reinforce the energy given with praise.

Step 2. *Awareness/Nurture*: Repeat step 1, becoming aware of what kept it from making sense: was there a hold in the extreme mask? If there is a hold—fast being simply fast without change, high being high with little or no variation—it will sound *unareba*: "High is not high, low is not low, fast is not fast, slow is not slow." What other in-time categories need greater blending with the extreme musical mask to help it make sense? What spices does the recipe need to satisfy the hearing palate? Are there holds in other in-time categories besides the extreme mask? (It is very common to place the other in-time categories—particularly rhythm—on automatic pilot as the performer works with one of them.) Reinforce the energy given with praise.

Step 3. *Release-Replace/Nurture*: Repeat step 1, choosing only one hold to release or one musicality statement to replace. In playing with the vocal mode, it is particularly important not to try and solve the whole complex of challenges at one time. It is also very important to reinforce the energy given with praise. Do not wait for a solution before affirming your energy efforts—reinforce *any* movement in the desired direction.

Step 4. *Awareness/Nurture*: Repeat step 3, this time becoming aware of any diminution or change in the extremity of the vocal mask chosen for step 1. Reinforce the energy given with praise. Continue the entire process as desired.

This is the simplest version of the hearing-vocal extreme mask process. The step-1 assignment can be made as challenging as desired. The reader is referred to *Performing Power* for an extended list of hearing-vocal exercises, which combine the categories in various ways and work with progressions as well (pp. 126–27). Each of them can be adapted for use with the four-step spiral exercise process.

Applying the Vocal Flex to Singing

Earlier we clarified the inner and outer aspects of the spoken vocal flex: the voice itself (the outer process) exercises its capacity to make whatever sounds are desired; simultaneously, the inner process (MIM and IMP) exercises its capacity to make mental and/or emotional sense out of those sounds. While this example applies to the musicality spectrum, the distinction will hold for the other two spectra as well. For the vocal-emotional spectrum, we will connect new and unfamiliar outer sounds with known inner emotional meanings. The vocal-quality spectrum will connect unusual vocal sounds with an expanded acceptance of those sounds, thus allowing a wider range of vocal expression and a greater measure of psychological and physical freedom with respect to vocal production.

With that inner-outer differentiation in mind, we will exercise the singing vocal flex emphasizing, as always, the need for an attitude of play and a focus on process rather than product. This is especially important in approaching the singing voice that is hedged in by "serious," technical, product demands from the beginning. Here, even more than with the speaking voice, we need to explore fully the spectrum that has *serious, product* at one end and *free play* at the other.

The play principle is the same in either case: explore freely, and do what you wish without prediction or judgment. Check all preevaluation at the door of the play space, knowing that whatever you do, you will not be harming Mozart, Verdi, or Puccini, and you will not "unlearn" what you already know. You may, on the other hand, learn things you can find out in no other way. Let us remind ourselves once again that all learning and growth is preceded by a movement into the unknown, and making that move can be easy and even inviting if you give yourself permission to play.

What does that suggest in approaching the singing process? Among other things, it means making different musical and interpretive choices from those you are accustomed to, or from those you have been asked to make. It does not mean suddenly becoming more "creative" — although allowing PIM to interact more freely with MIM is certainly a useful part of the process. Playing can be as simple as asking yourself questions: not "What should I do?" questions, which can be paralyzing in their lack of focus, but "What if?" questions that invite exploration in specific directions.

For example, as you prepared to sing an aria or song in a practice session, you could ask yourself, "What if I sang the aria faster than I have ever sung it?" If you did so, you would have moved into the unknown in a tangible way and given your system a specific interpretive challenge to work with. Other questions would follow automatically: "What does it mean to sing the aria faster? How does that affect the concept of the character? How do I need to change my idea of the character and the music in order to make sense of the faster tempo? What other musical adjustments do I need to make to allow the faster tempo to make sense?"

Notice that there are no value judgments involved at this point: we are simply exercising. We are practicing what we cannot do or have not done — which are not necessarily the same thing, although the two are often confused; and we are not trying to do it "right," or achieve a product. We are exercising our capacity to make new choices and to make sense of those new choices. Our intuitive, sense-making capacity needs all the exercise it can get, and the new outer choices provide the material for that exercise.

You may prefer some choices over others, or have interpretations that you especially like; it would be unnatural and unuseful if you didn't. But we need not identify with the choices we favor. If you only have one choice available, it is impossible to know that that choice is "the best one." Only when you have a number of possibilities to choose from — when you have genuine choice in the matter — is it possible to know the value of the one you have learned, are accustomed to, and therefore prefer.

Applying the vocal flex to the singing process, for example, is like a series of rapid-fire extreme vocal masks. It can also be thought of as a sequence of responses to a stream of questions about musicality choices: What if I sang fast? soft? staccato? slow? loud? legato? and so on. The questions are not verbal, of course, but instead address your intuitive musical awareness with as little MIM monitoring as possible. The responses are similarly intuitive, musical, and nonverbal.

Having said that, it is also useful to pose the questions separately from the singing process, in order to clarify the choices that could be made. In this way we can prime the pump of PIM's process, so to speak, and facilitate the flow of intuitive energy.

Specifying and clarifying the possible questions will also help generate the awareness of step 2 when applying the four-step spiral process. (That process is always applicable even when we do not give specific examples.) Before beginning a vocal flex or playing with a song, it may be useful to address the following list of questions to MIM and PIM, with the understanding that they are *not* to be answered in words. Nor is the result to be figured out before following their implicit instructions. One cannot not *know* the meaning of singing something faster—or louder, or more legato, and so on—without actually doing it; everything else is guesswork

Questions to Expand the Interpretive Process

What if I were to sing it louder? Softer?

What if I were to sing it more *staccato*? More *legato*?

What if I were to play with the articulation, moving between precise and loose?

What if I were to play with the quality of *sostenuto* (sustaining each note) as I sang?

What if I were to play with singing *sotto voce*?

What if I were to use consistent *portamento* (gliding) as I sang?

What if I were to move between *parlando* (a singing quality that sounds spoken) and regular singing as I sang?

What if I were to sing more *cantabile* (smoothly and lyrically)?

What if I were to change tempo frequently as I sang?

What if I were to make a number of *crescendi* and *diminuendi* as I sang?

What if I were to play with *rubato* (to slow down and speed up) freely as I sang?

What if I were to play with *accelerandi* and *ritardandi* as I sang?

What if I sang with more *marcato*?

What if I actually played with the pitch in places? (This question, if actually experienced, may raise all sorts of judgmental bogeymen. Changing the pitch of various notes in a song seems to be more *taboo* than almost anything else a singer can do. It is worth experiencing for that very reason, not to find a new interpretive possibility—although that may happen—but to expand the boundaries around the "sacredness of the score." Release one barrier, and other interconnected barriers may also begin to release.)

It is the 25-positions approach applied to the interpretive process. It is the expansion and cultivation of your interpretive field of choice potential until it blooms with an infinity of interpretive flowers from which to pluck your preferred performance bouquet. It is not necessary to judge the quality of any one of those flowers, but simply to nurture and enjoy them. You will always have the choice of which flowers to select, and it may be that one of the conductors or coaches you work with prefers a choice that you do not. How useful in that case to have nurtured that flower—or one like it—and have it available for presentation.

The list of questions deals with some of the outer aspects of the vocal process. It is like asking for various kinds of muscular effort with the face. The singing vocal flex would involve going through a rapid-fire series of changes based on as many of those questions as possible. The four-step spiral exercise process applied to the singing vocal flex would be as follows.

Step 1. *Increase/Nurture*: Do the vocal flex while singing your aria, using as many question categories as possible. Reinforce the energy given with praise.

Step 2. *Awareness/Nurture*: Repeat step 1, becoming aware of what categories you do not use. (You could also become aware of how the flex affects your singing process, or the facial and kinesthetic modes.) Reinforce the energy given with praise.

Step 3. *Release-Replace/Nurture*: Selecting only one of the awarenesses generated by step 2 for releasing-replacing, repeat step 1. Reinforce the energy given with praise.

Step 4. *Awareness/Nurture*: Repeat step 3, becoming aware of how the flexing energies of step 1 were affected by the releasing-replacing. Reinforce the energy given with praise. Continue the process as desired.

The list of outer interpretive questions, which are for use with the flexing process, are based upon standard musical score markings. However, there are a great many other musical directions and expressive markings that move into the area of *emotional* interpretation. This can and does create confusion: the musical meaning of *fast*, for example, is more easily agreed upon than is the musical meaning of *angrily*. The first is an outer direction; the second is inner.

In creating a flex process for the inner, we will ask a whole series of questions based upon traditional musical but emotionally suggestive markings such as *dolce*, *scherzando* and the like. We will also draw upon emotions from our list of arbitrary attitudes.

Drawing on the Inner for Singing Vocal-Emotional Play

These questions will take the general form: "What if I were to sing expressing a specific emotion?" Traditional musical markings often ask for such emotionally expressive qualities—*scherzando* (playfully), *agitato* (agitated), *animato* (animatedly), *risoluto* (resolutely), *dolce* (sweetly), and the like.

We can also go beyond the list of musical emotions. One coach developed an exercise using arbitrary attitude cards. Giving them to a singer, he asks them to translate that emotion into a nonverbal sound: a cry, a groan, a sigh, or any sound at all that conveys emotion for the singer. He then listens carefully for any entanglement interference in the production of that sound, and if he hears any asks the singer to rediscover the sound and release the interference, thus establishing a four-step spiral process. He then asks the singer to blend that sound with the singing process in a phrase from a song or aria, continuing the four-step spiral adjustments as necessary. One could continue this spiral for a full aria, blending the emotional sound with the singing, becoming aware of any unuseful relationship to the singing, releasing that interference, and blending it again from a higher place on the spiral of development. The important thing in this, as in all spiral exercising, is not to short-circuit the process by premature demand for closure and the achievement of product.

Singers could apply the process for themselves by simply asking the following questions. What if I were to sing: lovingly, angrily, passionately, sympathetically, bitterly, mournfully, joyfully, impudently, sarcastically, happily, indignantly, etc. The reader is referred to the attitude list in appendix A, and is encouraged to use attitudes and emotions of his/her own devising.

In working with this inner-to-outer process, it is worth repeating both a cautionary note and one that says, "Damn the entanglements, full speed ahead!" Awareness of the entanglement traps lurking in our emotional thickets is vital, as well as a means of exercising their transformation into choices. And since you have both the awareness and the exercises, do not be cautious about your use of energy: go for whatever it is you are doing with total commitment. The whole purpose of the four-step spiral process is to allow the performer to take one fully committed step at a time, and not to have to get everything right simultaneously. Not: "Play the emotion and get it right!" but rather: "Play the emotion; notice what happens in doing it that is not useful; do it again, releasing that interference, do it again, this time refocusing on the emotion; and so on, up the spiral." Each step of that process will be fulfilling in proportion to the totality of commitment brought to it; further, each step will expand in proportion to the fullness of the previous step. It is four-step spiral synergy in action.

Vocal Extreme Masks for the Singing Process

The previous lists of interpretive, qualitative, and emotional questions also apply to extreme singing masks. Here, however, the process focuses on one question at a time—whether it deals with musical markings, quality of sound, or emotions—working with it in depth, applying the four-step spiral as appropriate. In the singing vocal flex, the idea is simply to play at random, using a kind of stream-of-consciousness flow in the voice with the list of questions as stimulants to that flow.

In singing vocal extreme masks, one can proceed more methodically. Without losing the sense of play vital to developing maximum performing power, we can work with one musical, qualitative, or emotional interpretive mask at a time, exploring its integration with the aria or song in question. The following four-step spiral process applied specifically to singing vocal extreme masks illustrates this.

Step 1. *Expand/Nurture*: Choose an outer or inner question to apply to the aria or song. For example, "What if I were to play with the tempo?" or "What if I were to let joy be heard in my singing?" or "What if I were to sing with extreme nasality?" Go as far as possible with one choice or the other—do not hold back to make it "better," but go for it with total commitment. This is an *extreme* vocal mask exercise, and the first step is to move into the extreme unknown. After doing so, reinforce the energy given with praise.

Step 2. *Awareness/Nurture*: Repeat step 1, becoming aware of the effect of the technique or emotion on the singing and interpretive process: How do the tempo changes interact with the music? How might they be modified to heighten that interaction? What can be done with them to allow them to work more effectively? How do the tempo changes affect my singing process? If emotion was the choice: How does the expression of joy affect my singing or the music? What might I do with that expression to allow it to interact more powerfully with the music and/or my singing process? If a quality change was the choice: How does it interact with the interpretation? With the emotions? With the singing process itself? How might I enhance any of those interactions? (Note that we can also become aware of the effect on the other two modes, as discussed earlier. And it may be that some of the interferences sensed within the hearing-vocal mode may originate in its entanglement with the kinesthetic (number 7). For the moment, however, let us describe a spiral process that focuses within the hearing-vocal mode.) Reinforce the energy given with praise.

Step 3. *Release-Replace/Nurture*: Choose only one of the awarenesses generated in step 2, and make the adjustment suggested by that awareness as you repeat step 1. Reinforce the energy given with praise.

Step 4. *Awareness/Nurture*: Repeat step 3, becoming aware of how the original energies of step 1 are altered or modified by the adjustment: Did the original energies diminish more than necessary to do step 3? Could I rediscover the energies of the original step 1 without losing the qualities of step 3? Reinforce the energy given with praise. Continue the process as desired.

Working within the vocal mode allows us to bridge from an unknown technique to a sense of its meaning in steps 3 and 4. It is the arebacizing spiral discussed above: we exercise with an unfamiliar technique, which moves us into the unknown; then we spiral back into the known, modifying the technique to do so; then we spiral back out into the unknown again, moving toward the original statement, perhaps not as far (but possibly even further), with the idea of integrating the known and the unknown by arebacizing the unknown.

One could also choose to focus in step 2 on the relationship of the vocal technique to either the facial or the kinesthetic mode. In that case the arebacizing of the vocal unknown might be left on hold for the moment (although the total system is always working on integration, and simply *doing* a new technique sets that arebacizing factor in motion even when MIM thinks it is on hold).

We will conclude this chapter—the only one whose subject includes by its very nature the interactive process—with a further consideration of the coach-director relationship. The relationship of the voice to performance will automatically be touched by two part-teachers (the voice teacher and the musical coach), and if a director or acting teacher uses any of the information in this chapter in working with the singer-actor, the interaction multiplies. The quality of all those interactions is vital to the field.

Coach-Director Interaction Revisited

In reconsidering the coach-director interactions concerning the communication of emotion, there is no simple solution, nor any solution at all, for it is a process, not a problem. There are simply the individual teachers, coaches, and directors who can bring to that process their awareness of the complexity of the challenge, the nature of the human energy system, and the potential pitfalls in eliciting emotional communication from that system.

The ideal situation is for like-minded directors and coaches to work together in the coaching process: the director brings the eyes, the coach the ears, and together they can interact with the total process of the singer-actor, expanding the capacities of their ears and eyes respectively through the interaction. Then, when they are coaching by themselves, each can bring her heightened perception of the other mode to the process and be aware of the possible traps her own mode dominance can conceal. The director can learn to hear more wholly, and the coach can learn to see with greater clarity (and when unable to actually look at the singer, to be aware that many of the changes in the singing process may stem from what the singer is doing physically and/or facially).

The field of music-theater training needs more interacting in general on all levels if we are to cease "robbing the young singer-actor of his or her personal power" (recalling the Ford Foundation study from chapter 1). We need fewer horror stories like the following, which I heard from a young singer whom I coached while he was rehearsing an opera.

The director of the production (who shall be nameless) asked the singer to "emote" and wasn't satisfied until, as the singer put it, "I began to lose my voice from the tension interference." (He and I had only begun to work with the performing power technique, and he was not ready to play a strong emotion freely, on the spot, in rehearsal; but that was what was demanded.) To preserve his voice, he marked vocally for the rest of the rehearsal. Afterward, he asked the director if it didn't bother him that the kind of emoting he was asking for caused the singer to lose his voice. "I don't care about that," replied the director!

The most charitable assumption I can make about that kind of remark is that the director wanted the singer to learn to emote first, and then he could learn to put the two things together. The catch is that if the emoting in question creates vocal interference, it will always do so (unless it is understood for what it is and the entanglement is exercised out — and that will be doubly difficult if it has been drilled in during rehearsal and performance); otherwise, it will never be possible to put the emoting and the singing together healthily. But without interaction between that director and those who can hear, see, and understand the entanglement relationship between the emoting and the singing, and thus help the singer achieve them both, harmlessly, powerfully, and synergistically, the power robbing and diva disappearing continue. (Where the conductor was in all that, I did not think to ask, but there was an obvious lack of interaction.)

And make no mistake about it, the process of interaction is challenging. No matter how much respect we have for each other, each of us tends to think that *we* are perceiving the whole, and that it is the other person who is a bit myopic or slightly deaf. It is important to acknowledge that natural human characteristic, so that we can more easily allow our mutual awareness to develop in spite of it. The growth that can happen when we do so is immense and gratifying.

We all want to have full-spectrum performers, who are free to do whatever each of us may ask them to do without thereby jeopardizing the other parts of their performance. This book clarifies a process by which they can do that for themselves. The rest of us — teachers, coaches, conductors, and directors — can assist that process, help each other (and ourselves) by becoming guides with full-spectrum awareness. This book also serves that process, and the next and final chapters focus specifically on opening to the full spectrum of human energies in the service of the potential for radiant performing.

Chapter 13

The Full-Spectrum Performer I: Expanding the View

Choice and the Full Spectrum

The term *radiant performing* is, by definition, undoable. It cannot be made to happen, it can only be allowed, and the capacity to allow radiant performing is interdependent upon an instrument prepared to do so: a whole instrument capable of receiving the energies of the Radiant Whole, transforming them into specific physical, emotional, and vocal energies, and then communicating them freely and clearly. Up to this point, we have focused on the exercise and development of the parts of the whole instrument that create those transformations and communications—the body, the face, the inner emotional process, and the voice. Let us now consider the question of moving upward and inward: how can we best approach the other parts of the whole system and allow them as well to open more fully to the Radiant Whole? What are the principal ingredients in enabling those parts to do so?

Two ingredients that have been essential thus far—choice and the full spectrum—are also essential as we move up and in. We have singled out the capacity for choice as primary in expanding one's performing power. Whatever spectrum of energy one is exploring, freedom of choice over the full range of the spectrum is an essential ingredient in fulfilling performing potential. Thus the full-spectrum performer is capable of making any choice on any spectrum of energy. That does not mean she has to *make* all those choices, but simply that she is capable of it, *even if her instrument is not*. That is a key ingredient in radiant performing and an important point to which we will return.

How does the concept of full-spectrum performance relate to the radiant performing of roles that are not radiant in themselves? For while we speak of

340

the radiant performer, such a performer must play roles and portray characters who, to outward appearances, do not manifest radiance—often the contrary. How does full-spectrum freedom of choice intersect with this necessity to portray roles whose very essence is not free? One cannot change the character to reflect some sort of glamorized counterfeit of enlightenment or radiance. One must play Iago, Macbeth, or Lady Macbeth in all their grim and intense malevolence. Simultaneously, however, we want to give a radiant performance. Is that a contradiction in energy terms, or is there a way that these seeming opposites can coexist supportively? Let us examine the field from which all our choices are made, our field of choice potential.

Finite and Infinite Fields of Choice Potential

The universal field of energy that supports everything we do—our radiant source, the Radiant Whole—is a field of infinite freedom of choice. We may call it the universal or infinite field of choice potential (FCP). At each moment of our existence we "collapse" that infinite FCP into one specific choice—and then another, and another, and so on. After a time, these choices begin to define our *finite* field of choice potential. We repeat many of the choices we make and they become predictable—the rut principle takes over—and our finite FCP in the area of those choices becomes fixed and narrow. While some of this repetition and predictability may be inevitable, our personal power diminishes in proportion to the overall predictability of our choices, and to the resulting reduction of our finite FCP.

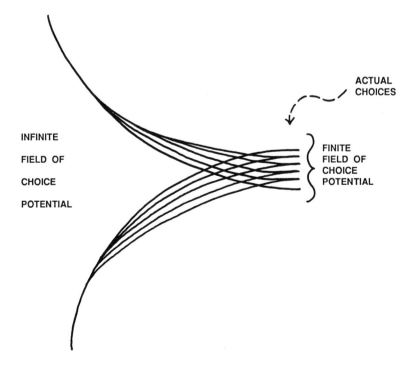

We can expand our finite FCP (and thus our personal power) by practicing other choices until they also become available for regular use. Once those choices can be freely made, they increase the size of our finite FCP. While it is not possible to make an infinity of choices in the three-dimensional world, any expansion of our finite FCP allows a fuller opening to the power of the infinite FCP. And that expansion begins with the awareness that we truly do have a freedom of choice beyond what our conditioning ruts would have us believe. Each new choice we practice and make available to ourselves carries with it the knowingness of other, related choices that we have not made but could make, and that expands the finite FCP even further without the need to actually practice those choices.

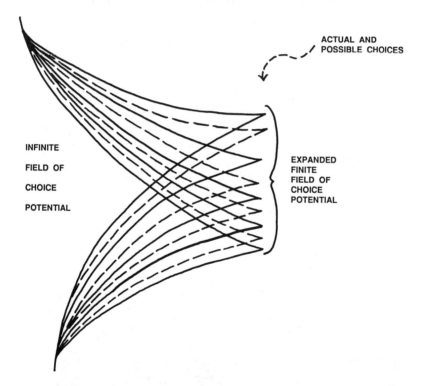

Our finite FCP is created both by actual, practiced choices and by those that are known but unpracticed (a concept clarified below). The more the finite FCP expands in the direction of our infinite FCP, the greater our personal and performing power. As our finite FCP expands toward the infinite in its freedom, we become increasingly able to open to the radiant power of the infinite. And with that we return to the concept of the radiant performer, who must simultaneously project what we think of as distinctly unradiant qualities.

Paradox: Radiance Experienced through Density

All our energies, projective communication and otherwise, come from within. While we have focused on the transformation of that inner energy into projective communication, we have also called attention to the source of it all—the undefined, formless power of the Radiant Whole. In the movement from formless, inner radiance to the external forms of communication, there often seems to be little or no relationship between the two. This is especially true for the performer who, in playing the character of Macbeth, for example, must portray the act of murder. For the character, that is clearly a perverse and hideous transformation of the radiant energies that are drawn upon to inform it.

But what of the performer who must portray that perversion of light, and who wishes to do so as freely and radiantly as possible? Can he portray dense energies—"a kind of energy characterized by slow, heavy vibrations with such qualities as negative, harmful, thick, illusionary and possibly evil" (Ray, *ERM*, p. 30)—and transcend them simultaneously? Can he, in short, give a radiant performance of Macbeth (or Othello)? The answer is clearly yes—however rarely such performances may occur. But how can we clarify the path through this performance paradox? One approach can be found in the crucial difference between the character and the performer with respect to the concept of choice.

Iago has no choice in what he does: first of all, he is a character in a play; second, even if he were a real person (and, like all of Shakespeare's great characters, he is about as "real" as a character can get) he is not enlightened and does not act with a conscious awareness of his freedom of choice. (We all have that freedom, but only the enlightened truly *know* it.) Within a broad range of interpretive possibility, Iago's actions and attitudes are clearly defined: he must do what he does, and he does not (cannot) *know* that he is free.

The performer, however, is in a different situation. He is free—although, like Iago, he may not know that as yet. The performer, however, can *develop* a freedom of performance choice that will give his every action a different quality than if he did not know that freedom of choice. This is a somewhat mystical but down-to-earth principle that one of my very bright students christened "the synergy of the known but unused." It means that each individual choice has power in proportion to the number of other choices that could have been made even if these choices have not been actually practiced. An example from athletics makes the principle clear.

In playing football, a great running back may run eighty yards for a touchdown. At every point in that run he makes specific choices that allow him to escape being tackled. Another running back could study a film of that run and practice making those same choices until he could execute them perfectly. But if, in a real game, he tried to run eighty yards by duplicating those choices, he would be lucky to gain five yards. If the choices he has practiced—however effective they were in the original situation—are the only ones he can make, they will be limited in their power. The first running back could have made many other choices at every point in his run—and his power as a runner is proportionate to the number of those choices. He is unpredictable because he has freedom of choice, and although he is limited to one choice at each moment as he proceeds down the field (like everyone else in the three-dimensional world), those particular choices are granted a power beyond themselves by the quantity and quality of the others that could have been made.

Two singers sing the same high note and the same coloratura passage with seemingly equal skill; the first, however, is capable of singing four steps higher than the given note, and can sing the passage in question at a much faster tempo; the second, on the other hand, is singing her highest or fastest. All other factors being equal—the size and quality of the voice, for example, about which we have little choice—the first singer's performance will have greater power. Or, as I often say in classes in referring to the power of kinesthetic repose, "Baryshnikov and I can both be in a state of repose, but his power in that state is far greater than mine because of the much broader range of potential kinesthetic choice surrounding it."

When Kenneth Tynan said that the reason for Sir Laurence Olivier's power as a performer was that he seemed to endanger his performance, he was, I believe, speaking to the many genuine choices palpably available to Olivier at any moment—including the possibility of destroying the performance itself (which he never did, but which seemed available in his field of choice potential). In examining his radiant performance of Othello, we have seen his field of choice potential to be a significant factor. Olivier may have had the largest field of choice potential of any actor in this century, and the scope of that field was essential to his radiant performance.

Consider in this context the capacity to make choices even though our instrument is not capable of executing them. The freedom to choose to fail is as important to our field of choice potential (and thus to our performing power) as knowing all the choices we could make successfully. The absolute power of the FCP is directly proportionate to the measure of true freedom in that field, which means just that: the freedom to do anything. In all cases, there is a powerful synergy at work between what one could choose to do but does not, and what one actually does.

Creating the energy field in which that synergy can take place means moving from the known to the unknown in the exercise process. It does not mean encompassing all of the unknown—that would be impossible in any case. It does mean sampling portions of the unknown that interconnect with and make available other, unpracticed choices over as broad a spectrum as possible. Practicing choices from all sectors of the unknown is necessary, especially from those sectors that are the most challenging to the performer. One need only practice as many choices as necessary to open the field as a whole to a conscious *knowing* that all choices are possible. True freedom of choice is interdependent upon the experience of having actually practiced either the choices themselves or a range of sufficiently related choices.

The process can be seen in three unfolding stages: (1) acknowledging our capacity for radiant performing and our infinite potential within that capacity; (2) actualizing and expanding through direct experience consciousness of our field of choice potential by the exercise of selective choices; and (3) developing increasing trust in and use of that expanding field of choice potential as we move toward radiant performing.

Of course, total performance freedom of choice is complex, involving as it does combinations in three and four dimensions. There are two aspects of the exercise process to be aware of as we proceed: the exercise itself, and the field of energy in which we exercise. The first is the exercise of the three projective modes individually and in any combination in any way; the second is the quality of full-spectrum awareness we bring to that exercise-expansion of our field of choice potential. These two factors also interact synergistically, for the qualities with which we approach the exercise process can allow that process the greatest freedom (or can interfere with it); conversely the developing trust in the actual exercise choices we make allows an expansion of the field itself.

When we experience radiant power in performances of Iago and the Macbeths (as well as Othello), that power will be interdependent upon the expansiveness and freedom of the performer's finite FCP. The experience of a person who allows rage to flow through his system but who is truly free to make many other choices in expressing that rage, is different — for the person as well as for observers — from that of a person expressing rage in the same way, but who has no choice in the way it is done, or who does so from an entangled condition (which is also choiceless). In the first case, the synergistic radiance of the infinite FCP, the power of the whole, supports and empowers the expression of rage in a way that may transcend in radiant performing the malign density of its expression. In the second case, the finite FCP has been reduced to a single choice, which is a reduction of its potential for radiant expression as well; the radiant power, as we have seen, is wasted internally in entangled short-circuiting. In the first case we have a radiant performing that allows us to open to its transcendent wholeness even as we are horrified by its specifics; in the second, the experience has been reduced to the horror of its specifics.

Life Expansion through Performance

Let me emphasize here that we are speaking of performance only; none of this is to be construed as justifying or rationalizing in some way the act of murder — or any other act — simply because the person committing it claims to be "enlightened" or "has an infinite field of choice potential." The wonder of performance is that it allows us to participate in such experiences in harmless and potentially transcending ways. What an extraordinary privilege it is! To perform means exploring the human energy system in an art where freedom of choice is not just a good thing, it is a requirement of the form. And to develop ourselves fully as performers we must practice many different choices without identifying with them; we must appear to be totally committed to them — which means to understand them completely as they are — without becoming attached to them — another way of saying entangled with them.

In life, identification with our various parts — the body, the mind, the emotions, our actions, opinions, roles, status, and so on — is the source of much distress and dis-ease. In performance we can learn to practice choice commitment without being trapped by identification with our choices. We can expand our finite FCP in the safety and harmlessness of performance and, if we wish, we can also draw upon the knowing of those experiences for our life process as well.

The extraordinary opportunity that performance allows for personal as well as performance process expansion is emphasized by Richard Moss in his remarkable book, *The Black Butterfly*. While we are discovering and exploring ways to empower our performing process (our singing, our physical dance, our emotional communication, and our mental relationship to those energies) by opening that outer process to the inner, Moss approaches it from the other direction. He investigates the process of enlightenment, and sees singing, dancing, and allowing a free emotional process as vital steps in contacting higher energies.

> To work with the whole bodymind, energy must be invoked through dance, song, speech, bioenergetic exercise—any dynamic that invites participation of all modes of consciousness (i.e., cognition, sensation, feeling).
>
> . . . .
>
> Exercises like the singing and dancing are constructed to make the process of invoking energy conscious, to invite expanded awareness in which the whole bodymind, not just the intellect or the emotion or the physical self, participates. We learn to release the higher consciousness and free energy from smaller egoic patterns, while at the same time training the whole bodymind so it can become a channel for the spontaneous and natural expression of higher energies.
>
> [Singing can] carry us . . . to the point where controlling and letting go become one and the same. This creates a doorway between the physical, egoic self and the infinite, unbounded being. In this doorway the psyche unifies, and we can receive and express a far larger dimension of aliveness. We learn to recognize that our multidimensional natures are capable of accesssing more energy than we allow ourselves to express within the confines of our usual egoic patterns. (pp. 87, 88)

Another name for those "egoic patterns" is *entanglements*. In chapter 6 we pointed out that our entangled nature requires assistance from higher inner energies if it is to fully release its conditioned bonds. For example, all projective, physical-emotional entanglements need awareness and understanding from the higher vantage point of MIM; the judgmental entanglements between MIM and the projective modes can be aided by PIM's freedom and playfulness; HOBS's awareness of all the foregoing can assist their process of release; and all of the preceding energies can be allowed to open to the Radiant Whole in fulfilling their potential. Moss reinforces that view.

> It is crucial for us to understand that *our problems cannot be resolved at the same level of consciousness from which they originate; we must move to a higher level of energy* [Moss's italics]. Most problems in life stem from the autonomous

functioning of the various modes of consciousness. At our usual
level of energy, thought and feeling tend to remain separate. We
think about something and it engenders a feeling (or vice versa)
which in turn generates new thoughts. Thought itself can only go
so far before it turns back on itself and begins to circle round and
round, a process that can become quite disturbing when our
energy heightens and we are trapped in our heads. We must move
to another mode of energetic activation and expression to free the
energy from such a cycle. There is an intrinsic nonrationality in
physical movement or singing that transcends conception or
emotion alone.

. . . .

The movement to a higher level of energy is a movement
toward a unification of the psyche, so that feeling, ideation,
sensation and the sense of ALL, which is really behind and above
our experience of reality, begins to merge. At a lower energy the
intellect tends to operate separately from our deeper feelings. We
live in our ideas and emotions, and there is a brittleness to our
lives. When the psychic energy heightens, as it does in the singing
the moment the process becomes effortless and unselfconscious,
there is sufficient energy to bring intellect and the deeper feeling
states together. (pp. 88, 89)

While we will continue to focus on expansion of our performance process,
rather than using performance to expand our personal process, Moss follows
the latter course to its ultimate unfolding.

As the energy level goes even higher, sensual perception,
physicality, conception, and feeling begin to unify. The body
becomes Light, flooded with a feeling that is both sensual and
intelligent. The mind is quiet in the usual sense and the
conception at this level is shared with the whole bodymind. This
state marks the awakening of the deeper psychical energy. . . . But
rather than a dormant process that resides in the body, it is more
an aliveness that is only possible at certain levels of energy. . . .
Yet even at this level there remains a sense of an experiencing self
that is somehow separate or other than the experience. There are
even higher levels of energy in which the whole subjective and
objective reality becomes a single divine Consciousness. This is
what we call Enlightenment. (p. 89)

The remarkable privilege and opportunity afforded us in exploring the performance process is that it can also allow us to move in the direction of an
expanded personal process. In addition to emphasizing those aspects of our
development that are solely performance oriented, we have the choice of simultaneously giving additional energy to our personal process as well (rec-

ognizing that it is impossible to isolate the two totally, for personal and per-formance processes are deeply inter-and innerconnected).

Returning then to the expansion of the performance process, let us ex-amine specific ways of moving in the direction of full-spectrum perfor-mance, beginning with the inner and the outer of the full-spectrum per-former.

The Inner and the Outer of the Full-Spectrum Performer

In expanding that finite field of choice potential in performance—the ongo-ing subject of this book—we have examined in detail the concept of entan-glements. Entanglements can be thought of as the rut principle in action. They are a conditioned lack of choice, and releasing their interference with freedom of choice in the three projective modes has been a major issue thus far. In exploring the three projective modes, we have dealt with the inner and outer aspects of each of them. A key to the inner part of each mode has been the expression of emotion. Emotion and its public expression—planks and a passion—is a basic issue in what we call the acting and singing-acting processes.

If we look at another model of the human energy system—this time a linear, top-to-bottom model—we can see that the spectrum of inner and outer, as we have used it thus far, falls far short of a full spectrum for the whole human energy system.

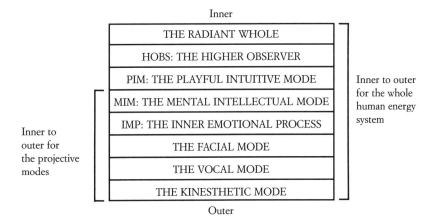

The pentagon of performing energies specifies parts of the human en-ergy system that can actually be exercised and developed by the performing power technique—MIM, IMP, the body, the face, and the voice—as well as those of which we can become more aware and draw upon in proportion to our awareness—PIM and HOBS. We have also seen an expansion of that model which places it within the field of the Radiant Whole.

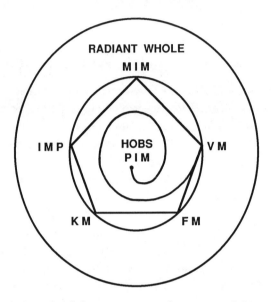

By exercising each of the energies on the points of the pentagon, and developing their freedom of choice on the full spectrum of *isolating* and *integrating*, we allow them to open more fully to the energies of PIM, HOBS, and the Radiant Whole, which lie above/within/around them. We have concentrated thus far on four points on the pentagon of performing energies. At this point, let us move to the awareness and expansion of MIM and the inner energies of PIM and HOBS in applying the concept of the full-spectrum performer to the other parts of the human energy system. Following that, we will examine briefly the concept of the Radiant Whole, which contains and supports them all, and we will examine more closely The Radiance Technique as a means of drawing directly upon the power of that Whole if we choose. We will begin this expansion from the outer to the inner with MIM.

A Coaching Tool for MIM: The Pentagon of Preparation (for the Opening to Radiant Performing)

MIM's basic function, as we suggested in chapter 1, is that of a coach or guide for the projective modes and IMP. Using three of its principal powers—analyzing, remembering, and imagining—MIM does the research, the homework, and then gives assignments to the three projective modes. If MIM is wise as well as intelligent, she will allow them to carry out their tasks in their own unique and, often, MIM-transcending ways. As a tool for assisting MIM in this process of awareness, choice, and exercise, the pentagon of preparation is especially useful.

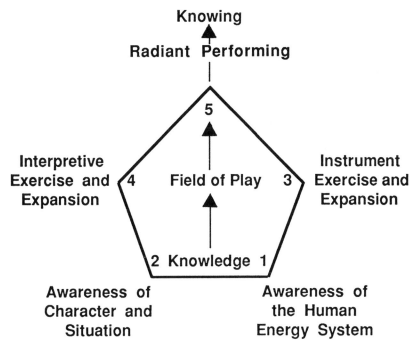

The points on this pentagon relate to the following issues. Points 1 and 2 both concern awareness. Together they form a knowledge base of understanding about the performer's instrument (point 1) and the character and situation being performed (point 2). This awareness and knowledge is to be transformed into knowing by moving through the steps of preparation contained in the pentagon.

Point 1 is the performer's awareness of his/her instrument—the human energy system and how it functions. That, of course, is the basic subject matter of this book.

Point 2 is the performer's awareness and understanding of the character and situation being portrayed. Along with the information in point 1, it forms the basis for making exercise and performance choices. It should be emphasized that having knowledge of the character and situation is only that—knowledge—which must be transformed into communicative knowing through exercise. At the same time, that knowledge is vital information on which to base the exercise process. Expanding that base of awareness and knowledge will be facilitated by the questions that follow, which suggest areas for investigation.

Points 1 and 2, then, establish the awareness-knowledge baseline for MIM; that foundation then supports the performer's move in the direction of knowing, which begins by exercising the projective mode system.

Points 3 and 4 can be dealt with in any order, although exercising the instrument itself before proceeding to interpretation is often the most useful sequence. However, the two points are always interacting, regardless of which one is approached first, and in the expansion-spiral phase of the exercise process they are combined.

Point 3 is the expansion of the performer's instrument and, again, is one of the fundamental subjects of this book, particularly in chapters 9 through 12.

Point 4 has two steps: (1) basic communication of the knowledge arrived at in investigating point 2; and (2) expansion of that fundamental interpretive capacity through the application of the full-spectrum, 25-positions concept.

Point 5 is the opening to radiant performing, and the movement to knowing through the application and direct experience of all the principles of awareness and exercise we have discussed. The pentagon as a whole rests upon a field of infinite play, which underlies and supports all the exercises.

Viewing the entire pentagon from point 5, one can create exercises that draw upon the four points in various combinations. For example, the four-step spiral process can be used to blend points 3 and 4. This kind of blending integration can also be applied to points 1 and 2 through the study of this book, and by answering the lists of questions about one's personal and performance process and the questions about character and situation. For example, the level of personal performance capacity can suggest areas of useful interpretive expansion (my face can do more than the traditional interpretation suggests—perhaps I can expand that traditional model); and interpretive possibilities can motivate the expansion of personal performance capacity (the character's body is more expressive than mine—I will expand my kinesthetic capacity to fulfill the character through exercise).

The following questions covering each point on the pentagon are for MIM's use in guiding the movement from knowledge to knowing, beginning with awareness and proceeding to the exercise process, concluding with a simplified checklist for use in creating a personal exercise process.

Establishing the Knowledge Baseline: Instrument Awareness

1. Am I aware of which of my projective modes are the strongest, and which need strengthening to be in better balance with the whole?

2. Are there aspects of my projective modes that need special attention? For example, the focus process, my gestural capacity, my vocal flexibility, and so on?

3. Have I become experientially aware of all seven entanglements in myself?

4. Am I able to observe them without judging them?

5. Have I found specific ways to exercise and make choices of those entanglements?

6. How fully and freely am I able to accept my entanglements as a part of me and as potentially useful choices?

7. Am I aware of which specific uses of energy bring my entanglements into play? For example, strong emotion, singing, gesturing, and so on?

8. Do I repress those energies in life and performance in order to keep from experiencing my entanglements?

9. Is there a gap between what I am doing and what I think I am doing?

10. Am I experientially aware of that gap? If I am not, how can I become more aware of it?

11. What am I doing to narrow the illusion-actuality gap?

12. How do I feel about using my body and gestures in performance?

13. How expressive am I facially? Does my level of facial projection match the level of my inner feelings?

14. How do I know my level of facial expressivity?

15. How free do I feel emotionally? Is that the way I am perceived by others? How do I know that?

16. Do I feel I need to limit the way I use my voice, my emotions, and my body in performance?

17. Is there a gap between the impression I make upon people and the impression I have of myself? How do I know that?

18. What am I doing to change my thinking about myself?

19. Am I aware of qualities in me that do not support my process? For example, am I easily discouraged? When asked to do something unfamiliar or unknown, do I resist? And so on.

20. Am I aware of qualities in me that support my process? For example, when I feel discouraged, do I persist? When asked to move into the unknown, do I embrace the opportunity? And so on.

21. Am I able to let go of nonsupportive choices, and make new, supportive choices in their place?

22. Am I able to celebrate my process?

23. Am I able to hear and accept information about myself and my performance from other people without judging myself or resisting the information?

24. Can I also distinguish between clear information of that kind and biased information? For example, all information is useful as such, but not all of it needs to be incorporated by the performer. (This question raises the issue of authority dependence: ultimately a performer must take responsibility for the choices he or she makes, and not all authority figures give clear information.)

Completing the Knowledge Baseline: Character Awareness

1. What happens in the piece? What is the story? What is the dominant emotional mood of the story?

2. How does my character interact with the events of the story? Who is she/he? What does she/he do in her/his life?

3. How does the music interact with and interpret the story? How does the story interact with the mood of the music?

4. How does the music define my character? How is my character's music different from the rest of the score?

5. What is the climax or crisis of the story? How is it interpreted musically?

6. What is the climax or crisis for my character? How is it interpreted musically?

7. Is my character sympathetic or unsympathetic? How is this reflected musically?

8. What changes take place in my character during the piece? Are there changes I could make besides those suggested by the story? Does the music suggest the same changes, different changes, or fewer changes than

those of the story? Where are the transitions in the music and the story? Do they happen at the same time?

9. What are my character's needs and desires? Likes and dislikes? How important are they to her/him? What will my character do to get what she/he wants? Does she/he get it? Where in the piece are these needs and desires most clearly communicated?

10. Who opposes or aids my character? Who likes or dislikes my character? What is the relationship of my character to the other characters in the piece?

11. How intelligent is my character? How sensitive? How does she/he express her/himself? Forthrightly? Vaguely? What are my character's beliefs and convictions?

12. How does my character feel about each of the other characters in the piece? How do they feel about my character? Does my character know how they feel about her/him? What do the other characters say about my character? Are they speaking truthfully? Why do they react as they do?

13. Is my character facially expressive? Are there any clues in the text about that, or is it a choice I can make on my own?

14. Is my character physically expressive? Are there any clues in the text about that, or is it a choice I can make on my own?

15. What facial and physical means do I use to communicate the mental and emotional qualities of my character?

16. What physical actions are implied by what my character says? How are these implications modified or expanded by the music?

17. Drawing only upon the words, I will describe my character in detail, including age, social and economic status, personality, physical characteristics, temperament, including character qualities such as openness, courage, optimism, emotionality, and so on. Next, I will draw a description of my character based on the suggestive qualities of the music accompanying whatever my character says or does. Then I will notice whether the two descriptions agree, and make a new, complete description blending the two.

18. Next, I will make a similar description of myself, and compare my characteristics with those of my character. Then I will make choices in the way I use my physical, facial, emotional, and mental energies that will allow the two portraits to interact most powerfully.

19. Having done all (or part) of this MIM-based analysis, am I able to release it and explore, without resistance, other choices suggested by directors or coaches?

20. Am I able to explore other choices with my body and my face, even though they seem contradictory to MIM's analysis? Am I able to blend those new, seemingly arbitrary choices with the more logical, analytical ones?

Further Support for the Knowledge Baseline: Aria/Ensemble Awareness

1. What has happened just before the aria/ensemble?

2. What is my character's emotional state as the aria/ensemble begins? Am I able to communicate that state clearly and freely with my facial-emotional mode?

3. What is my character's physical state as the aria/ensemble begins? Am I able to communicate that state without unnecessary physical tension?

4. Whatever the state of being of the character, am I able to sustain an appropriate state of readiness and support for my total performance process?

5. If there is an introduction to the aria/ensemble, what happens to the character mentally/emotionally during that introduction to allow the first sung phrase to grow out of it?

6. What kind of focus search and emotional progression do I use to lead into the initial singing focus?

7. What happens during the aria/ensemble? Can I state clearly the mental/emotional event of the aria/ensemble for my character? For example, in Mozart's "Dove Sono," from *The Marriage of Figaro,*" the Countess moves from a condition of psychological fearfulness and timidity to hopefulness and confidence, which allows her to take charge of the outcome of the opera.

8. When do the focus shifts occur in the aria/ensemble? Am I able to make clear, with my use of the focus process, my character's thought process (which means both the musical and verbal process)?

9. How many of the focus points are thought process, and how many are environmental?

10. Have I made clear emotional choices for each point of focus? The emotional process will change during some focus points, while others will be sustained. Have I made useful choices with respect to those possibilities?

11. What is the overall emotional progression during the aria/ensemble?

12. Are there interludes when my character does not sing during which I can use a search-focus process? Have I made clear, communicating emo-

tional choices during those interludes? Do the interludes relate to what my character has just sung, do they lead into what will be sung next, or do they do both?

13. How does my character express her/himself physically and gesturally? Am I able to make useful kinesthetic choices in doing this?

14. Am I aware that *I* frame the aria/ensemble, that the character's experience begins *before* the accompaniment begins and concludes *after* the accompaniment has concluded? Is my accompanist aware of this (in audition situations), and have I worked that out with her or him?

15. If I am singing in a foreign language, do I know the meaning and implication of every word and phrase both literally and figuratively?

16. Do I know how the aria/ensemble relates to the rest of the piece?

Preparing for the Movement toward Knowing: Energizing the Play Space

1. Have I made play an integral part of my exercise process in releasing the power-robbing interference of judgment?

2. Do I include some or all of the following play exercises as a part of my daily exercise process: gibberish (spoken and sung), sound and motion, sound and emotion/motion, impulse play, impersonations as I sing or speak memorized material, seeking out and playing with things I am afraid to do in performing or exercising, and simply playing freely with any mode?

3. Am I able to establish a relatively judgment-free environment within which to exercise and expand both my instrument and my interpretive power?

4. Am I able to allow my imagination to play freely?

5. Am I able to allow whatever I imagine to be freely expressed by my body, face, and voice?

6. Do I exercise my power of imaginative play regularly? (For further information, see *The Complete Singer-Actor*, questions to energize the imagination, pp. 138–39.)

Beginning the Movement toward Knowing: Instrument Exercise Expansion

1. Do I understand that when I am exercising my total performing instrument, no product judgment of any kind is appropriate? And that for maximal development of my communicating power, I must be as free of

judgment as possible when exercising any part or combination of my total process?

2. Do I exercise regularly with some or all of the following facial-emotional exercises: focus-process play (the focus process also to be a part of all the following facial-emotional exercises), facial flex, extreme masks, extreme mask release and return, arbitrary attitude expansion, rapid-fire masks, rapid-fire attitudes, rapid-fire extreme masks, rapid-fire expanded attitudes, attitude combinations, and attitude linking? (See chapters 9 and 10 for specific descriptions and clarification of any of these exercises.)

3. Do I exercise regularly with some or all of the following kinesthetic exercises: gesture flex isolations, body flex isolations, extreme body masks, extreme gesture masks, combinations of these, head-flop-space-flop-bod-flop sequences, and arbitrary gesture sequences? (See chapter 11 for descriptions and clarification of any of these exercises.)

4. While most singers will have a regular vocal exercise process, there is always room for exploration and expansion; and for actors, it is vital. Do I exercise regularly with some or all of the following exercises: the hearing-vocal flex, hearing-vocal extreme masks, and arbitrary musicalities, both isolated and in various combinations? (See chapter 12 for descriptions and clarification of any of these exercises.)

5. Do I do some combining of these mode-isolation exercises each day? For example, facial flex plus a head-flop sequence, or gesture flex plus singing, or an arbitrary gesture sequence plus hearing-vocal extreme masks, or arbitrary attitude expansion plus singing and so on (the number of possible combinations is immense).

Continuing the Movement toward Knowing: Interpretive Exercise and Expansion

1. Am I able to actually communicate the awareness knowledge of point 2 as I exercise and perform? (If what I would like to communicate and what I actually communicate are not the same, it is useful to return to point 3 to expand the appropriate instrumental capacity to narrow the gap between the two.)

2. Simultaneously with exercising the capacity to communicate the awareness knowledge of point 2, am I aware that I can also begin to exercise other interpretations and thus expand my range of interpretation?

3. Have I made the 25-positions concept a part of my daily exercise

process through the use of some or all of the following exercises with my actual performance pieces: arbitrary kinesthetic stances, arbitrary attitudes, arbitrary gestures, head-flop sequences, and arbitrary musicalities?

4. Am I aware in applying the 25-positions concept in all these ways that I need not throw out the awareness knowledge of point 2? That I can blend any of the arbitrary choices with that basic understanding of the piece in question? (It is also useful to remember that blending may involve the four-step spiral process — first making the arbitrary statement without concern for its appropriateness, then becoming aware of the gap, then blending, and finally becoming aware of the diminution of the arbitrary statement through the blending process, and repeating the spiral on a higher level if desired.)

The Cutting Edge of the Movement toward Knowing: Infinite Play for Instrument and Interpretation

Viewing the pentagon from point 5 includes all the exercise processes. It also allows us to see it from the infinite-play perspective, which serves as an integrator of those two points, expanding the performance process in a way not as easily accessible to either of them separately.

The basic technique here is to make a playful leap into the unknown while performing memorized material. This leap is facilitated through the use of instrument-expansion exercises, which by their nature will have unknown connotations. For example, while singing an aria or song, one could do the gesture flex or the facial flex; once that was done, one could arebacize it, moving back toward the known until the flex was sufficiently modified to blend with the known and "made sense" again; from that point, one could move back toward the unknown, carrying the meaning along with that movement as far as possible, but allowing it to drop when necessary as one continues the expansion, returning to the known again, and so on. It is the four-step spiral process applied to the juncture of interpretaion and instrument expansion: leap into the unknown with step 1, during which step-2 awareness is generated; the step-3 arebacizing movement generates the awareness of step 4, and the process continues.

Any of the instrument-expansion exercises can be used for this exercise. The advanced performer-exerciser can practice combinations, for example, a head-flop sequence and extreme masks. Whenever you can't think of anything fresh, this is a sure way to open up the interpretive process.

A Simplified Checklist for the Daily Exercise Process

There are so many exercise possibilities that performers with whom I regularly work have asked for simplified guidelines in approaching the process. The following checklist of suggestions is a response to those requests.

1. It is useful to refresh your point-1 awareness of the functioning of the human energy system, and particularly your personal relationship to that awareness.

2. It is also useful to rekindle your point-2 awareness of the characters and situations you are playing, perhaps digging in a bit deeper each time, as the interpretive process expands through exercise and different interpretations become possible.

3. Before exercising points 3 and 4, establish the play space in which to exercise them. Use whatever means necessary. Play as much as you wish, but play enough to create the right to play.

4. For point-3 instrument expansion, select one isolation exercise per day for each mode. In addition, select one integration exercise between two modes each day.

5. For point 4, select one interpretive expansion exercise per day for each mode. In addition, select one mode combination for interpretive expansion each day.

6. For point-5 infinite-play combinations, use the known-to-unknown, arebacizing spiral in exercising and expanding at least one instrument-interpretation combination each day.

Seven Interactive Questions for Discovery and Rediscovery

Since the pentagon of preparation concentrates largely on the development of the individual process, and in expanding the power of our processes in making choices, let us consider briefly the relationship of our own process to that of others. Our performing power is proportionate to the scope of our field of choice potential. But as we interact with others, their choices also become a part of our process. And our performing power will become interdependent upon our capacity to allow those new choices to interact freely with our personal field of choice potential.

The question is simple: Can we expand our power of choice to include the choices of others: coaches, teachers, directors, conductors, and colleagues? While a part of what we do in performance is our personal choice, we also find ourselves in constant interaction with the choices of others. We will be asked to perform those choices, and our interaction with them can offer us opportunities for expansion. The accompanying spectrum can be explored with the same freedom we use to explore our own spectrum of choice. As a guide in this process, we may use the seven interactive questions for discovery and rediscovery.

OUR CHOICES — — — — — — — — —THE CHOICES OF OTHERS

1. Can I identify the energy spectrum I wish to explore? (Is it a tension-relaxation spectrum? A control-release spectrum? An isolation-integration spectrum? A do-more/do-less spectrum? A naturalistic-stylized spectrum? A self-character spectrum? A known-unknown spectrum? A serious-play spectrum? A discipline-freedom spectrum? A sustain-change spectrum? A memorized-improvised spectrum?)

2. Can I describe the choices I usually make on that spectrum? (Am I aware of how the rut principle has created a habitual choice on the spectrum I wish to explore?)

3. Can I discover other choices on that spectrum?

4. Can I *rediscover* any of those choices? (Rediscovery means making a choice one has already made with the spontaneity of its discovery.)

5. Can I rediscover any given choice as often as I wish? (Can I experience the spontaneity of discovery each time the same choice is made—finding the feeling of the first time each time?)

6. Can I discover the choices suggested by others as freely as I discover my own choices? (Can I bring the same total commitment and wholeness of performing energies to choices that are not my own as I do to my own?)

7. Can I rediscover any choice suggested by someone else as often as I (or they) wish? (Can I make the choices of others again and again with the same sense of spontaneity and "first-timeness" each time?)

With all the preceding tools for MIM's use in preparing the conditions of radiant performance, let us continue our move inward and upward to the energies which inform that kind of performance.

Chapter 14

The Full-Spectrum Performer II: Further Up and Further In

Expanding PIM: Opening to Your Spontaneous Self

Having established a new view of the full spectrum — one that relates to the energies of the whole human system — and provided MIM with the coaching tools for the performing energies, let us continue to move inward and upward on that spectrum as we approach the Radiant Whole. (That is a paradox in itself, for we cannot move either away or toward the Radiant Whole since it is everywhere — and nowhere. And whatever our relationship to the Radiant Whole, we can open always to its energies more fully wherever they are or are not.)

With that step we encounter the playful intuitive mode or, as we have dubbed it, PIM. The intuitive mode promotes MIM's capacity for imagination and creativity; and, as Barbara Ray has said, "Enhanced capacities of imagination and creativity are often described as playful" (*ERM*, p. 55). Thus our emphasis on the capacity to play when exercising will in turn expand our access to the intuitive mode. Thus there is no abrupt change of process in exercising PIM: we will simply continue to explore our ongoing development of the intuitive mode.

In the middle of Philip Goldberg's very useful book, *The Intuitive Edge*, he cites research indicating that intuitive people tend to have certain kinds of personality characteristics. Among other things, intuitive people tend to be unconventional (and comfortable with it), confident, self-directed, willing to explore uncertainties and entertain doubts without fear (or as we might put it, are able to move into the unknown despite fear), willing to receive criticism, and able to accept or reject it as necessary, willing to change when it seems appropriate, independent, foresighted, and spontaneous. A portrait emerges describing "a constellation of features: self-assured, highly motivated nonconformists who can tolerate ambiguity, change and uncertainty and are willing to risk looking foolish or being wrong" (p. 109).

It is interesting to contrast that portrait with the characteristics of the addictive system as sketched by Anne Wilson Schaef: defensiveness, judgmentalism, the need for control, authority dependence, and so on (see chapter 3). As Goldberg says:

> When faced with uncertainty and ambiguity, people without [the traits of the intuitive person] might try to restore equilibrium by imposing as much predictability as they can, adhering like glue to rigid rules and procedures, or seeking the often false security of statistics. They might define problems in an overly simple way, gather information from only obvious places, and consider only safe, predictable alternatives. In this way they discourage their intuitive minds from functioning effectively. Those who enjoy, or at least tolerate, uncertain conditions and who are adaptable and independent are more likely to encourage their intuition and give it room to operate. (p. 109)

This might suggest an obvious approach for anyone who wanted to develop his or her intuitive capacity: *act* like a person who is strongly intuitive. Goldberg continues:

> It might be tempting for anyone who wants to become more intuitive to try cultivating the attributes and style of the intuitive personality. This should be approached with caution, however. It is dangerous to adopt certain external behaviors in hopes of becoming transformed internally. The strain of trying to be something you are not can be a bigger barrier to intuition than behavioral traits. (pp. 109–10)

It is easy to recognize in that warning the same "unless it comes from the inner, it isn't valid" criterion that led to the constipated, inner-oriented imbalance of the American acting process for so many years. The reinforcement of that existing imbalance in society as a whole as well as in performance may be unnecessary. To warn people who are already cautious, predictability prone, and nonintuitive about the dangers in acting other than they feel and the need for additional caution if they do so would ensure that such people (most of us) will remain exactly where they are: in a careful, risk-free, nonintuitive space. It is reminiscent of the paragraph warning against gesture discussed in chapter 11: the fear and trembling is already built in; what is needed is a way to exercise its release.

Fortunately, Goldberg does not dwell upon that cautionary note, and in fact has many specific behavioral exercises for developing the intuitive process; yet it is an underlying misdirection that needs awareness and clarification. At our radiant centers, we are all flexible, confident, spontaneous, self-responsible, self-sufficient, and creative. Our conditioning leads us to think, feel, and behave otherwise. We can learn to recognize both our outer conditioning—what we "are" and can choose to change—and our radiant potential—what we "are not" so far as our outer behavior, thoughts, and feelings are concerned, but what we can learn to manifest more freely and fully. We can accept what and where we actually are in the present even as we choose to move in the direction of our infinite potential.

If we do not acknowledge and accept what and where we are, and instead, judge it, deny it, repress it, and guilt ourselves for it, then, yes, it can be "dangerous to adopt certain external behaviors in hopes of becoming transformed internally" (Goldberg, p. 109). But it is not the inner (on the deepest level) that needs transforming; it is the outer levels—including the mind and the emotions—that need to be aligned with and transformed by the wholeness of our radiant interior. If we recognize that necessary interaction between the inner and the outer—another of our continuing themes—it will not only be safe to explore "certain external behaviors," but doing so will be positively vital to the expansion of our total performing process.

Freeing, activating, and exercising PIM moves that interaction one step closer to our radiant center. At the same time, for the performer, PIM—like MIM—operates through the three projective modes. Most books on intuition focus strongly on the inner creative process, allowing it to remain within or to be developed as an inner process over a period of time. For the purposes of performance expansion, we will take the view that intuitive power, like radiant power, is present in everyone and only awaits release through properly prepared channels. As with the expression of thoughts and emotions, we will focus on the overt and tangible expression of intuitive impulses through the three projective modes, either individually or in combination.

In *Performing Power*, I referred to the "mode minds," the three nonverbal, nonintellectual minds of the emotions, the body, and the voice. (For the voice, this intuitive impulse lies in the music it makes in speaking or singing, as differentiated from the words themselves.) Being nonverbal, and therefore outside the specific territory of MIM, the mode minds are intuitive capacities that can be aided or hindered by the predictive, judgmental control patterns that MIM can exercise automatically and addictively: "By trying to control the intuitive processes, the intellect (MIM) reduces the complexity of their energies, robbing them of part of their flow and life" (p. 25).

Our task is twofold: (1) to release the blocking processes that interfere with the flow of PIM's energies, and (2) to exercise the freedom of the three projective modes to express PIM's impulses. Books on intuition, like Goldberg's valuable effort, are concerned with differentiating between the useful, "true" intuitive hunches and the "merely" emotional — separating the wheat from the chaff. Our effort, on the other hand, will focus on the *exercise* of allowing the intuitive impulse to be expressed first, and *then* shaped or discarded. For the performer, overconcern with the appropriateness, usefulness, value, or truth of the intuition can bring MIM into play and kill the impulse before it can be expressed. And MIM can preevaluate and render a negative judgment on *any* performance impulse before it is actually expressed. A performance intuition can *only* be evaluated *in process*, as a direct experience. Preevaluation of projective, performance intuition is worse than useless — it is destructive.

Let us stress that point. A common and logical approach in training intuition is to stress the importance of examining the intuitive hunch or impulse before it is put into action. PIM flashes a message, MIM acknowledges it, and then evaluates it. For the nonperformer, this is fine. But for the performer, intuitive impulse examined in that way is already dead; performance flows in time and there is no time-out to examine the intuitive impulse for its usefulness. What needs to be developed is not the mental process of screening the intuitive impulse, but rather the capacity of the projective-modes system to respond instantly to the free-flowing energies of PIM. Encouraging and exercising that capacity to respond will be our focus even as we exercise simultaneously the expansion of PIM's freedom of flow.

This does not suggest that all impulses should be followed in public performance. Here again, we are speaking of the missing exercise process — when you exercise, practice what you cannnot do; when you perform, allow what you can do — and of finding a way to *exercise* the projection of intuition rather than let it wither by subjecting it to the inevitable judgmental rigors of public performance. It is true, of course, that as we learn to trust PIM's capacities in the exercise process, those capacities will expand into an increasingly useful resource for performance itself; but that will happen in and of itself as the interacting system of PIM and its projective messengers grows in strength and confidence.

Once the intuitive impulse has been actually expressed, it is possible to examine and describe it with a question-asking process. Some of the distinctions suggested by Goldberg include the following: Is it intuition or impulsiveness? Do we simply *want* the intuition to be true or useful? Is it intuition or image-making? (That is a tricky question for the singer-actor.) Is it intuition or rebelliousness—the urge to be different? Is it intuition or intellectual laziness—substituting spontaneity for homework on the character? Is it intuition or fear of uncertainty—any decision being more comfortable than ambiguity? Is it intuition or simply an emotional response or interpretation? But the important thing is to first let it flow with no concern for evaluation—to exercise and develop the intuitive capacity without judgment.

A large portion of *The Complete Singer-Actor* was devoted to exercises that drew upon those intuitive, imaginative, creative, spontaneous energies within us all. Many of those exercises have become a continuing, deepening part of my work with the singer-actor. I would like to take a brief tour of parts of that book, noting the exercises that are pertinent to the expansion of PIM, describing how they function, and broadening our awareness of what they can do.

In exploring the nonverbal portions of PIM's playground (and it is vital in developing the capacity for intuitive flow to focus initially on the nonverbal), there are two exercise tools relating specifically to the nonverbal energies of the body, the emotions, and the music of language (spoken or sung). They are gibberish and the sound and motion.

Games for PIM's Playground

Gibberish: A Musician's Language

To play with gibberish is to make up a language without verbal content; and since the verbal meaning does not exist, the music of gibberish *is* the meaning. It is a useful tool and plaything for singers and actors alike: no expertise or preparation is needed, anyone can do it, and it is impossible to be right or wrong in the process. Thus in exercising with gibberish there is no possibility of judgment in how the voice is used (although performers have proved to be capable of judging almost anything they do, whether it makes sense to do so or not).

When I first began introducing gibberish as an exercise tool, there were often performers who could not utter a "word" of gibberish. They were so deeply conditioned to avoid doing anything wrong that having to make a choice where there *is* no right or wrong was petrifying. Since then, however, the energy field around gibberish and improvisatory exercises in general has changed: performers are more capable of jumping in and going with the process of improvisatory play. My experience with it can be seen as corroborating Rupert Sheldrake's morphogenetic field theory: as more and more performers have become familiar and free with the exercises, it has expanded the field of possibility for everyone: the exercises are more available, psychologically and on other levels, for those who have never done them. As more performers expand into the field of the unknown, that field becomes more accessible for everyone, newcomers and veterans alike.

As I put it in *The Complete Singer-Actor*:

> The experience (of playing with gibberish for the first time) is
> invariably both strange and liberating. There is nothing for singer-
> actors to fall back upon. They have been told what to do all their
> lives, but now there are no stock phrases, no correct responses,
> nor any route that "should" be followed. (p. 115)

Gibberish is easily introduced in a group. The leader simply explains it very briefly and then begins a gibberish conversation with one person, which is then passed to the next, and so on. Group energies generally erupt in a vigorous, playful fashion as the freedom and lack of judgment become clear.

Gibberish is a liberating means of expressing the musical emotions of a soliloquy or song without worrying about its verbal content or meaning. One performer can give another a gibberish "line reading," which the other performer can then "mirror," or allow the spoken energies to interact with an actual line. This is a simple and playful way of expanding the musicality of language without giving actual line readings (with all the attendant judgmental and control patterns connected with that technique).

Gibberish is also useful as a tool for singing improvisation. In one sense, one is already "singing" and improvising simultaneously when practicing gibberish, and it is only a short step from there to actual singing improvisation (without the difficulty of simultaneously improvising a coherent verbal text).

As with all the exercises we will suggest to expand the capacity to respond to PIM, gibberish is playful — there is nothing to judge about it. However, description of the musicality of a gibberish phrase can be a helpful ear-training exercise. It is also a way of leading into the next PIM exercise, the sound and motion.

The Sound and Motion: An All-Purpose Music-Theater Exercise

The sound and motion is an exercise that has continued to evolve and expand over the years. It began as abstract play with the body and the voice in combination in various ways (see *The Complete Singer-Actor* for the original description). In its simplest form, it involves the following: With performers in a circle, one of them will make a sound-phrase of any kind. (Yes, any kind: The sound can be verbal or abstract, sung or spoken, gibberish or actual language—all of which is best clarified by a demonstration.) The sound is accompanied by a physical action of any kind—big or small, full-body or part, realistic or abstract. The other members of the group then mirror the sound and motion. Following that, the next performer will create another sound and motion for the group to mirror, and so on.

With that as a basic pattern, there are innumerable variations possible. Both the sound and motion (S&M) and gibberish are purely intuitive exercises, and can be used to play impulse-release games at any point. The leader says "impulse" and points at someone who then responds instantly with a burst of gibberish or an S&M—with no preevaluation by MIM.

One of the most significant additions to the basic sound and motion came in response to the clarification of the total projective-modes system. When the sound and motion was first created, the facial-emotional mode had not been defined, and was not included in the exercise. With the addition of the third mode, the sound and motion (S&M) becomes the sound and emotion-motion (S&EM), and attains the status of a total, all-purpose music-theater exercise. Since all conceivable combinations of the three modes are available, it is possible to exercise the complete music-theater performance process with that tool alone.

While writing this chapter, I worked with an ensemble of advanced performers, some of whom had had contact with the S&M in earlier years. To a person, they were astonished and excited by the pertinence of the new S&EM to their present process. From their previous experience with it, they had thought of the S&M as a fun warmup, an inhibition releaser, and an ensemble-promoting exercise, which was how I had previously approached it. One did S&Ms for five minutes or so at the beginning of an exercise session, and then moved on to the singing of actual scored material. How surprised they were when we played for an hour and a half every day for a week and hadn't begun to exhaust the learning and growth potential in the exercise. (Another performer who had been exploring S&EM's over a period of time said, "I've been doing S&EMs for five years and I learn something new each time I do them.")

Exploring Varieties of the Sound and Emotion/Motion

The following is a partial list of possibilities that can be explored in working with a three-mode approach to the sound and motion/emotion exercise. As with all the exercises we have discussed, the S&EM is useful both as an awareness exercise and as an exercise for use with the four-step spiral exercise process. We will include entanglements, interferences, and energy uses to watch for as we discuss the exercise.

In the basic form of the S&EM, an attitude card can be shown to the individual prior to performing the exercise, which makes the emotion in question a part of the total process. However, by bringing the emotional process into play in this way, the response of the body and the voice will usually be affected by entanglement. For example, the emotion of anger, by calling into play controlling tensions in the body, could affect both the sound and the motion: the sound might become, literally, an angry sound — that is, constricted and blocked in the throat, which also indicates tension in the body. To help free the energy system from this entanglement and make the S&EM a true music-theater exercise, we can take the following approach.

Let us draw a parallel between singing a song and the S&EM. As we have seen, the act of singing a song is an unnatural act that we want to appear to be as natural as possible. It is unnatural because it combines the three projective energies in ways unlike anything in our everyday life process. The voice is doing something magnificently artificial (singing); the emotions are generally at a higher level of intensity than is customary in life (and, in any case, would not be combined with the singing process in the ordinary circumstances of life); and the body needs to be supporting the singing process, which means functioning in a very different way than it would in normal life if it were responding to the increased intensity of the emotional process. The body is clearly the key: not only must it *not* do what it would ordinarily do in reaction to the emotional process, it must learn to do something entirely different in response to the needs of the singing voice.

It is precisely the same with the S&EM: the body, the voice, and the emotional process (the face) are called upon to do three different things at the same time. That is the essential definition of a complete singing-acting exercise: the juggling of the three projective-mode energies in ways that are unlike ordinary, habitual life. Thus we can use the S&EM to serve this essential exercise process in the following ways.

An individual does an S&M (without adding the emotional component); then the leader gives that individual an attitude (either aurally or visually), which is then combined with the original S&M to make an S&EM *without changing either the sound or the physical aspects of the original S&M*. In most cases, of course, adding the emotion *will* change the vocal and the physical in some way—which is as elegant a demonstration of the entanglement process as one could devise. The performer will become very aware of the difference, and so will the observers. When the rest of the group mirrors the process, they will become aware of the effect in themselves as well. In fact, the most useful process seems to be as follows: (1) One person does an S&M; (2) the rest of the group mirrors the S&M; (3) the leader gives the group an attitude to combine with the S&M to make an S&EM; and (4) all the members of the group can become aware of the entanglement process in themselves—it will be different for each of them—and can then repeat the S&EM combination several times on their own, practicing releasing the entanglements using the four-step spiral process, before a new sequence of S&M to S&EM is initiated.

It has been illuminating for performers to experience so directly and concisely the existence of entanglements within themselves—a fact of the human energy system that could otherwise remain an intellectual, nonexperiential construct. In this form, each S&EM is like a miniature act of music theater: the song being sung is the sound, the physical action accompanying that song is the motion, and the attitude informing the song experience is the emotion. The singer-actor's process involves the simultaneous interconnection *and* isolation of all three components.

A way of further isolating the three energies is as follows. One performer provides the motion, a second performer provides the sound (without having watched the motion, so as to ensure a random combination), while the group leader or a third performer provides the emotion (by showing an attitude card, calling out an attitude, or creating a facial-emotional statement to be mirrored). A fourth performer then puts that all together, followed by the group as a whole. The exercise can also be done in stages, with the fourth performer first doing the motion all by itself, then adding the sound and the emotion successively.

Variations on this exercise can be practiced with actual aria or song phrases. A singer selects a phrase or two from her repertory; without knowing what that phrase is, another performer provides the motion, and another the facial-emotional energy. The singer then puts the three together. As the words *facial-emotional energy* suggest, that component can be anything involving the face from a facial flex to an extreme mask to an arbitrary attitude.

And just when one thinks all the possibilities of S&EM exploration are exhausted, a new combination turns up. After this chapter was written, I was exploring the practice and uses of the inner floppy release with another advanced group. We returned to specifying the emotion in advance, asking the performers to do an angry, joyful, or astonished S&EM without trying to release the entanglement—which, as a result, would be virtually automatic. Then they would repeat the S&EM, sustaining the outer statement as clearly as possible, only this time they would add an inner floppy release. Simple as it is, the exercise was revelatory in its expansion of awareness, and in developing the capacity for doing the floppy release in actual performance.

Improvisation: Playing with What We Fear

Improvisation is a basic means of exercising our access to PIM's storehouse of creative energy. When one is improvising with any mode, any MIM judgmental control will interfere with the process and be evident to performer and observers alike. Even though MIM may say, "I can't think of anything to do"—a common statement when first working with improvisation—there is *always* something to do—it's just that MIM can't always predict what those nonverbal physical, emotional, and musical things might mean, where they might lead, or how they might be judged. And that is what MIM cannot "think of"; the actual things to do are innumerable—just turn the body, voice, and face free to do them. The basic issue is often simple fear: fear of judgment (from any source, including oneself) about what one might do. That fear is often the single most powerful blocking factor preventing us from drawing on PIM's energies freely.

The title of Susan Jeffers's useful book, *Feel the Fear And Do It Anyway*, is excellent counsel in itself. She follows that injunction with a vital insight: as long as you are growing—and moving into the unknown—the fear will be there. If you wait for it to go away to make the move, you will never do it— for the fear will always be there, intensified by never having been tested. Further, the cumulative sense of powerlessness that comes from being controlled by those fears is far more frightening than pushing through them. Each fear overcome reduces that residue of helplessness; each fear submitted to increases its power over us.

There is only one way to deal with both issues—to get rid of the fear of something, and to start releasing the powerlessness that untested fears breed—and that is to actually do the thing feared. Once that is done, the fear will almost always be exposed for what it is: an illusion made up of one part actuality and nine parts preevaluative fantasy. All the dire predictions— "If I do thus and so, I will be laughed at, look inferior, reveal something dangerous about myself, violate something," and so on—is revealed as illusory. The fear itself is real; it is simply the basis for it that is an illusion; expose the illusion and the fear vanishes as well. But one can only expose the illusion by acting out whatever it is that one is afraid to do: thus, the game of doing what we fear.

To play this game, it is obvious that the kind of safe, nurturing, honest, descriptive, do-whatever-you-want-to-do-without-judgement environment we have described in previous chapters is vital. Once that is established, it is profoundly useful to ask performers to look within and see if they can become aware of energy uses they fear. That in itself is a challenge, for such fears are often very carefully concealed—a logical thing for the human system to do: out of sight, out of mind, where they can't cause trouble for MIM. They are in the unknown. They have not been acted upon, at least not for a long time. They may have been acted out once, judged harshly and then repressed on that basis.

However, these fears can usually be identified in some form, and when they are actually put into play, the process is inevitably one of release, expansion, and a more powerful performance. A telling example: Fifteen performers were involved, and the fears they dealt with spanned the full spectrum of possibility. Six of them worked with the fear of being boring, or of doing too little, or of simply using their own unmodified energies. All of these fears, acted out, emerged in low-key versions that were powerfully alive, very different, and very useful for the performers in question. Many of the rest worked with the fear of doing too much, of being phony, of being ugly, of exposing a part of themselves they were ashamed of. In almost every case, it was the most powerful and compelling performing they had done (and they were a talented group). When a second round of the same exercise was done—to exercise the fear of not being able to do it again—they were all able to rediscover the freedom they had found (albeit in different ways); it wasn't a one-time shot. In succeeding days, however, they all reexperienced in various ways that fear of not being able to do it again: "What we did was so exciting — maybe it was just an accident — so let's not even try." We continued to explore that fear as well — fear begetting fear — and as each fear was brought into the open, it was revealed for the illusion it is.

Opening to PIM: Tuning in to Higher Energies

In exploring the process of opening to PIM, and to the many layers of intuitive and creative energies that are available to us, MIM can do little except to allow it. And to allow it is far from a simple, passive injunction that will just happen. On one hand, as Goldberg puts it, "Intuition can't be ordered, commanded, implored, or contrived." On the other, "We simply have to be ready for it" (p. 155). We have to prepare ouselves in some way to allow it, to be ready for it.

One of the ways we can prepare and open ourselves to the universally available flow of creative, intuitive, nonverbal energies is by aligning the outer energies — MIM and the three projective modes — to the qualities of the inner energies. We might compare the process to tuning in a radio: there is a certain frequency of energy — radio waves — available all around us; for example, some of them may carry the music of the Boston Symphony. We only need to tune in to that frequency with the appropriate technique and technology. The energy is there, but unless we tune (the technique) our radio (the technology) to its frequency, we will not receive the glorious music it has to offer us.

Just so with our heavily conditioned, entangled communicating system: there are incredible energies available to that system in each of us — the technology is us — but if we do not tune in to them with the appropriate techniques, their "music" will not be available to us in its full power. We will receive occasional hints of what could be, or we will hear it dimly, through static and interference, but the wholeness of its potential will be only partially experienced. That is another way of looking at the inner and outer relationship: the idea of attuning the outer to the inner; allowing the outer energies to be in synch with the qualities of the inner, and therefore receptive to them.

We have discussed previously some of the ways of tuning in to those inner energies. In *The Complete Singer-Actor*, for example, there is a series of questions to energize and attune MIM and PIM to the free reception of intuitive and creative energies (2d ed; pp. 137–42). In this volume, the energies of infinite play (as well as all of the seven guiding principles for radiant performing) are viewed as qualities that allow us to be in tune with the energies of wholeness within us. As we focus within and open ourselves more fully to the energies of the Radiant Whole, I would like to expand upon that process, by drawing upon HOBS, our higher observer-higher consciousness. While HOBS does not speak (MIM is the last bastion of the verbal world on our move inward), he/she can be aware of and bring our outer attention to the availability of higher energy principles flowing from the Radiant Whole. With that awareness, we can align the outer energies of MIM, IMP, and the projective modes to those principles.

HOBS: Gateway to the Radiant Whole

As we saw at the beginning of this chapter, the universal energy field of the Radiant Whole is an infinite field of choice potential (FCP). There are qualities of that infinite FCP to which we can open, and which can expand our finite FCP. These are qualities that, like the field of their origin, are unlimited in their scope and inclusive in their relationship to all the parts of life they support. By allowing those qualities to support our processes in rehearsal and performance, we will be expanding our finite FCP.

With the aid of HOBS, then, let us address ourselves to the nature of some of the supporting and nurturing principles and qualities of higher energy that can allow us to open our performing process more fully to the Radiant Whole.

This will expand upon the exploration begun with the seven guiding principles for radiant performing. As with those principles, we must recognize that, in the context of this book, we can do so only with words rather than with the energy principles themselves. There are words available to us that attempt to open to such principles, and we can use them to point in the direction of the energy lying behind them. Words, as we have seen, will always be reductions of higher energy principles; yet used with clarity, they can also serve as tools for guidance and support as we open to those higher energy principles. As Barbara Ray has put it:

> Different principles (kinds) of energy have different essential
> natures and qualities. *Parts* have qualities which are characteristic
> of the vibration of the partial planes. The Whole has qualities
> which are *vastly* different in vibration and essence from partials.
> Some qualities of the universal, innate *within* the fabric of radiant
> energy, are expressed in words (limited as words are) such as
> Clarity, Radiance, Joy, Celebration, Abundance, Acceptance,

Balance, Bliss, Honoring, Here Now, Always, Integrity and Universal. The reference is to the whole quality of energy behind these English language words. The quality of energy exists *before* the words in any language are created to "describe" it. (*ERM*, p. 91)

The energy principles we will consider, like the seven guiding principles, are not one end of a spectrum: they have no useful opposites in themselves. HOBS doesn't use words, but if he/she did, the selection would be drawn from the translation of higher energy principles into those words that most nearly reflect them. As much as is possible in the word world, then, we want to experience these higher energy principles as lying behind and encompassing the inherent duality of words.

As we examine some of those word guides, let us do so with the idea of allowing the qualities behind them to expand our finite field of choice potential. Some of them are familiar, but seen in this context, they can have a new and different relationship to our process. Any one of them can inform, support, and guide our process on the three-dimensional level; they can become part of our choice process as we practice, rehearse, and perform, and direct us beyond the time-and-space-bound energies of MIM and the projective modes.

Let us remember that aligning our outer energies with the inner qualities of wholeness is not a process of repression or denial. Those energies— MIM, IMP, and the modes—have been conditioned to deny our access to inner wholeness, a denial reflected most clearly in our entanglements. We can acknowledge the state of the outer processes, and accept them without judgment or guilt. As we disentangle them, we can support that process by tuning in to the qualities of wholeness whenever we remember to remember—one of MIM's principal powers. And when we remember that we have forgotten, we can choose not to blame ourselves for that either, instead beginning now, always in the present, allowing our wholeness to come into play.

It is often useful to have a list of questions to assist the remembering process. These questions can be thought of as cues to HOBS, who becomes a kind of prompter. An actor in rehearsing a scene will say "Line?" when he cannot remember what comes next, and the prompter will then speak the next few words to support him. In opening to qualities of wholeness, HOBS can be our prompter: whenever we feel that a different quality of energy would be useful in practice or rehearsal, we can activate HOBS by saying (either aloud or in our mind), "Energy?" And through HOBS—from our

Radiant Whole—can flow an abundance of choices that PIM, then MIM, IMP, and the modes, can translate into new and more useful outer energy behavior. The questions to facilitate this process are as follows.

1. Is there a quality of energy that would allow me to support my process (or the group process) more fully?

2. Do I choose to open to that quality of energy?

3. Am I resistant to doing so?

4. Can I acknowledge and accept that resistance and choose to open to a different quality of energy anyway?

5. If I cannot (or choose not to) say yes to question 4, am I able to experience and know the block that stops me?

6. Am I remaining free of judgment and guilt, whatever choices I make in response to the previous questions?

Higher Principles of Energy: Qualities of Wholeness

With those questions as memory cues, let us explore some of the qualities of wholeness that can be opened to when the request "Energy?" is made. This particular list of the qualities of wholeness (and of radiant performing) draws extensively on the work of Barbara Ray. All quoted sequences are taken from *The Expanded Reference Manual of The Radiance Technique®*.

Abundance

> In higher consciousness, abundance is a quality of universal energy . . . an energy which is limitless. (p. 7)

There is always more available to us from the whole. Our potential expansion is always greater than MIM can know. Our parts do not have the capacity to know or judge those limits, and we can learn to open to the abundance that is there and trust in it even though it may manifest itself in a different way than we expect.

Acceptance

> As an energy of higher consciousness [acceptance] refers to your capacity to be truly present in the here-now moment and to be able to see clearly "what is" without illusions (interpretations, projections, assumptions, prejudices). Acceptance allows you to move and "opens the gate" on the evolutionary (upward, counterclockwise) spiral of your . . . unfolding process. It allows

for expansion and movement, for growth, transformation and
enlightenment. (p. 7)

Aspire

In higher consciousness, your ordinary desire to achieve [to
aspire] becomes a higher aspect of your will as you consciously
direct your life's breath, your life force energies, toward your
higher aspirations, your journey of awakening. (p. 10)

We can always move in the direction of our highest aspirations however
far away they may appear to be to our outer, partial selves.

Awareness

Refers to watchfulness and consciousness. Your awareness of all
planes of existence can be limited or can be in an ongoing
process of expanding. (p.11)

Awareness and remembering are fundamental to all the processes we
have touched, and are primary on any list of performing energy principles.

Balancing

In higher consciousness, [balancing] describes harmonious
resonance with universal energy . . . an *interaction* of a higher
order energy principle with that of a lower order [which] allows
for the process of expanding, transforming and harmonizing of
the lower (denser) energy to the higher opening, the gate for it to
be what it *really is* in nature. A mind becoming in harmony and
balance with radiant, universal energy is different from an
unnatural, polluted, ruptured, out-of-order mind. (p. 15)

For the performer, we can speak of balancing the projective modes by
releasing their MIM-induced attachment-entanglement with the lower, controlling tensions of the physical and opening to the higher, free-flowing flexibility of the Radiant Whole.

Beginning Now

In higher consciousness [the energy of "beginning now"] brings
your awareness to the "here-now" present and guides you to go
from here without being trapped in past patterns. Each moment
of Life is full and complete, is within itself, whole and "beginning
now" centers you in its *wholeness*. (p. 15)

The sixth *P*, patience in the present, also supports the importance of always
beginning now in the performance process, as well as in life.

Celebration

In higher consciousness [celebration] refers to a *quality* of

universal, whole, radiant energy which has its source in the inner
planes of your Being—in the Soul and Spirit. *Celebration* is a
quality of wholeness *within which* are various degrees of polarities
of up/down, positive/negative and so on. (p. 21)

There is nothing in our performance and exercise process that cannot
be expanded by the quality of celebration. *Everything* in our process will
unfold more fully and develop more powerfully in the nurturing energy of
celebration—even the performance of the choices of others (directors or
conductors) that we would prefer not to make as our own.

Centering

In higher consciousness, "centering" means focusing on your
Inner point of Light, your Seed or point of wholeness *within* you
and within all Life forms from which the outer planes manifest.
(p. 21)

Centering is sometimes thought of as a physical act. In this use of the
term, the center is a different quality of energy that can indeed transform
and center the energies of MIM and the modes. Further, that energy is not
found in MIM and the modes, and is an unknown to them.

Choice

In higher consciousness, "choice" refers to your ability to discern
higher from lower, whole from partial, limited from unlimited,
denser from lighter, inner from outer energies. . . . [T]he process
for moving from an outer to an inner consciousness . . . is one
which requires your mastery of clear discernment of different
kinds of energy and the development of your power/ability to
make *conscious choice* of a higher order. (p. 22)

With awareness of the ways our projective modes are entangled, we can
begin to free them and discern more clearly the differences between them.
We can then begin to choose among them for the purpose of performing
power and clarity. Simultaneously, we can begin to discern energy differences on inner levels, and this process may be facilitated by discernment on
the outer levels. "Mastery of the outer planes is an essential awareness on the
journey of awakening to the consciousness of the Inner Planes and (of) the
differences in energy of the Outer and Inner Planes" (p. 79). If we are confused (entangled) as performers about the difference between MIM and the
modes, it can also simultaneously distract from our discernment on the
inner.

Clarity

Refers in higher consciousness to the quality of *clearness*—one of
the qualities of the kind of energy called universal, radiant. Clarity
means seeing things *as they really are* without illusions, without
attachments. (p. 23)

Becoming a performing artist means getting what you think you are doing and what you are actually doing to be the same thing; it means being
clear about your performance as it really is.

Conscious

In ordinary use [conscious] refers to a state of being aware of
yourself and your environment, of being awake not asleep, not
unconscious. In higher consciousness, "becoming conscious"
refers to the capacity to expand into deeper, inner realms of
life—"to become awakened from sleep." (p. 24)

The levels of sleep, of robotic, unconscious behavior in performing begin on the outer with the physical. Our conditioned entanglements can so
distract us (without, unfortunately, awakening us) that we are even less able
to move our attention from those outer processes and open to the inner. It is
the rut principle in action on a more general behavioral level.

Courage

In higher consciousness [courage] refers to an inner *quality* of
Light, a quality of the soul. The word itself comes from "cour" in
French, meaning of the heart, and means an inner energy of the
"inner heart" which is steady and ongoing no matter what the
process of the outer polarities and cycles. (p. 25)

It takes great courage to look clearly at what one is actually doing. It
takes even more to make changes in that behavior. However, the courage to
do both things does not come from the level of the behavior one is changing.
If we *try* to find it there, we may diminish our capacity to open to the true
source of that courage—the inner heart.

Discovery

In higher consciousness growth [the discovery process] refers to
. . . being able to move into the unknown without preevaluating
the experience, without trying to limit by comparisons and
analysis. Discovery is going beyond the known limits or
boundaries. Discovery is a natural inner energy which nature has
implanted within our fabric, yet this process is often blocked,
repressed and denied in early programming. The discovery

> process is "like a young child" in expansion, growth and freedom
> of expression and this quality must be activated, expanded and
> nurtured from within. (p. 31)

When, as performers, we try to repeat what we have done, it is easy to
lose the power of discovery. No matter how often we may have performed
something, we always do it for the first time every time—whether we know
that consciously or not. The discovery process is vital to our learning and
growth, and what we may call "the rediscovery process" is equally important
to the performance process (often referred to as "the feeling of the first time
each time"). Without it the powerful energy of spontaneity is not available.

Flexibility

As a higher principle of energy, flexibility refers to the capacity to respond freely, fully, and swiftly to changing outer circumstances. The responses may range from persistence in what one is doing, at one end of the
spectrum of choice, to a reversal of one's actions at the other end—or any
possibility between them. Flexibility involves the capacity to see clearly what
actually is, and to accept that and respond to it in the here-now present without judgment about what "should be" or expectations about what one wants
it to be.

Gratitude

> In higher consciousness [gratitude] refers to an *inner* energy
> which expresses from within, with no external cause, spontaneous
> feelings of wholeness, of fullness, of radiance. (p. 46)

Gratitude is a vital energy for the performer. It means recognizing that
every situation, no matter how unpleasant it may seem on the outer, is an
opportunity for even greater growth than that which will occur automatically because of our inherent capacity for development. We are always growing and changing, and awareness of our capacity to enhance and expand that
growth through more conscious participation leads to gratitude for whatever
is. Gratitude for all the opportunities enfolded in whatever is allows us to
open more fully to them, and to make maximum use of their potential (even
if the choice means asserting the right to leave the situation—to "shoot the
dog").

Humor

> In higher consciousness, it is your capacity to let go of
> attachments and enjoy all aspects of your life expression with the
> polarities and degrees of ups and downs, good and bad, positive
> and negative, and so on. (p. 51)

Interacting with gratitude and flexibility, humor also allows the performer to make greatest use of the opportunities for growth present in all coaching, rehearsal, and performance situations. It is a quality of great value in the challenging, often daunting environment of music-theater training, rehearsal, and performance.

Interconnection

Refers to a link between or among things that connects them and can be used as a way to describe relationships between parts in a system and subsystems. In higher consciousness, interconnection refers to the "inner-connection" from *within*, from the Inner Seed of Life and Light of all living things. All life is inner-connected from *within* at the same *vibrational* point of Light. (p. 57) [In working with the dualistic thinking of ordinary consciousness,] as you begin to become a "knower" of the interconnected relationships within the Whole, it is not possible to see the extremes of being "for" or "against" something as the only choices. (p.32)

For the individualistic, often solo-oriented context of music theater, interconnection is a powerful energy in supporting the dynamics of ensemble. The interconnection within can nurture interconnection in the outer, both between performers and between performers and the audience.

Joy

Joyousness is a quality of your True, Inner Self, a quality of universal energy and of *wholeness*; it is *not* a characteristic of partial, outer plane energy, *not* an energy of polarity. "Joyousness" is an energy of the inner planes, of the soul expressed from within, radiating outward *through* the outer personality and can express with and beyond the fluctuations, polarities of the outer self. When you are expressing *Joy*, you are in touch with your Real Self, with the inner to outer expression of your universal life energy. (p. 61)

Joy interconnects with celebration in supporting a constant inner flow of energy that is there in its greater reality, regardless of the outer densities of a characterization, a rehearsal situation, or a performance. Even on the limited outer planes we have seen the capacity of the emotional process to combine seeming opposites, for example, to blend outer grief and happiness in the well-known phenomenon of "smiling through tears." How much greater is the capacity of the whole system to support all outer processes with the energy of joy regardless of their density.

Love

[There is] love of the outer heart—love with an object. This kind
of love is the warm feeling of affection felt or sensed from the
chest/heart area, love from the lower planes. This kind of love is
different from the love known as . . . universal, radiant Love that
simply *IS* without external, outer stimulus or object. (p. 66)

While the word *love* has been much abused and reduced in its outer
implications, the energy behind the word remains the most potent factor in
life as a whole and in the music-theater environment in particular. Like
James Carse's play and infinite Play, there is love and infinite Love. Infinite
Love is unconditional: it requires nothing, it expects nothing, and there is no
diminution in its availability, regardless of outer circumstances.

Opening

In higher consciousness [opening] refers to the process of
allowing yourself to move into the unknown unobstructed, to
move into greater consciousness without restricting and in a
natural growth process as a flower opening or unfolding
according to the principle of Life from within it. (p. 79)

Opening our outer process—MIM and the modes—to the energies of
the unknown inner is a key and a gateway to the expansion of our performing (and personal) power. Power in this sense is the potential to open to and
communicate more fully the higher energies of love, joy, gratitude, celebration, support, and all the other qualities of our inner radiance.

Support

[Support is] the inner quality of universal, whole energy which
sustains unconditionally and interacts with both positive and
negative, moving always transformingly in the direction of Light,
Wholeness. (p. 102)

Our continuing outer support for ourselves, for each other, for our colleagues, teachers, coaches, and directors is a way of aligning our outer energies to the unconditionality of our own radiant support, thus creating greater
synergy between our inner and outer processes.

Transformation

The process of moving from one way of being to another
according to natural growth stages, openings from within the
blueprint of the seed. Change is a natural law of the cosmos.
Transformation and change are powerful energies *within* the very
fabric of Life energy. (p. 109)

Transforming Process

The dynamic interaction which is fundamental to the *very nature* of existence on all planes of Being. Breathing, eating, drinking, emoting, thinking and so on are transformational processes. All energy is in motion, is not static and is always interacting and in a transforming process. Your entire energy dynamic is in movement, interacting and transforming. (p. 109)

Our conditioning, the rut principle, our habitual patterns all resist the natural process of change and transformation, as does our tendency to make products of everything, including our own processes. Thus the energies of awareness, acceptance, consciousness, clarity, choice, discovery, and courage are all a vital, interconnected field of support energy for transformation and the transforming process.

Universal

[Universal] means pertaining to or pervading the whole, all-embracing, all-reaching, constituting the whole, entire, not limited or restricted, can be used for all kinds, all forms. From its base it also means of the *one*—of the Whole—of the Cosmos. As a principle or *kind* of energy—cosmic, transcendental, Radiant—different from others such as physical, mental, electrical, nuclear, solar; as a *quality* of energy refers to wholeness and the characteristics of the Whole (non-partial and *not* the part). (p. 113)

The Radiant Whole is our universal source of energy. It contains and supports all the energies we have discussed (and could discuss), and is always there in infinite availability. We can allow that infinite supply to support us in proportion to our outer capacity to open to it. Opening to our inner radiance can be exercised in many different ways on the outer, interdependent upon which level of outer energy is in question. The physical, emotional, vocal, mental, and intuitive energies have been addressed in detail as we have established an exercise process for each of them and for the whole system. To these outer exercises we have added one more: Remembering to ask, "Energy?" whenever alignment to the inner is useful (which is *Always*—another quality of whole energy in itself).

Always

In higher consciousness [always] refers to the quality of universal energy that is "forever"—and inner energy—beyond and transcending the limits of time as we know it in the ordinary outer world (p. 9).

There is never a moment, not a millisecond, waking or sleeping, active or passive, that we are not being supported and nurtured by our radiant source whether we are conscious of it or not. With that quality as a model, we can open to its power: We can *always* become more aware of the choices we make in practicing, rehearsing, and performing that do *not* reflect the radiant qualities of our infinite field of choice potential.

We can *always* choose to align ourselves more fully with that radiant field. Without changing what we are called upon to do in practice, rehearsal, or performance, we can *always* call upon HOBS, our universal prompter: "Energy?" we can ask, and then open to the radiant reply.

The Radiance Technique and the Performing Power Technique: Differentiating and Clarifying

Having examined many of the partial energics of the human energy system, and how we can develop ways of allowing each of them to open more fully to the Radiant Whole, it remains to address, briefly, The Radiance Technique, which allows us to draw directly on the Radiant Whole.

There have been occasional misunderstandings and confusion about the relationship between the performing power technique and The Radiance Technique. While the difference between the two techniques is clear and has been carefully delineated, it is not surprising that confusion might arise, given the fact that we have no consensual vocabulary for discussing human energies beyond the levels of the physical, the mental, and the emotional. Let us clarify further both the differences and the interacting, synergistic potential of the two techniques.

The primary difference between them has to do with their relationship to the Radiant Whole. On one hand, we have the concept of *opening to* the Radiant Whole (the performing power technique), and, on the other, *accessing directly and drawing upon* the universal energy of the Radiant Whole (The Radiance Technique). The performing power technique works with the outer plane energies of the body, the emotions, the voice, and the mind, disentangling their energy relationships so they are free to fulfill their individual capacities as well as interact with each other in mutually supportive ways. In doing this, those outer energies also open more fully to inner-plane energies and to the Radiant Whole. This is an important and challenging process in itself. As Barbara Ray has put it:

The Outer Planes originate from the Inner Planes and are inner-connected to the Inner Source. They are manifested form coming from the inner plane blueprint. In relationship to vibration, these planes [the physical, emotional, and mental] are experienced differently than the inner planes. In higher consciousness, *mastery of the outer planes is an essential awareness on the journey of awakening to the consciousness of the Inner Planes.* (ERM, p. 79; my italics)

Mastery of the outer planes in performance is the purpose of the performing power technique. As I put it in another context, "The Performing Power Technique provides a unique means of developing and integrating into a greater whole the various parts of our communicating system—the physical, emotional, vocal, and mental modes. In doing this it allows each of those processes to become more responsive to the unlimited, universal energy of the Radiant Whole. Our relationship to that infinite potential expands *in proportion to the capacity of those external modes to open to it.*" In moving toward mastery of the outer energies, the outer planes will also open more fully to the energies of the inner planes, and specifically to the energies of the Radiant Whole.

Simultaneously, The Radiance Technique accesses and amplifies that flow of energy directly from the Radiant Whole, *from the source itself.* Thus the two techniques, while having no overt connection with one another, can become a powerful and synergistic combination. Practiced together, they create a mutually enhancing, full-spectrum synergy between the inner and the outer, between the infinite capacity of the Radiant Whole and all the parts of the communicating system. The more they open, the more it flows; the more it flows, the more they open!

One need not be a performer to use The Radiance Technique, of course; it can be learned and practiced by anyone. Conversely, one can use the performing power technique without having any knowledge of The Radiance Technique. There is also a difference in how the two techniques can be learned. The Radiance Technique cannot be learned from a book, but only from an instructor certified by Radiance Stress Management International, Inc. The performing power technique, however, can be learned in a variety of contexts, this book being one of them, as well as in special seminars and institutes. It must, of course, be practiced and experienced directly to be actually learned, but this can be done individually without an actual teacher (although a teacher can be very helpful).

We may also note that confusion has arisen in connection with the use of the term *Reiki*. Reiki is a coined Japanese word (like *vita-life* or *energy-rich* in English) meaning universal life energy. It may be used generically by anyone to designate anything and is not synonymous with The Radiance Technique. Thus a person teaching Reiki is not teaching The Radiance Technique. This clarification has emerged since the writing of *Performing Power*, and is included for the information of performers and consumers in general. The Radiance Technique and the performing power technique are both sciences of the energies they deal with. They encompass fields of knowledge and energy and include instructions that, if followed, lead to direct experiences of those fields. It is vital to approach them both with clarity, accuracy, and validity as we exercise and develop our performing energies.

For further information about The Radiance Technique, write:

American Radiance Technique Association International
P. O. Box 40570
St. Petersburg, FL 33743-0570

Guidelines on the Path to Radiant Performing

As we conclude this journey, it seems appropriate and useful to suggest a series of steps or guidelines in creating the conditions for radiant performing. While the knowledge and awareness in some steps are necessary for others, the guidelines as a whole are not to be thought of chronologically: most of them are processes that will be interacting simultaneously. The numbers in parentheses refer to the chapters that relate to each guideline. We will use the three vital ingredients established in chapter 1 as an overall structure for these guidelines.

Aligning to Purpose

1. Establish personal purposes that both engage MIM's power of participation (fulfilled performing potential), and transcend MIM's power of predictive control (radiant performing) (1, 2, 4, 6, 13).

2. Open to HOBS and to the qualities of higher energy of the Radiant Whole (1, 4, 14).

3. Practice all of these steps regularly and consistently, persistently and patiently, and always in the present (6, 14).

4. Be ready, always, for the unknown of radiant performing (4, 14).

Assessing Reality

5. Develop clarity about the requirements of singing-acting (2).

6. Develop clarity about the nature of the human energy system (1, 4, 5).

7. Develop clarity about your conditioning and how it is manifested in entanglements (3, 5).

Activating the Exercise Process

8. Using the pentagon of preparation, develop self-and role awareness (13).

9. Using the pentagon of preparation, develop an exercise process to allow the human energy system to serve singing-acting (7–12).

10. Create a play space in which to exercise, a space in which you can open to PIM, and move freely into the unknown (1, 6, 14).

11. Strengthen the communicating power of your performing energy system—MIM, IMP, body, face, and voice (7–12).

12. Transform the entanglements among your performing energies into choices (7–12).

The Radiant Performer: A Description

Finally, let us create a portrait of a radiant performer, with the understanding that we are talking about a process and not a finished product.

A radiant performer has a mental intellectual mode (MIM) that

- sees clearly the kind of performing it wants to cocreate with the whole performing system;

- can assess and accept the reality of his/her current state of development without judgmentalism;

- has the courage to do what is needed to move toward a fulfilled performing potential, and can be honest with and about oneself, and follow one's inner convictions;

- can use its principal powers of observing, analyzing, remembering, imagining, and intuiting to choose with discernment, playfulness, and courage;

- can draw freely upon its power of creative imagining;

- can intelligently analyze musical and dramatic scores, and thus make clear performance choices;

- can sustain concentration;

- is willing and eager to take risks;

- is free from judgmental inhibition, defensiveness, and resistance in exercising and rehearsing;

- is artistically and intellectually curious; and

- is open to and enthusiastic about the possibility of radiant performance, and aware of the control it may have to relinquish if that occurs.

A radiant performer has an inner emotional process (IMP)

- to which he/she has free access, both to positive and negative ends of the spectrum;

- that he/she understands (i.e., knows its functioning and special qualities);

- that he/she is able to draw upon and relate to in performance; and

- that he/she can allow to flow freely, and that is freely available in performance without entanglement tension in the body, voice, or face.

A radiant performer has a face

- with eyes that can be used expressively and that have the qualities of intensity and command;

- that uses the focus process freely and effectively;

- that can be transparent to a full range of positive and negative emotions, or, for purposes of characterization, can modify or mask any of them without entanglement;

- that feels alive and potent to the viewer even when it is not expressing a strong emotion; and

- that is free to make its own independent statements, regardless of those being made by the voice and/or the body.

A radiant performer has a body

- that is both relaxed and ready at all times, particularly in moments of emotional intensity, and is always fully available for vocal breath support;

- that has a strong sense of presence and is physically commanding and magnetic;
- that is physically fit, flexible, and strong;
- that moves through space with freedom, grace, and power and has a varied vocabulary of movement;
- that is grounded, centered, and focused in its use of energy and is a free channel for expression; and
- that has gestural freedom, range, expressivity, and variety.

A radiant performer has a voice

- that is free to be emotionally expressive without entanglement;
- that is freely produced and capable of a wide range of musical, vocal, and emotional expression;
- that is well supported by the breathing process;
- that realizes the performer's maximum musical, vocal, and expressive potential;
- that is flexible and has a wide dynamic and pitch range and a good sense of and capacity for rhythmic expression; and
- that is well projected without effort.

A radiant performer has a total instrument

- that is capable of adapting with power and flexibility to the differing needs of music theater of all kinds;
- that has an instinct for theatrical and musical/theatrical statement;
- that has minimal entanglements between emotions and voice, facial expressivity and body, gestures and body, voice and face, and voice and body;
- that has a flair for risk-taking boldness, for chutzpah (which, in Kenneth Tynan's words, combines "cool nerve and outrageous effrontery");
- that expresses the singer-actor's full personality power and can use that power to portray characters completely unlike the actor; and
- that is capable of fulfilling the performer's potential and thus creating the conditions for radiant performance.

Appendix A: Arbitrary Attitudes

Afraid
Aghast
Ashamed
Astounded
Astonished
Annoyed
Awed
Arrogant
Apologetic
Alarmed
Ardent
Angry
Amused
Bitter
Bold
Condemning
Condescending
Contrite
Cynical
Confident
Compassionate
Contemptuous
Curious
Cheerful

Contented
Cool
Defiant
Disgusted
Doubtful
Disappointed
Depressed
Desperate
Derisive
Eager
Embarrassed
Enraged
Exultant
Ecstatic
Excited
Elated
Fierce
Flirtatious
Frightened
Frantic
Flippant
Furious
Grief-Stricken
Gracious

Giddy
Groveling
Hurt
Haughty
Happy
Horrified
Impudent
Ironic
Ingratiating
Insolent
Indignant
Inspired
Insane
Innocent
Jubilant
Joyful
Jealous
Loving
Melancholy
Mad
Mournful
Miserable
Majestic
Mocking

Mischievous
Pleased
Proud
Puzzled
Pleading
Pitying
Pompous
Passionate
Playful
Regretful
Reverent

Rapturous
Surprised
Sulky
Shocked
Suspicious
Sullen
Sarcastic
Savage
Seductive
Sympathetic
Satisfied

Sorrowful
Troubled
Tragical
Tender
Thrilled
Teasing
Terrified
Wistful
Wondering
Wary

Appendix B: Arbitrary Gestures

Hand over head
Hand to head
Hand to back of head
Hand to forehead
Hand to nose
Hand to mouth
Hand to cheek
Hand to ear
Hand to opposite ear
Hand to neck
Hand to back of neck
Hand to shoulder
Hand to chest
Hand to stomach
Hand to side
Hand touching opposite side of
  body
Hand on hip
Hand on opposite arm
Hand on other elbow
Hand caresses body
Hand out, palm up
Hand out, palm down
Hand out, palm in

Hand out, palm out
Hand pointing
Hand behind back
Both hands over head
Both hands to head
Both hands to back of head
Both hands to forehead
Both hands to mouth
Both hands to cheeks
Both hands to ears
Both hands to neck
Both hands to back of neck
Both hands to shoulders
Both hands to chest
Both hands to stomach
Both hands touch opposite sides of
  body
Both hands on hips
Both hands on one hip
Both hands caress body
Both hands clasped
Both hands out, palms up
Both hands out, palms down
Both hands out, palms out

Both hands pointing
Both hands held out to sides
One hand out, one over head
One hand behind back, one on hip
Arms crossed
One hand to head, one over head
One hand to head, one to neck
One hand to head, one to shoulder
One hand to head, one to chest
One hand to head, one to stomach
One hand to head, one hand out
One hand to cheek, one to head
One hand to cheek, one to neck
One hand to cheek, one to shoulder
One hand to cheek, one to heart
One hand to cheek, one to stomach

One hand to cheek, one hand out
One hand to heart, one over head
One hand to heart, one to eye
One hand to heart, one to neck
One hand to heart, one to stomach
One hand to heart, one to hip
One hand to heart, one out to side
One hand to heart, one fist out
One hand to heart, one hand held
    out
Fist out
Fist over head
One fist out, one fist over head
Both fists out
Both fists over head

References

Balk, H. Wesley. *The Complete Singer-Actor*. 2d ed. Minneapolis: University of Minnesota Press, 1985.
_____. *Performing Power*. Minneapolis: University of Minnesota Press, 1985.
Blair, Lawrence. *Rhythms of Vision*. New York: Schocken Books, 1976.
Bohm, David. *Wholeness and the Implicate Order*. London: Routledge & Kegan Paul, ARK Paperbacks, 1983.
Bower, B. "Getting the Drop on Blood Pressure." *Science News*, June 27, 1987, 405.
Brook, Peter. *The Shifting Point*. New York: Harper & Row, 1987.
Bruder, Melissa, Lee Michael Cohen, Madeleine Olnek, Nathaniel Pollack, Robert Previto, and Scott Zigler. *A Practical Handbook for the Actor*. New York: Random House, Vintage, 1986.
Campbell, Jeremy. *Grammatical Man*. New York: Simon & Schuster, 1982.
Carse, James P. *Finite and Infinite Games*. New York: Macmillan, The Free Press, 1986.
Carson, Richard D. *Taming Your Gremlin*. New York: Harper & Row, 1983.
Cohen, Robert. *Acting Power*. Palo Alto, Calif.: Mayfield, 1978.
Cole, Toby, and Helen Krich Chinoy, eds. *Actors on Acting*. New York: Crown, 1970.
Cottrell, John. *Laurence Olivier*. Englewood Cliffs, N.J.: Prentice-Hall, 1975.
Csikszentmihalyi, Mihaly. *Flow*. New York: Harper & Row, 1990.
Emmons, Shirley, and Stanley Sonntag. *The Art of the Song Recital*. New York: Schirmer Books, 1979.
Fritz, Robert. *The Path of Least Resistance*. New York: Fawcett Columbine, Ballantine, 1989.
Gawain, Shakti. *Creative Visualization*. New York: Bantam, 1982.
Goldberg, Philip. *The Intuitive Edge*. Los Angeles: Jeremy P. Tarcher, 1983.
Goleman, Daniel. "Brain's Design Emerges As a Key to Emotions." *New York Times*, Aug. 15, 1989, Cl, C9.
Gourlay, Logan, ed. *Olivier*. New York: Stein & Day, 1974.
Helmstetter, Shad. *What to Say When You Talk to Yourself*. New York: Simon & Schuster, 1986.
Holden, Anthony. *Laurence Olivier*. New York: Atheneum, 1988.
Jeffers, Susan. *Feel the Fear and Do It Anyway*. New York: Fawcett Columbine, Ballantine, 1988.

Kogan, Judith. *Nothing But the Best*. New York: Random House, 1987.

Kriegel, Robert, and Marilyn Harris. *The C Zone*. New York: Fawcett Columbine, Ballantine, 1984.

Landau, Terry. *About Faces*. New York: Anchor, 1989.

Lawrence, D. Baloti. *Massage Techniques*. New York: Perigee, 1986.

Maslow, Abraham H. *Motivation and Personality*, 3d ed. New York: Harper & Row, 1987.

Mekler, Eva. *The New Generation of Acting Teachers*. New York: Viking Penguin, 1987.

Mitchell, Richard G., Jr. *Mountain Experience*. Chicago: University of Chicago Press, 1983.

Moss, Richard. *The Black Butterfly*. Berkeley: Celestial Arts, 1986.

Olivier, Laurence. *On Acting*. New York: Simon & Schuster, 1986.

_____. *Confessions of an Actor*. New York: Simon & Schuster, 1982.

Peck, Stephen Rogers. *Atlas of Facial Expression*. New York: Oxford University Press, 1987.

Pryor, Karen. *Don't Shoot the Dog*. New York: Bantam, 1985.

Ray, Barbara. *The Official Handbook of The Radiance Technique*®. San Francisco: The Radiance Technique Association International, Inc., 1987.

_____. *The Expanded Reference Manual of the Radiance Technique*®. St. Petersburg, Fla.: Radiance Associates, 1987.

Schaef, Anne Wilson. *When Society Becomes an Addict*. San Francisco: Harper & Row, 1987.

Schumacher, E. F. *A Guide for the Perplexed*. New York: Harper & Row, 1979.

Tynan, Kenneth. *The Sound of Two Hands Clapping*. New York: Holt, Rinehart & Winston, 1975.

Wilber, Ken. *Eye to Eye*. New York: Anchor/Doubleday, 1983.

Index

Compiled by Eileen Quam and Theresa Wolner

About Faces (Landau), 217
Abundance: defined, 376
Acceptance: defined, 376–77
Acting: classes, 40, 44, 51; defined, 248; techniques, 215–16
Acting Power (Cohen), 34
Acting-singing. *See* Singing-acting
Actor Prepares, An (Stanislavski), 44
Actor's Studio: and realism, 47
Addiction: and music theater, 58–59; to process, 58, 63; and singing-acting, 58–59. *See also* Society
Addictive Organization, The (Schaef), 148
Adler, Stella: and Stanislavski method, 248–49
Alexander technique, 96, 271, 272
Allowing: in emotion, 223–25, 248–49
Always: defined, 383–84
American acting technique: basis of, 261; vs. British, 215; and IMP, 222, 318
American Gothic, 122
American New Music Theater Festival (Philadelphia, 1987), x
Analysis: and singing-acting, 66
Anticipatory entanglement, 108, 114–17, 115, 273–79 *passim*, 296
Anti-emotionalists, 215
Apprentice artists: training of, xx–xxi, xxiii
Arbitrary attitudes, 262, 391–92; exercise, 251–56, 260, 300–301; and extreme mask, 265; and personal experience, 260; and singing, 335
Arbitrary gestures, 393–94
Areba: defined, 20, 25; and rapid-fire attitudes exercise, 220; and stage time, 219; and vocal mode, 324–26
Arias: and awareness, 356–57; and PET, 255–56; and thought process, 229
Art of the Song Recital, The (Emmons and Sonntag), 291–95 *passim*
As-if behavior. *See* Dishonesty
Aspire: defined, 377
Astaire, Fred: on repetition, 193
Atlas of Facial Expression (Peck), 217
Attitudes: arbitrary, 251–56, 260, 262, 265, 300–301, 335, 391–92; combining, 255–56; expanding, 266–68; rapid–fire, 220, 246, 253–55
Audience: interaction with, 53, 91, 98
Authentic/real/believable. *See* Areba
Authority dependence, 164–69; on Adler, 249; balancing, 167–69; and drawing out emotion, 249–50; freeing self of, xxiv; as limitation to growth, 57; and mutual addiction, 164–65; shift, xviii; and validation, 164–65
Awareness: aria, 356–57; character, 354–56; conscious vs. unconscious, 174–75, 211–12; defined, 377; ensemble, 356–57; and growth, 174–75; integrative pledge

of, 242; kinesthetic, 275–78; and MIM, 242, 352

Balancing: defined, 377
Balk (Wesley) Summer Opera Music Theater Institute: Barber and, xiv
Barber, Joan Susswein: on radiant performance, ix–x, xiii–xv
Beginning now: defined, 377
Behavior change: negative methods for, 178–82; positive methods for, 208–13; shaping, 184–202, 275
Behavioral psychology: and higher energies, 85
"Bill of Opposites, The" (Balk), 133
Bing, Rudolf: success of, xix
Biology: and IEI process, 85
Black Butterfly, The (Moss), 347–48
Blame: as addictive characteristic, 64–65; and responsibility, 64–65. See also Guilt; Shame
Blocking: breaking through, 257–58, 306–7
Blood pressure: and awareness, 174
Body flex, 279–80, 282
Bohm, David: on fragmentary thinking, 52; on fragmentation and wholeness, 38–39; on language, 4
"Book of Days" (Monk), xi
Brando, Marlon, 216
British technique: vs. American, 215
Broadway: Barber and, ix; and opera, 47
Brook, Peter: on opera, xix, 48–49, 74
Building a Character (Stanislavski), 44

C Zone, The (Kriegel), 198
Callas effect: and rapid-fire attitudes exercise, 220
Campbell, Jeremy: on play, 153
Candide: performance, 72
Carmen: knowledge of, 14, 15, 18
Carroll, Lewis: and language, 20
Carse, James: on play, 151–52
Carson, Richard D.: on radiant whole, 29
Celebration: defined, 377–78
Center for Neural Science (NYU), 23, 215
Center Opera Company. See Minnesota Opera Company
Centering: defined, 378
Challenging: and comfort zone, 198

Character: awareness, 354–56; singer-actor as, 93
Choice: defined, 378. See also FCP
Choice, field of. See FCP
Clarity: defined, 379
Cleveland Institute of Music: Foldi and, ix
Coaching: -directing interaction, 338–39; and faces, 317; and inner processes, 312–13; and MIM, 350–60; music, 40, 51
Cohen, Robert: on acting power, 34
Communication: modes of, 101, 199–200. See also specific modes
Complete Singer-Actor, The (Balk), xiv, xvii–xix; on energies, 373; on exercises, xvii–xviii, 366, 373; on gibberish, 367; on imagining, 250; on opposites, 60, 133; on wholeness, 36
Concealing: in emotion, 223–25, 301
Concentration: and FOCUS, 227
Conditioning. See Environment; Society
Confusion: as addictive characteristic, 74–76
Control: entanglements, 105–6; vs. flow, 99; illusion of, 73–74; territorial, 74. See also Judgmentalism; MIM
Courage: defined, 379
Creating a Role (Stanislavski), 44
Csikszentmihalyi, Mihaly: on flow, 92
Cuing: and behavior change, 208, 210–11

Defensiveness: as addictive characteristic, 65–66
Density: and radiance, 343–46
Dependency: as addictive characteristic, 63–64; and external referents, 63
Descartes, René: on judgment, 61
Desdemona: and transparence of hurt, 224
Diction classes, 40
Discovery: defined, 379–80
Dishonesty: as addictive characteristic, 69–72
Don't Shoot the Dog! (Pryor), 177–78, 184
Dualism: as addictive characteristic, 60–61; of inner-outer processes, 44–45; transcending, 137–39. See also Opposites

Ego: and MIM, 158
Einstein, Albert: criticism of, 86; on intuition, 83
Ekman, Paul, 217

Electra: Polus portraying, 215
Emmons, Shirley: on gesture, 291–95 *passim*
Emotion: and acting, 214–69 *passim*;
    allowing vs. concealing, 223–25; and
    kinesthetic mode, 271–73; and tension,
    271–72; and vocal mode, 311, 315–20.
    See also Facial-emotional complex; IMP
Emotionalists, 215
Energies: higher, 79, 85–90, 137–38,
    373–74, 376–84; source of, 343;
    transforming, 302–3; working with, 168.
    See also Human energy system;
    Projective modes
Ensemble: in music theater, 76–77
Entanglements, 99–132, 347; anticipatory,
    108, 114–17, 202; controlling, 105–6;
    and cuing, 210–11; and defensiveness,
    65–66; defined, 53–54, 99; and emotion,
    315–16, 317; and exercise process, 59,
    172, 189–92; and external energies,
    53–55; facial/kinesthetic, 108, 119–23,
    188, 232; harmful, 102; hearing-vocal/
    facial, 108–9, 125–27; hearing-vocal/
    kinesthetic, 108, 127–32; as human
    condition, 99–101; judgmental, 107–8,
    109–14; linking, 105; and motivation,
    212; nature of, 102–4; origin of, 102–4;
    part/part facial-emotional, 108, 123–25,
    238; part/whole kinesthetic, 108,
    117–19; revealing, 171–73, 183–213;
    sympathetic, 104–5; and tension,
    256–57, 286; and trainers, 186; varieties
    of, 104–7; and vocal/facial, 108–9,
    125–27, *126*, 236; vocal/kinesthetic, 108,
    127–32
Environment: changing, xxiii; and
    entanglements, 55; of music theater,
    55–57, 74; and potentiality, 9–10. *See
    also* Society
Error correction, 139–40
Exercise process: with arbitrary gestures,
    290–91; daily checklist, 360; of facial-
    emotional complex, 214–69 *passim*; of
    FAMUS, 236–40, 243–46; of FOCUS,
    233–36; of IMP, 251–56; intention of,
    xvii–xviii, 7, 48; of kinesthetic mode,
    270–303 *passim*; and knowledge, 19–20;
    and negative methods, 178–82; vs.
    performance, 175–77, 269; for the
    performer, xviii–xix, 6, 98, 162–63,

183–213, 353–60; and potentiality, 6,
    10–11; and repetition, 192–94; as
    secondary, 176; sound and emotion/
    motion, 369–71; sound and motion,
    368–69; steps in, 188–92; for the
    teacher, xviii; 25-positions concept,
    202–8; of vocal mode, 204–39 *passim*.
    See also Four-step spiral process;
    Practice; Shaping; Training
*Expanded Reference Manual of The Radiance
    Technique, The* (Ray), 12, 97, 343,
    376–83 *passim*
Expansion, Spiral of, *169*, 169–71, 205–8,
    206
Experiential focus, 230–32
External referents. *See* Authority
    dependence; Validation
Extinction: as behavior change, 181–82;
    defined, 181
Extreme masks, 243–46, 265–66, *266*; of
    body, 280, 281, 282; of gesture, 281,
    282; of vocal, 323–24, 330–31, 336–38
Eyes: as focus process, 226; shutting, 230.
    See also FOCUS

Face: interest in, 217; in opera, 217; and
    self-consciousness, 219–20, 238. *See also*
    Facial mode
Facial-emotional complex, 27, 53, 214–69,
    317; exercise process of, 214–60 *passim*,
    305
Facial flex, 236–40, 321
Facial/kinesthetic entanglement, 108,
    119–23, *120*, 188, 232
Facial mode, 101, 218–22; assumptions
    about, 219–21; vs. body, 218, 272;
    components of, 226; and entanglement,
    218; expanding, 241–46; and IMP,
    221–22; and invisible/inaudible, 222–23;
    isolation of, 218–19; neglect of, 218;
    primary function of, 218, 225; and
    repression, *103*; vs. vocal mode, 305,
    318
Facial musculature process. *See* FAMUS
FAMUS, 226–28, 232–39, 318; defined,
    226; exercise process, 236–40, 243–46;
    functions of, 232–33
FCP, *341*, 341–43, *342*, 343–46, 374
Fear: and improvisation, 371–73

Feel the Fear and Do It Anyway (Jeffers), 371
Feelings, frozen: as addictive characteristic, 68–69, 102
Field of choice potential. *See* FCP
Finite and Infinite Games: A Vision of Life as Play and Possibility (Carse), 151
Fitzgerald, F. Scott: on intelligence, 133
Flexibility: defined, 380
Floppy release, 285–88
Flow: and addictive characteristics, 76; vs. control, 99; criteria for, 92–93; defined, 5, 92, 102; and performance, 32–33, 53. *See also* Peak experience
FOCUS, 226–36; and concentration, 227; defined, 226; exercise process, 233–36, 289; functions of, 227–32
Foldi, Andrew: on radiant performance, ix, xii–xiii
Ford Foundation: study on singer-actor training, 51–52
Four-step spiral process, 189–92, 204–5, 206, 207, *207*; and arbitrary attitudes, 253, 300–301; attitude expansion, 267–68; and extreme mask, 245–46; and facial flex, 239–40; and facial mode, 125, 239–40, 245–46, 253, 254, 282–85; and gesture motivation, 297–98; and kinesthetic mode, 281–85; and personal experience, 259–60; and rapid-fire attitudes, 254; and singing vocal flex, 334–35; three mode, 329; and vocal extreme mask, 330–31, 336–38; and vocal mode, 326–31, 330–31, 334–35, 336–38
Fragmentation: defined, 38; of language, 4; and loss of performing power, 36, 51–52; of training, 40–41, 56–57; vs. whole, 38–39
Freud, Sigmund, xii, 86
Fritz, Robert: on judgment, 61–62; on path of least resistance, 141; on problem-solving vs. creating, 177; on secondary vs. primary choices, 177
Frozen feelings: as addictive characteristic, 68–69, 102

Galileo: and logic, 81
Garrick, David, 215–16

Gesture: arbitrary, 290–91, 393–94; flex, 280, 282; and inner connection, 298–300, 314; motivating, 295–98; slow-motion, 285
Gibberish, 366–68
Go-too-far rule. *See* GTF rule
Goldberg, Philip: on intuition, 362–64, 365, 366, 373
Gould, Glenn: on technical problem, 209–10
Grammatical Man (Campbell), 153
Gratitude: defined, 380
Group Theater: and realism, 47; and Stanislavski method, 248
Growth, spiral of: of Cs, 174–75, *175*; of Rs, *172*, 172–73
GTF rule, 167
Guidance modes: and projective modes, 28, 101
Guide for the Perplexed, A (Schumacher), 134
Guilt: as harmful, 70; releasing, 44–46; of singer-actors, 51. *See also* Blame; Shame
Guthrie, Tyrone: on music theater, xix, 158; on transcending difficulty, 137

Habits: letting go of, 285–88; old, 275, 328
Head-flop sequence, 288–90
Hearing mode: dominance in, 199
Hearing-vocal/facial entanglement, 108–9, 125–27
Hearing-vocal/kinesthetic entanglement, 108, 127–32
Hearing-vocal mode, 53, 304. *See also* Vocal mode
Helmstetter, Shad: on emotional energy flow, 102
Higher energies. *See* Energies
Higher observer. *See* HOBS
HOBS, 23–25, 27–28, 30, 34, 79, 83, 98, 138, 197; defined, 23; and entanglement, 106–7; and radiant whole, 374–76; and wholeness, 30, 88, 101, 374–76
Hologram: as metaphor for individual in addictive system, 58
Human energy system: and addictive characteristics, 76; conditioning of, xviii; defined, xxiii; and facial mode, 221; and higher energies, 79; and kinesthetic mode, 271, 273; and performing power,

xxiv, 33, 82–85, 90, 98; and projective modes, 25; and singing-acting, xvii; and wholeness, 82–85, 101
Humor: defined, 380–81

Iago: and concealment, 224
IEI process, 164; applied, 98; defined, 80–81; and investigative process, 80–82, 85–87
Imagining, 250
Immobility/mobility spectrum, 278–79
IMP: and coaching, 312–13; defined, 23–25; and emotion, 103, 216; encouraging, 248–53; exercising, 98, 251–56, 300–301; and facial-emotional complex, 124, 215, 221; and higher energies, 83; inner processes of, 44; vs. MIM, 106, 248; and performing power, 90, 92, 96, 98, 101; and vocal mode, 311, 316; and wholeness, 26–28, 34
Improvisaton, 371–73; defined, 371; and gibberish, 367; and MIM, 371, 372; and PIM, 371
Injunction/intuitive apprehension/communal confirmation. See IEI process
Inner emotion process. See IMP
Instructional/experiential/interactional process. See IEI process
Interconnection: defined, 381
Interpretation: expanding, 333–34; playing with, 306–9; and 25-positions, 334
Intuitive Edge, The (Goldberg), 362–64
Intuitive mode. See PIM
Investigative process: of higher energy levels, 79–82; and radiance technique, 96–98
Isolation/integration spectrum, 278–79

Jaw: as entanglement, 239
Jeffers, Susan: on fear, 371
Joy: defined, 381
Judgmentalism: as addictive characteristic, 61–63, 166, 180–81; as condemnation vs. discernment, 62, 170; and creative process, 62; and entanglements, 107–8, 109, 109–14; freedom from, 63; and interruption, 200; of MIM, 102, 108, 110, 116; and play principle, 331–32; preevaluative, 62–63, 170–71;

premature, 196; vs. process, 166, 168–69; and teaching, 168
Juilliard School: addictive behavior in, 67
Justification: and defensiveness, 66

Kinesthetic mode, 53, 101, 270–303; and doing, 271, 273–74; dominance in, 199; and emotion, 271–73; and MIM, 273–74, 302; and repression, 103
Kinesthetic focus shift, 229–30 passim. See also Narrative focus
Kinesthetic tension: and defensiveness, 65; and FOCUS, 228
Knowledge: and knowing, 14–20, 256, 353–60; of unknown, 11–14
Kogan, Judith: on addictive behavior in academia, 67
Kriegel, Marilyn: on challenging self, 198
Kriegel, Robert: on challenging self, 198

Landau, Terry: on faces, 217
Language: and fragmentation, 4; and knowledge, 20; music of, 43, 324–25
Lawrence, Baloti: on Alexander technique, 271
Learning: and assimilation, 196; and defensiveness, 65; defined, 11–12; process, 11–14; rate of, 198; and reviewal, 201; spiral model of, 12–13, 18. See also Knowledge
Ledoux, Joseph: on emotions, 23, 216
Lewis, Jerry, 111
"Living Process System" (Schaef), 76
Love: defined, 382
Lying. See Dishonesty

Mamet, David: on acting training, 46, 179
Marketplace: and art forms, xxii
Maslow, Abraham: on artists, 133–34; on forces in psychology, 85; on peak experience, 29–30, 90, 92; on wholeness, 29–30
Massage Techniques (Lawrence), 271
Mental-intellectual mode. See MIM
Meredith Monk Ensemble, ix, x
Method acting, 216
Metropolitan Opera: Bing and, xix; Foldi and, ix
MIM: and awareness, 242; and blocks to growth, 167; and character oneness, 93;

and control, 72, 96, 102, *103*, 105–6, 112, 158; and defensiveness, 65–66; defined, 21–26; and emotion, 216; as guidance mode, 28, 101; and higher energies, 83, 88; vs. IMP, 248; and improvisation, 371, 372; as inner process, 44, 72, 318–19; judgmentalism of, 102, 108, *110*, *116*; and kinesthetic mode, 273–74, 302; and Olivier performance, 32; and pentagon of preparation, 350–60, *351*; and performing power, 90, 92, 96, 98, 144; vs. PIM, 197; and rapid-fire attitudes exercise, 220; and rationality, 81, 122; and wholeness, 30–34, 96, 107, 144
Minnesota Opera Company, xxii; Balk and, xvii, xx
Minnesota Opera New Music Theater Ensemble: Barber and, ix–x, xiv; development of, xxiii; Monk and, xi
Minutia mania: defined, 74
Mitchell, Richard: on flow, 92–93
Models, 88
Modification spectrum, 223–25
Monk, Meredith: on radiant performance, ix, x–xii
Morphogenetic field theory, 367
Moscow Art Theater, 43
Moss, Richard: on enlightenment, 346–48
Motivation/nonmotivation spectrum, 296
Mountain Experience (Mitchell), 92–93
Movable laboratory, xvii, xviii, xx, xxii
Movement classes, 40, 51
Music: coaching, 40, 51; of language, 43, 306–9; of vocal mode, 26
Music theater, ix–xv, xvii–xxiv; control-oriented, 74; defined, ix, xi; demands of, 48–51; environment, 55–59, 74; as metaphor for society, x; musical comedy as, ix, x; opera as, ix, xii, xxi; parts-whole relationship in, 41; performer and, xviii; and potentiality, 9; purpose of, xxi; spectrum of, ix, xi; stylization, 285. *See also* Singing-acting
Musical comedy: as music theater, ix, x
Musicality: and emotion, 315; and inner meaning, 318; spectrum, 308–9

Narrative focus, 230–31

National Association of Teachers of Singing, 202, 236, 258, 284–85
National Theater, 94
NATS. *See* National Association of Teachers of Singing
Naturalism. *See* Time
NBC rule, 167
Negative reinforcement: as behavior change, 180–81; and judgmentalism, 180–81
Negativism: as addictive characteristic, 66–67
Neutral reading, 320–21
Never-be-careful rule. *See* NBC rule
Non-Western theater: vs. Western, x
Nothing but the Best: The Struggle for Perfection at the Juilliard School (Kogan), 67

Official Handbook of The Radiance Technique, The (Ray), 33, 97
Olivier, Laurence: on acting, 95–96; as method actor, 216; and *Othello* performance, 3, 5, 16, 31–32, 91, 94–97, 144, 344; and peak experience, 94; as powerful performer, 344; on radiance, 3; on rehearsal, 95
On Acting (Olivier), 95–96
Opening: defined, 382
Opera: as artificial, 49; bad productions of, xix; on Broadway, 47; change in, xix–xx; as music theater, ix, xii, xxi; as natural, 49
Opera America: panel, x
Opposites, 60, 133–35, 138–39
Othello: and modification of hurt, 224; Olivier as, 3, 5, 16, 31–32, 91, 94–97, 144, 344

Part/part facial-emotional entanglement, 108, *123*, 123–25, 238
Part-teachers, 41, 42, 50, 51, 74
Part/whole kinesthetic entanglement, 108, *117*, 117–19
Parts. *See* Fragmentation
Path of Least Resistance, The (Fritz), 61
Patience: as guiding principle, 138, 155–57
Peak experience: and acting-singing, 5, 31; criteria for, 90–91; and performing, 31–32, 34, 90–92; and wholeness, 29–30. *See also* Flow

Peck, Stephen R.: on faces, 217
Pentagon models: purpose of, 11; trio of, 8–9. *See also* Performing energies, pentagon of; Potentiality, pentagon of; Preparation, pentagon of
Perfectionism: as addictive characteristic, 67–68, 166; and hopelessness, 68; and potential, 68; and shame, 68; and workaholism, 148
Performance: vs. exercise, 175–77, 269; full-spectrum, 340; and life expansion, 346–49
Performer: counterconditioned, 56–78; vs. environment, xxiii; as essence of music theater, xxiii–xxiv; external energies of, 10; full-spectrum, ix, 349–50; internal processes of, 10, 349–50; and potentiality, 10; as product, 165; self as, 63. *See also* Radiant performer
Performing energies, pentagon of, 349; function of, 89–90; and higher energies, 88–90, *89*; and repression, *103*
Performing Power (Balk), xiv, xvii–xix, xxii; on energy, 83; facial-emotional mode in, 214–15; on FOCUS, 226; on fragmentation damage, 52; on hearing-vocal mode, 304–5; on inner-outer processes, 45, 221; and interest in faces, 217; on judgmentalism, 61, 100, 109; on language musicality, 324–25; on MIM, 26; on mode minds, 364–65; on old habits, 275; on projective modes, 25, 53; on radiance technique, 33, 96; on singers, 47; singing voice in, 305; speaking voice in, 305; on synergy, 37; on time, 285; on training concepts, xxii; on vocal mode, 304–5
Performing power technique, 164; and higher energies, 88; and human energy system, xxiv, 33, 90, 98; and performance, xiv, 90–94; and radiance technique, 97–98, 384–86; and radiant whole, 384; and wholeness, 87–88, 384
Permission: and process, 167, 168
Persistence: defined, 155; as guiding principle, 138, 155
Personal experience: and arbitrary attitudes, 260; four-step spiral process, 259–60
PET: of arias, 255–56

Physicality: dominance in, 199; and posture, 202–3
PIM, 24–25, 27–28, 34, 79, 83, 98, 197; defined, 24; and entanglement, 106–7; exercises for, 366–74; expanding, 362–66; and higher energies, 88–89, 373–74; and improvisation, 371; and wholeness, 88, 101
Plateau phenomenon, 192
Play: as guiding principle, 138, 150–54, 331–32; space, 357; value of, 153–54; and work, 151–52
Playful intuitive mode. *See* PIM
Plowright, Joan: performance of, 3
Polarization. *See* Dualism
Polonius: on practice, 113
Polus: as Electra, 215
Positive reinforcement, 208–13; and babies, 180; and interruption, 186–87; occasional, 192–93, 242; for self, 184–85, 187, 192
Posture: good-student, 275, 276; and singing, 202–3
Potential: defined, 5, 6; as guiding principle, 138–39, 157–60; as purpose, 7, 33
Potentiality, pentagon of, *9*, 9–11, 55; and awareness, 18; dualism in, 44–45; exercise process in, 161–62, *162*; as whole system, 36
Practice: avoiding, 163–64, 165; dualities of, 148; as guiding principle, 138, 148–50
Preparation, pentagon of, 350–52, *351*, 360
Present patience: as guiding principle, 138, 155–57
Prevailing emotional tonality. *See* PET
Problems: convergent, 134–37; divergent, 134–37; solving, 134–37
Process: addiction, 58, 63; defined, 145–46; as guiding principle, 138, 145–48
Product: performer as, 165, 171
Projective modes, 25, 49, 53, 84, *84*; energy flow in, 104, 218, 318; functions of, 217–18; and guidance modes, 28; and higher energies, 83, *84*, 90; and inner modes, 318–19, 343; and performing power, 90; source of, 343; training, 101. *See also* Facial-emotional complex; Kinesthetic mode; Vocal mode

Pryor, Karen: on changing behavior, 178–82, 184–87, 209, 212; on learning, 195, 196, 198; on reinforcement, 192, 209; on removing attention, 200; on shaping, 184–87
Psychoanalysis: and higher energies, 85–86
Punishment: and behavior change, 178, 179–80; positive, 200–201
Purpose: aligning to, 7; as guiding principle, 138, 139–45

Radiance: defined, xxiii, 3
Radiance technique: and investigative process, 96–98; and performing power technique, 97–98, 384–86; purpose of, 33; and radiant whole, 33–35, 87–88, 97, 138, 384, 384; and *reiki*, 33, 386
Radiant performer: defined, ix, 387–89; purpose of, 143
Radiant performing: and choice, 340; conditions for, 5–6, 340; defined, 4–6, 5; and full spectrum, 340; guidelines for, 386–87; principles for, 133–60; and radiant whole, 340; as rare, 37; spiral path to, 141–42
Radiant whole: blocking of, 37; defined, xxiii, 28–29, 343; direct access to, 33–35; flow of, 37; and freedom of choice, 341; and HOBS, 374–76; and human energies, 79, 83, 96; MIM and, 107; and pentagon, 350, 350; and performing power, 90, 96, 98; and radiance technique, 33–35, 87–88, 97, 138; and singer-actor, 159; as universal, 383
Rapid-fire attitudes exercise, 220, 253–55; and extreme mask, 246
Rationalization: and defensiveness, 66
Ray, Barbara: on dense energies, 343; on energies, 343, 374–75; on intuition, 24; on judgment, 61; on learning, 11–12; on play, 362; on radiance technique, 33, 97, 384–85; on wholeness, 376–83 *passim*
Realism: and acting, 47
Reality: assessing, 7
Rehearsal: as fragmentation, 40–41
Rehearsal-teaching, xxii. *See also* Training
Reiki. See Radiance technique
Reinforcement. *See* Negative reinforcement; Positive reinforcement
Repetition: effectiveness of, 192–94, 197

Repression: equals expression, 102–4, *103*, 130
Responsibility: as addictive characteristic, 64–65; and blame, 64–65
Ristad, Eloise: on communication modes, 199
Rut transformation, 322–23

SAD: defined, 127; as vocal/facial entanglement, 127
Scarcity: as addictive characteristic, 76–77. *See also* Zero-sum model
Schaef, Anne Wilson: on addictive society, 57–60, 77, 363; on blame, 64–65; on confusion, 74–76; on control, 73; on dependency, 63; on dishonesty, 69–72; on honesty, 72, 112; on judgmentalism, 63; on perfectionism, 68; on responsibility, 64–65; on self-centeredness, 76; on workaholism, 148
Schumacher, E. F.: on education, 135; on problem-solving, 134–35, 137
Science: and investigative process, 82, 96–97
Scores: interpretation of, 305–9
Search: and FOCUS, 227–28, 233
Select: and FOCUS, 228, 233
Self: as central, 76; interaction with, 98; as performer, 63
Self-centeredness: as addictive characteristic, 76–77
Serious/anxious/deadpan. *See* SAD
Shame: and perfectionism, 68; releasing, 44–46. *See also* Blame; Guilt
Shaping: laws of, 185–202; vs. training, 184; and varying modes, 198-200. *See also* Behavior change
Sheldrake, Rupert: on human energies, 83; morphogenetic field theory of, 367
Shift: and FOCUS, 228–29, 233–36; kinesthetic, 229–30 *passim*; thought-process, 229–230
Shifting Point, The (Brook), xix, 48–49, 74
Shut: and FOCUS, 230
Sills, Beverly: on sound, 309
Singing-acting: and character portrayal, 93; characteristics of, 48–50; as complex system, 23; and conditioning, 58–78; demands of, 48–51; and higher energies, 82–85; and inner radiant performing, 91; parts-whole relationship of, 38–41, 47–48; and potentiality, 9; training, 36–55; as unnatural, 48; as whole, 159. *See also* Music theater

Society: addictive characteristics of, 57–78; conditioning by, 58–78; music theater as metaphor for, x

Solo: and self-centeredness, 76

Sonntag, Stanley: on gesture, 291–95 *passim*

Sound and emotion/motion, 369–71

Sound and motion, 368–69

Spiral process. *See* Four-step spiral process

Spoken vocal flex, 320–23

Squeeze. *See* Vocal/kinesthetic entanglement

Stanislavski, Konstantin, 43–44, 46, 47, 71–72; adaptation of, 248–49; on emotion, 216

Strasberg, Lee: and Stanislavski method, 248–49

Support: defined, 382

Sustaining: and FOCUS, 228, 233–36; holding as, 221

Sway. *See* Vocal/kinesthetic entanglement

Sympathetic entanglements: defined, 104–5

Synergistic Performance, The (Balk), xvii

Synergy: and environment, xxiii–xxiv; and potential, 5, 6; and singer-actor, 37, 47–48; 160; and wholeness, xxiii, 36, 90

Taming Your Gremlin (Carson), 29

Teaching: environment in, 168; principles of, 184; and shaping, 185, 186, 197–98

Tension: and emotion, 271–72, 338–39; entanglements, 256–57, 286, 297, 298; and floppy release, 286-87; -relaxation spectrum, 274

Theory: vs. pragmatic reality, xiii

Thought process: in arias, 229; communicating, 218, 225; shift, 229, 230. *See also* Experiential focus

Time: real vs. stage, 219, 285

Total-performance nautilus. *See* Exercise process

Training: and addictive characteristics, 57–78; of artists, xx, xxi, xxiii; cause-and-effect blaming in, 64–65; entangled, 186; fragmented, 40–41, 56–57; and interaction, 338; and projective energies, 50; vs. shaping, 184; of singer-actor, 36–55, 198, 306; of speaking voice, 318. *See also* Exercise process; Rehearsal-teaching

Transformation: defined, 382; rut, 322–23

Transforming process, 383

Transparency: and allowing, 224, 225

Transpersonal psychology: and higher energy levels, 79, 85

25-positions concept, 202–8; and anticipatory entanglement, 275; and body flex, 280; and four-step spiral process, 204–5; and interpretive process, 334; and tension/relaxation spectrum, 274

Tynan, Kenneth: and Olivier, 94, 344

Universal: defined, 383

Validation: and authority dependence, 164–65; self-, 165

Verbal mind. *See* MIM

Vocal-emotional spectrum, 310–13, 319–20, 335–36

Vocal/facial entanglement, 108–9, 125–27, *126,* 236

Vocal flex, 320–23, 324, 328, 331–35

Vocal/kinesthetic entanglement, 108, 127–32, *128*

Vocal mode, 53, 101, 304–39; and areba, 324–26; and emotion, 315–20; and extreme mask, 323–24; and facial mode, 218, 305, 318; and IMP, 311, 316; integrating inner/outer, 313–15; and repression, *103;* spoken, 320–23

Vocal-musical play, 306–9

Vocal-quality spectrum, 309–10

Voice. *See* MIM

Voice lessons, 40, 51

Warm-up, facial, *240*

Western theater: vs. non-Western, x

What to Say When You Talk to Yourself (Helmstetter), 102

When Society Becomes an Addict (Schaef), 57, 148

Wholeness. *See* Radiant whole

Wholeness and the Implicate Order (Bohm), 4, 38

Wilber, Ken: on higher energies, 79–81, 86

Wodehouse, Barbara: on training, 100

Wood, Grant: and facial expression in painting, 122

Words. *See* MIM

Workaholism: and perfectionism, 148; and repetition, 192–93

Young, Stark: on Moscow Art Theater, 43

Zeffirelli, Franco: on Olivier's *Othello,* 31

Zero-sum model: as corollary to scarcity model, 76–77

H. Wesley Balk is professor of theater at the University of Minnesota and Director of Performer Development for the New Music Theater Ensemble of the Minnesota Opera Company. His directing credits include the New York City Opera, Santa Fe Opera, San Francisco Opera, Houston Opera, Washington Opera, Central City Opera, and Minnesota Opera Company.